Lean DevOps

Lean DevOps

A Practical Guide to On Demand Service Delivery

Robert Benefield

✦Addison-Wesley

Boston • Columbus • New York • San Francisco • Amsterdam • Cape Town
Dubai • London • Madrid • Milan • Munich • Paris • Montreal • Toronto • Delhi
Mexico City • São Paulo • Sydney • Hong Kong • Seoul • Singapore • Taipei • Tokyo

For information about buying this title in bulk quantities, or for special sales opportunities (which may include electronic versions; custom cover designs; and content particular to your business, training goals, marketing focus, or branding interests), please contact our corporate sales department at corpsales@pearsoned.com or (800) 382-3419.

For government sales inquiries, please contact governmentsales@pearsoned.com.

For questions about sales outside the U.S., please contact intlcs@pearson.com.

Visit us on the Web: informit.com/aw

Library of Congress Control Number: 2022937306

Copyright © 2023 Pearson Education, Inc.

Cover image: Vinap/Shutterstock

ISBN-13: 978-0-13-384750-5
ISBN-10: 0-13-384750-0

1 2022

Author: To my beautiful love, Gabrielle, my "little people" Aidan and Talia, and all of those who have enriched my life and, in the process, made the world a better place.

Contents

Foreword   *xv*
Acknowledgments   *xviii*
About the Author   *xx*

Introduction   1

Chapter 1: The Problem with IT Service Delivery   7
    Approach #1: Reduce Delivery Friction   9
        The Downsides of Targeting Delivery Friction   11
    Approach #2: Managing Service Delivery Risk   12
        The Downsides of Targeting Service Delivery Risk   14
        The Essence of Delivery   15
    Beginning the DevOps Journey   17
    Summary   18

Chapter 2: How We Make Decisions   21
    Examining the Decision-Making Process   22
    Boyd and the Decision Process   23
    The OODA Loop   26
    The Ingredients of Decision Making   29
        Ingredient 1: The Target Outcome   30
        Delivering Measures over Outcomes   36
        Ingredient 2: Friction Elimination   39
        Ingredient 3: Situational Awareness   42
        The Challenge of Trust   44
        The Fragility of Mental Models and Cognitive Biases 45
        Ingredient 4: Learning   48
        Failing to Learn   48

The Pathway to Improved Decision Making   53
Summary   54

Chapter 3: Mission Command   55
    The Origins of Mission Command   56
      Learning How to Lead Effectively the Hard Way   57
    Managing Through Unpredictability   58
      Knowledge and Awareness Weaknesses   59
      Misalignments   60
      Misjudgment of Ecosystem Complexity   61
    The Anatomy of Mission Command   62
    Commander's Intent   63
      Brief   66
      Situational Overview   67
      Statement of the Desired Outcome or Overall
        Mission Objective   67
      Execution Priorities   67
      Anti-Goals and Constraints   68
    Backbriefing   69
    Einheit: The Power of Mutual Trust   71
      Creating Einheit in DevOps   74
      Continual Improvement   75
      Staff Rides   78
      After Action Reviews   79
    Organizational Impacts of Mission Command   80
    Summary   81

Chapter 4: Friction   83
    Understanding Ohno's Forms of Waste   84
      Muda (Pure Waste)   86
      Muri (Overburden)   109
      Mura (Fluctuation and Irregularity)   113
    See the Whole   125
    Summary   126

Chapter 5: Risk   127
   Cynefin and Decision Making   128
      Ordered Systems   *131*
      Unordered Systems   *134*
   Reimagining Risk Management   143
      Have Clear and Understood Target Outcomes   *144*
      Make the Best Choice the Easiest Choice   *145*
      Continually Improve Ecosystem Observability   *147*
   Summary   151

Chapter 6: Situational Awareness   153
   Making Sense of Our Ecosystem   154
   The Mental Model   157
      The Problems with Mental Models   *158*
   Cognitive Bias   161
   Gaining Better Situational Awareness   163
   Framing   164
      Finding and Fixing Framing Problems   *165*
   Information Flow   169
      Why Ecosystem Dynamics Matter   *169*
      Meeting Your Information Flow Needs   *172*
   Analysis and Improvement   181
   Summary   182

Chapter 7: Learning   183
   The Emergence of Skills Attainment Learning   184
      The Rise of the One Right Way   *186*
   Outcome-Directed Learning   188
   Creating a Learning Culture   191
      Day-to-Day Kata   *191*
      Improvement and Problem-Solving Kata   *192*
      The Coaching Practice   *193*
   Summary   195

Chapter 8: Embarking on the DevOps Journey 197
    The Service Delivery Challenge 204
        Traditional Delivery Fog in the Service World 205
        The Challenge of the "ilities" 207
    The Path to Eliminating Service Delivery Fog 209
        The Role of Managers in Eliminating Service
            Delivery Fog 210
        Identifying What You Can or Cannot Know 214
        Ways the Team Can Eliminate Service Delivery Fog 219
    Summary 220

Chapter 9: Service Delivery Maturity and the
            Service Engineering Lead 221
    Modeling Service Delivery Maturity 223
        The Example of Measuring Code Quality 224
        Service Delivery Maturity Model Levels 225
        Service Delivery Maturity Areas of Interest 228
        Configuration Management and Delivery Hygiene 232
        Supportability 235
        Single Point of Failure Mitigation and
            Coupling Management 239
        Engagement 241
    The Service Engineering Lead 243
        Why Have a Separate Rotating Role? 244
        How the SE Lead Improves Awareness 246
        Organizational Configurations with the SE Lead 248
    Challenges to Watch Out For 250
        Incentivizing Collaboration and Improvement 251
        Developers Running Production Services 253
        Overcoming the Operational Experience Gap 254
    Summary 256

Chapter 10: Automation   257
    Tooling and Ecosystem Conditions   258
    Building Sustainable Conditions   260
        5S   *261*
        Seeing Automation 5S in Action   *278*
    Tools & Automation Engineering   283
        Organizational Details   *285*
        Workflow and Sync Points   *285*
    Summary   287

Chapter 11: Instrumentation and Observability   289
    Determining the "Right" Data   291
        Know the Purpose and Value   *293*
        Know the Audience   *297*
        Know the Source   *302*
    Making the Ecosystem Observable   307
        Instrumenting for Observability   *310*
        Instrumenting Development   *310*
        Instrumenting Packaging and Dependencies   *314*
        Instrumenting Tooling   *316*
        Instrumenting Environment Change and
            Configuration Management   *317*
        Instrumenting Testing   *319*
        Instrumenting Production   *320*
        Queryable/Reportable Live Code and Services   *321*
        Presenting Task, Change, Incident, and
            Problem Records Together   *321*
        Environment Configuration   *322*
        Logging   *323*
        Monitoring   *324*
        Security Tracking and Analysis   *325*
        Service Data   *326*

Pulling It All Together   327
    Instrumenting a Wastewater Ecosystem   328
    Instrumenting an IT Ecosystem   331
Summary   333

Chapter 12: Workflow   335
Workflow and Situational Awareness   336
Managing Work Through Process   337
Managing Work Organically   339
The Tyranny of Dark Matter   340
    Learning to See the Disconnects in Action   343
    Resolving Disconnects by Building Context   347
Visualizing the Flow   349
    Workflow Board Basics   351
    State Columns   352
    State Columns for Operations   353
    Swim Lanes   355
Task Cards   358
Preventing Dark Matter   359
Using the Board   362
Seeing the Problems   363
Limiting Work in Progress   365
The Limits of a Workflow Board   367
    Managing the Board   367
    Managing Flow and Improvement   368
Summary   368

Chapter 13: Queue Master   371
An Introduction to the Queue Master   372
    Role Mechanics   374
    "Follow the Sun" Queue Mastering   384
Queue Master Rollout Challenges   389

Team Members Don't See the Value   389
More Traditionally Minded Managers
   Thwarting Rollout   390
Pushy Queue Masters   391
Junior Team Members as Queue Masters   391
Queue Masters Who Struggle to Lead Sync Points   394
Summary   394

Chapter 14: Cycles and Sync Points   395
Inform, Align, Reflect, and Improve   396
Top-Down Alignment Control Approach   397
Alignment Through Iterative Approaches   397
Service Operations Synchronization and Improvement   400
The Tactical Cycle   400
Important Differences Between Kickoffs and
   Sprint Planning   404
Daily Standup   408
Retrospective   411
General Meeting Structure   413
The Learning and Improvement Discussion   415
The Strategic Cycle   421
Strategic Review   424
General Review Structure   426
A3 Problem Solving for the Strategic Review   427
Summary   432

Chapter 15: Governance   433
Factors for Successful Governance   434
Meeting Intent   435
No Target Outcome Interference   437
Maintain Situational Awareness and Learning   438
Common Governance Mistakes   440
Poor Requirement Drafting and Understanding   440

Using Off-the-Shelf Governance Frameworks   445
Out-of-the-Box Process Tooling and Workflows   450
Tips for Effective DevOps Governance   453
Understand Governance Intent   454
Make It Visible   454
Propose Reasonable Solutions   456
Automation and Compliance   458
Be Flexible and Always Ready to Improve   458
Summary   460

Appendix   461
Index   463

Foreword

Just about everyone can remember being inconvenienced by a computer outage at sometime during their lives. I particularly remember walking into the Melbourne airport on a sunny Saturday morning and discovering that the computer which ran all the check-in terminals was down. It stayed down all morning, exposing just how time-consuming and awkward the manual check-in process was. Some of us made it to our destinations many hours late; others were not so lucky. And I remember the hours-long check-in lines at the Baltimore airport many years later; the computer running Southwest's check-in kiosks was out and this time there was no manual backup process. After multiple long lines, we raced to our gate just in time to board before the door closed on a half-empty plane.

As I stood in those lines, I imagined the scene in the data center where "emergency responders" were no doubt scrambling to bring the system back up; after all, I had been there. Some years ago, I managed a factory data center, and we knew that any outage longer than a half hour would seriously curtail pack-out. It only happened once, and believe me, that was one time too many.

At last, we have a book written for the people on the emergency response side of a computer outage. It's not a book focused on being agile or lean; it's a book that focuses on being ready: ready to prevent serious service delivery problems, ready to limit the damage when they happen, and ready to uncover the cause of any incident and keep it from happening again. You would think, given our increasing reliance on technology, that there would be a lot of information about how to do these things well. But I haven't seen a lot of guidance for those who hold this challenging job, at least until now.

We have decades, if not centuries, of experience handling emergency situations in fire departments, hospitals, and military organizations. But rarely have we thought to apply that experience to the technical world, probably because we don't consider a technical failure to be a matter of life or death. But as Robert demonstrates throughout this book, lessons from other domains can be surprisingly relevant for those seeking to prevent computer outages and, when they do (inevitably) occur, limit their damage and ensure a rapid, safe recovery.

Service delivery teams do a lot more than minimize outages and smoothly handle any that may arise; they provide a critical interface between their organization and its consumers. This book is based on a simple premise—the purpose of a technical system is to bring about expected outcomes for its consumers, and the purpose of service delivery teams is to ensure those expectations are met. They do this by understanding consumers' intent when using the service, discovering what prevents consumers from achieving the outcomes they expect, and learning how to improve the system and close the gaps.

This book is not about meeting service delivery targets; it's about paying attention: paying attention to consumers, being aware of their expectations, and being attentive to their frustrations. It's about paying attention to the ways in which complex technical systems interact, how information flows through organizations, and how decisions are made and executed. It's about paying attention to and improving the way work gets done and the outcomes that are delivered.

Be warned that focusing on delivering outcomes is a novel concept for IT teams, because historically, there was a large time and distance gap between technical teams and their consumers. Most "standard" IT practices, including Agile practices, presume that an intermediary translates consumer intent into proxy features and goals, which then guide the decisions of the technical team. This book eliminates such proxies, and in doing so, it may contradict some of your views on appropriate roles, responsibilities, and processes. Therefore, you might want to check your confirmation bias at the door as you enter, because, as the saying goes, "It ain't what you don't know that gets you into trouble. It's what you know for sure that just ain't so."

This is an important book. It is well written and engaging, with great stories and easy-to-understand analogies. It simultaneously challenges readers and offers very practical advice. I highly recommend it.

Mary Poppendieck
January, 2022

Register your copy of *Lean DevOps* on the InformIT site for convenient access to updates and/or corrections as they become available. To start the registration process, go to informit.com/register and log in or create an account. Enter the product ISBN (9780133847505) and click Submit. Look on the Registered Products tab for an Access Bonus Content link next to this product, and follow that link to access any available bonus materials. If you would like to be notified of exclusive offers on new editions and updates, please check the box to receive email from us.

Figure Credits

Cover image:	Vinap/Shutterstock
Figures 2.1, 2.2, 2.4–2.11, 3.1–3.9, 4.1–4.7, 4.9–4.17, 5.1–5.11, 6.1–6.10, 7.1–7.4, 8.1–8.8, 9.2–9.8, 10.1–10.6, 11.1–11.8, 11.10, 12.1–12.9, 13.1–13.8, 14.1–14.7, 15.1–15.4:	Courtesy of Gabrielle Benefield
Figure 2.3:	John R. Boyd

Acknowledgments

I am far from a natural at writing a book. Its linear format feels overly constraining to the way that I think. Books also feel like a permanent record, while life to me feels more like a constant quest to test ideas, gain knowledge, and correct mistakes to improve yourself and, if you are lucky, maybe make the world a little bit better along the way.

This made creating this book rather arduous. In my desire to help you, the reader, get the most coherent message, I spent an inordinate amount of time rewriting and shuffling content around. I probably would still be at it today if it weren't for the immense help and patience of several key people along the way.

The person most central to helping turn this book into reality, and the one who drew the great illustrations in this book, is my wife and partner-in-crime Gabrielle Benefield. With her product innovation background and my delivery experience, we constantly challenge each other to understand what so often goes wrong with teams and organizations in order to find the best way to help others sustainably deliver the outcomes that really matter. This book, along with the Mobius Loop innovation framework, have come out of years of deep discussion and collaboration to bring out the best in people in order to overcome the problems and dysfunction that so often thwart organizational success.

I also cannot thank Mary and Tom Poppendieck enough for their help and inspiration throughout this process. Both so generously spent the time challenging me to dig deep into my experiences to try to best convey to the world *why* the key pillars of this book are so critical to DevOps success.

I want to extend a special thanks to Colonel David A Hopley OBE RM (Retd). I learned and adopted many of the principles of Mission Command by working alongside many talented military veterans early on in my career. Despite my hazy awareness of their origins and understanding of the nuances that make them so effective, the approach not only resonated with me but always seemed to work better than traditionally run teams. Being the formal commanding officer of the UK Special Forces (SBS) and as a member of the teaching staff at the Joint Services' Defence College, Colonel Hopley helped improve upon my lay description of Mission Command.

I also want to thank those who hung in through thick and thin reviewing the many iterations of the manuscript, some who also spent several hours helping me clarify my often-jumbled thoughts. This includes: Steve Freeman, James Duncan Davidson, David McNab, Jeff Sutherland, and Tim Beattie. I am also grateful for the patience of the editorial and production team at Addison-Wesley, including: Haze Humbert, Chris Guzikowski, and Menka Mehta. Your help turned this book into something that I am proud of.

Finally, there are a number of people who were instrumental as sounding boards to help clarify many of the ideas in this book, including (in no particular order): Peter Webb, Priit Kaasik, Heikko Ellermaa, Martin Sulg, Ainar Sepp, Sarah-Jane Mason, Chris Matts, Ademar Aguiar, and Henrik Kniberg. You helped me express *why* the approaches in this book not only work, but can help others on their own journey to learn, improve, and maybe make the world a little bit better for all of us.

About the Author

Robert Benefield is an experienced technical leader who has decades of experience delivering robust on-demand services to solve hard problems in demanding ecosystems including banking and securities trading, medical and pharmaceutical, energy, telecom, government, and Internet services. His continual eagerness to learn and work with others to make a difference has taken him from building computers and writing code in the early days of the Internet at Silicon Valley startups to the executive suite in large multinational companies. He shares his unique experience in the hopes that others can continue to build on it without having to collect quite as many scars along the way.

Introduction

Delivering on-demand services well is never easy. Your success hinges on having both the capability and capacity to deliver what your customer needs while doing so at high speed with the consistency, reliability, security, privacy, and cost effectiveness that they expect. This is just as true whether you are providing an IT service or a more traditional courier or electric utility service.

However, unlike more traditional services, IT service providers are far less restricted by organizational size or physical location. With so many quickly deployable tools and cloud capabilities available, even the smallest IT service providers can now instantly scale to address nearly any identified market need globally.

Where IT service delivery providers do struggle is predictably and reliably delivering services that match customer expectations. This, of course, matters. No one wants the frustration and disappointment of a service that falls short of what is needed. What makes this particularly frustrating is that such shortfalls are not caused by misunderstanding the market need or the functionality customers are looking for. If anything, IT is flooded by tools and techniques that allow businesses to analyze and validate ideas quickly. Instead, the problems arise from awareness gaps caused by the way organizations deliver and manage the services themselves.

As IT service stacks grow in complexity, it becomes far more difficult to determine, let alone ensure, that the dynamics between service components and the delivery ecosystem match what the customer expected. Rather than put measures in place to improve their awareness and understanding of these dynamics, delivery teams have focused on other factors like delivering more faster, using the latest cloud technologies and architectural approaches, or adopting the process or methodology most in fashion. Unfortunately, in the process the delivery teams unknowingly create further disconnects that fragment the information flow and context necessary to understand those dynamics.

As the resulting gap between what delivery teams *believe* they are providing and what is *actually* delivered grows, the team's ability to maintain sufficient context to make effective decisions steadily degrades. Even when disconnects are found, organizations often double down on more processes and misunderstood tooling that do little to effectively bridge the gaps. This creates a vicious loop that creates more frustration as the team drifts further away from being able to deliver to meet customer expectations.

Learning How to See

It is not inevitable that delivery teams have to fall into such a dysfunctional spiral. To break the cycle, you first need to understand the many ways you can lose your situational awareness, from deeply entrenched bad habits that fragment information flow to biases and perceptions that distort your understanding of a situation and what is important. Only then can you begin to put measures in place to counteract these tendencies and improve everyone's situational awareness.

Sharpening your situational awareness is like gaining a new sense or superpower you never knew you had. I like to think of it as learning how to see.

The primary objective of this book is to help you on that journey so that you and your organization can close the awareness gap and deliver services that your customers can use to reach their target outcomes. This book is geared primarily for two audiences. The first comprises the individual contributors, like software developers and IT Operations staff, who are in the trenches delivering the services. The other key audience comprises the managers and leaders who are responsible for building and directing those delivery teams.

For individual contributors the journey begins by looking at the delivery process itself. The first step is how you determine the objective of the work you are performing. Can it be used to check how well what is delivered aligns with the target outcomes of the customer, or are the measures more output-focused, such as the number of features or service uptime? Then there are the ways you acquire, understand, learn, and improve your ability to deliver. There are a number of misperceptions that inject flaws into our decision making, and ultimately the effectiveness of our actions.

To break this cycle, in this book you will find various techniques to help you measure and improve your situational awareness and the quality of information flow across your organization so that you are able to make better delivery decisions that move your services closer toward meeting your customer's target outcomes. Along the way many of the excuses people make for not changing their behavior and way of working, from managing work to governance procedures, will be debunked so that you and the team can continue to make progress.

Here, managers and delivery leadership will find strategies to help delivery teams spot and eliminate awareness gaps and misalignments that hinder effective delivery. This begins by identifying the various problems that arise from many of the management styles, requirements management techniques, processes, communication styles, and incentive structures that have traditionally been relied upon to direct and control people. These lead to poor decision making, conflict, reduced learning and improvement, and ultimately failure to deliver in a way that meets customer expectations. You will also learn about the power of Mission Command, as well as ways to communicate, inspire, and support the members of your team to effectively deliver to the organization's vision and the outcomes customers are trying to achieve.

Those who do not fit neatly in one of the two audiences described likely will also find value within these pages. For example, you might uncover and correct your own misperceptions about service delivery. This can help you better understand and more effectively interact with service delivery teams.

The thinking and techniques in this book are part of the larger Mobius outcome delivery approach, which you can find at https://mobiusloop.com. Mobius has been developed by a community dedicated to harnessing the power of innovation and delivery excellence to more effectively achieve the outcomes that matter.

How to Use This Book

This book can be divided into three parts. The first part introduces the key dynamics that underlie the service delivery challenge. It sets the scene for how those of us in IT service delivery are constantly in danger of focusing far too much on removing delivery friction or reducing perceived delivery risk, often at the cost of maintaining situational awareness and ensuring teams have the ability to learn and improve.

Understanding these dynamics is important for any IT service delivery organization, and especially for those that wish to pursue the promise of DevOps. Overlooking them and missing their effects are what causes so many who pursue DevOps and Agile delivery approaches to fail to meet their promise from the start. This lack of awareness and appreciation of the way they can distort how we perceive the delivery ecosystem is also where many automation tooling and artificial intelligence/machine learning (AI/ML) approaches so often fail.

The second part of the book dives into each of the key elements and the role they play in service delivery. It explores their importance, how they are so often misapplied, and the repercussions to service delivery and the team. I personally feel that this is the most important part of the book, and the one that is so often missing from most guides out there.

The third and last part of the book is a practical guide to help you improve your own service delivery effectiveness. It includes ways to determine the maturity of your team to ensure you have the key elements in place to deliver consistently and effectively. It also has a number of suggestions for how to organize and manage the flow of work, build and deploy instrumentation and automation solutions, and deal with governance associated with internal controls and those required to meet legal and regulatory requirements.

My Own Journey

This book draws from my own journey working in the trenches as an individual contributor and, later, a technical leader to build great IT services and improve the effectiveness of the teams delivering them. I know from firsthand experience that every ecosystem has different challenges, and what I have learned from my own missteps along the way has kept me levelheaded and practical. More than anything, I want this book to be a useful addition to your bookshelf for a long time. This is why the focus of this book is to help you better understand your circumstances so that you and your organization can deliver more effectively, not to talk about some specific process or set of technology that will quickly be supplanted by the next big fad.

I have been blessed throughout my career to have met and worked alongside a number of people far smarter than I am who early on in my career exposed me to revolutionary concepts and ways of working. Some had worked alongside John Boyd's "Fighter Mafia." Others were Training Within Industry (TWI) veterans, or had to come up with ways to deliver highly reliable services long before the existence of concepts like cloud computing or continuous delivery. Only later did I realize that what I learned along the way is what has allowed me to quickly cut through delivery ecosystem noise to help teams overcome seemingly intractable problems. At times it has felt like a superpower, one that I hope I can share to help you reduce your own delivery pain and frustration to secure success.

Chapter 1

The Problem with IT Service Delivery

Tell me and I forget. Teach me and I remember. Involve me and I learn.

Benjamin Franklin

In the fast-moving hypercompetitive world of today, innovation is as crucial as it is hard. People want ever better solutions faster. This requires pushing the envelope, taking chances into the new and unknown. While such bets do not always succeed, playing it safe risks a slide into irrelevance.

September 23, 2010:

Blockbuster Entertainment filed for Chapter 11 bankruptcy protection after suffering from challenging losses due to strong competition from Netflix and other video on-demand services. Despite having a commanding lead in home video rentals and an offer to enter the video on demand business as early as 1999, Blockbuster failed to foresee the growing popularity of mail-order and streaming movie services.

Few industries face expectations for innovation as high as those the IT industry faces. From smartphones and the applications and services that bring new capabilities instantly to our fingertips, to the advanced analytics engines that help us understand ourselves and the universe around us ever faster and more accurately, we have grown to expect a continuous stream of revolutionary breakthroughs that both titillate and improve the quality of our lives.

But this increasingly rapid flow has hardly been cost free.

January 3, 2018:

Security vulnerabilities Meltdown and Spectre were revealed to the world. Each exploits weaknesses in the speculative execution features found on most modern microprocessors, allowing an attacker to reveal and extract targeted private data. Being at the hardware level, these vectors thwarted both system and virtualization security protections. This created particularly damaging risks to cloud service providers and their customers. IT providers dependent upon legacy software were left with the choice of painful upgrades and patches or remaining vulnerable. To make matters worse, many of the initial firmware, operating system, and virtualization patches were haphazardly created and rolled out. These created instability, unwanted reboots, and occasional bricking of systems. Patches also degraded system performance between 2 and 19 percent.[1]

Each innovation brings with it additional layers of technology, increasing the level of complexity in the operating stack. With so many moving parts produced by an ever growing list of providers, it is difficult for any one person to definitively know everything there is to know about an IT stack they rely upon or are responsible for. Like a building with an unknown foundation, this complexity creates a level of uncertainty that makes innovation more difficult. It also threatens to add fragility that drives up the likelihood of failure.

At the same time that technical stacks have increased in complexity, customer patience for failure has eroded. As demands for using IT solutions to solve problems have grown, IT has become deeply embedded into nearly every aspect of our lives, large and small. Now everything from our household appliances and cars to banks and emergency services relies upon an increasingly intricate web of software and IT hosted services to function. Any one failure can cascade into something both crippling and costly for both the user community and the provider. What constitutes a failure has also expanded to include not just faults and broken functionality but also poor usability and missed expectations.

1. "Speculative Execution Exploit Performance Impacts - Describing the performance impacts to security patches for CVE-2017-5754 CVE-2017-5753 and CVE-2017-5715," Red Hat: https://access.redhat.com/articles/3307751

August 1, 2012:

The major market maker Knight Capital Group suffered from an error in its SMARS algorithmic router software that led to a $460 million trading loss over the course of 45 minutes. This exceeded the total assets of the firm, eventually pushing the company to be acquired.

Solving for innovation speed, reliability, and expectations matching has kicked off a competition between two approaches: *reducing delivery friction* and *managing service delivery risk*. This competition is important as it affects how organizations approach DevOps, and ultimately its chances for success. However, while each approach does address some important factors, each also contains a number of serious flaws. These not only cause frustrating delivery problems themselves, but can actually hinder the organization from achieving the single most important aspect of service delivery: effectively helping customers reach their target outcomes.

Approach #1: Reduce Delivery Friction

September 7, 2017:

Credit reporting agency Equifax announced that hackers broke in and stole the personal information of up to 143 million American consumers. The break-in was reported to have occurred sometime in May through an exploit of a previously reported Apache Struts vulnerability. Despite a patch being readily available since March that fixed the problem, Equifax appears to not have taken the necessary precautions to remove the vulnerability until well after the breach. Unnamed sources claim that the decision to delay might have occurred due to resource contention with other software development activities.

Being perceived as too slow to respond to events, regardless of whether it is fixing a new bug or vulnerability or addressing some new customer demand or regulatory requirement, can be not only embarrassing but fatal to a business. It undermines trust and confidence in an organization's competence.

What is worse, speed is not only a matter of how many minutes or hours are needed to respond, but also whether the organization responds more quickly than its competitors. With it becoming increasingly easier to find and change to a new supplier, such perceptions can lead to a rapid loss of market share.

This desire to increase speed and agility has, not surprisingly, kicked off a rush to optimize delivery response. The most obvious place for delivery teams to start has been to look for any sources of delivery friction in the environment that can be eliminated.

Delivery friction is anything that reduces delivery speed, throughput, or responsiveness. As there are real gains that can be achieved by eliminating delivery friction, the industry has been flooded with solutions.

For instance, Agile methodologies like Scrum and Kanban target the traditionally long delivery cycles that make changing delivery priorities and getting solutions to market slow and cumbersome. Breaking work into small batches as these methodologies prescribe also has the added benefit of gaining feedback more quickly, which can help reduce the waste caused by misunderstood or misaligned requirements.

Likewise, the coding practices and release engineering tooling improvements that accompany DevOps' continuous integration/continuous delivery initiatives often push developers toward more frequent code check-ins into less complicated code repository structures. These together with more rapid build, integration, and testing cycles increase the amount of feedback developers get during delivery. This allows problems to be spotted and addressed far more quickly while context is still fresh in people's minds. Pair programming, unit tests, and code reviews also help developers write more elegant code while improving the knowledge of the code base across the team.

The move away from architectural monoliths to more self-contained modular services running on cloud instances that can be spun up and down nearly instantly makes the process of scaling and changing out aging and no longer suitable components potentially much faster and less daunting. Platform-as-a-Service (PaaS) and open source software solutions allow developers to share and borrow solutions to common problems, further speeding up the time it takes to get solutions to market. Configuration and orchestration automation tools like Puppet and Kubernetes allow thousands of service instances to be managed globally by a handful or tens of engineers.

All of these friction reduction improvements sound great. However, they can have a number of dark sides that few openly acknowledge, let alone fully understand. These not only create headaches for people in the delivery organization, they also get in the way of delivering the outcomes that customers care about.

The Downsides of Targeting Delivery Friction

The first challenge with fixating on eliminating delivery friction is that it is easy for delivery teams to focus on building as much as they can as quickly as they can rather than on trying to understand what the customer is trying to accomplish and how their solution might help them achieve it. Some believe that by simply delivering more you will eventually deliver something customers find useful. Others who have been influenced by traditional financial accounting often translate building more assets while expending the same number of man hours as a financial win regardless of their utility. Both are incredibly wasteful and count on success being little more than a matter of chance.

This cycle of producing as much as you can as fast as possible is often reinforced by delivery teams being evaluated on how much they can deliver in a period of time. At first glance this might not seem like much of a problem, but if you feel that your throughput is falling below expectations, it can be extremely tempting to push friction elimination to the extreme by cutting corners and take on unnecessary risks for the benefit of speed.

March 22, 2016:

Open source developer Azer Koçulu unpublished more than 250 of his own modules from the NPM package manager due to a trademark disagreement. One of those, left-pad, was a mindlessly simple module used to pad out the lefthand side of strings with zeroes or spaces. Despite being only five lines long, left-pad became a critical dependency for tens of thousands of projects, including widely used Node and Babel. Its disappearance caused development and deployment activities worldwide to fall over, exposing the brittleness of the NPM system.

This push to release faster has also been far from inclusive. The development-centric nature means that most improvements have focused on making the lives of developers easier, often to the exclusion of others. QA, and especially operational teams, often find themselves being pushed or worked around for the sake of increasing delivery speed. As these groups are usually measured by metrics such as service uptime and the frequency and severity of production problems, they feel that this rushing is against their best interests, jeopardizing their ability to perform their jobs effectively. It also doesn't help that many developers only have limited awareness of, and often little interest in, the technology stack they are deploying into. This increases the odds of something going wrong.

January 31, 2017:

Source code hosting service Gitlab.com experienced a major service outage due to the accidental removal of data from their primary database server. While troubleshooting a production problem on a secondary server, an engineer accidentally wiped the data in the primary server's database. None of the backups were in a state to be sufficiently useful to restore all lost data. In the end it is estimated that 6 hours of data, including 4979 comments and 707 user accounts, were lost in 5037 projects.

Operationally focused teams have pushed back. While they are not opposed to reducing friction, they favor actions that minimize problems arising in the first place. This has given birth to our second approach, managing *service delivery risk*.

Approach #2: Managing Service Delivery Risk

February 29, 2012:

Microsoft Azure suffered a massive 36-hour outage due to a leap year bug in the SSL transfer certificate handling code that manages communications between host agents and their virtual guest agents. Certificates were given invalid dates that created errors that ultimately caused entire clusters to error out and go offline. This problem was made worse by a code rollback attempt that failed due to incompatibility problems between the rollback code and newer networking plugins. This created further complications that extended the length of the outage.

Being able to respond quickly to failure is great. But service support and IT Operations teams know that failure can be costly, often in ways that others fail to understand until it is too late. It not only consumes massive amounts of support resources to respond and deal with production problems, it also damages trust with the customer. It is better to try to avoid failure in the first place.

Teams that feel this way instead favor trying to manage service delivery risk directly. Anything that is unknown, poorly documented, or insufficiently understood is an unmanaged danger that puts the organization at risk of failure.

To mitigate such dangers, teams that prioritize risk management attempt to make all risks knowable up-front. Because undocumented variation is considered the largest source of unmanaged danger, such organizations typically begin by mandating that all delivery activities follow standardized "best practices." These practices are heavily documented and include most day-to-day activities spanning from maintenance and troubleshooting to making infrastructure and service changes. The idea is that the danger of undocumented variation can be minimized by forcing everything to follow a heavily documented standard.

Knowing that not all needed changes can be completely standardized, nonstandard changes are put through a process that attempts to make them known enough that the risks they might create can be captured and assessed. This is done by documenting details about the changes, how they will be performed, and their potential impact, and then submitting them through a governance review and controls process where they can be reviewed by responsible parties to determine whether any potential risks from the proposed changes are acceptable. If they are not, the party wanting to make the change needs to abandon the change or make modifications to it to make it acceptable.

Documenting every possible standard practice is both tedious and time consuming. Rather than coming up with all of these processes themselves, most organizations adopt them from one of the many popular IT service management frameworks such as ITIL[2]. These frameworks have the benefit of being known as industry best practices full of lots of easy-to-use

2. "What is ITIL," https://www.itgovernance.co.uk/itil

templates and procedures that many IT organizations are familiar with. They are also widely recognized by auditors for legal and regulatory compliance.

The Downsides of Targeting Service Delivery Risk

Implementing an industry best practice to minimize unknown variation and enable responsible parties to review nonstandard changes before they are pushed live sounds like a good idea. While all the extra processing might introduce additional delivery friction, it seems like the sort that might help the organization deliver more effectively. Isn't having a service that performs as expected a critical part of what a customer needs?

The problem with this approach begins with the fact that it makes four flawed assumptions:

- Work will be predictable.
- People will correctly follow a documented process.
- People in authority are capable of making effective decisions.
- Industry-certified frameworks are less risky than noncertified or lesser-known approaches.

The first assumption is that the vast majority of work needing to be performed in production will necessarily be predictable enough that all necessary steps to get to a satisfactory result can be documented beforehand without any need for variation.

This leads us to the second assumption, which is the belief that everyone will follow all documented processes exactly without any variation. Even though service management frameworks demand an audit trail, the vast majority accept the change script and checklist that engineers follow as sufficient evidence without any real programmatic means to ensure that someone hasn't miskeyed an action, done something out of order, or taken shortcuts along the way.

There is also the reliance on "responsible parties" chosen to sit on a Change Advisory Board (CAB) to review changes to determine whether the risks they pose are acceptable. The members of these CABs are usually selected from managers, heads of functions, and key stakeholders of areas affected by the change. While CABs usually can catch such problems as scheduling conflicts and communication gaps, they are usually far enough away from the day-to-day details that it is difficult for them to have enough awareness and understanding of the potential risks the changes pose to the ecosystem and the dangers they might have for the customer.

The final problem with this approach is that it silently makes the assumption that the current state is by default somehow less risky than any nonstandard one. Not only is that not necessarily true, inaction can actually *increase* the risk to the organization. I have personally seen organizations get caught in this trap a number of times. Sometimes it is a critical customer threatening to leave, or demands from some regulatory body under the threat of major fines and legal action, if a particular change they absolutely had to have was not made by a certain date. Other times a dangerous defect has been found in a critical service, usually one involving some commercial third party, that requires an extended downtime window to fix. In such cases it can be extremely difficult to push through a change quickly, even when not doing so can jeopardize the future existence of the organization.

The Essence of Delivery

The customer inevitably finds themselves stuck in the middle of this conflict between those who try to optimize for delivery speed and attempt to manage risk. Naturally, customers want both quick delivery and no faults. They simply do not understand why they cannot have both. Meanwhile, each team thinks their approach is right and their goals should be prioritized. Do the IT Operations staff not understand the time and innovation pressures in the market? Is the work of the delivery team as risky as is being implied? They both seem to care deeply about the success of the company. How can these two technical teams have such opposing views?

Can DevOps be a solution?

Before answering those questions, it is worthwhile to first consider the purpose for why we are doing IT delivery in the first place.

At the most basic level, delivery is nothing more than a chain of interrelated decisions. Like any decision, they are made to reach some sort of preferred, or at least less bad, state than the current trajectory. In the context of service delivery, they are made for the purpose of helping customers achieve their target outcome.

A *target outcome* is a set of desirable or otherwise important conditions that the customer wants to reach. Delivering to achieve a target outcome is more than simply delivering an output or meeting a promise of a service reliability level. Reaching a target outcome means functionally satisfying a need, whether it is to solve an existing problem, minimize or prevent one from occurring, exploit an opportunity, or to otherwise improve the current condition.

The connection between an outcome and the tool or service attempting to deliver it can be straightforward ("I want to stay informed about today's weather so that I know if I need to alter what I wear"), complex with many solutions ("I want better global weather and market information so that I can choose the best crop to farm"), nested ("I want better climate information to design buildings that have a lower carbon footprint but stay comfortable for its inhabitants"), or even part of an aspirational journey ("I want to reduce man's impact on the environment worldwide"). The target outcome provides us with a direction or purpose to deliver toward.

In order to reach an outcome, you need to have some idea of current conditions. What is the size of the gap between the current state and the desired state? What are the means available that can be used to attempt to close that gap, what obstacles might get in the way that need to be avoided or overcome along the way, and how can we tell if we are making material progress toward the target outcome? The answers together are what we call our *situational awareness*, the idea that we know what is going on around us to make better decisions more rapidly.

Any good decision maker reflects on the impact of the decisions they make. Did they result in the changes we were expecting, and did those changes result in progress toward the target outcome? Understanding what did and did not go well and why helps us learn and improve our decision making, and thereby our ability to deliver more effectively, in the future.

Beginning the DevOps Journey

March 2015:

Woolworths Australia completed a 6-year project to replace a 30-year-old in-house ERP system with SAP. The project's lack of understanding of day-to-day business procedures quickly led to the breakdown in the company's supply chain. Shelves quickly became bare while suppliers and stores struggled to get orders through the new system. Store managers lost the ability to get profit and loss reports for 18 months, limiting their ability to manage profitability at the store level. These failures contributed to a $766 million loss and the layoff of hundreds of employees.[3]

Unfortunately, in emphasizing outputs and uptime we assume but do not check that we are actually delivering solutions that help customers get to their target outcomes. The reason for this comes back to how we have become accustomed to working. It would seem odd to most people working in delivery to be expected to figure out themselves what the customer is trying to achieve and how to deliver it to them. We instead expect to be told what features or requirements need to be delivered. This removes a lot of ambiguity and eliminates the need for any direct customer contact.

Having trackable lists of requirements also makes it far clearer how we will be evaluated. Managers can simply measure delivery outputs like how much work was done and how well it aligns to what was asked for.

While unambiguous and easy to manage, measuring the delivery of outputs provides little incentive for workers to check that customers are able to use what was delivered to reach their target outcomes. The fact that managers tend to be measured on their ability to deliver requirements on time and on budget only compounds this problem. It is as if any gap between what was asked for and what the customer needs is the customer's problem. This is far from a sustainable strategy for any business.

3. "Three ERP failure case studies and what you can learn from them," ERP Focus, https://www.erpfocus.com/erp-failure-case-studies.html

Being disconnected from target outcomes also changes what factors are considered when making delivery decisions. With evaluation metrics taking center stage, focus turns to any actions that can turn them favorable. Teams soon learn how to quickly game measures such as velocity (by breaking up jobs into many small tasks), bug counts (closing, deprioritizing, or reclassifying them as "features"), and code coverage (creating poorly constructed unit tests that do little to test the underlying code), undercutting their intended value.

So what does all this have to do with DevOps?

To be truly successful, a DevOps implementation has to remove all the barriers and disincentives that prevent the delivery organization from helping customers reach their target outcomes. This takes systematically moving away from traditional beliefs, habits, and approaches about IT service delivery and establishing a more situationally aware, outcome-based, and continually learning and improving approach.

As you will see, this transition is incredibly difficult to do. Habits and beliefs are hard to break with. This takes a lot of convincing, especially when it challenges traditional systems used to assess people and work product performance.

The best way to take people on this journey is to begin with making the dysfunction visible. The best approach is to strip the delivery process back to its core, the decision.

One person, a US Air Force pilot and military strategist named John Boyd, pursued such a search in order to understand what is necessary to optimize the decision-making process. As you will see, his journey provides a useful lens to better understand the decision-making process itself and how improving your decision making can help you deliver the target outcomes that matter.

Summary

IT service delivery organizations commonly feel that they must choose between optimizing for output and speed by targeting delivery friction, and managing risk by minimizing unknown variation through defined practices and review processes. Not only are such approaches flawed, they cause teams to lose sight of the fact that service delivery is about delivering solutions that help customers achieve their target outcomes.

To deliver more effectively, teams should instead think of service delivery as a decision-making process. By understanding how decisions are made, decision-making can be improved to deliver the target outcomes that matter.

Chapter 2

How We Make Decisions

Prepare for the unknown by studying how others in the past have coped with the unforeseeable and the unpredictable.

George S. Patton

Decisions act as our steering wheel that guides us through the pathways of life. This is true whether a decision is simple, like deciding whether to have a cup of coffee, or complex, such as choosing the best architectural design for a new critical service. Decisions are also how we guide our own actions when delivering IT services, whether it is in how we approach coding a new feature or troubleshooting a production problem.

However, being effective at decision making isn't an innate skill. In fact, it is one that is surprisingly difficult to learn. For starters, effectiveness is more than how fast you decide or how adeptly you execute that decision. It must also achieve its objective while accounting for any conditions that might change the dynamics and thereby the outcome trajectory of your actions in the executing ecosystem.

In this chapter, we take a deeper look at the decision-making process itself. We will also explore the ingredients necessary for effective decision making, how they impact the decision process, and how they can become impaired.

Examining the Decision-Making Process

Decision making is the process of pulling together any *information* and *context* about our situation and evaluating it against the *capabilities* available to progress toward the *desired outcome*. This is an iterative, rapid process. To work well we have to determine with each cycle whether the decision progressed us toward the outcome. If so, how effective was it, and if not, why not? We also have to look to see if anything unexpected occurred that can tell us more about the situation and the efficacy of our current capabilities that we can use to adjust and adapt.

Figure 2.1

Figuring out the right mix of context and capabilities for decision making can be challenging.

Even though we make decisions all the time, the process for making them can be surprisingly complex and fraught with mistakes. Consider the example of taking a friend to a coffee shop. While the task is inherently simple, there are all sorts of elements involved that, without the right level of scrutiny, can cause problems. You may find that you have the wrong address (*wrong or incomplete information*), that you took a wrong turn because you thought you were on a different street (*flawed situational context*), or that your car is having engine trouble and the coffee shop is too far to walk to (*mismatched capabilities*). It is also possible that your capabilities, context, and information to get to the coffee shop are all fine, but your friend is angry because the shop has no Internet service and she only agreed to go there with you because she assumed she would be able to get online (*misunderstood target outcome*).

Spotting and rectifying mistakes under such simple conditions is easy. However, as the setting becomes far more complex, particularly as decisions take the form of large chains like those needed in IT service delivery, mistakes can far more easily hide under several layers of interactions, where they can remain undiscovered all while causing seemingly intractable problems. As these mistakes mount, they steadily degrade our understanding of our delivery ecosystem in ways that, unless found, undermine the overall effectiveness of future decisions.

The military strategist John Boyd became captivated by the importance of decision making while trying to understand what factors determined the likelihood of success in combat. He studied how simple mistakes could cascade and destroy any advantage a unit might have, and sought ways to improve decision-making processes in order to create a strategic advantage over the enemy. His work soon came to revolutionize how elite units, and many Western militaries, began to approach warfare.

Boyd and the Decision Process

Like many of us, John Boyd began his search for what factors increased the likelihood for success by looking at the tools (in this case weapons) of the victor. Boyd was an American fighter pilot who had served in the Korean War, where he flew the highly regarded F-86 fighter jet that dominated the skies against Soviet-designed MiG-15s. He knew firsthand there were differences in each aircraft model's capabilities. He theorized that there must be a way to quantitatively calculate an aircraft's performance so that it could be used to compare the relative performance of different types. If this were possible, one could then determine both the optimal design and the combat maneuvers that would be the most advantageous against the enemy.

His work led to the discovery of Energy-Maneuverability (EM) theory. It modeled an aircraft's specific energy to determine its relative performance against an enemy. The formula was revolutionary and is still used today in the design of military aircraft.

From there, Boyd looked to combine his theory with the optimal processes to fully exploit an aircraft's capabilities. He used his time at the Fighter Weapons School in Nevada to develop *Aerial Attack Study*, a book of aerial combat maneuvers first released inside the US military in 1961. It is considered so comprehensive that it is still used by combat pilots as the definitive source today.

Having both a means to create the best tools and processes to use them, most of us would figure that Boyd now possessed the formula for success in warfare. Despite all of this, Boyd was still troubled.

When he ran his own formula against some of the most successful weapons of World War II and the Korean War, he found many instances where the "successful" ones were far less capable than those of the enemy. Particularly disturbing to him, this included the highly regarded F-86.

Figure 2.2

Searching for the ingredients to air superiority was difficult.

As Boyd went back to earlier wars, he found that this was hardly unique. In fact, throughout history, having superior weaponry seemed to rarely be a relevant factor in determining the victor. As Boyd continued to research, he repeatedly found instances where numerically and technically superior forces lost spectacularly to their poorly equipped opponents. That meant that despite his revolutionary work on EM theory, combat success couldn't be determined by any one formula or set of maneuvers.

Boyd studied great military tacticians from Sun Tzu and Alexander the Great to the Mongols, Clausewitz, and Helmut von Moltke. He also interviewed surviving officers of the most successful German Army units during World War II to understand what made them different. He soon realized that battlefield success hinged on which side could make the right decisions more quickly and accurately to reach a given objective. This was true even in cases where the victor possessed inferior weapons, fewer soldiers, poorer training, and battlefield terrain disadvantages. Not only that, but he noticed that this decision-making advantage could be gained just as well by either optimizing your own decision-making abilities or by thwarting those of your opponent.

This realization led Boyd to examine more deeply how the decision-making process works and what can make it more or less effective. In the process, he invented what is now known as the *OODA loop*.

Operation Millennium Challenge

A good recent demonstration of outmaneuvering superior enemy forces happened in the *Operation Millennium Challenge 2002* war game event held by the US Armed Forces in the Persian Gulf. On one side was the "Blue" side with the latest US weapons, while on the other was an unknown "Red" adversary armed with little more than light weaponry.

The Blue side had built elaborate plans to make the most of its superior firepower. What they had not counted on was the savvy leadership of the Red team under Lt. General Paul Van Riper. Van Riper knew there was no way he could win head-to-head against his more capable opponent. Instead, he used his ability to adapt rapidly to outmaneuver and overwhelm the Blue side. He used motorcycle messengers and World War II–style light signal communications to avoid Blue's sophisticated electronic surveillance. He then launched a surprise raid on the Blue fleet by using lightly armed speedboats to locate the fleet followed by a large salvo of missiles. This approach not only eliminated any advantages Blue had, but also used Blue's size and rigidity of command as friction against itself.

Despite Red's seemingly long odds, the Blue side's ability to react was subsequently overwhelmed, resulting in 16 ships being "sunk," including an aircraft carrier, ten cruisers, and five of the six amphibious ships involved. In all, 20,000 Blue service personnel were "lost" by the surprise maneuver, greatly embarrassing the US military.

The OODA Loop

Boyd hypothesized that all intelligent creatures and organizations undergo decision loops continuously as they interact within their environment. Boyd described this as four interrelated and overlapping processes that are cycled through continuously and which he called the OODA loop, depicted in Figure 2.3. These processes include the following:

- **Observe:** The collection of all practically accessible current information. This can be anything from observed activity, unfolding conditions, known capabilities and weaknesses present, available intelligence data, and whatever else is at hand. While having lots of information can be useful, information quality is often more important. Even understanding what information you do not have can improve the efficacy of decisions.
- **Orient:** The analysis and synthesis of information to form a mental perspective. The best way to think of this is as the context needed for making your decision. Becoming oriented to a competitive situation means bringing to bear not only previous training and experiences, but also the cultural traditions and heritage of whoever is doing the orienting—a complex interaction that each person and organization handles differently. Together with observe, orient forms the foundation for situational awareness.
- **Decide:** Determining a course of action based upon one's mental assessment of how likely the action is to move toward the desired outcome.
- **Act:** Following through on a decision. The results of the action, as well as how well these results adhere to the mental model of what was expected, can be used to adjust key aspects of our orientation toward both the problem and our understanding of the greater world. This is the core of the *learning* process.

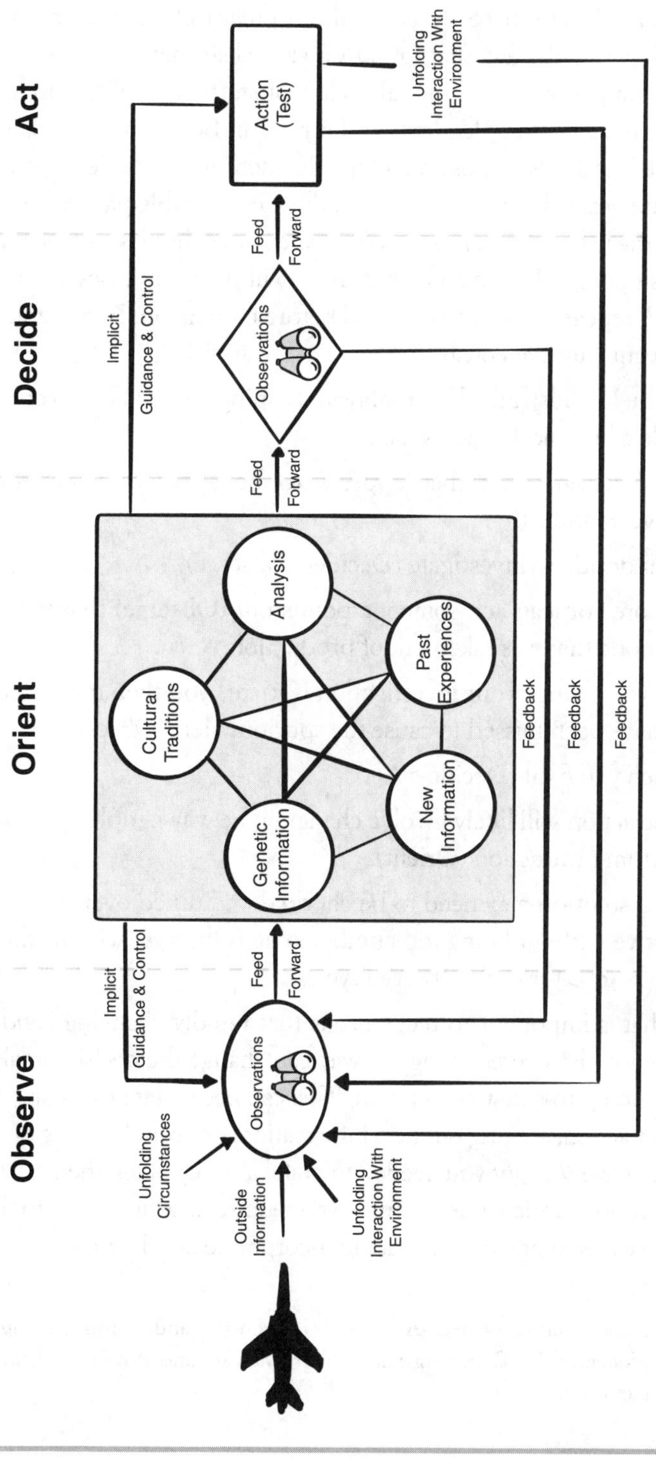

Figure 2.3
OODA loop.

Many who compare OODA to the popular PDCA cycle[1] by W. Edwards Demming miss the fact that OODA makes clear that the decision process is rarely a simple one-dimensional cycle that starts with observation and ends with action. The complex lines and arrows in Boyd's original diagram visualize the hundreds of possible loops through these simple steps in order to get to the desired outcome. As such, the most suitable path is not always the next in the list. Instead, it is the one that ensures there is sufficient alignment to the situation. That means that there will be many cases where steps are skipped, repeated, or even reversed before moving on. In some situations all steps occur simultaneously.

To help illustrate this nonlinear looping, let's take a very simplistic example of a typical process failure.

You get an alert that appears to be a failed production service (Observe->Orient).

You decide to investigate (Decide->Observe).

Before you can act, someone points out (Observe) that the alert came from a node that was taken out of production.

As you change your investigation (Orient) you then may go to see what might have been missed to cause the spurious alert (Observe).

Then you fix it (Decide->Act).

The action will likely involve changing the way people approach pulling nodes from production (Orient).

This solution may need to be checked and tuned over time to ensure it is effective without being too cumbersome (Observe, with further possible Decide->Act->Orient->Observe cycles).

What is important to recognize is that rapidly changing conditions and information discovered along the way can change the decision maker's alignment, leading to a new orientation. This can necessitate canceling or revising a plan of action, seeking out new information, or even throwing out decisions you may have *thought* you needed to make and replacing them with different and more appropriate ones. It may even require knowing when to throw away a once well-used practice in order to incorporate new learning.

1. Known as "Plan-Do-Check-Act," it is a control and continuous improvement cycle pioneered by Demming and Walter Shewart and now used heavily in Lean Manufacturing.

With the loop in hand and understanding how changing conditions can affect the way it is traversed, Boyd became interested in exploring the ways that one could not only out-decide their opponent, but also disrupt their decision process. Was there a way to overwhelm the enemy by changing the dynamics on the battlefield beyond the enemy's ability to decide effectively?

Boyd ultimately called this "getting inside" your opponent's decision cycle. Increasing the rate of change beyond the enemy's ability to adjust effectively can overwhelm their decision making enough to render them vulnerable to a nimbler opponent. He realized that the path to do this started with traversing the OODA decision loop to the target outcome faster than your opponent can.

With this knowledge, Boyd tried to identify the ingredients necessary to drive effective decision making.

The Ingredients of Decision Making

Figure 2.4
Success is having sufficient amounts of the right ingredients.

Just like any recipe, decisions are only as good as the quality of the ingredients on hand and the skill used putting them together. While the importance of any one ingredient can often differ from one decision to the next, they all play an important role in determining the efficacy of the decision-making process.

In order to understand more, let's take a look at each of these ingredients.

Ingredient 1: The Target Outcome

An effective decision is one that helps you in your pursuit of your *target outcome*. Target outcomes are the intended purpose of the decision. The better any target outcomes are understood by those making decisions, the better the person making the decision can choose the option that is most likely to lead to progress toward achieving those outcomes.

Figure 2.5
The target outcome.

Besides helping to highlight the better option in a decision, awareness of the target outcome also helps to determine decision efficacy by providing a means to measure any progress made toward it. This aids in learning and improvement, making it far easier to investigate cases where progress did not match expectations. This can help answer questions like:

- Was the decision executed in a timely and accurate way? If not, why not?
- Did the decision maker and others involved in executing it have sufficient situational awareness of current conditions to make an optimal match? If not, why not?

- Was the decision the best one to execute, or were there other, more suitable decisions that could have been made that might have had a more positive impact on outcome progress? If better alternatives existed, what can be learned to make it more likely to choose the more optimal decisions in the future?

The third point is the most important of these to note. While there are other ways to find awareness and execution improvement areas, it is far more difficult to determine whether the decision chosen to pursue, as well as the process for choosing it, could itself be improved without an adequately defined target outcome to measure it against. Remaining unaware that the target premise used to decide which decisions you need to make is flawed is incredibly corrosive to the efficacy of your decision-making abilities.

Despite their importance, target outcomes rarely get the attention they deserve. The problem begins with the fact that most decision frameworks spend far more time focusing on how quickly you execute a decision and not whether the decision is the one you need to make. This is especially true in IT, where far more value is often placed on team responsiveness and delivery speed. What information IT teams do get about outcome intent is usually a description of an output, such as a new feature, or performance target, like mean time to recover (MTTR).

There are also challenges around the communication of the outcomes themselves. Some people simply do not think delivery teams need to know anything about the desired outcome. More frequently, however, target outcomes are not clearly communicated because the requestor may not have a clear idea themselves of what they are. This "not knowing" your target outcome may sound strange but is surprisingly common.

To illustrate this, let's go back to our coffee shop example.

When we say we want a cup of coffee, what exactly is our underlying intent? It probably isn't to simply have one in our possession. In fact, most of us would be pretty upset if all we had were the disappointingly tepid remains of one.

Figure 2.6
Tepid coffee rarely
sparks joy.

Typically, what we are looking for are the conditions that we associate with obtaining or consuming a cup of coffee. We might like the taste, the warmth, or the fact that it helps us feel more alert. It is possible that we don't actually care about the coffee but are more interested in the opportunity to relax or chat with friends or colleagues. Getting a coffee may be an excuse to find a convenient place to finalize a business opportunity. It might even be as simple as creating an opportunity to get Internet access, as it was with our friend earlier.

What sometimes makes achieving target outcomes tricky is that changing conditions can alter its intent or invalidate it altogether. For instance, stepping out of the office into a hot day can cause someone to change their order to an iced coffee. Suddenly finding yourself late for a meeting can throw out the idea of relaxing at the coffee shop, possibly eliminating the trip entirely. If we are with our Internet-obsessed friend, we might go to a different coffee shop where the coffee is less enjoyable and choose a smaller size or a different blend than we would normally have.

As a result, not only is all the hard work put in to enact the wrong decision a waste, but any measures used to gauge progress can at best be meaningless and at worst perpetuate the problem. Even if by chance you reach your desired outcome, the initial flaw means that your ability to learn from your actions to improve and replicate the success has been undermined, opening you up for surprise and disappointment when it eventually fails.

The military faces very similar challenges. It is easy for a commander to order his troops to march up a hill or send a squadron to bomb a target. But if the commander's intent is not known, conditions might change and destroy any advantage the commander thought the action might have attained at best, or at worst lead to the destruction of the unit.

For this reason, Boyd and others found that it was better to turn the problem on its head, focusing instead on communicating to troops the target outcome rather than the actions they should use to try to achieve it. He became a strong proponent of Mission Command as a means for commanders and subordinates to communicate and build a true understanding of the target outcomes desired from a given mission. Mission Command, as discussed later in Chapter 3, "Mission Command," is an approach to communicate the intent and target outcomes desired that still gives those executing to achieve them the ability to adjust their actions as circumstances require them to do so.

This Mission Command method is useful in the service delivery world of DevOps. Not only does it enable teams to adjust to changing delivery conditions more quickly than more top-down approaches, it also enables teams to better discover and correct any flaws found in their understanding of the target outcomes themselves. Anyone who has worked in a delivery team knows that such flaws happen all the time, mostly due to the fact that few ever get to meet, let alone discuss, target outcomes with the actual customer. Most delivery teams instead have to rely upon proxies from the business or make intelligent guesses based upon their own experience and the data available around them.

It is in these proxies and guesses where things can go very wrong. The worst of these is when the focus is not on the actual outcome itself but on the solution itself, the method used to deliver the solution, or measures that have little connection to the target outcome.

To understand better, let's go through some of the common patterns of dysfunction to see why they occur and how they lead us astray.

Solution Bias

How many times have you been absolutely certain you knew exactly what was needed in order to solve a problem only to find out afterward that the solution was wrong? You are far from alone. It is human nature to approach a problem with a predetermined solution before truly understanding the problem itself. Sometimes it is the allure of a solution that misguides us, while at other times we fail to take the necessary time and effort to fully understand the expected outcome.

We commonly encounter solution bias when vendors push their products and services. Rather than spending any effort figuring out the problems you have and the outcomes you desire, vendors try to create artificial needs that are satisfied by their solution. Some do it by flashing fancy feature "bling." Others list off recognized established companies or competitors who are their customers in the hopes that this will entice you to join the bandwagon. Some look to become your answer for your "strategy" in a particular area, be it "cloud," "mobile," "Agile," "offshoring," "DevOps," or some other industry flavor of the month.

Solution providers are notorious for assuming their offering is the answer for everything. They are hardly the only one who suffers from solution bias, however. Even without the influence of slick marketing literature and sales techniques, customers are just as likely to fall into this trap. Whatever the cause, having a solution bias puts those responsible for delivery in an unenviable spot.

The School Bell

Figure 2.7
School bell.

Architect Alastair Parvin provided an illustrative example of this very problem in a story he gave at a TED talk in 2013.[2] A school had approached his architecture firm to redesign the school building. It was Victorian era with narrow hallways so cramped that it was difficult for students to get through between classes. The school administration had accepted that the construction was going to be expensive, but needed the problem to be solved.

At first glance the problem looked straightforward. The school wanted a new school building with spacious halls to accommodate the students moving between classes. Most of us would take that as a signal to start roughing out a design and a project plan for the school administration to look over.

The architects in Parvin's firm took a different approach. They started by looking more closely at the problem (crowded hallways) and the desired but only indirectly requested outcome (allowing students to move easily between classes). Anyone who has worked with flow problems knows that short, intense bursts can be a real mess. It is better to find ways to have lower and more even flows. This gave the architects an idea.

They came back to the school and recommended that instead of a new building they should redesign the bell system so that smaller school bells went off in different places at different times. This would allow for student traffic to be distributed more evenly, effectively eliminating congestion at a much lower cost. The solution worked brilliantly. By moving away from a predetermined solution the school managed to save millions.

Execution Bias

Figure 2.8
Bill let it be known he was completely focused on the execution.

2. "Architecture for the People by the People," Alistair Parvin: Ted Talk, https://www.ted.com/talks/alastair_parvin_architecture_for_the_people_by_the_people/transcript?language=en

Requesting and delivering inappropriate solutions is not the only way we stray from the target outcome. We all carry any number of personal biases about *how* we, or others on our behalf, execute. There is nothing in itself wrong with having a favorite technology, programming language, process, or management approach. Our previous personal experience, the advice of people we trust, and the realities of the ecosystem we are working in are inevitably going to create preferences.

The problem occurs when the method of execution eclipses the actual target outcome. As Boyd discovered, knowing all the possible maneuvers is of little benefit if there is no target to aim for.

In technology, execution bias can take the form of a favored process framework, technology, vendor, or delivery approach regardless of their appropriateness. When execution bias occurs, there is so much focus on how a particular process, technology, or approach is executed that any target outcomes get overlooked. This is why there can be so many excellent by-the-book Agile, Prince2, and ITIL implementations out there that, despite their process excellence, still fail to deliver what the customer really needs.

Delivering Measures over Outcomes

Good metrics measuring the effectiveness in moving toward achieving a target outcome can be very useful. They can help spot problem areas that require addressing, guide course correcting, and ultimately help teams learn and improve. However, it is far too easy to place more focus on achieving a metric target than the outcomes it is supposed to be aiding. There are two rather common causes for this.

The first is when the target outcomes are poorly understood or, as in our coffee example, more qualitative in nature. It may take a number of attempts with the customer to provide enough clues to really understand what they are looking for. This can seem arduous, especially when multiple teams who have little to no direct interaction with the customer are delivering components that together provide the solution. In many cases teams might find it too hard or time consuming to even try. Instead, they opt to track more easy-to-measure metrics that either follow some standard set of industry best practices or at least might *seem* like a reasonable proxy to measure customer value.

The other cause is the more general and long-held practice by managers to create measures to evaluate the individual performance of teams and team members. In Frederick Wilson Taylor's book *The Principles of Scientific Management*, management's role was to tell their workers what to do and how to do it, using the measures of output and method compliance as the means to gauge, and even incentivize, productivity.

Both cases encourage the use of measures like number of outputs per period of time, found defects, mean time to recover, delivery within budget, and the like. All are easy to measure and have the added benefit of being localized to a given person or team. However, unless a customer is paying only for outputs, they rarely have anything but the most tenuous link to the actual desired outcome.

Encouraging more outputs may not sound like such a bad thing on its face. Who wouldn't want more work done in a given time, or higher uptime? The former nicely measures delivery friction reductions, while the latter provides a sense that risk is being well managed. However, the problem is two-fold. The first and most obvious is that, as we saw in our coffee story, few outcomes are met simply by possessing an output. This is especially true if an output is only a localized part of the delivery. Likewise, few customers would be happy to have a great database on the backend or a high uptime on a service that doesn't help them achieve what they need.

Another challenge comes from human behavior when they know they are being assessed on how well they meet a target. Most will often ruthlessly chase after the target, even if doing so means stripping out everything but the absolute minimum required to achieve it. This is extremely problematic, especially if there is only at best a loose connection between the measure and the desired outcome. I have personally observed teams that have sacrificed service quality and maintainability by reclassifying defects as feature requests to meet defect targets. The defects were still there, and often even worse than before, but as the count of what was being measured was dropping, the team was rewarded for their deceit.

The Objectives and Key Results (OKR) framework tries to overcome this by using a common set of clearly defined qualitative objectives that are intended to provide targeted measures. However, many find doing this well to be difficult. The best objectives are directly tied to the pursuit of the outcomes the customer wants, with key result measures that are both tied to those objectives and have sufficiently difficult targets (to encourage innovation) that they are reachable only some of the time. In this way the targets form more of a direction to go in and a means to measure progress toward rather than some definitive targets that staff and teams feel they are being evaluated against. Unfortunately, this thinking goes against many of the bad assessment habits many of us grew up with in school. Instead, organizations tend to turn objectives into the same traditional output performance criteria with outputs becoming the key results to be quantitatively measured, thereby losing the value and original intent of OKRs.

Lost Bills

The dysfunction caused by output-based metrics is bad enough when everyone involved is in the same organization. It is even worse when such metrics form the basis of compensation between two different firms.

One large company was looking to streamline the operational support of various backend systems used to support the business. The old operational approach had led to many small teams that felt very protective of their space. Rather than fight with them, the CIO decided to wipe the problem away by outsourcing the entire mess.

The systems, much like the business, were stable and mature. The CIO decided that the most effective way to structure the outsourcing contract would be to pay for the number of incident tickets handled.

One of the outsourcing targets was the billing system. Even though billing was one of the most critical parts of the company, and one of the most interconnected, it was generally very stable. The billing process ran every night from 1 to 3 a.m. As it required locking customer records in both the CRM and billing databases, it was important that the process complete well before the Sales and Customer Support teams needed to access the system during the business day.

After a few months, the billing runs started to fail. The outsourced support investigated and noticed a read error of data in the cache containing customer records being processed. They cleared the cache, restarted the billing process, and everything continued seamlessly. The error began to happen more and more frequently. One of the support people decided to automate the recovery with a script. This eliminated the manual work, sped up recovery, and as it opened and closed incident tickets associated with the error, the outsourcer would reap income from the work. Everyone seemed to win.

Another few months went by. Customer Support started noticing that the number of complaints about incorrect bills had been growing significantly. The problems were very strange, with customers being billed for services they had never had. Eventually, it got the attention of the executive staff and a team of engineers was sent in to investigate. What they found was startling.

A CRM system upgrade had turned on the ability for Sales and Customer Support staff to insert double byte and other special characters in the customer database. The billing batch processes could not handle these and would throw an exception when encountered, halting the billing process. Such failures are never good and indicate that there are likely awareness and quality issues in the delivery process.

But this particular problem was far worse than that.

The script that the outsourced support had written "solved" the offending error by dropping the customer identification database records that had been loaded before the special character was hit. The now orphaned billable assets would then be appended to subsequent customers as the process was restarted. This caused three types of errors:

Some customers were billed for products and services they never used.

Some customers were not billed for products and services.Some proportion of these customers also disappeared entirely from the customer and billing databases.

As the outsourced operational support staff were paid by the number of tickets they handled, they had little incentive to find the root cause of the problem, let alone fix it. Instead, they were measured and rewarded for efforts that ultimately ruined the integrity of the customer and billing databases and the overall billing process.

Ingredient 2: Friction Elimination

Figure 2.9
Friction elimination needs to be strategic, not random.

As mentioned in Chapter 1, friction is anything that increases the time and effort needed to reach a target outcome. It can arise at any point along the journey. This includes the decision cycle itself. We can be affected by it from the time and effort to gather and understand the information surrounding a situation through one or more of the various steps needed to make the decision, act upon it, and review its result. Friction can be so potent as to prevent you from reaching an outcome entirely.

Eliminating delivery friction, whether in the form of provisioning infrastructure, building and deploying code, or consuming new capabilities quickly, is what attracts people to DevOps and on-demand service delivery. There is also a lot of value in trying to mitigate many of the sources of wasteful friction whenever possible. But as Boyd found, and what so many of us miss, is that eliminating friction only provides value if it actually results in helping you reach your target outcome.

Many confuse friction elimination with increasing response and delivery speed rather than reaching the outcome. Teams dream of instantly spinning up more capacity and delivering tens or even hundreds of releases a day. Organizations will tout having hundreds of features available at a push of a button. We do all this believing, with little strong supporting evidence, that being fast and producing more will somehow get us to the outcome. It is like buying a fast race car with lots of fancy features and expecting that merely having it, regardless of the type of track or knowing how to drive effectively on it, is enough to win every race.

The gap between the lure of possessing a "potential ability" and effective outcome delivery is often most pronounced when there is friction in the decision cycle itself. "Red" side's win over "Blue" in *Operation Millennium Challenge 2002* is a great demonstration of this. The "Blue" side's superior weaponry was not sufficient to overcome its inferior decision loop agility against the "Red" side.

This same decision cycle friction was likely at work in Boyd's analyses of Korean War era fighter aircraft. The superior abilities of enemy MiG fighter jets over the F-86 that Boyd found was often made irrelevant in the battlefield due to the relatively higher friction in communication flow and command structures of Communist forces compared to those of the US. This friction made it far more difficult for Communist forces to quickly understand and adjust to changing battlefield dynamics, as well as to catch and learn from mistakes. American pilots did not have such problems and exploited these differences to their own advantage.

While the IT service delivery ecosystem does not face quite the same adversarial challenges, these same friction factors do have a significant impact on an organization's success. Teams can have an abundance of capabilities to build and deploy code quickly, yet still have so much decision-making friction that they are prevented from delivering effectively. Such friction can arise from such sources as defects and poorly understood target outcomes to poor technical operations skills. Interestingly, symptoms of decision friction do not necessarily manifest as problems of delivery agility. Often they take the form of misconfigurations, fragile and irreproducible "snowflake" configurations,[3] costly rework, or ineffective troubleshooting and problem resolution. All of these not only impact the service quality that the customer experiences but also can consume more time and resources than former traditional delivery methods did.

Even when delivery agility is a problem, it is not always caused by poor delivery capabilities. I regularly encounter technical delivery teams with nearly flawless Agile practices, continuous integration (CI)/continuous delivery (CD) tooling, and low friction release processes that stumble because the process for deciding what to deliver is excessively slow. At one company, it typically took *17 months* for a six-week technical delivery project to traverse the approval and business prioritization process in order to get into the team's work queue.

Another frequent cause of delivery friction occurs when work that contains one or more key dependencies is split across different delivery teams. The best case in such a situation is that one team ends up waiting days or weeks for others to finish their piece before they can start. However, if the dependencies are deep or even cycle back and forth between teams, such poor planning can drag out for months. At one such company this problem was not only a regular occurrence but in places was *seven* dependencies deep. This meant that even when teams had two-week-long sprints, it would take a *minimum* of 14 weeks for affected functionality to make it through the delivery process. If a bug in an upstream library or module was encountered or if the critical functionality was deprioritized by an upstream team, this delay could (and often did) stretch for additional weeks or months.

3. https://martinfowler.com/bliki/SnowflakeServer.html

Delivery friction can also come from behaviors that are often perceived to improve performance. Long work weeks and aggressive velocity targets can burn out teams, increasing defect rates and reducing team efficiency. Multitasking is often a method used to keep team members fully utilized. But having large amounts of work in progress (WIP), along with the resulting unevenness and predictably unpredictable delivery of work, as well as the added cost of constant context switching, usually results in slower and lower-quality service delivery.

Friction in feedback and information flow can also reduce decision, and thereby delivery, effectiveness. I have encountered many companies that have fancy service instrumentation, data analytics tools, and elaborate reports and yet continually miss opportunities to exploit the information effectively because it takes them far too long to collect, process, and understand the data. One company was trying to use geolocation data in order to give customers location-specific offers like a coupon for 20 percent off a grocery item or an entrée at a restaurant. However, they soon found that it took three days to gather and process the information required, thus making it impossible to execute their plan for just-in-time offers.

These are just a small sampling of all the types of delivery friction. Others can be found in Chapter 4, "Friction," which goes into considerably more depth. Understanding the various friction patterns that exist and their root causes can help you start your own journey to uncover and eliminate the sources of friction in your delivery ecosystem. The next decision-making ingredient, *situational awareness*, not only can aid in this search, but is the key ingredient for building enough context and understanding of your delivery ecosystem to make effective decisions.

Ingredient 3: Situational Awareness

Figure 2.10
Never overestimate your level of situational awareness.

Situational awareness is your ability to understand what is going on in your current ecosystem, and combine it with your existing knowledge and skills to make the most appropriate decisions to progress toward your desired outcome. For Boyd, all this gathering and combining takes place in the OODA loop's *Orient* step.

It makes sense that having information about your delivery ecosystem provides a level of insight into its dynamics to improve the speed and accuracy of the decisions you make in it. It is gaining this edge that has been the draw for everyone from investment banks and marketing companies to IT services organizations to invest in large-scale Big Data and business intelligence initiatives as well as advanced IT monitoring and service instrumentation tools.

But while the desire to collect as much information as possible seems logical, collecting and processing information that is unsuitable or has no clear purpose can actually harm your decision-making abilities. It can distract, misdirect, and slow down your decision making.

What makes information suitable depends heavily upon the right mix of the following factors:

- **Timeliness:** Relevant information needs to be both current and available in a consumable form at the time the decision is being made to have any positive impact. Information that arrives too slowly due to ecosystem friction, is now out of date, or is buried in extraneous data will reduce decision-making effectiveness. Collecting just enough of the right data is just as important.
- **Accuracy:** Accurate information means fewer misdirected or inaccurate decisions that need to be corrected to get back on the path to the target outcome.
- **Context:** Context is the framing of information in relation to the known dynamics of the ecosystem you are executing in. It is how we make sense of our current situation and is an important prerequisite for gaining situational awareness. We use context to not only understand the relevance of information to a given situation, but also to gauge the level of risk various options have based upon our grasp of the orderliness and predictability of the ecosystem. How all of this works, and how it often goes wrong, is covered in considerable depth in Chapter 5, "Risk."

- **Knowledge:** The more you know about the relative appropriateness of the options and capabilities available to you, the greater the chance you will choose the option that will provide the most positive impact toward achieving the target outcome. How much knowledge you have and how effectively it can aid your decision making depends heavily upon the decision-making ingredient of learning effectiveness.

Assuming you are able to obtain suitable information, you then need to combine it effectively to gain sufficient situational awareness. There are many ways this process can fall apart, making it the most fragile component of the decision process. Boyd was intrigued by this, and spent the rest of his life trying to understand what conditions could damage or improve it.

Understanding these conditions is both important and discussed more fully in Chapter 6, "Situational Awareness." For the purposes of this chapter, it is important to point out the two most common places where situational awareness can silently deteriorate, often with chronic if not catastrophic consequences. These are the challenge with trust, and the fragility of mental models and cognitive biases.

The Challenge of Trust

Most of us cannot acquire all the information directly ourselves and instead rely upon other people, either directly or from tools they build and run. If any of those people do not trust those who consume the information or what they will do with it, they may withhold, hide, or distort it. This can be done either directly, if they are handling the data themselves, or by suboptimizing the data collection and processing mechanisms they are asked to build and manage.

Lack-of-trust issues are surprisingly common. The vast majority of the time they arise not out of malice but out of fear of blame, micro-management, loss of control, or simply fear of the unknown. They are also just as likely to be caused by problems between peers as well as between managers and individual contributors in both directions. Many of these issues can develop out of anything from simple misunderstandings caused by insufficient contact or communication to larger organizational culture issues. Whatever the cause, the resulting damage to decision making is very real and can be far reaching.

The Fragility of Mental Models and Cognitive Biases

Human brains have evolved to rely upon two particular shortcuts to both speed up and reduce the amount of mental effort required to make decisions. These shortcuts, the mental model and cognitive bias, are generally quite useful when we are in stable, well-known environments. However, as you will see, these mechanisms are particularly susceptible to flaws that can severely degrade our decision-making abilities.

Mental models are sets of patterns that our brains build that are internal representations of an ecosystem and the relationships between its various parts to anticipate events and predict the probable behaviors of elements within it. Mental models allow us to quickly determine what actions are likely the most optimal to take, dramatically reducing the amount of information that needs to be gathered and analyzed.

Mental models are valuable, which is why people with experience are often quicker and more effective than a novice in situations that are similar to what they have been through previously. However, this mental model mechanism has several serious flaws. For one, a mental model is only as good as our understanding of the information we use to build and tune it. This information may be partial, misconstrued, or even factually incorrect. Boyd knew that this would inevitably lead to faulty assumptions that damage decision making.

The most obvious threat to mental model accuracy is having a rival try to intentionally seed inaccurate information and mistrust of factual information and knowledge. Studies have shown that disinformation, even when knowingly false or quickly debunked, can have a lingering effect that damages decision making.[4,5] In recent years such behavior has moved from the battlefield and propagandist's toolbox to the political sphere to discredit

4. "Debunking: A Meta-Analysis of the Psychological Efficacy of Messages Countering Misinformation"; Chan, Man-pui Sally; Jones, Christopher R.; Jamieson, Kathleen Hall; Albarracín, Dolores. *Psychological Science*, September 2017. DOI: 10.1177/0956797617714579.
5. "Displacing Misinformation about Events: An Experimental Test of Causal Corrections"; Nyhan, Brendan; Reifler, Jason. *Journal of Experimental Political Science*, 2015. DOI: 10.1017/XPS.2014.22.

opponents through overly simplistic and factually incorrect descriptions of policies and positions.

But incorrect information, let alone active disinformation campaigns, is far from the most common problem mental models face. More often they become flawed through limited or significantly laggy information flow. Without sufficient feedback, we are unable to fill in important details or spot and correct errors in our assumptions. When an ecosystem is dynamic or complex, the number and size of erroneous assumptions can become so significant that the affected party becomes crippled.

Like mental models, cognitive biases are a form of mental shortcut. A cognitive bias trades precision for speed and a reduction of the cognitive load needed to make decisions. This "good enough" approach takes many forms. The following are just a handful of examples:

- *Representativeness biases* are used when making judgments about the probability of an event or subject of uncertainty by judging its similarity to a prototype in their mind. For instance, if you regularly receive a lot of frivolous monitoring alerts, you are likely to assume that the next set of monitoring alerts you get are also going to be frivolous and do not need to be investigated, despite the fact that they may be important. Similarly, a tall person is likely to be assumed to be good at playing basketball despite only sharing the characteristic of height with people who are good at the sport.
- *Anchoring biases* occur when someone relies upon the first piece of information learned when making a choice regardless of its relevancy. I have seen developers spend hours troubleshooting a problem based on the first alert or error message they see, only to realize much later that it was an extraneous effect of the underlying root cause. This led them on a wild goose chase that slowed down their ability to resolve the issue.
- *Availability biases* are the estimation of the probability of an event occurring based on how easily the person can imagine an event occurring. For instance, if they recently heard about a shark attack somewhere on the other side of the world, they will overestimate the chances they will be attacked by a shark at the beach.

- **Satisficing** is choosing the first option that satisfies the necessary decision criteria regardless of whether there are other better options available. An example is choosing a relational database to store unstructured data.

When they are relied upon heavily, it is extremely easy for cognitive biases to result in lots of bad decisions. In their worst form they can damage your overall decision-making ability.

Unfortunately, we in IT regularly fall under the sway of any number of biases, from hindsight bias (seeing past events as predictable and the correct actions obvious even when they were not at the time) and automation bias (assuming that automated aids are more likely to be correct even when contradicting information exists) to confirmation bias, the IKEA effect (placing a disproportionately high value on your own creation despite its actual level of quality), and loss aversion (reluctance to give up on an investment even when not doing so is more costly). But perhaps the most common bias is *optimism bias*.

IT organizations have grown used to expecting that software and services will work and be used as we imagine they will be, regardless of any events or changes in the delivery ecosystem. A great example of this is the way that people view defects. Defects only exist in the minds of most engineers if they are demonstrated to be both real *and* having a direct negative impact, while risks are those situations that engineers view as likely events. This extreme optimism is so rampant that the entire discipline of Chaos Engineering has been developed to try to counteract it by actively seeding service environments with regular failure situations to convince engineers to design and deliver solutions that are resilient to them.

Another serious problem with mental models and cognitive biases is their stickiness in our minds. When they are fresh they are relatively malleable, though if you were ever taught an incorrect fact you likely know that it will still take repeated reinforcement to replace it with a more accurate one learned later. The longer that a mental model or bias remains unchallenged in our minds, the more embedded it becomes and the harder it is to change.

Ingredient 4: Learning

Figure 2.11
Learning isn't just school and certifications.

The final and frequently misunderstood piece of the decision-making process is *learning*. Learning is more than the sum of the facts you know or the degrees and certifications you hold. It is how well you can usefully capture and integrate key knowledge, skills, and feedback into improving your decision-making abilities.

Learning serves several purposes in the decision process. It is the way we acquire the knowledge and skills we need to improve our situational awareness. It is also the process we use to analyze the efficacy of our decisions and actions toward reaching our target outcomes so that we can improve them.

Learning is all about fully grasping the answer to the question *why*. This could be why a decision did or did not work as expected, where and why our understanding of the target outcome was or was not accurate, or how and why we had the level of situational awareness we did. It is the core of various frameworks, including Lean, and it is how we improve every part of the decision-making process.

The best part about learning is that it doesn't need to occur in a formal or structured way. In fact, our most useful learning happens spontaneously as we go through life. This should help us constantly improve the quality of our decisions—that is, if we remain willing and able to learn.

Failing to Learn

Learning is a lifelong pursuit, one we like to think we get far better at it with experience. However, it is actually really easy for us to get *worse* at it over time. We even joke that "you can't teach an old dog new tricks." What causes us to get worse at doing something so fundamental?

A common belief is that any problems we may have are merely a result of having less dedicated time for learning. It is true that learning requires time to try things out, observe what happens, and reflect to really understand the reasons we got the results we did so that we can apply that knowledge to future decision making. However, the problem is far deeper.

For learning to occur we also need to be amenable to accepting new knowledge. That is pretty easy to do if you have no prior thoughts or expectations on a given topic. But as we gain experience, we start to collect various interpretations and expectations on a whole raft of things that we can use to build and tune our mental models. When they accurately reflect our situation, we can speed up and improve the accuracy of our decision making. But, unfortunately, not everything we pick up is accurate. Sometimes we learn the wrong lesson, or conditions change in important ways that invalidate our previous experiences.

As we discussed earlier, these inaccuracies can create serious flaws in our situational awareness. They also can damage our learning ability. When confronted with new knowledge that conflicts with our current view, we will sometimes simply ignore or overlook the new information because it does not meet our preset expectations. Other times we might actively contest the new evidence unless it can irrefutably disprove some interpretation we hold, even if the view we hold cannot itself stand up to such a test. This high bar creates friction that can slow or prevent us from learning.

The causes of this resistance have roots that go back to our formal schooling days.

"But That's Just a PC"

There are a lot of scenarios where long-held habits and beliefs can get in the way of our ability to learn. Sometimes the outcome we are targeting becomes so ingrained that we fail to learn when our customers' needs change. Other times we get so used to the idiosyncrasies of our environment that we fail to see important problems or risks in the state of our code and repository health, the suitability of our long-held processes, or challenges in skill and relationship dynamics in our teams. These can all make life far more difficult than it needs to be and even put the business in jeopardy.

An energy company fell into such a predicament. Only after struggling to overcome their established beliefs did they discover that these very beliefs were endangering the core of its business.

The company had long relied upon a critical internally built application written in Fortran. It was designed to calculate how much electricity each power plant should generate across each service area, hour by hour each day over the entire 24-hour period. This information was critical for managing the health of the generation plants and the power grid, as well as the quality and availability of the electricity supply. Even more importantly, the generated results also had to be provided to government regulators. While generation and distribution had some buffer to allow things to coast along for a couple of hours with no data, failing the regulator's requirement meant millions in immediate fines.

Even though this application and the data it provided were so important to the business, few company employees were aware of its existence. For decades the application had run with little fanfare on a large mainframe in the basement of a building at one of the power stations. It only came to light when the building it was in was slated to be demolished.

In the process of trying to figure out what to do, management discovered that all of the original application developers had long since retired. The mainframe itself, while impressively large, was so ancient that the manufacturer had long gone out of business.

The situation seemed dire, but the business didn't seem to fully recognize the risk it had. The setup had been running so seamlessly for the most part that, at first glance, all that was required was to move the equipment. It didn't help that there was a strong belief that mainframes are by their nature failure-proof. That this one had been running since the 1970s only seemed to solidify that thinking.

The team I was leading at the time was tasked with coming up with a workable solution to the problem. What confidence others had quickly faded when we began to understand the complexities of the situation. We quickly swarmed the problem, with one part of the team looking into the problem of moving the existing system, while the rest of us looked for other alternatives.

Along the way we managed to dig up the source code and, while it was ancient enough to require some effort to port to a more contemporary platform, doing so would be fairly straightforward. We were also fortunate enough that some of us had long ago become well versed in the intricacies of Fortran.

After a few weeks we managed to port the entire application to Linux. Eager to see if it would work, we ran it alongside the existing system. The hourly process took on average 50 minutes or so end-to-end, so we wanted to make sure the ported application would be not only just as accurate but could also fit in the same execution window.

That was when the real fun began.

At its first execution, the new setup executed the entire process in less than one second. After the main system completed its work we compared and found identical results. In disbelief, we continued running both in parallel for several weeks, each time coming up with the same results. Decades of technology innovation meant that what had once required a huge mainframe and nearly an hour of calculation time could now run on a tiny virtual machine instance in almost no time.

Convincing the business that the new setup was a far superior approach that was both cheaper and had the side effect of removing a massive business risk was extremely difficult. People had long grown to believe that mainframes are far superior in every way to a standard PC. Even though there was ample proof that doing so was safe and expedient, moving such an important application to an ordinary computer, let alone a virtual machine, seemed in many people's minds to be far more dangerous than the existing setup. They were simply too set in their ways to easily accept this new knowledge.

After yet more testing and a lot of pressure to decommission the mainframe, the management team finally gave in and migrated to the ported application.

The Shortcomings of the Formal Education System

Overcoming preexisting beliefs about a solution is not the only problem that can negatively affect our ability to learn. Preconceptions about learning and the learning process can also play a major factor.

Most of us spend a large chunk of our childhood being formally educated in school. While this is useful for kickstarting our life of learning, many of the techniques used can lead to unhealthy habits and expectations that can impede our ability to learn later in life. The worst of these is creating the expectation that there is only one right way of working.

Having only one right method is easy to teach and test for in a standardized way. The problem is that life is not so black and white. Oftentimes, especially in IT, either there is no single right answer or the right answer no longer is right later down the line. However, the expectation of singular permanence makes people resistant to learning new and potentially better ways of working.

This problem is compounded by the fact that standardized teaching is done in a top-down way. It creates an expectation that there is an all-knowing authority that is there to judge our ability to follow instructions. Such an approach is not only unrealistic and noncollaborative, it also discourages critical thinking and innovation.

Hindsight Bias and Motivated Forgetting

Failing to learn is never good. But the problem is far more than simply missing out on knowing some information. It also can make it a great deal harder to improve our overall decision-making abilities. Ironically, the places where learning is often the most dysfunctional are those officially designed to encourage it. This includes everything from incident postmortems to sprint and project retrospectives, end project reports, and lessons learned reviews.

The reason for this goes back to some of the dysfunctions covered earlier. Being subconsciously predisposed to believe that the world operates in a particular way makes it incredibly easy to believe that events are more predictable than they are. This *hindsight bias* causes us to overlook the facts as they were known at the time and misremember events as they happened. This creates false narratives that can make any missteps appear to be due to a lack of skill or a total disregard for what seem to be obvious facts.

When this is coupled with a lack of trust and fear of failure, people can be motivated to avoid blame by actively forgetting or obfuscating useful details. This creates a culture that is not conducive to learning.

The Pathway to Improved Decision Making

We have discussed how the quality of decisions is dependent upon the strength of our understanding of the problems and desired outcome, the friction in our decision process, our level of situational awareness, and our ability to learn. We have also covered many of the ways that each of these key elements can degrade. How can we begin to improve our own decision-making abilities?

As you probably could have guessed by now, the journey is not as simple as following a set of predefined practices. We have to first dig deeper into how we go about making decisions and answer the following questions:

- Do you and your teammates understand your customer's target outcomes? Do you know why they are important. Do you have a good idea for how to measure that you are on track to reaching them?
- What factors in your ecosystem are causing rework, misalignments, and other issues that add friction that slows down and makes your decision-making and delivery processes inefficient?
- How does the information you and your teammates need to gain situational awareness flow across your ecosystem? Where is it at risk of degrading, and how do you know when it is happening and its potential impact on your decision making?
- How effectively does your organization learn and improve? Where are the weak points, and what effect are they having on your decision-making effectiveness?

Effective DevOps implementations not only can answer these questions with ease, but can tell you what is being done to fix any challenge the team faces. Each implementation journey is different, and there is no one answer for what is right.

This book takes the same approach.

If you think you have a good grasp of the service delivery problem space and are ready to dive straight into practical application, you can jump ahead to Section 3. In those chapters I have written a number of techniques and

---

approaches that I have used in numerous organizations large and small and found extremely helpful for everyone across the organization.

However, if you are like me, you may feel that you need to understand a bit more about the thinking behind this approach to feel more comfortable with it before making any serious commitment. This deep dive begins with Chapter 3, "Mission Command," in the next section.

Summary

Even though we make decisions every day, becoming an effective decision-maker is a skill that takes a lot of time and effort to master. John Boyd's OODA loop shows that the process is iterative and continual, with success dependent upon the following:

- Understanding the target outcome desired
- Gaining situational awareness through observing and understanding your capabilities and the dynamics of the ecosystem you are operating in
- Identifying the impacts of friction areas to gauge what decision options will most likely help you progress toward the outcome desired
- Following through with the action, and observing its impact so that you can determine how far you progressed, and if there are new details or changes that must be learned and incorporated into your situational awareness

Boyd showed that continually honing situational awareness and learning are at least as important as the speed of decision-making itself. Damage to any ingredient harms decision quality, and with it the ability to succeed.

and relay complex situational information, have it received, understood, and considered on the other side, and then for a decision to be made and codified in suitably detailed actions, relayed back, understood, and acted upon is just too long to be workable. There is simply too much nuanced information to communicate, and even if it all could be relayed, the sheer quantity would, much like the alerts of an overzealous monitoring system, overwhelm central command.

All of this friction creates a cloud of uncertainty that compromises the entire decision cycle, rendering commanders incapable of keeping up with events while preventing subordinates closer to the action from taking the initiative in exploiting any momentary opportunities exposed to them.

Some military leaders, such as Alexander the Great and the Mongols, found ways of not just overcoming such chaos but also using it to their advantage. As a result, they repeatedly dominated the battlefield by using rapid and unpredictable change as a weapon to defeat far superior adversaries.

Despite knowing of those successes, as well as the fact that the victor in a battle rarely wins by destroying the physical fighting capacity of the enemy, most military organizations hung onto rigid traditional top-down organizational techniques. It was not until the 19th century, in the wake of the brutal defeat of the Prussian Army by another such military leader, Napoleon, that serious efforts were made to codify the techniques that Alexander and others had so lethally wielded.

Learning How to Lead Effectively the Hard Way

During the Napoleonic Wars, the Prussian army was one of the most powerful in Europe. It was larger, more experienced, and better equipped than any rival. Despite all of that, it repeatedly found itself outmatched in the battlefield against Napoleon's far smaller decentralized forces. At the battles of Jena and Auerstedt in 1806, for instance, Prussian forces outnumbered the French forces nearly 2:1 and yet were soundly defeated.

It became clear that the traditional centralized command structure and rigid planning of the Prussian forces was degrading its ability to effectively deploy and lead troops in the battlefield. Rather than take the initiative, troops were expected only to execute what they were ordered to do. With battlefield conditions changing rapidly and no way to effectively communicate their subtleties to commanders to understand and adjust orders effectively in response, the Prussians found themselves continually outmaneuvered and unable to exploit their superior capabilities.

The top-down approach also completely disregarded the skills and experiences that the Prussian troops brought with them. This further constrained the speed and potential effectiveness of Prussian decision making, all at a time when such capabilities were needed most.

Over time, Napoleon came to believe that his success was due to his own tactical brilliance and not the freedom he gave his troops to decide and act in the field. As a result, he slowly succumbed to the lure of more traditional centralized command as he struggled in the freezing battlefields of Russia, where his fortunes turned. This did not go unnoticed by the Prussians. Noting that a significant factor in Napoleon's early battlefield successes seemed to be tied to devolving authority to his officers in the field who could adapt quickly to changing battlefield conditions, the Chief of the Prussian Army's General Staff, General David Scharnhorst, noted that Napoleon put together a reform commission to overhaul decision making throughout the chain of command. Carl von Clausewitz, who later wrote *On War*, participated on the commission and introduced the concept of the "fog of war" to describe how changing conditions and incomplete information can affect decision making.

Scharnhorst and the commission decided the best way forward was to train staff officers to act decisively and autonomously in the heat of battle. They soon developed techniques and military schools to teach them to a professional officer corps chosen on merit alone. Later, Helmuth von Moltke took over as Chief, expanded upon the commission's work, building the core of the doctrine of *Auftragstaktik*, or what we call Mission Command.

Managing Through Unpredictability

The best way to understand the thinking behind Mission Command and the importance and interplay between its various components is to understand how its approach to unpredictability differs from other management methods. To do this, let's start by introducing the potential sources of unpredictability in your ecosystem and how other management methods attempt to tackle them. These potential sources are flawed knowledge and awareness, misalignments, and misjudging ecosystem order and complexity.

Knowledge and Awareness Weaknesses

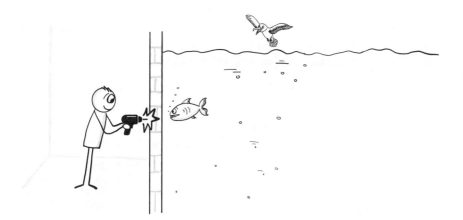

Figure 3.2
Little did Bill know, his remodeling project was about to take a turn.

Not everyone in the delivery ecosystem is likely to always possess all the relevant knowledge and awareness needed to make the best decision. Sometimes they might lack the relevant skills and experience, or be unaware of some key aspect about the dynamics and interdependencies within the ecosystem to identify and suitably solve the situation they find themselves in.

Like most centralized command structures, most management approaches attempt to tackle this problem by trying to separate the duties of decision making from those of performing most of the actions required to execute the decision. Being on top of the team hierarchy and peers with managers of other functions, it is assumed that managers should be best placed with enough bandwidth to understand what is going on across the ecosystem. This allows staff to be treated much like any tool or material, with each possessing known capabilities and capacities that can be applied by managers to complete defined tasks using approved methods.

The problem with such approaches is that they count heavily on managers maintaining sufficient situational awareness for everyone, all while separating them from directly witnessing many of the details that will likely be uncovered which could improve future decisions. As ecosystems become larger and more complex, the ability to capture and stay sufficiently aware of all aspects necessary to make effective decisions becomes increasingly difficult. Dividing work based on skills often exacerbates this, leading to the fragmentation of work across more specialized teams. As a result, the work, and often the reward and recognition structure for performing it, becomes separated from the target outcome. Not only does this make it more difficult for the outcome to be achieved, it removes much of the incentive to share information that might not be directly relevant to the work of function that discovers it but provides critical insight necessary to achieve the target outcome.

Finally, such approaches also overlook the fact that users and customers are also important actors in the ecosystem. Failure is just as likely if users and customers do not know enough about how to use your services or how they will meet their expectations. To them, a solution that is impenetrable to use or seems irrelevant can be worse than no solution at all.

Misalignments

Figure 3.3
Misalignments.

The second source of unpredictability is caused by misalignments. People can misunderstand a task that needs to be done, misjudge what others might do, misprioritize, or simply forget all or part of the task. This can be caused by everything from lossy or slow communication to a lack of trust or commitment.

Misalignments are a common affliction, enough so that I spend a lot of time looking at how information moves through an organization, is understood, and is acted upon to help me hunt down and fix their sources. This is especially useful when misalignments are endemic or concentrated in a particular part of the ecosystem.

Traditional management recognizes the problem and expects managers to use detailed tasking and assessments to find misalignments when they occur. This approach suffers from the same limitations that create knowledge and awareness gaps. It also does little to protect against another type of misalignment of missing the outcome the customer is trying to achieve. Staff focus on completing the tasks to the standard they are asked to meet, not whether the work leads to the outcome desired. This leaves finding and course correcting to managers, many of whom will likely be so busy directing people that they can easily overlook or misjudge the details of what is needed. Also, being one or more steps away from the activity, managers are more likely to struggle to determine what course corrections are needed to deliver what is required.

Misjudgment of Ecosystem Complexity

The third source of unpredictability is caused by misjudging the dynamics of your operating ecosystem domain. As we explore in Chapter 5, "Risk," not all ecosystems are ordered and predictable. This poses a problem for traditional management techniques, which are designed to expect that either managers or the experts they hire can determine from what is happening what actions need to be taken.

The more unordered an ecosystem is, the more likely that causality cannot be determined until, at best, after the fact. Expecting orderliness in your delivery ecosystem when there is none leads to misjudgment of the situation and ultimately poor decision making. What makes it worse is that this same unordering effect can also make it difficult to understand why a decision was poor and learn from it.

The Anatomy of Mission Command

Figure 3.4
"...and this is where you find our mission's intent."

Both Clausewitz and Moltke recognized and wrote extensively about each form of unpredictability. They knew that they were so endemic to warfare that, at best, only the very beginning of a military operation could be planned with any sort of precision. However, they also found that there were ways to minimize the effects of each. Some, such as staff rides and war-gaming (both covered later in this chapter), tackle some aspects head on. Others avoid problems altogether by fundamentally restructuring how orders are given.

Key to all of this is the realization that, regardless of whether the activity was a single mission or the overall strategy for victory over an enemy, the *target outcome* should remain stable throughout. In Moltke's view, this means that the main objective of any leader is to share and be clear about the intent behind any action with subordinates. The leader should *not* instruct subordinates of what specific tasks to perform or specify what methods have to be used, but instead needs to ensure that they understand what the target outcomes are and how the mission or campaign needs to contribute to achieving it.

By focusing on the target outcome rather than specific actions and methods, subordinates are free to choose the most optimal options and make the most sensible decisions for whatever situations they encounter that best achieve the target outcome. This approach is fundamentally different than what most of us are used to. In traditional organizations, the outcome is less something subordinates pursue and more something that the manager is seen orchestrating subordinate tasks to reach.

There are a number of important components to Mission Command that must be present together to make it work. These are *commander's intent*, *backbriefing*, *einheit*, and *continual improvement*.

As we examine each of these components to understand what it is and how it works, you might notice a number of parallels that many of the components have with concepts that are central to Lean and Agile. These parallels are not accidental. However, it is important to note that many of the failures that organizations have when adopting Lean or Agile often begin by only implementing some and not all of these components.

Commander's Intent

Commander's Intent is where the journey for defining the target outcome begins. Along with backbriefing, it is the way that the commander or manager provides subordinates with the clearly defined objective, or *intent*, that forms the anchor point to guide decisions throughout any mission or scenario. This is necessarily more than simply telling subordinates of a target outcome. Leaders need to be confident that their subordinates understand enough of the nuances of what it means so that if any plans fail or conditions change, they can alter their approach and adapt to still reach the target outcome.

This is actually far more involved than it might sound. Even when trust levels are high between leaders and subordinates and both share many of the same values, there are a lot of places where subtle yet important details can be lost. This is enough of a challenge that I often encourage team members to, if at all possible, first check to see if the intended outcome behind any request, task, requirement, or job duty is clear, meaningful, and actionable before beginning work. I call this passing the "Pony Test."

Figure 3.5
"Wanting a pony doesn't mean you must have one in your bedroom!"

The "Pony Test" is a quick sanity check. It is designed to catch whether any important information about the intent of a work item is missing or unclear. The name originates from the actions of a particular product manager who, one manager later noted, acted like a child demanding a pony. This product manager was known for regularly failing to give any reasons beyond "because I want them" for why certain requirements were being asked for, and refused to take seriously any repercussions for delivering them. After one particular disaster, the organization decided that anyone who wanted to make a request needed to both have a meaningful purpose or reason for it *and* consider any costs or consequences to ensure it didn't become an open-ended headache.

The test is simple, and asks the following questions:

- What is the target outcome? How does this differ from the current situation? Is it a current problem or need that can be measured, or a future issue or opportunity?
- Is there a timeframe within which the need must be met? If so, why and what happens if it is missed?
- Are there any priorities that we need to be aware of, both within delivering the need and in the larger scope of our other duties? If so, what are they and how do we resolve conflicts?
- Are there any constraints that we must abide by?

What is good about the Pony Test is that it works just as well for new requests as it does for guiding triage and incident activities. For instance, one commonly ill-defined requirement that hits DevOps teams is the meaning of "uptime." Everyone wants high uptime, but few bother to articulate what uptime actually means, why they need it, when they need it, what the relative value of different uptime conditions is, or what happens when they do not have it.

Anyone who has run a service knows that when it comes to uptime, not all times, conditions, or services are equal. No one cares if a service is down when no one needs it, but everyone is irate when it is down at a critical point. Knowing and understanding these nuances can help staff make better decisions on how to approach problems. When faced with time and resourcing constraints, they might spend more time designing and testing the reliability or redundancy in one area over another, or start triaging a more important data integrity issue over restarting a service. As services become increasingly complex, managers need to spend more time ensuring that any nuances are shared and understood by all.

Understanding the desired outcome is critical before establishing delivery targets and measures. This is especially true for service environments. As every service environment is different, I use an old broadcasting fiasco as an example of how uptime and availability can have different meanings under different conditions. Conflicting definitions can cause a lot of costs and expended effort to all go to waste. For instance, no one really cares if there are cameras broadcasting the playing field at a stadium if nothing interesting is happening. Yet people will be absolutely furious when something exciting is happening and the broadcast feed is unavailable.

This very thing occurred on November 17, 1968. The Oakland Raiders were playing their then rival the New York Jets in an American Football League game. With just over one minute left in the game the Jets were winning 32–29. The game had run long due to penalties and was threatening to encroach on the primetime schedule of NBC, which was broadcasting the game. NBC, seeing the potential conflict and believing there was no chance that the Raiders would come back with so little time remaining, decided to cut away from the game to broadcast the children's movie *Heidi*. Little did NBC know, they had just cut away from what at the time was considered one of the most exciting comebacks in the sport, with the Raiders managing to score two touchdowns to win 43-32. Fans were furious, and shortly after the debacle the National Football League inserted a clause into its TV contracts that guaranteed that all future games would be broadcast in full in their home markets.

To ensure that Commander's Intent was understood and acted upon, Moltke and others developed a means to convey it that answers the same questions as our Pony Test. This is called the *brief*. As you will see, it can be heavily repurposed for our own needs.

Brief

In order to ensure that subordinates feel free to determine how they are going to reach the target outcome, orders need to look far less like the instructions that most people think of and more like a description of what that desired outcome means and why it needs to be achieved. This description needs to strike a balance that can direct subordinates toward the intended outcome but is not so detailed and prescriptive that it impinges on any creativity and initiative they might need to reach it.

Rather than calling these "orders," which most associate with a laundry list of what to do, they are often referred to as *directives*. In order to effectively capture strategic intent, a commander's directives typically follow a particular pattern of roughly four or five short elements, described in the following sections.

Situational Overview

A situational overview is a brief description of the current situation. Its goal is to both make clear what is going on and provide some relevant background behind what needs to be done.

In an IT setting, a situational overview could be something like "Our business push to increase the number of customers has steadily raised the load on our systems. We are now at the point where at peak periods service performance, defined by reasonable service responsiveness without timeouts or errors, threatens to dip below what customers expect."

The situational overview is very much a starting point. Unless subordinates are already familiar with the situation, it is likely that they will need to obtain more information before attempting to deliver a solution in pursuit of the target outcome.

Statement of the Desired Outcome or Overall Mission Objective

In the next step the manager or commander covers the essential objective that needs to be achieved, and the "why" behind it. This is not some fluffy statement, but something with a meaningful objective that enables those receiving the statement to take short-term actions that can provide results toward achieving the conveyed intent. It often contains elements of who, what, when, where, and why, but avoids specifying how. This is the essence of the information necessary to answer the first question in the Pony Test.

Sticking with the current example, this could be "We need to ensure that production service performance stays in line with customer expectations. This needs to be done in order to maintain customer loyalty as well as to allow us to gain greater market share."

Execution Priorities

Whether we are on the battlefield or in an office, it is rare that we are delivering every aspect of a service alone in a vacuum. We inevitably need to coordinate with and seek help from others. The leader needs to help make the subordinate aware of the themes and priorities of activities of such groups. The leader may suggest reaching out to certain teams or individuals in order to help the subordinate make key decisions to best achieve the envisioned end state.

In our example, a leader might state: "We need your team to work out the most expedient and effective way to allow us to seamlessly accomplish this. Marketing wants to put together a campaign that, if successful, may result in dramatically increasing our customer base. They have been planning to target mid-level companies who might benefit from certain aspects of our services. Jane from Marketing can work with you to provide details and can feed back to her team in case they need to make any adjustments based on your work. We are also in the middle of a contract renewal with our most important customer, who has brought up concerns about our ability to scale. Joe in Sales is available to help. Other than triage support this is the highest-priority item in the Technical division. The CEO and board are supportive of investing, but need to understand what might be entailed and what impact it might have to our capex and ability to deliver other projects."

Anti-Goals and Constraints

Figure 3.6
"No, we cannot start a real disaster to test our DR processes!"

It is rare for a mission or activity to lack any boundaries or constraints. Sometimes these are caused by upcoming events that subordinates may not be fully aware of, or limitations in time or resources that need to be accounted for in future decisions. Similarly, anti-goals are explicit items that *cannot* be allowed. This helps clarify the scope of action available.

To complete our example, let's see what constraints our "commander" has laid out: "We know that some customers are at a critical point in their business cycle where, for the next month, they are particularly sensitive to any interruptions in the availability of our service. Severe interruptions not only could cause us to lose customers, but would damage our reputation severely. That could force us to exit that market and to scale back our growth plans. Your team needs to look for ways to minimize customer impact. We also know that the Business Intelligence team is working on improving real-time analytics, which could involve some of the same systems you might decide to look at. They need to be aware of any potential changes in their area. Finally, any improvements absolutely cannot impair our production security in any way."

Throughout the directive briefing, the subordinate is expected to ask questions, challenge details, and point out any potentially erroneous information. The purpose of this is not to challenge the capabilities or authority of the leader, but to help clarify and ensure that the subordinate fully comprehends and has what is needed to stay oriented to the outcome. As we all know, anything that can be misunderstood often will be.

Backbriefing

Figure 3.7
"With this approach we should be able to achieve that outcome."

The brief is never enough for the manager or commander to be confident that subordinates fully understand and have what they need in order to progress the commander's intent of a directive. This is why subordinates are expected to follow up a directive briefing by providing what is called a *backbriefing*.

The purpose of a backbriefing is not to provide a typical detailed plan. It is very much an opportunity for subordinates to both get the answers to any important questions they might have about the directive as well as demonstrate that they understand its underlying intent, their role in achieving it, and the relationship between their mission and the mission of others who may be involved. In this way it acts as a quick check to eliminate any ambiguity or misunderstanding.

The backbriefing also serves as a check to help the leader gain additional clarity of the implications of their own directives. Being closer to the details, subordinates have a more granular view of potential risks and needs that may jeopardize the mission's success. It is possible that these details may result in the directive being altered or eliminated altogether.

Backbriefings also allow subordinates in different work areas to compare notes and ensure alignments across the organization. This can further improve situational awareness and decision accuracy.

Backbriefings happen relatively soon after the initial directive. For small and well-understood directives, they might run back-to-back with the brief. However, I find that there is a lot of value in giving subordinates some time to think about the directive, do some short checks on some of its important aspects, and to put together a loose outline of an approach. For single-person tasks or team-sized tasks, this could be as short as a few hours or a few days. Such investigation is typically done as a spike within the weekly cycle. For larger initiatives, as well as when subordinates have their own teams and staff, more time will likely be needed to allow teams to be briefed and coordinate with each other to provide a meaningful backbriefing.

In our earlier example, the subordinate may come back with information regarding recent performance degradations that pinpoint potential bottlenecks in the database and data structures. The work in this area might be particularly risky. Data schema changes might also impact the work being done by the BI team, and might also have an unforeseen impact on potential integration efforts with an external tool that have been discussed. The subordinate might also come back with data showing that increased load has not been the result of additional customers, but is due to unexplained changes in the way that one particular customer uses the service.

Einheit: The Power of Mutual Trust

Figure 3.8

"Trust makes us stronger."

To work well, Mission Command needs more than some back and forth about the outcomes and intent of any activities. There also needs to be some level of mutual trust between the leader and subordinates. The leader needs to be confident that the subordinates will understand and carry out what is desired, while subordinates need to trust that they will be supported when exercising their initiative. Without it information flow and shared awareness will wane at the very moment when they are needed most: when conditions cause decisions and plans to go awry. Even the hint of losing support or incurring blame can cause people to become protective of important yet potentially embarrassing details, feel prevented from asking necessary probing questions, and feel unable or unwilling to reach out for help.

The Prussians observed that trust and a commitment to a shared cause was a major factor that improved the cohesiveness and fighting ability of Napoleon's army. Scharnhorst's early reforms helped set in motion a number of the key factors that Moltke later made part of the fabric of Mission Command in the Prussian Army. It became known as *einheit*, which roughly means "unity" and "oneness" in German.

Despite being a foreign term to non-German speakers, einheit is a useful way of describing the dynamic that creates team cohesiveness. Not only does it have far less baggage than the often overused word "trust," it also expresses two other important factors of trust that are so often overlooked. One is the idea of building a shared commitment to an objective. The other is personal insight, understanding, and rapport that members of a team have for each other.

Having shared commitment to an objective means that no one has to worry that some hidden agenda or ulterior motive might get in the way of achieving the stated outcome. Everyone can be confident that the stated target outcomes are the primary goal that matters and no manager or subordinate is going to act in a way that is going to undermine efforts to reach them.

Familiarity and shared experiences between team members is another important part of einheit that can also significantly aid alignment. The more you know the strengths and weaknesses of each other, the ways each other communicates, and the way each other will think about, approach, and solve problems, the more seamlessly you can work together toward the objective.

Strong team member familiarity can help fill in any situational awareness gaps needed to make a good decision. For instance, you might approach discussing a topic in a different way if you know that it will help your team-mate or manager understand it better. You might pair with someone who is strong in an area you are weaker in for help or to strengthen your knowledge. You might even look to share your own knowledge in an area others are unfamiliar with. All of these can help you and your team perform more effectively.

People who have worked in close-knit teams know that there is no better way to build an additional level of shared context than to spend time building shared experiences, and with it trust, within and across teams. Moltke taught his troops to recognize the importance of shared context and trust themselves. From there he showed them that this level of rapport gave their own intuition an extra level of accuracy that they could then rely upon. This meant that they could reduce the level of confusion and misalignment that might otherwise lead to inaccurate and conflicting conclusions. As everyone took part, this "going and seeing" provided a far superior level of situational awareness across the entire organization.

Regular interaction and mutual trust had the added benefit of encouraging implicit communication to develop among the team. Think about a family member or someone you have been close to for a long time. If you've known them long enough, you can often gain a clear sense of the state of a situation from little more than body language or the tone of their voice, even without being explicitly told its details. Implicit communication and mutual experience can provide a means for information to travel quickly and accurately. Subtle differences, from the tone of a voice to a slight change in the way that someone behaves, can convey large amounts of information very rapidly and accurately.

Prussian commanders spent a great deal of time in the field working closely with their subordinates, learning the nuances and capabilities of one another across the collective unit as they interacted within the environment. The intuitive awareness that staff gained gave them the ability to act quickly and in unison with little in the way of discussion.

This implicit knowledge greatly improves situational awareness. It also sharpens appropriate responsiveness to escalating situations. It was so effective that after German unification in 1871 it was integrated into the wider German military.

In German such awareness is referred to as *Fingerspitzengefühl*, which means "fingertip feel." It is conceptually similar to English sayings like "keeping one's finger on the pulse."

As John Boyd had discovered in his interviews of former German officers, Fingerspitzengefühl was at the heart of the successes of the German military during World War II. It allowed troops and officers to quickly establish important and meaningful relationships between disparate pieces of information as they became available. Their shared experiences helped them intuitively know how to respond, even when the information received was incomplete. Officers were able to build a mental map of the battlefield, allowing them to continuously stay oriented and respond with speed and determination.

Many who have studied Toyota have likely also encountered similar discussions of the importance of building up intuitive knowledge and trust within the organization. Some at Toyota compare it to the way that samurai once practiced until their long swords became extensions of their arm. In the same way, the individuals in the organization can build the same connections to work as one.

Creating Einheit in DevOps

As an IT leader, I spend a lot of time and effort to foster a sense of einheit across the organization. I find that it starts with spending time with teams as they go about their daily work. I watch how communication flows between team members and how they share new ideas and discoveries. I look at how information flows across teams and the larger organization to see where it gets lost, distorted, or simply slows down. These are all places where einheit is likely absent.

I do encourage teams to have regular team lunches, "brown bag" discussions, and team outings. I also utilize the regular sync points that are discussed in Chapter 14, "Cycles and Sync Points." I find that the amount of focus and value put into both retrospectives and strategic reviews by both team members and managers can determine how much einheit will develop. When both retrospectives and strategic reviews are taken seriously and are seen as valuable, team commitment will go up. People take notice when there is dedicated investment in helping the team improve.

The Queue Master role, as discussed in Chapter 13, "Queue Master," also can help build the feeling of "oneness," especially when those holding the role are positioned to realize that they are there to look for patterns and help guide the team to success. The role itself is usually eye-opening, allowing individuals to take a step back and look at the dynamics across the team. When paired with retrospectives, it can be a powerful motivator toward encouraging collaboration.

Einheit can also be created across teams as well as between geographically distributed team members. When faced with coordination challenges in such situations, I look for opportunities to encourage team members to spend quality time face-to-face with their counterparts in their own surroundings. This helps people understand and build the rapport that creates einheit. When done well, I find that as people really get to know each other, any expense is more than paid for by the value from the reduction in organizational friction and mistakes.

The final aspect I try to rid the organization of is the idea that there needs to be someone to blame for a mistake or negative event. This is always hard to accomplish. Most people have a natural tendency to look for fault in someone's actions while simultaneously avoiding blame on themselves. Negative events are typically caused by the loss of situational awareness, and if there is any "blame," it is the system that enabled it to occur and not the people in it. Negative events rarely happen because someone intended for them to occur. Finding the cause of the loss, learning why it happened, and finding a way to prevent it from happening again, all while not blaming the person or people who were involved, will go a long way toward improving team trust.

Continual Improvement

Figure 3.9
Continual Improvement.

Having the autonomy to adjust to unpredictability only works if there is also a culture in place that is willing and able to discover and incorporate new knowledge and approaches to better attain the target outcome. This type of culture is surprisingly uncommon, and not because people are resistant to improving their abilities and knowledge. One reason, explored in Chapter 7, "Learning," comes from the way that many of us approach the learning process, assuming that learning comes top-down and that there is one absolute truth for everything and that it does not change. Another comes from how constrained people feel to objectively challenge accepted norms and beliefs in pursuit of the target outcome.

Challenging the status quo, whether it is attempting to validate assumptions or seeking solutions that are better or more effective than existing favored approaches, is never easy. For one, the status quo is familiar and generally accepted as "good enough" to get the job done. Unlike new approaches, favored approaches need little justification for use. This holds true even when the usual assumption or method is known to have significant flaws that damage its suitability.

This need to justify any new investigation or ideas is where learning and improvement enthusiasm so often falter. Trying something new, innovative, or unconventional is risky, especially if there is low tolerance in the organization for mistakes. Failure is not fun at the best of times, but it can be devastating if it puts your job at risk. Besides negatively affecting anyone's willingness to experiment, intolerance for mistakes can also cause people to hide important information that is needed to be situationally aware of a situation and improve it. This is true even when an organization touts continual improvement. Without explicit managerial cover and support, few feel safe enough in their positions to take a chance of being blamed, or worse, for a mishap.

There are numerous examples of this tendency to "play it safe" throughout IT, whether you are talking about the lag and dysfunction of improving project planning and management techniques, problematic postmortems structured to lay blame on a person or team, or the way that new technologies and techniques struggle to be adopted and used effectively. One example that is regularly overlooked yet particularly relevant to DevOps is the journey to modernize software installation and configuration management.

Even though manually installing and configuring software is people intensive and error prone, IT teams have long found it to be completely normal. In the early days when there were only a handful of systems to install and configure, it hardly seemed worthwhile to spend time building a robust revision-controlled automated provisioning system that could authoritatively report a current node configuration state. But even as the number of installations and configuration complexity have increased to warrant deploying such tools and supporting processes, many IT teams remain reticent to use them despite their real benefits. When it does occur, the initiative is usually management-led, typically with either a vendor who can take the blame or an internal sponsor who is willing to take the political risk.

John Boyd, Helmuth von Moltke, and others realized that relentlessly challenging the validity of our assumptions and approaches needed for continual improvement is critical for success. In his 1976 paper "Destruction and Creation,"[1] Boyd stated that in order to shape and be shaped by our changing environment, we must continually destroy and re-create the mental patterns that we develop to comprehend and cope with it. It is only through continual learning and improvement that we can adjust to take advantage of these changes to "improve our capacity for independent action."[2]

Moltke also understood that punishing one case of misjudgment would kill off every attempt to encourage initiative. He was famously tolerant of mistakes. He felt that as long as the commander's intent was recognized and understood, mistakes made in the pursuit of the objective should be accepted and viewed as occasions to learn and improve. He instructed superior officers to refrain from punishment or harsh criticism of mistakes, and instead praise the initiative and correct the troops in such a way that they learn.

Both Boyd and Moltke also knew that learning and improvement need fast and regular feedback in order to increase ecosystem understanding and build up the overall body of knowledge that is available for use in the future. Some of the most valuable feedback often comes from uncovering what went wrong, and any fault or blame would only encourage people to withhold this valuable information.

1. http://pogoarchives.org/m/dni/john_boyd_compendium/destruction_and_
   creation.pdf
2. Boyd, John, "Destruction and Creation," p. 1.

Over time, two techniques to improve experimentation and reflection have emerged from the ideas of Boyd and Moltke. These have been widely adopted by a number of Western militaries and have analogs both in Lean Manufacturing and in Agile methodologies such as Scrum. In the military they are called *staff rides* and *after action reviews*. The purpose of each is important for IT organizations to understand as it is so often lost in their IT equivalents.

Staff Rides

Like most military commanders, Moltke had his troops regularly practice. Where Moltke was different was that he was less interested in critiquing how well troops marched in formation or how closely they followed orders. He was more interested in getting them to think about how to use their capabilities to successfully navigate a dynamic ecosystem. He did this through competitive war-gaming. The most innovative of these were his staff rides.

A staff ride would begin with Moltke taking select officers out to an area where a significant military event, such as a battle or major deployment, was likely to occur. Using the latest topographical maps and military intelligence, he would construct hypothetical scenarios and "what if" situations for his officers to work through. To make it real, at times the rides were combined with practice maneuvers incorporating troops and weaponry.

The rides tested staff on their ability to take in information in their environment and construct actions from that context. The unpredictability and fluidity of warfare meant the officers had to think on their feet and improvise. They learned that success belonged not to the team that followed an order exactly as prescribed, but the one that achieved the desired outcome. This also happens to be the essence of the art of learning to think.

Participation did not end after the action. After a muddy day out in the field, Moltke would sit with his troops and insist they review the day, analyzing what happened and finding ways to incorporate what they learned. This combination of strategy, practice, and analysis in a real-world setting helped his officers be better prepared to think creatively on how best to achieve the outcome.

Chaos Engineering has turned into one form of the IT equivalent of a staff ride. By actively creating real failure scenarios that technical staff need to navigate in their code and supporting systems, they start to think beyond the idealized "happy path." I usually take this much further with my teams by "war-gaming" out scenarios to get the entire team to think together rationally about various problems. Such war-gaming can either be a paper exercise or, preferably, involve actual actions taken in a war-gaming environment. Other times it might simply involve walking through either a past event but within the context of the current or some future ecosystem configuration, or some hypothetical scenario that business or market conditions might eventuate. I use opportunities like new initiative planning, strategic reviews, and audits that naturally bring the team together to minimize disruption and distractions.

Most teams are skeptical of the value of such activities at first, missing that the focus is less on *how* but *why* they would act in a certain way during a particular scenario. Often people are surprised to find their assumptions are flawed, or that there might be a far simpler or more elegant solution. Everyone learns along the way, and it is a great way to encourage people to think about how to hone and improve.

After Action Reviews

Review and reflection were brought directly to the battlefield during World War II with the development of the after action review, or debrief. Immediately following action, survivors were brought together with technical information surrounding the event. The goal of the review is focused on helping teams reflect upon and continuously learn from their experiences. Importantly, ranks are intentionally put aside to ensure candid discussion.

The US military discovered a number of benefits with the after action review. For one, they allowed teams to work together to better understand and learn from the action. Each person carried a piece of what happened from their personal experience, but rarely did they have the full picture. Being able to review and reflect helped teams make sense of what happened, to make the experience meaningful. They found that this improved unit readiness and built cohesion. It also contributed to the larger knowledge of the military, helping with future action.

In IT, retrospectives should play a very similar role to the after action review. They should encourage open and candid discussion in a way that helps the team reflect and learn.

Organizational Impacts of Mission Command

The Mission Command approach is vastly different than what people are normally used to. It requires both more independent and more holistic thinking by staff, which creates more shared ownership in the target outcomes, as well as higher awareness of the interdependencies and need for alignment across teams at the individual contributor level. If done well, this goes a long way toward helping teams minimize the sources of decision friction that make delivering effectively in an unpredictable ecosystem so difficult.

Moltke made gaining such awareness much more explicit. He required every subordinate to be trained to function effectively at two levels of command above his appointment. This doesn't mean that they needed to have lots of extra skills and certifications in order to be able to do their job. That is impractical. The purpose was to build the skills for them to think about the bigger picture of the *system* that they are operating in.

Lean practitioners tend to call this "systems thinking." Some IT types, especially those who have been in the industry a long time, remember when there was a need to deeply understand the dynamics and interactions across complex IT ecosystems. Back in those days such a skill was sometimes referred to as "systems engineering."

Such systems thinking is increasingly important in a service delivery world, where service components and service consumers can be both numerous and diverse. By ensuring that the intent and any necessary constraints are clear and understood, all while ensuring that the flow of information about current conditions is free of blame, teams can make the necessary decisions and improvements to deliver the target outcomes.

Summary

Teams that are told a desired outcome are far more effective than those that are told what actions they must perform, because it enables teams to quickly and independently adapt to previously unknown or changing conditions. Briefings and backbriefings are mechanisms that arose from the Prussian military and were later adapted in the civilian world. They can help leaders and staff align on the intended outcomes, any execution constraints that must be followed, and what resources and support the team might need when pursuing them.

For this framework to work, there must be mutual trust within the team and between the team and management. Team members also must be encouraged to work closely together to reduce communication friction and improve shared situational awareness. When done well, einheit is established, allowing the team to deliver smoothly as one, with few misalignments and little conflict.

Chapter 4

Friction

Only three things happen naturally in organizations: friction, confusion, and underperformance. Everything else requires leadership.

Peter Drucker

When it comes to service delivery, most of us equate friction with those elements that hinder our delivery speed and throughput. It is what drives so many of us to automate our builds and deployments, purchase cloud services, and adopt various Agile practices. But thinking about friction so narrowly can cause us to suboptimize, or worse overlook, everything else that is getting in our way of achieving the desired outcomes.

For John Boyd and Helmuth von Moltke, discussed in the previous two chapters, friction is what degrades our situational awareness and impedes learning. Boyd's Energy-Maneuverability (EM) theory proved that even if you were faster and more capable than your opponent, you could still fail if you did not sufficiently adapt to changing conditions or incorporate learning effectively along the way.

Lean takes friction a bit further. In product and service delivery, Lean practitioners note that you can succeed at delivery and yet still fail if you are less effective than the competition at helping your customer achieve their desired outcome. To avoid this, team members in Lean organizations know to explicitly search for and try to eliminate anything that hinders or does not directly add value in any way that the customer can perceive, declaring it *waste*.

For Taiichi Ohno, who is credited with creating the Toyota Production System, waste takes three forms: pure waste (*muda*), overburden (*muri*), and irregularity (*mura*).

What is powerful about this approach is that it makes us openly question everything we do under the lens of how it contributes to the target outcome. The idea of removing friction and waste quickly reminds us that it is not how fast you can go that is important, but rather how far you can progress toward the target outcome. This different perspective on delivery forces us to challenge the status quo, driving us to continually experiment, learn, and improve to better achieve those outcomes.

Understanding Ohno's Forms of Waste

Lean and the idea of targeting waste came out of the US government's "Training Within Industry" (TWI) program,[1] which was designed to improve productivity of war production efforts and overcome labor scarcity during World War II. One of its most valuable components, Job Methods (JM), specifically targeted waste reduction through continuous improvement.

Workers using JM were encouraged to constantly look for ways to improve the methods used to perform their work by thinking about why they were necessary and how they contributed to the intent behind the work. Were there unnecessary steps or details that could be eliminated? Could steps be rearranged or simplified to reduce mistakes or the time needed to complete a job? Workers who came up with improvements were celebrated and encouraged to share them widely.

1. https://www.lean.org/search/documents/105.pdf

These ideas were brought to Japan by US Army General Douglas MacArthur, the Supreme Commander for the Allied Powers in Japan after Japan's defeat in World War II. He was in charge of reconstruction after the war and was eager to find ways to speed it up to improve the living conditions of the Japanese citizenry. One of the approach's early adopters was Taiichi Ohno, a Toyota plant manager and later vice president of Toyota, who needed a way to help his struggling company compete against more resource-rich competitors like GM.

Ohno pushed these ideas to everyone across the company, from the worker on the assembly line to the executives at the top. To get everyone willing to pitch in to find ways to continually improve, he had to encourage them to change the way they viewed their jobs. Rather than just following instructions, they needed to continuously and critically examine everything that went into delivery. Anything that either got in the way of delivery or otherwise did not directly contribute to meeting the customer's needs needed to be viewed as a form of waste that needed to be eliminated.

Ohno and the Toyota teams found that waste can take many forms. Being familiar with these types and their effects can help with identifying and minimizing their presence in your own ecosystems.

Friction vs. Waste

At this point you might be thinking "Hey, I thought this chapter was about friction! Why is he talking about some Japanese guy's definition of waste?"

In short, waste is a form of friction. The extensive body of knowledge from Lean has many lessons that apply to IT. I believe it is worthwhile to introduce many of its concepts in the original language to both minimize confusion and to allow you, the reader, to be able to investigate other Lean literature further.

However, like a lot of Lean terms, the term "waste" is easy to misunderstand, misapply, or view as irrelevant in the IT context. Most people think of waste as a useless but mostly harmless byproduct of some process. It might not be desirable to have, but unless you know it is causing real problems, it is viewed as being safe to ignore. This is especially true in IT, where waste is neither physical nor usually visible.

Friction, however, is seen as a real thing in IT. Whether it is in the form of poorly written requirements, buggy code, poor tools, not enough deployment environments, or slow processes, friction hinders our ability to progress and successfully deliver.

Friction is also viewed less as a personal affront than waste. I know that I am far more open to finding an easier, more "frictionless" way of doing something than finding a "less wasteful" way.

Finally, labeling something as friction more clearly describes its impact to our knowledge-driven decision-making industry. Anything that makes us slower to reaching a solution, whether it is working on useless tasks, having to redo a task, or waiting for a slow process to complete, is friction.

If it is helpful to you as you progress through this chapter, please feel free to replace the word "waste" with "friction" in your mind.

Muda (Pure Waste)

Figure 4.2
Muda is as bad as it looks.

Muda is the Japanese word for waste as well as uselessness, idleness, and futility. By definition it is an activity that the customer wouldn't willingly pay for. Contrary to popular belief, the target isn't to figure out how to do things cheaper. Rather, it is to identify and remove anything that doesn't tangibly contribute to achieving the desired outcome.

Seeking out Muda is more than just finding useless things to eliminate. Muda can help us identify places where situational awareness has been lost, where customer outcomes have been misunderstood, or even where learning has been hobbled. It also gets us to better understand the underlying intent for all the things we are told we need to do in order to meet any legal, regulatory, or internal requirements that do not provide direct tangible value to the customer. For Ohno, these requirements were also a form of Muda. While they may be difficult to eliminate, it doesn't mean that we cannot somehow minimize or streamline any friction they may create and still meet their intended purpose.

Shigeo Shingo, one of the creators of the Toyota Production System, helpfully identified seven types of waste in manufacturing. Over the years, an eighth was added (non-used employee talent), creating a helpful list for teams to use in their efforts to root out waste. To guide us on our journey I have created a useful analog in the DevOps world, which is shown in Table 4.1.

Table 4.1

Seven Types of Waste in Manufacturing and Their Corresponding Terms in DevOps

Manufacturing	DevOps
Defects	Defects
Overproduction	Overproduction
Waiting	Systemic impediments
Non-used employee talent	Overspecialization
Transportation	Handoffs
In-process inventory	Partially done work
Motion	Task switching
Excessive overprocessing	Excessive processes

This may seem like a somewhat obvious list of things not to do. But it takes more than just declaring that you are not going to do them. It is important to understand why they happen, as well as how they degrade our decision making. Doing so should help you understand the power of many of the mechanisms, from Workflow and Queue Master to Service Engineering Leads and sync points, that I heavily rely upon both to make it obvious when they are occurring and to help teams eliminate them.

To better understand these types of waste, let's step through each of them.

Waste 1: Defects

Figure 4.3
Even subtle defects can be deadly.

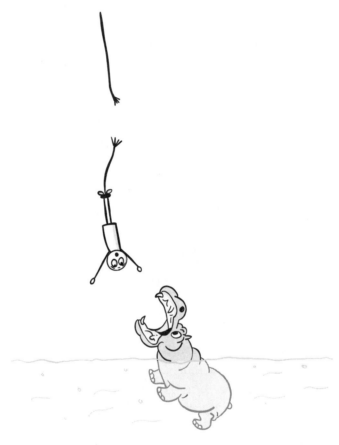

Whether they are bugs or shortcomings in a service, no one needs to be told that defects are obvious waste. They are a failure that gets in the way of a product or service performing as the customer needs.

Not only does no one intentionally create defects, no one likes to be known for doing so. The friction they create can slow down delivery in embarrassing and unexpected ways. As most teams are judged on how quickly they can deliver, this combination means that defects are often underplayed, hidden, or labeled as "features."

Allowing a defect to fester only makes the situation worse. Defects found shortly after they are created are far easier to fix. The person who created a defect is far more likely to have enough context to know where it is located. As time goes on, context is lost, memories fade, and other changes may further obscure the root cause and thereby make it harder to find. Once a defect makes it into production, costs go up astronomically. Not only does this make it far more difficult to triage and fix, but now customers have likely been impacted.

Defect-ridden code is also hard to work with. It makes meeting deadlines far more unpredictable. Not only do defects need to be fixed, but they also make it easy to unintentionally create additional ones. Few people like working in such dangerously unpredictable conditions. Even the knowledge that an area has rotten code can make it incredibly difficult to attract and retain good delivery staff to work on it, making it that much more difficult to deliver effectively.

The best way to prevent defects from occurring is to understand their causes. As covered in Chapter 5, "Risk," defects are the result of insufficient situational awareness of your delivery ecosystem. To demonstrate this, here is a list of the most common causes of defects:

- Misunderstood requirements
- Errors and poorly worded instructions
- Lost or insufficient context within the problem space
- Inconsistent or poorly structured and/or managed code, configuration, and/or data
- A lack of, or hard to follow, dependency management
- Poorly tracked or understood build and/or run environment management
- Nondeterministic/nonreliable/nonrepeatable installation and rollback functions
- Using an unsuitable or unfamiliar tool or language
- Typos

Each one of these is an example of lost awareness. Some, like misunderstood requirements or lost context, are obvious. However, even more subtle causes like typos or tooling/language mismatches that seem minor on their face can cause very real, and often hard to find, problems.

Lean tackles this problem by trying to "mistake proof" the delivery line. It uses techniques designed to do this in two ways.

One approach is to design the system in such a way that it is impossible to make certain mistakes. Manufacturers do this regularly with tools and parts by creating a shape that can only be put together in one correct way. An example is the asymmetrical shape of an HDMI connector. In IT this can be done by creating tools that prevent dangerous commands or invalid configurations from being executed by accident. I cover some strategies for this in more length in Chapter 10, "Automation."

The other way is to put in place mechanisms that make it far easier to spot mistakes and potentially hazardous conditions in the first place. Lean manufacturers use multiple techniques to bring immediate attention to anything abnormal or out of place.

One example is to use a clear marking such as color coding or symbols. Colors and symbols are great ways of providing a lot of information quickly with little overhead. Lean manufacturers use different colors for certain parts, trays, carts, and even places where tools are placed.

This simple technique is very helpful, and a familiar one for any heavy IDE (integrated development environment) tool user. I also use it heavily with color coding management interfaces and terminal windows between environments, color coding datacenter cabling and connectors, as well as color coding between different types of alarms and graphs. I have even worked with teams to "color code" tools, frameworks, and languages to the types of tasks that they are most suited for. Sometimes this "color code" is the use of distinct symbols or markings like stripe patterns in case someone is color blind. Using such coding mechanisms both encourages people to use the most appropriate option for the job and gets them to ask, and if needed debate, why a certain tool or technology is not favored for a particular job type.

Another example of a mechanism for spotting mistakes is what in Lean is called "stop the line." In a Lean factory there will be *Andon* cords placed throughout the assembly line that activate an alarm to alert everyone of a defect. If the defect is not fixable immediately, the assembly line is halted. This exposes where a fault was found, aiding efforts to find the source, and prevents the failed product from moving further up the line where the fault can be concealed or create additional faults.

In IT such mechanisms are more difficult to put in place. We can and do stop builds and delivery pipelines when a failure condition is encountered. However, problems are not always obvious in the heat of the moment, when it is difficult to step back and see the whole. This is why I recommend having both a Queue Master, as detailed in Chapter 13, "Queue Master," who can help find problems directly, as well as a Service Engineering Lead, as detailed in Chapter 9, "Service Delivery Maturity and the Service Engineering Lead," who can help the larger team build the maturity to see more effectively themselves.

A shift toward such mistake proofing makes environments safe for teams to work in and repositions teams to view defects as a failure of the system that needs to be addressed to help all rather than as their own personal failure, which they might be tempted to conceal from others.

Waste 2: Overproduction

Figure 4.4
"But I only ordered one!"

You can have too much of a good thing, especially when if it is rarely, if ever, used.

Overproduction occurs when something is produced that has no paying customer. For manufacturers this excess results in inventory build-up that needs to be stored, discounted, or thrown away. This is obviously a Bad Thing To Do. Not only do you have to decide whether it is better to pay to store it or throw it away, the resources used to create it remain tied up in something that is not providing any value.

While IT overproduction is caused by many of the same forces as in manufacturing, namely a focus on outputs over outcomes, it is both far less visible and more destructive.

IT overproduction lurks in the form of unused or unneeded features, excess code, and unwanted activities that provide little demonstrable value. People may claim that customers want the unused features, but never bother to see if this is true or how it contributes to the overall outcome. Internal processes and tools may look useful but the output may be ignored or no longer provide any value.

What many IT professionals miss is that all of this overproduction is not just wasteful, but also introduces a lot of excess friction into delivery. Excess features and code might not be used but they have to be integrated, tested, deployed, and managed in production. If they are not, they can end up turning into dangerous landmines that can inadvertently destroy a company, as happened with Knight Capital (as detailed in Chapter 10, "Automation").

Excess code and features also obscure our overall understanding of our ecosystem. They make it far more difficult to find problems, understand what code is and is not being exercised as customers use it, and figure out the best place to make changes and add features and functionality that customers actually do need.

To counter overproduction, I always try to make it obvious what the costs of doing it are to the organization. I track the extra support and maintenance costs, the added infrastructure costs, and the increase and variability of delivery times and defects it causes. I also try to capture actual usage patterns to make it easier to spot features that are rarely, if ever, used. This allows for the technical teams to hold a fact-based discussion with the business to ensure that what is being done is in the best interests of the organization and the outcomes of its customers.

Making the Wrong Numbers

Anyone who has worked at a telecommunications company knows voice service is still considered a keystone in the industry. This is despite the explosive growth of packet-switched networking and Internet-based services.

One such provider was looking to consolidate and upgrade their many legacy voice products. They built and acquired many over the years that served a myriad of consumer and business needs. But as time went on, these systems were growing increasingly unstable and expensive to manage. Many of these systems were also not compatible with newer fiber lines. Despite this clearly growing problem, few stakeholders could agree on the best way to resolve it.

Marketing and Sales were fearful that any loss of features would not only look bad but risked losing customers. As a result they demanded that any new solution include all 200 existing features found across all systems currently in place.

This left the delivery teams in a conundrum. There was simply no system on the market that contained every one of these features. The only way any solution could accommodate it would require either integrating several commercial solutions together with custom code or building everything from scratch in-house. Either approach would be both costly and take years to implement. As Marketing, Sales, and Support all strongly pushed back anything that did not have feature parity on Day 1, there was no way to easily phase in a solution.

The teams struggled with this problem quarter after quarter with little to show for it. The company became increasingly concerned as the risk of system failures grew with no solution yet in sight.

This seemingly insurmountable problem actually had a rather simple solution. Customers didn't really want every feature. They only wanted the ones that were valuable to them. Some features were for long-obsolete needs or ones that could be better handled in another way. Also, not every customer or market was equally valuable to the company. If a feature had to be built and supported at a loss for a customer, it needed to be agreed as to why.

Keeping all this in mind, one team decided to dig in to see which features were actually being used by which customers along with the revenue each generated. They found that there were roughly six features that were heavily used, along with another seven that were infrequently used by customers who were important enough to the company that it made sense to include them. All of these features were so common as to be included in most solutions available on the market. The vast majority of the remaining 180 features had either never been used or not been used for the past five years.

The data was so obvious that the other three teams backed down. Soon after, a solution was delivered with all the necessary features. This was then rolled out to friendly parties to try. Not long after, we migrated the rest and then proceeded to shut down all of the legacy systems.

Figure 4.5
"Please wait for the next available representative…"

Even with all of the focus over the years on new tools and processes designed to reduce delivery friction, we still struggle to get things done. Much of this is caused by a wide array of systemic impediments that IT teams manage to inflict upon themselves, either out of habit or through a lack of communication and understanding. Each one inevitably degrades our ability to make effective decisions.

While the most obvious impediments cluster around operational areas, many exist throughout the service delivery lifecycle. Common forms include frustrating bottlenecks, misalignments, and hard blockers that stop you from being able to make any progress at all until they are eventually removed. They result in delivery delays, rework, missed customer expectations, and frustration that can increase tension across the organization.

Identifying Systemic Impediments

The first step on the path to eliminating this form of waste is to first recognize the causes of systemic impediments. Frequently the cause grows out of a previous problem or goal that is no longer valid. Other times, communication issues and misalignments in goals or understood target outcomes create contention that hinders progress. Uncovering these causes and their costs to the organization can help bring attention to, and ultimately remove, an impediment.

To help you on your journey, here is a list of some of the most common systemic impediments:

- **Communication challenges:** Distance, whether physical or organizational, limits timely high-bandwidth face-to-face communication. Instead, we are left to rely upon more lossy, out-of-sync communication mechanisms such as email and documents that lose context and can be misinterpreted in ways that reduce our situational awareness and cross-organizational alignment. As you will discover in Chapter 6, "Situational Awareness," the increasing globalization of IT also can introduce language and cultural background differences that can lead to further problems and create distrust.

- **Poorly configured work environments:** In our increasingly virtual world, many organizations miss the value of a well-designed shared work environment. This is a place where team members can meet to work collaboratively with minimal outside interruptions. It also acts as an information store and sync point, creating a useful structure to capture and share information, as well as catch and correct misinterpretations. Without a shared work environment, whether due to limited space, geographical distribution, or a global event such as a health crisis, sharing becomes more informal and uneven. Without concerted effort to implement tools that improve information sharing, collaborative working, and conflict resolution, information can be lost, and trust can be hindered.

- **Poor environment management:** Environment hygiene, from all the components that make up the service to the software, operating systems, patch levels, configurations, and physical and/or virtual layers of coding, testing, and operating environments, is important to keep track of and maintain. Any lack of hygiene introduces potential variation where situational awareness can be lost, thereby reducing the efficacy of decision making.

- **Poor code management:** Code that is poorly written, commented, tracked, or updated makes working with it slow and error-prone. Supporting development tools and their usage, from code repository tools and structures to build and test tools and the artifacts they generate, are also important for code health. Anyone who has worked in a place with a large number of code branches and infrequently checked-in code knows how painful merging and integration is. This pain is caused because there has been so much disjointed change that no one person has the full context of the code. The gaps in awareness this creates across the team are difficult to close and also distract from the target outcomes you are trying to deliver.

- **Excessive tight coupling:** Components, systems, and services can grow to become so interdependent upon each other that any change to one has a significant and immediate ripple effect on another. Tight coupling forces affected parts to be treated as a single unit. This reduces flexibility by forcing any changes in one to be treated as changes in all. It multiplies the effort required to deliver, manage, and troubleshoot. It can also increase the amount of downtime required to make a change, as affected parts cannot be swapped out or changed individually, as well as reduce the number of options available to easily scale those areas.

- **Competing objectives:** Organizations can fall into the trap of having individuals or teams with different or even conflicting objectives. This can lead to disagreements, rivalries, and blocks that hinder progress. Not only do competing objectives impede business and create an impenetrable fog that obfuscates the strategic intent of the organization, they can divide and be heavily demoralizing to staff.

Friction-Filled Clouds

I am impatient by nature, and waiting unnecessarily for something is a particular pet peeve of mine. However, I am not so impatient that I am willing to rush through something if it means more work and friction later. Deploying services on the cloud is probably the place where this balance comes most to the forefront.

Many organizations transition to using the cloud to work around internal impediments. A common catalyst is all the friction involved in waiting for new hardware and software to be installed and made available. This can make going out and instantly provisioning an AWS or Azure instance quite alluring, especially when the alternative can take weeks or months.

I commonly see IT Operations organizations miss the problem that developers and others across the organization are trying to solve. Instead, they focus on the technology of cloud computing. Many try to build "internal clouds" or put in place yet another lengthy provisioning process for using an external provider. One company I was at even went so far as insisting that each service provisioned needed to go through a weeklong design process for each new virtual machine or container to "make sure that everything was documented and approved."

Process is hardly the only source of friction. A second common friction-filled mistake occurs when teams fail to manage their cloud service configurations. Cloud consoles become full of one-offs, while configuration and orchestration tools like Puppet, Docker, Kubernetes, and Terraform are either not used at all or are so full of untracked one-offs that it becomes difficult to know what is in production or how to reproduce it.

A third mistake is to so tightly couple cloud services as to lose much of the flexibility that moving to cloud services would otherwise afford. This forces teams to take down, update, and bring back up such services together in a resource-heavy coordinated fashion.

Waste 4: Overspecialization

Figure 4.6
Bill misinterpreted when they told him that his specialization would take him to high places.

When you face very deep and complex problems, having specialized expertise available to help can be very useful. Likewise, becoming the trusted go-to person for certain types of problems can even be ego-boosting. Acquiring those skills takes time and practice, with more difficult or rare skill sets often commanding premium compensation rates. This encourages people to specialize.

So what could possibly be wrong with this?

The problem begins with how specialists are deployed. When the skills are rare or expensive, many companies look to maximize their investment. They single out specialists, funneling all work requiring that expertise toward them. This creates problems that ultimately degrade situational awareness and weaken organizational trust and learning.

One such problem is the risk of separating work from its overall context. Specialists spend so much time working on tasks that fit their specialty that they often get left out of what is happening in the larger ecosystem, and with it the overall objective of the work. Similarly, those outside the specialty do not get enough of a view to understand what the specialist has done and why. This degrades feelings of ownership for everyone across the lifecycle, creating fertile ground for finger-pointing and blame.

Another such problem is the issue that the worker's identity and value often become associated with their skill type rather than their ability to help the company achieve its target outcomes. The worker's specialization is currency, and the rarer it is, the more the worker is worth. This disincentivizes specialists from sharing what they are doing with others for fear of endangering their value.

It is important to note that larger organizations are the most vulnerable to the specialization problem. The reasons are myriad:

- **Skill-focused hiring:** Specializations are far easier to define as a need and hire as a position, making managers easily tempted to organize teams by specializations. Being narrowly scoped, work must then be passed from silo to silo to be completed. Hiring approaches that put applicants through specific tests that follow a narrow band of acceptable solutions often bias toward like-minded people. This makes teams more susceptible to tunnel vision and specialization "not invented here" groupthink.

- **Lack of ownership and insufficient understanding of the work:** When there is a lack of ownership or insufficient understanding of the work, awareness of the larger ecosystem and responsiveness to events within it often break down. Work easily loses meaningful priority as it bottlenecks at handoff points between silos. Teams optimize based upon what is most expedient to them, even if it is at the expense of suboptimizing the larger organization. Temptation for finger-pointing and blame inevitably builds as work becomes blocked and problems that cross disciplines arise.
- **Fight against obsolescence:** Rapid technology or strategy changes can render specialized skills obsolete. Incumbent specialists who see work shifting away from their area of expertise may attempt to stall or derail change, hindering an organization's ability to adapt.
- **Lack of personal engagement and buy-in:** The compartmentalization of duties creates a rigid and less stimulating workplace environment. Not feeling like a collaborative part of solving for an outcome can limit creativity and the adoption of new technologies and solutions. Limited management understanding of these underlying dynamics can further slow organizational responsiveness.

The best way for an organization to free itself of this waste is to continuously look for opportunities to minimize the need for specialization. One way is to avoid overly complex solutions that need deep specialization skills. Another is to rotate roles as well as find creative ways to regularly help members of the team cross-train each other.

Where specialized work is unavoidable, there are ways to reshape specialist roles and teams to minimize its drawbacks. The best is to embed specialists as subject matter experts in teams that own the end-to-end lifecycle. This model is similar to Spotify's squads and guilds approach. Rather than performing all the specialist work themselves, the specialists can advise and train others to help ensure activities are done right. This not only improves flexibility by improving the size and liquidity of the pool of staff skill sets, but it creates an attractive incentive for employees to continually learn new skills. Specialists can still hone their skills, jumping into deeper challenges and sharing with other experts in a wider interest group. The wider exposure helps people become "T-shaped," with both deep specialist knowledge in one area and broad competency across many others.

Overspecializing Dysfunction

I frequently encounter companies that over-rely on specialists for frequent activities, creating all sorts of bottlenecks that hinder the ability of other teams to get work done. The three most common are database administrators (DBAs), network engineers, and IT security specialists.

Being a specialist or having specialists in a delivery team isn't necessarily bad. I often recommend having some. When they are part of a diverse and skilled team they can help everyone make better technical decisions. They can also help coach others to code and perform maintenance tasks using better approaches, and can tackle those hard problems that can otherwise limit your ability to meet customer needs.

However, specialists themselves need to be regularly challenged and stretched so that they can stay interested and grow with the team. When they are not, they often place all of their worth to the team on what work they alone can perform. This inevitably makes them act overly possessive of their area to the point where they become a single point of failure.

I had this very problem at one company with DBAs and network engineers. There had been a policy that all database work required a DBA, while on the network side most access was controlled by access control lists (ACLs) that needed to be signed off and then performed by a network engineer. Both policies made changes and deployments painfully slow. While DBAs and network engineers liked the respect and feeling of importance, the pressure on them was high and the work was both tedious and uninteresting.

So I changed around the dynamic, starting with the DBAs.

I sat down with some of the top DBAs in the organization. They were extremely talented, and arguably some of the best I have ever worked with. I was keen to make the bottlenecks go away. But I also valued their knowledge and wanted them to feel that they were being challenged and were growing.

I proposed that they come up with tools and other ways that would allow others to perform simple, low risk tasks. Alongside, we created a point system that allowed for engineers who showed that they could responsibly perform them to steadily gain more privileges to perform other, slightly riskier tasks. Those who could not would lose points, and with it their privileges.

I then created a Database Engineering (DBE) discipline that would be in charge of future database architectural decisions, research new promising technologies and data optimization strategies, as well as work with developers to improve coding and data structure practices. As with the engineers, the DBAs were given a point system. Those who created and improved tools and practices that enabled work to be handed off would be given the ability to become a DBE and drive their interest area. Those who were not interested would stay working on database administrative tasks but might find themselves working for the very engineers that they were slowing down.

The approach was extremely popular, and in a short time the bottlenecks had mostly melted away. We also had a big win in that our best DBEs were now tackling some of the latest technological problems, allowing our capabilities to leapfrog over many of our competitors.

I took a similar approach with network engineering. The team soon found ways to throw out the network ACLs and replace them with technologies that eventually formed much of the backbone of software-defined networks (SDN). This enabled delivery teams more flexibility while still ensuring that the networks remained both secure and performant.

Waste 5: Handoffs

Figure 4.7
Handoffs.

Handoffs are a fact of life. Not everyone can always do everything all the time. Sometimes it may even be prudent, or a legal requirement, to intentionally separate responsibilities across teams.

Handoffs, however, introduce two challenges. The first is that people and teams do not always share the same set of priorities. When priorities differ, work can easily become trapped along a handoff chain. Whether a team is waiting for another team to complete a piece of work they need or a partially completed item is waiting to be picked up and completed, the delay it causes appears the same from the customer's perspective.

The second challenge is that handoff and integration points become opportunities for information and context to be lost. The resulting flawed assumptions can lead to errors and rework, as well as complicate the troubleshooting of any problems that cross the handoff or integration boundary.

The most common form of handoffs are those between specialist roles and domain experts brought in to complete an activity. I have personally seen back-and-forth loops between DBAs and engineers or developers and testers that drag on for days or weeks.

Another common challenge is caused by the overly tight coupling between components as well as nonsensical splitting of responsibilities across teams. Ironically, such splitting is often done under the belief that more teams with fewer responsibilities will automatically result in faster delivery regardless of how tasks are divided up. This usually leads to dividing tasks at the very bottlenecks that lead to excessive handoffs.

The Serial Loopback

At one company such responsibility divisions led to a long handoff chain that ultimately became debilitating to the company. The service had been broken up across 20 different Agile teams under the belief that together they could deliver everything in one or two 2-week sprints. Unfortunately, the way that they were divided left 14 teams with tight library and other dependencies that needed to be first delivered by another team before they could confidently complete their own tasks. In a number of cases these dependencies were cumulative, with a team dependent upon a library from another team that was dependent upon another element from yet another team and so on. This ultimately serialized the very deliveries they were trying to speed up, in some cases increasing delivery times by upwards of six months.

What was worse, if a bug or other problem was found midway through the chain, the process would effectively have to loop back to the team responsible for fixing it and traverse the chain from that point again.

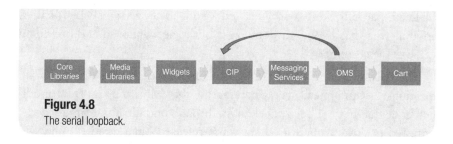

Figure 4.8
The serial loopback.

It is important to understand where handoffs exist within your ecosystem. Workflow boards like those discussed in Chapter 12, "Workflow," in conjunction with the Queue Master discussed in Chapter 13, "Queue Master," can help you spot excessive handoffs. I also encourage teams to identify and discuss handoffs at retrospectives and Strategic Review sessions.

Encouraging staff to find ways to reduce handoffs wherever possible improves organizational responsiveness and flexibility. It also can improve situational awareness, as well as reduce errors and misunderstandings that result in wasteful rework.

Waste 6: Partially Done Work

Figure 4.9
Partially done work.

In Lean, partially done work is called "work in progress" (WIP). WIP is anything that has had work done on it but is not deployed and providing value to the customer.

Partially done work, or WIP, is a common scourge of IT delivery organizations. It can appear everywhere across the delivery cycle, from modified code that has not been checked in, through unbuilt/unintegrated code, untested packages, unreleased software, released but turned off code, to partially completed operations tickets.

There are a lot of problems with partially done work. It is easy to focus on how it can create a lag in gaining value from the work, or how not checking in a big batch of code delays potentially useful feedback. Both are meaningful. But perhaps the worst problem with WIP is that it tends to create *more* work for people who believe what they are doing is making them more efficient.

Think through a time when you were juggling multiple pieces of work. Each time you cycled to the next item you had to put in some effort to regain context. Where did you leave it? In what direction were you trying to take the activity? Did something change while you were not attending the task that altered the dynamics enough that you have to course correct or even throw away what you have?

Another issue with temporarily losing context is that it creates an opening for mistakes. Dynamics can change in ways that you might not notice until it is too late. We can also misremember what was going on or what we were doing in ways that introduce unintentional defects or rework.

The best way to tackle partially done work is by making it and its effects visible. Workflow boards that show the amount of work in progress are one good form. This is also where Queue Masters are extremely helpful. They can spot not just when WIP is happening, but also some of the patterns that might be causing it. This can help teams find ways to work together to break their bad habits

One such common bad habit is our next waste: task switching.

Waste 7: Task Switching

Figure 4.10
Task switching.

Whether you are building, testing, or operating services, IT work requires a lot of deep concentration and building up context. Interruptions are hazardous for both. Yet in the desire to maximize output, we willingly accept frequent task switching as normal, whether in the form of interruptive fault troubleshooting or the sudden reprioritization of work.

It is easy to fall for task switching, and it often goes hand in hand with partially done work. Some love the thrill of racing off to be the hero in an outage firefight. Others feel that by having several activities on the go at the same time they are somehow more indispensable to the organization. Often an organization is particularly bad at prioritizing and tracking work, and every task becomes an opportunity for someone to lobby hard for it to be done immediately.

Switching between tasks is not just distracting, it fractures context, which slows our progress and degrades efficiency as partially done work builds up in the queue. Task switching also erodes our situational awareness, our ability to spot patterns, and ultimately our ability to learn and improve. Not only do we end up losing track of what is going on, but we risk losing touch with the outcomes that we need to accomplish. At best this can result in higher-priority items being delayed or neglected. At worst our ability to make sensible decisions fails.

Many IT teams, especially those with a heavy operational support element, resign themselves to widespread task switching. It is easy to believe that it is simply the nature of the job, but, as we will demonstrate later with the Queue Master role, restructuring the way that work hits the team can greatly reduce disruption. By being the entrance point for work, the Queue Master also can see across the ecosystem, noticing patterns and ultimately helping the team learn.

Workflow visualization techniques can also help uncover task switching, including lingering tasks and a build-up of work in progress. It is also important to actively look for and reduce the number of sources of task switching. As discussed in Chapter 13, "Queue Master," I encourage Queue Masters to help the team investigate ways of restructuring long-running people-intensive tasks, as well as work that seems to flow in circles between teams or requires a great deal of back and forth.

Waste 8: Excessive Processes

Figure 4.11
"Why do I have to fill out all these forms to replace my keyboard?"

Processes can be helpful. They standardize the shape and direction of work to ensure a reliably repeatable outcome. If deployed and maintained properly, processes can reduce errors and rework. They also are good ways of capturing knowledge that can enhance the capabilities of the team.

However, you can have too much of a good thing. For IT, having and following the processes can become more important than the customer outcome, sometimes to the point where it is even declared as the objective that the customer is looking for. This is true even when the processes themselves do not seem to do much to improve delivery or service effectiveness.

Some of the worst process waste is done under the banner of "industry best practice," even when it is clear that the process is hindering the business. Over time, this divergence in purpose can reduce an organization's ability to respond in a timely and flexible way to the demands placed upon it. Learning and improvement seem to slow to the point where there is nothing significant that directly correlates to improved effectiveness and progress toward customer needs. Tensions and stress rise from increased frustration, workloads, and rework.

Excessive processes tend to develop one or more of the following attributes:

- **Inflexibility:** IT lives in an ever more dynamic ecosystem. Customer and business needs can shift at an even faster rate than technology. The combination of condition changes means processes need to be continually reviewed, altered, and sometimes even eliminated in order to stay aligned. Inability or resistance to adapt processes reduces their efficacy and creates waste.
- **Excessively prescriptive:** A useful process is typically a repeatable pattern that helps us understand the situation and navigate toward a successful outcome. However, excessively prescriptive processes can be so detailed that they become a mindless straightjacket that actively prevents people from adjusting to changing conditions. Such processes should be reviewed to determine whether the process is a workaround hiding a larger problem.
- **Demonstrate little to no discernible customer value:** Some processes are put in place with the best of intentions. However, due to either habit or misunderstanding of the actual need, they struggle to provide any appreciable value. These processes are typically poorly constructed or are ill fitting for their deployed environment. Sometimes they have been taken verbatim from another environment or official list of "best practices." For instance, one company required physical signatures for certain change procedures. There were no legal or regulatory requirements for the procedure, and later I found that the only reason it was there was because the process had been copied from a company that did have such requirements.

    Such processes should be reviewed to determine what problem they are trying to solve and whether the problem exists and needs solving in the target environment. If it does, the process should be altered to make the intended desired value far more apparent. If it doesn't, the process should be thrown out. It is far safer to have no process than to shoehorn in one that is not fit for purpose.

- **Execution-knowledge mismatch:** Sometimes a process ends up being executed by people who either do not understand the underlying reasons for it or lack the knowledge, awareness, or skills required for executing it. IT organizations are often filled with such processes, and they don't just occur at the junior support technician level. In fact, in my experience they are most common where a process requires sign-off by senior management, like change board approvals and official governance processes. The lack of sufficiently shared situational awareness degrades the approver's ability to effectively execute their intended procedural duties. It can be caused by ineffective internal communication flows as well as poorly structured information.

  When mismatches happen, it is imperative to quickly find out how they have developed so they can be rectified. Is there a more appropriate way of achieving the intent behind the process? Perhaps the process can be executed at a level where the right situational awareness exists, or the quality and flow of information can be improved such that the approver can effectively perform his or her duties.

- **Regularly broken or circumvented:** Sometimes processes seem to be regularly broken or circumvented. One very common one is breaking a purchase into a lot of small transactions in order to work around a very slow process for anything over a particular value. Another is reusing old code or systems to avoid having to spend lots of time porting to some substandard "official" technology.

These are all symptoms that a bigger problem exists. Rather than resorting to strict enforcement, the process needs to be reviewed to see why it is not followed. It is possible that the process is overly cumbersome, doesn't match actual conditions, or that its value is not understood by those who should be using it. Occasionally, much like the fact that certain statutes require that some financial transactions use fax technology, the process is simply no longer needed.

Each of these symptoms is a good indicator that you have excessive processes. It is important to review processes regularly, whether or not there are obvious signs of problems. I usually encourage teams to look at whether any processes appear problematic or questionable at regular cycle sync points like retrospectives and strategic reviews, as discussed in Chapter 14, "Cycles and Sync Points."

Good processes need to clearly contribute to the larger objectives, the ones that the customer cares about. Processes that do not do that in the most effective way need to be changed or removed entirely.

Muri (Overburden)

Figure 4.12
"Surely there is room for just one more package in the release!"

Not every form of problematic friction is a form of "pure waste." One such form is known in Lean as *Muri*, or overburden.

Scientific Management and cost accounting have long trained managers to think of inputs as sunk costs that need to be fully exploited in the name of efficiency and cost management. People with such a mindset believe that anything less is "waste."

Such overburdening is never good, and it can take many forms. Most people concern themselves with overburdened systems and machines, knowing that their reliability degrades with each little push beyond what is reasonable. However, there are two often overlooked forms of overburden that can damage our ability to deliver and make effective decisions: *overburdening people* and *overburdening releases*.

Overburdening People

Overburdening people is extremely common. Not only are managers frequently cajoling their staff to give it their all, many who are ambitious or nervous about losing their jobs also want to be seen going the extra mile. But such behavior is actually quite risky. There are, of course, the challenges that it can lead to burnout and leave little slack to compensate for any problems that occur. However, a far more pressing issue is the way that it damages decision making.

When people are stressed or otherwise overburdened, they unconsciously narrow their attention to only the most critical aspects of the immediate task at hand. This forced myopia keeps the person from becoming overwhelmed, but at a significant cost.

Less awareness makes it far more difficult to notice important facts or changing conditions across the ecosystem, limiting people's ability to learn and adjust. Research suggests that overburdened people are less productive and make more mistakes.[2] Overwork also can cause those affected to miss important decision points along the way.

Another fact that many miss is that even one overburdened team member can affect decision making for the entire team. An overburdened team member is likely to feel too busy to share what information they do have, weakening the awareness of those around them. They are also more prone to miss deadlines and important sync points, and are typically far less willing to "waste time" reviewing a situation or aiding their own learning and that of others. They don't have to step back, consider the big picture, and find a better approach.

I run into overburdened people all the time. The worst part is that they are usually those that an organization can least afford to lose.

So how do you fix overburdening your teams?

2. https://www.uclan.ac.uk/news/tired-and-overworked-employees-pose-huge-risk-to-business-data

It starts by making sure that the overburdened people attend the sync points, especially retrospectives and strategic reviews. They will try to refuse, which is when managers and teams can stage an intervention, sometimes even using a review session as a way to figure out how to redistribute or otherwise reduce workloads. It is also good to rotate those people to other areas that are new or different to them within the team's scope. Their insight will usually be valuable, and it will give them time to step back and realize for themselves the damage they were causing to themselves and others in their efforts to help the team succeed.

Overloading Releases

Having occasional big releases consisting of lots of changes bundled together can seem like a good thing. It gives developers more time to work on meatier problems and gives testers more time to test. Operations people like the fact that there will be fewer release interrupts to worry about, while for customers a surge in new features can make a new release seem compelling.

So why are big releases a bad thing?

Rather perversely, many who favor the big release approach over having more frequent smaller ones usually end up increasing the very risk and delivery friction that many claim they are attempting to avoid. For starters, having fewer releases doesn't necessarily equate to less risk. In fact, bundling many changes means a thicket of new and different interactions. This creates a thick fog that obscures everyone's situational awareness. Which of the many changes might be the root cause of a new problem? It could be one or the interaction of many. If developers haven't fully thought out how each change might interact with others or, worse, if changes were made by several different teams, it could make troubleshooting and fault resolution far more difficult and time consuming.

Having fewer releases doesn't really help reduce delivery friction, either. Giving developers longer to work on features can encourage long-lived branches and fewer check-ins. This reduces transparency and can result in a painful integration problem down the road. It also lets developers off the hook from thinking defensively about changes and how they might interact in the ecosystem if they go live before they are complete.

Longer release cycles do not help testing, either. Shorter cycles require really understanding what is of high value to test. They also create an incentive to invest in improving test cycle times, allowing the organization to get more feedback more frequently. Longer cycles encourage generic testing with poorer focus and longer feedback cycles. This results in a poorer understanding of the health of the code, and often results in releases going live with lots of known bugs.

The same goes for governance processes. Those used to working with large releases often fool themselves into believing that the only way any organization can have robust governance is to require many checkpoints full of reviews and detailed documentation in order to spot and mitigate potential risk. However, having necessarily heavy governance processes can actually make it more difficult to manage risk. Nobody likes having to justify everything they do, and the documentation process can be tedious and feel wasteful for everyone involved. When change tracking is limited and governance boards are run by managers who are not deeply technical or into the detailed minutiae, many smaller changes are simply missed or obfuscated in the name of expediency.

There is also a time penalty. Change happens in more than software. People, usage patterns, business requirements, and regulatory requirements can all change, sometimes unexpectedly. More time means more opportunity for these changes to affect the operating environment of the service. A release that reflects the earlier conditions from when the project was started may be unsuited for current needs. Holding onto changes longer also delays customers and the business benefiting from their value, if their value isn't eroded away by changing conditions.

What to do?

All of these types of Muri can be avoided by looking at how work flows through each part of your system. As discussed in Chapter 12, "Workflow," visualizing workflow through effective use of Kanban boards and Queue Master rotations can go a long way to help spot problematic bottlenecks, including long wait times, deep queues, and lots of work in progress.

Another useful measure is to look at code repository structures and statistics, as well as build, test, and deployment statistics. Does work get trapped on long-lived branches? Are certain tasks always handled by a tiny minority of the team? Are there long integration and test cycles with complex conflicts and seemingly intractable long-lived bugs? Do deployments touch a lot of different areas? Is it expected that there will be unstable periods after a production release?

Understanding flow and Muri can help us create a sustainable balance that promotes the very awareness and learning needed to make better decisions and achieve our target outcomes.

Mura (Fluctuation and Irregularity)

Figure 4.13
"Well, this isn't much fun!"

Mura means unevenness, irregularity, or lack of uniformity in Japanese. For manufacturing, unexpected shifts in customer demand, uncontrolled variability in products, unreliable equipment, and poor training can cause irregularity or fluctuation that can lead to organizational stress, quality problems, unhappy customers, and waste.

IT also suffers from a variety of forms of fluctuation and irregularity, from sudden demand spikes to unexplained loading and configuration drift that hinders service delivery function and performance. This has become an even greater problem as IT services have become more demand based. Not only have service stacks become far more complex, potentially causing delivery and operational workload fluctuations, they are also shared, meaning that problems that once were localized, such as misconfigurations or instance failures, can have a widespread effect. Also, with shared usage, user uptake and usage patterns can compound in unique ways. This can lead to wild load fluctuations that can occur with little to no warning. These can cause large, complicated problems that can cripple a service and be challenging to rectify.

The biggest mistake that people make is believing mura is both inevitable and unavoidable. It is not. Mura itself is caused by a situational awareness gap interacting with friction points in the ecosystem. This unknown can be caused by anything from an externally driven demand to an irregularity within the ecosystem itself. The unexpected fluctuation or irregularity only causes a discernible problem when it catches on one or more friction points it encounters along the way.

Another interesting aspect of mura is that the way we respond to the problem can heavily influence the severity of the outfall from the variation. In fact, it is one of the most common places where our instinctive reaction to the problem is likely to cause a further cascade of irregularity and friction that can compound the damage caused.

As we will see, the best way to eliminate mura is to aggressively find and close situational awareness gaps wherever possible, all while simultaneously removing friction points and exploiting bottlenecks in the ecosystem.

To better understand, let's take a deeper look at the two most common patterns: *unexpected demand variability* and *unmanaged variability*.

Unexpected Demand Variability

We are all familiar with the concept of fluctuating demand. Demand inevitably ebbs and flows throughout the day, week, or even year. Most variability is only noticed when a bottleneck, such as a store checkout queue or a traffic backup, creates some sort of noticeable delay or failure. Such variability, while unpleasant, is tolerable when it follows predictable patterns that we can make adjustments for in advance to ease the pain.

It is a very different story when demand shifts unexpectedly. Whether it is a lack of toilet paper or a suddenly overloaded web service, customer frustration builds to the breaking point as suppliers scramble to respond and adjust.

For IT, demand-triggered variability is often a sign that the delivery arm has somehow become disconnected from the customer and their target outcomes. This loss in awareness makes it difficult to foresee even gradual changes until they cause a real problem. Crisis then ensues when the organization's response hits friction that makes it difficult to adjust sufficiently to deal with the situation.

These sorts of awareness gaps tend to have two common causes.

First, in some instances, Sales, Marketing, Product, and Support teams that do have regular contact with the customer want to reduce potential distractions and have more control over managing delivery team priorities by acting as a proxy between customer and delivery. While the reasoning can be sound, it often leads to information delays and context gaps. The end result is the delivery team seeing a stream of jobs that lack much of the important context of the actual outcome desired or the obstacles in the customer's way in reaching it. Not only do they have no easy means to build an understanding, they have no way of catching any mismatches that develop. This leaves a system full of awareness gaps and friction points where variability will thrive.

Second, awareness gaps more commonly form around the fragmentation of organizational silos. Looking at the ecosystem from their fragmented perspective, neither the business nor the delivery sides can be fully aware of the customer or of the dynamics that drive behavior in their environment. This is never a great spot to be in, but really becomes a serious issue when one or both sides fully *believe* they have the true picture and that any misalignments are just noise or the other side's fault. The problem gets compounded by a lack of understanding of the health of the delivery side or its ability to handle demand shifts.

In both cases, when the crisis hits, a cascade of problems erupts. Teams can become overwhelmed (*Muri*) or defensively fragment along functional lines (*Muda*) to avoid blame. The stress slows everything down, mistakes increase, and the organization's ability to deliver becomes severely disrupted.

Even in the most minor cases the team will not completely recover. Previously promised work will be missed or suffer quality issues. Unless actively countered, trust will further erode while the facts of what happened are hidden or obscured for fear of blame. This further degrades situational awareness and puts severe limits on organizational learning and improvement. The stress of the event can also leave people stressed and create bad feelings across teams, adding further delivery friction.

This may sound bad, but the problem rarely ends there. The awareness gap that caused the initial crisis often makes us misread what happened as a pure resourcing issue. Our instinctual response pushes us to make further inappropriate decisions that only exacerbate the actual problem. The C-suite is particularly vulnerable to this. In most cases the reality on the ground has been obfuscated by the streams of cheery reports C-suite members receive and heavily managed interactions they have with their subordinates, meaning that often they too have lost their situational awareness.

Let's take a look at what happens and why we often make things go from bad to worse.

The Bullwhip Effect

Figure 4.14
"Snap!"

A variability-triggered crisis can seem very scary. When first reactions prove to be insufficient and everything appears to be sliding further into chaos, it is tempting to overreact and throw resources at the problem. This can be in the form of more infrastructure, more people, additional project time, extra features, or even more teams and software.

On the surface, this response makes sense. More servers, software, and hands available to throw at a problem may feel like insurance, even if it increases costs and complexity. But the extra padding does little to solve the underlying problems. Awareness is, at best, no better. In fact, the extra resources may simultaneously *increase* friction and *degrade* awareness. This can further compound the original problem and provide the necessary fuel to create a *bullwhip effect*.

The bullwhip effect is a classic supply chain friction problem. It begins with a sudden unexpected shift in demand. This shift can start from a steady state or, as happened during the COVID-19 pandemic, be preceded by an abrupt demand drop that forces production to be dramatically reduced to a lower baseline. As you will see, the problem is not that there has been a demand shift but how much friction an organization needs to overcome to spot and adequately adjust to it.

In IT these shifts typically take the form of load spikes and feature demand. IT teams respond by frantically trying to increase supply. For capacity, it might be panic buying and setting up new capacity or stealing it from other areas. For code, it could be hiring lots of developers or outsourcing large swaths of development.

As demand hits the supply chain, the bulge hits friction points on the delivery side, creating a ripple effect of stress and delay. The more time and focus that growing capacity takes, the more the pressure to complete will build. Such stress inevitably will compel those in the supply chain to act without spending sufficient time investigating what is driving the demand, how long it might last, or the repercussions of their actions on other elements of the ecosystem.

This is where the real damage kicks in.

Once the situation has become stabilized, delivery friction now makes it expensive and painful to change direction and bring things back to normal. This forces the organization into an untenable situation. If you ordered new resources (servers, people, software, etc.) you still need to take delivery even though they may be of little use. If you stole resources from somewhere else, you need to find a way of dealing with those ramifications. If you temporarily outsourced much of your development, you will need to figure out how to cost-effectively understand the state of the code and how best to manage and support it moving forward.

The worst part of all of this is that there may be so much built-in friction that reversing any decisions made or mitigating the damage they might cause is often difficult or impossible. Budgets and project schedules are often blown, sometimes in ways that incur high ongoing costs, with little to show for it.

Another damaging element of the bullwhip effect is that, despite creating a whole new set of issues, the underlying problem that created the initial cascade remains unsolved. Until those friction and awareness gaps are addressed, there is nothing to stop this cycle from repeating over and over, wasting ever more precious resources as customers continue to feel neglected and underserved.

Unmanaged Variability

Not all variability is sudden or demand driven. It can just as easily live in our services and the wider environment. It might be caused by a slightly different configuration over here, subtle differences in understanding over there, customers with divergent usage patterns or needs, or even aberrations caused by differences in the ordering of events. These quietly build like so many layers of paint and grime on a wall, obfuscating the real state of the ecosystem in ways that make it increasingly less predictable and reproducible.

Rising complexity in technology stacks, along with the growing adoption of virtualization and containers, has only increased the number of opportunities for variability. Everything from varying hardware components in computers, differences in compiler-generated byte code and software patch version, to unseen resource contention that varies the sequence and timing of operations can cause subtle yet important variations in behavior. Even differences in client endpoints and the way they access services can have a noticeable effect. Increasing the number of moving parts only adds to the risk.

The growth and fragmentation of organizations hasn't helped matters. Organizational silos can create drift in interpretations and implementation details. It only takes one misunderstanding between individuals or teams to create havoc that can easily disrupt the service.

Despite this growing complexity, many in IT seem to approach these challenges optimistically unaware. Those who do concern themselves with unmanaged variability often mistakenly believe that it can be fixed simply by forcing everyone to follow prescriptive processes.

The Snowflake

Figure 4.15
Snowflakes are all
unique and fragile in
their own special way.

As children we are told that every snowflake is different. This makes its frag-ile beauty special because it is both one of a kind and ephemeral. Few would suggest that these are qualities that we want in our IT services. Yet, the ways in which many organizations build and manage environments make snow-flakes in IT frighteningly common.

In 2012 Martin Fowler wrote a blog post that coined the term "snow-flake server."[3] Snowflakes are server and software configurations that have organically grown and changed over time to the point where it is nearly impossible to exactly duplicate them. They can happen anywhere, from server and data configurations to external environment factors such as hid-den resource contention in virtualized or containerized environments.

More often than not this drift happens through special "one-off" tweaks, such as manual modifications to fix a problem and get things

---

3. https://martinfowler.com/bliki/SnowflakeServer.html

working. Other times the drift is caused by poor packaging and patching that leaves installation and update detritus scattered about. With the "job done," people often forget about the details of what or how it was done. As one-offs build, it becomes harder and harder to figure out everything that makes them different from what we think they should be. They become increasingly unpredictable and dangerous, sometimes to the point of paralyzing improvement and putting the business at risk.

Those who are faced with having to reproduce unknown one-off configurations often try to overcome the problem by simply imaging the disks of the deployed instances bit by bit. But as Fowler notes, such hacks not only perpetuate the buildup of cruft, they also do nothing to ensure consistent and understandable behavior.

Minimizing Mura

The best way to minimize mura is to look at tackling its root causes. That doesn't mean trying to avoid shifts and change. Ecosystem change is unavoidable. However, we can do something about minimizing problematic friction.

The first and most important thing to do is eliminate any avoidable gaps in situational awareness throughout your environment wherever possible. Regardless of whether we are a junior staff member or the CEO, we all unintentionally do things that can create false assumptions, communication breaks, and misunderstanding.

The following are some questions that you and the rest of your team might want to consider asking yourselves in an effort to minimize mura:

- Do organizational silos exist and, if so, are they necessary? If they do and they are somehow unavoidable, can software and infrastructural dependencies that cross team boundaries be minimized? Can work be restructured to improve transparency and communication across organizational boundaries in a way that improves situational awareness, collaboration, and trust?
- Have you eliminated all "single points of failure"? These are places where only a small number of people know an element within your environment. This could be code, configuration, how to deploy, how

to use, how to troubleshoot, or anything else that is important within the service lifecycle. The best way to test this is to see how well tasks can be rotated among people in the team. If only a small fraction can do the work, they should pass on their skills so that others can do it as well as they can.

- Does every API have an owner? If so, do the owners ensure that API compatibility and coupling best practices are in place to allow for changes to be made by one team with minimal impact to others?
- Have similar things been done at the data level, where every piece of data has an owner, and the data quality, rate of change, and importance are understood? Have dependencies been minimized wherever possible so that they can be easily managed?
- Are there ways that you can authoritatively know what is out in your environment, including how everything is configured?
- Can everything be easily reproduced exactly without resorting to imaging?
- Can software be deployed and configured atomically?
- Are differences between deployments and versions captured, known, and understood?
- Do you avoid uncontrolled one-offs? The best way to test this is to check that every release and patch is fully version controlled, all changes made by scripts are fully transparent, logged, and auditable, and if shell access cannot be eliminated, that write and execute privileges are both minimal and fully logged and auditable.

Minimizing variation wherever possible does help. Unfortunately, eliminating all of it is nearly impossible. Your services may depend upon shared infrastructure and services that you neither control nor have full transparency into. You may be dependent upon technologies and data that you do not have direct access to examine, or your customers may be unwilling to reveal enough about what they are doing and why to help you forecast patterns ahead of time. You may even have legacy "snowflake" servers, software, and processes. One thing you can do is design your environment to be resilient to chaos. I refer to this as the "Defend against the Madman" approach.

The way this model works is simple. If your service has an element that lacks sufficient transparency, imagine that it is in the hands of a madman and try to figure out the worst damage that that element can do, and how it might do it, to the parts of your service that you know. If it is a cloud service, imagine someone taking resources away randomly or loading things down where clock ticks become distorted. How would you track its effect and engineer against it? What sorts of user activity could be dangerous, how could you spot that activity, and what could you do to manage the situation? If the component or service lives in a snowflake configuration, imagine a malicious and crazed person running through the halls and in the data center with an ax. What could that person destroy that would be difficult, painful, or just plain impossible to replace or recover from? Is there a server or disk array that is really important and difficult to replicate? Are there particular people who have knowledge or skills that no one else possesses? As equipment goes offline, what are users experiencing with the service? How can you make any friction visible, and what can you do to mitigate it?

All of this probably sounds improbable, but it does the job of breaking the overly optimistic happy-path approach that seems to pervade the IT industry. If you take it seriously, you begin to approach challenges defensively, thinking through failure modes and how variability might strike. This also moves us closer to reducing the level of variability that we, and ultimately our customers, are exposed to.

This concept is hardly new in our industry. It goes to the root of much of the thinking behind test-driven development (TDD), where you write the tests first that capture the various use cases that your code might eventually be exposed to before you write your code. This helps with thinking through the problem set before you code rather than being colored by the way you put it together after the fact.

Netflix and Their Variability Monkeys

Anyone who has been dependent upon a supplier for critical infrastructure or services has probably experienced at some point problems with service predictability and reliability. Some of the more famous ones, such as the data-center power outages at 365 Main in 2007, the severed undersea cables off of Egypt in December 2009, and some of the larger AWS outages, caused major disruptions for thousands of businesses and millions of people.

Figure 4.16
Are your services resilient against the Simian Army?

As services become ever more complex, chances are that variability will get worse. Anyone who has built infrastructure at massive scale can tell you, the more moving parts that you have, the higher the probability that something will fail. Urs Hölzle, VP of Technical Infrastructure at Google, once gave a metric that if you have a cluster of 10,000 servers, each consisting of components with a rated Mean Time Between Failure (MTBF) of 10,000 days, you can expect at least one failure a day.[4] When you combine outsourcing and scale, the chances of having a failure that you have little control over can become extremely high.

Fortunately, few of us work at a scale with mission-critical services where such failures are severe enough to be fatal to a business. That said, with the growth in adoption of cloud services stacks, this problem is becoming more and more prevalent to enterprises. Netflix is an extreme example of a company that has taken such concerns into account and come up with a novel solution for dealing with them.

4. *The Datacenter as a Computer: An Introduction to the Design of Warehouse-Scale Machines* (p. 77), Luiz Andre Barroso and Urs Hölzle, 2009.

Not long after Netflix began to offer video streaming services, they looked to leverage external infrastructure providers to allow them to more rapidly and elastically scale. At the time, demand for streaming services was unclear. In such conditions investment in lots of expensive infrastructure could prove fatal to the business.

However, outsourcing core services can also be dangerous. Outsource providers may not sufficiently understand your business or may provide services that do not quite meet customer expectations. Netflix decided to depend heavily upon Amazon's AWS cloud services. This exposed large parts of Netflix's streaming business to the risk of service delivery shortfalls from AWS.

Rather than optimistically expect stability and reliability, Netflix took a different path. Their early work with AWS made them realize that there would be a lot of instability. They saw that AWS's co-tenancy model was not set up to provide the level of predictability or reliability Netflix's complex workload required. Such variability meant Netflix could not rely on having sufficient integrity for every process.

Instead, Netflix decided to build their services to expect and accommodate failure at any level. To this end, they built a series of tools they called the Simian Army that roam over their services, randomly killing and degrading servers and applications to ensure failure. They feel that if they are not constantly testing their ability to succeed despite failure, then it is not likely to work in the event of an unexpected outage when it matters most.

Unlike most companies that try to do this in protected test environments, Netflix runs these tools in production. That way, they remove all the uncertainty that simulation creates, and firmly ensconce in the minds of engineers that their code will be put to the test in circumstances that matter and that they will have to pay attention to. Engineers have to build far more defensively, understand what will happen when things go wrong, and put in safeguards to recover. By dealing with the variation as a given, it stops being an issue, resulting in far more robust and resilient services.

See the Whole

As you might imagine, it is rare for most sources of friction in the service ecosystem to neatly fit in one category or have one simple root cause. Often, they layer on top of one another, creating a tangled mess of dysfunction.

For this reason, Lean embraces examining the whole value stream from the time an order is received until a solution is delivered to address it. Leaders are encouraged to walk the floor ("go to the Gemba") to look at the end-to-end flow with their own eyes. They do this not to tell people on the floor how to do their jobs, but to help find the impediments that reduce awareness within the workspace as well as across the line.

To improve awareness and reduce bottlenecks, the structure of work in Lean organizations tends to be more fluid, with fewer sharply defined roles. In Lean Manufacturing, people are encouraged to work together to make adjustments to the structures of their work stations and their way of working to improve flow and reduce errors. Information can flow naturally, allowing workers flexibility and awareness that helps shape meaningful continuity between their work and the end product.

Lean organizations also reach out to customers and suppliers in order to understand and work together toward achieving the desired outcome.

When Toyota decided to enter the US minivan market, they had their design team drive around the US in a minivan to understand the needs and desires of the market. Similarly, they drove European luxury cars in Europe and the US before embarking on Lexus. Toyota also regularly works with suppliers to help them understand and adopt Lean practices, knowing that their improvements will help both Toyota and their customers in the end.

Summary

Focusing only on improvements that increase delivery speed and throughput does little to ensure you and your team deliver effectively. Friction "wastes" in your delivery ecosystem can damage responsiveness and increase team workload, all while reducing your ability to deliver the outcomes that your customers expect and your organization needs to be successful.

As you will see in the next chapter, gaps in your situational awareness caused by friction and your inability to understand your delivery ecosystem also have a significant impact on delivery and service operational risk in ways that reduce the efficacy of traditional IT risk management mechanisms.

Chapter 5

Risk

Nothing will ever be attempted if all possible objections must be first overcome.

Samuel Johnson

The idea of risk conjures up feelings of danger of personal or organizational safety. While some people find flirting with danger exhilarating, everyone ultimately wants to avoid its repercussions. For IT, risk is the probability of not reliably delivering a product or service to the right people at the right time in a sufficiently safe and secure fashion that allows them to successfully pursue their target outcomes. With IT embedded in critical parts of our daily lives, avoiding IT failures is increasingly important. This makes it important for the provider, the customer, and their staff to have confidence in the way any probable and intolerably dangerous hazards are identified, assessed, and mitigated.

Unfortunately, managing IT risk has become more difficult. Rather than the single locally run piece of software of old, IT solutions are far more likely to consist of a large number of interdependent components. These services are frequently delivered by multiple organizations, many who rely upon global supply chains themselves to deliver their piece of the puzzle. Such complexity breaks many of the techniques of traditional risk management. Having so many providers in the delivery chain makes it difficult, if not impossible, for any organization to see deeply enough across the technology stack to count on compliance procedures to expose and control risk. As the SolarWinds hacks of 2020 spectacularly revealed (see sidebar), it takes only one hazard from a single link in the chain to affect everyone.

Modern IT solutions require a better way to assess and manage risk. Rather than continuing to rely upon using compliance processes to find potential hazards and then mitigate their risks, we need to look at what we know about the delivery and operational ecosystem. This includes how much visibility we have into the elements that comprise the ecosystem, as well as the predictability and orderliness of its dynamics.

In this chapter, we will explore how order and predictability affect risk and the decision-making process. We will also cover a number of techniques to help mitigate risks from unknown and unknowable hazards in your ecosystem.

Cynefin and Decision Making

We know that environments can differ in complexity. The more complex and dynamic an environment, the more context and situational awareness we need to confidently make effective decisions in it. However, being complex and dynamic doesn't necessarily equate to there being more, or more severe, risky hazards. For instance, a meat cutter in a meatpacking plant works in a far less complex environment than a commodities futures trader, yet most would agree that the meat cutter faces a higher risk of injury or death from a bad workplace decision.

Where there is a difference is in the way that decision risk is managed. While the risks for the meat cutter are more severe, their number is small and well known. Most risks to the meat cutter can be mitigated through scripted procedures that can be closely monitored, such as ensuring that cutting tools are sharp and in good working condition, only using such tools in particular ways, and avoiding slippery surfaces.

The commodities trader, on the other hand, faces a wide variety of ways that seemingly sound decisions can go bad, from bad weather and pest outbreaks to unexpected bumper harvests and political events that dramatically change the supply and demand dynamics of the market. For commodities traders, a scripted set of procedures would do little to uncover, let alone manage, any risks. Instead, they have to constantly seek out the most up-to-date relevant contextual information and adjust their positions within the bounds of their risk tolerance accordingly.

This relationship between contextual dynamics and the suitability of an approach became apparent to David Snowden while working on the problem of knowledge management and organizational strategy. From his work he developed a sensemaking framework called *Cynefin*. His framework is a complexity thinking tool designed to help people sense the situational context in which they are operating in order to make better decisions.[1] Snowden has continued to work and tune the framework, which has grown into a particularly useful guide to help people recognize the dynamics of the domain they are working in and understand why an approach that worked well in one context can fail miserably in another.[2]

1. David J. Snowden and Mary E. Boone, "A Leader's Framework for Decision Making," *Harvard Business Review*, November 2007 https://hbr.org/2007/11/a-leaders-framework-for-decision-making
2. The Cynefin Framework, https://thecynefin.co

Figure 5.1
Cynefin framework.

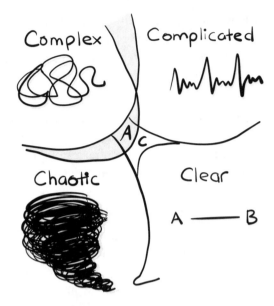

The Cynefin framework consists of five contextual domains: *clear, complicated, complex, chaotic,* and *confusion.* Each domain is defined by the nature of the relationship between cause and effect, with clear and complicated domains being two forms of *ordered systems,* while complex and chaotic domains are forms of *unordered systems.*

While some environments are more likely to find themselves in a particular contextual domain than the others, any number of developments can raise or lower complexity that shifts an environment into a different domain. This often not only breaks existing risk management but can create delivery friction and cause situational awareness to degrade.

Learning how to recognize which domain your organization is in at a given time can help you find the best approach to manage any risk. It can also be a useful way to spot and mitigate many of the common behaviors that often erode the quality of decision making in them.

Let's take a look at each domain to get a better idea of the different dynamics of each.

Ordered Systems

Ordered systems are those where a particular input or action will directly and predictably produce the same result. This clear and observable relationship between cause and effect holds true regardless of whether specific expertise is required to execute it. As such, the system can be pulled apart and put back together in a straightforward way like a machine.

As you will see, it is the level of expertise required to see the cause-and-effect linkage to make an effective decision that separates the clear and complicated contextual domains. This difference also plays a significant role in how best to manage risk in each.

Clear: "The Domain of Best Practice"

Figure 5.2
The clear domain —
simple and obvious.

Clear contexts are those where the problem is well understood and the solution is evident, thus making for perfect situational awareness. Snowden refers to these as "known knowns."[3] The act of problem solving requires no real expertise, just the ability to capture the issue, categorize it, and respond following established practice for the problem category. As the problem is already known, all the work can be scripted ahead of time, either in written form for someone to follow step by step, or as an automated tool that can be activated at the appropriate time.

The earlier scenario of a meatpacking plant is a good example of an ordered system operating in the Clear contextual domain. While an experienced meat cutter might be faster and less likely to get injured than someone

3. Ibid, p. 3

new on the job, there is little discernible difference from the actions of cutting up carcasses of the same type that cannot be scripted.

Clear contexts fit well for Taylorist method-driven management models, introduced in Chapter 2, "How We Make Decisions." Work can be defined and planned well in advance with instructions, coming from the top down, detailing clearly defined best practice. Likewise, risk can be managed by ensuring that workers closely adhere to instructions which explicitly check for known potential hazards, such as the state of tools and surfaces in the meatpacking example. The clear domain is the desired realm of Tier 1 helpdesks and support functions in traditional service management, as instructions can be placed in runbooks that can be searched and followed by the most junior technician.

There are two types of challenges that can plunge a clear contextual environment into chaos that is difficult to recover from. The first danger is that with so much of the actual thinking and directing happening from the top down, it is easy for conditions to shift that cause awareness gaps to form. With people working in such environments so used to following the routine, they often miss the warning signs of an imminent hazard until it is too late to react. Not only is this bad for delivery, the resulting failure and chaos can cause a precipitous drop in worker trust of management that further degrades organizational awareness.

Figure 5.3
Even if the domain is clear, you still need to see it.

There is also a second danger of the people working in the ecosystem becoming so attached to their past experiences, training, and successes that they become blind to new ways of thinking and struggle to learn and improve. Past rules become immutable in their minds, even when evidence of their diminishing suitability builds around them. Established firms that were once successful and large bureaucracies often fall into this trap, forfeiting success to more dynamic or suitable alternatives.

Complicated: "The Domain of Experts"

Figure 5.4
Some problems are complicated enough that they need an expert to solve.

The complicated contextual domain is the realm of the skilled expert. Unlike the clear domain, there are enough "known unknowns" that it is no longer possible for management to rely solely upon reusable scripts that an unskilled worker can follow to solve a situation. Instead, some level of domain expertise is required to both analyze what is going on and decide a suitably effective course of action. Typical examples of such expertise include an auto mechanic, an electronics repair person, or an IT desktop support specialist. Likely, all have been trained to match symptoms with known solutions they can confidently execute.

Rather than spending time scripting and enforcing methods, managers break the delivery domain by resource skill type, staffing and allocating tasks according to the perceived demand need. As a result, risk is usually managed through top-down change-gate processes. These are processes that serialize delivery into separate design, development, test, and release stages, each separated by a change management review at the end of each stage where conditions can be reviewed to uncover potential problems that need addressing.

Despite being seemingly straightforward, there are a number of challenges that traditional complicated contextual domain risk management processes tend to struggle to adequately address. One is the danger of becoming overly reliant on narrowly focused skilled specialists. As they are typically incentivized only on how well they perform their specialty, their narrow focus often fragments organizational situational awareness along functional or specialty lines.

Organizations that rely upon skilled specialists are also dependent upon them to deliver innovation and improvements. This can be problematic when specialists who are incentivized to justify their value feel threatened by any change that might diminish their value. They might overlook or dismiss new concepts that they do not know or that they feel endanger their value. Similarly, competing specialists can also engage in endless debates and "analysis paralysis" that create hard-to-solve decision friction that can prevent the organization from resolving an issue and moving forward.

Unordered Systems

Unordered systems are those where causality can only be determined in hindsight, if at all, even when the system is stable. Constraints and behavior evolve over time through the interaction of components. In such systems no amount of analysis will help with predicting systemic behaviors, making it impossible to deconstruct and reassemble like an ordered system.

Being that the cause-and-effect linkage is not immediately apparent, unordered systems are also ones where it is far from easy to use ordered system–style controls to manage risk. This makes shifts into an unordered system domain particularly perilous for organizations that rely upon clear and complicated risk management approaches. The disappearance of the relationship between cause and effect can make organizations miss fatal hazards entirely, or worse, not be able to handle them when they are encountered.

In fact, such a shift can seem so nonsensical that those expecting an ordered system may refuse to believe that any risk management breakdown is anything more than existing methods not being done with sufficient vigor. Rather than changing approaches, they increase the rigidity of their failing processes, adding additional processes, documentation, and governance that are of little help in eliminating the unpredictability emerging from the ecosystem itself.

In order to better understand what is happening, let's look at these two very different unordered system domains.

Complex: "The Domain of Emergence"

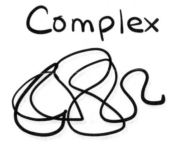

Figure 5.5
The complex domain.

When there are unknown unknowns in the ecosystem that cause the same action to produce different results when repeated, it is likely you have moved into a complex context. In the complex domain the environment is in constant flux, hiding cause-and-effect relationships in a mass of seemingly randomly moving pieces. Not only is it no longer clear if there is a right answer to a problem, but it can even be difficult to find the right questions to ask. Solutions that may seem obvious in hindsight only become apparent once they are discovered, or emerge, through continual experimentation.

This need to continually probe and test the dynamics of the ecosystem in order to problem solve and make effective decisions in it mirrors many elements of Boyd's OODA loop discussed in Chapter 2, "How We Make Decisions." It allows those in it to find ways to learn through an ongoing series of experiments to observe how system elements affect the behavior of the overall system. This increases the amount of feedback available to make it easier to spot shifts and emerging patterns that can then be used to improve decision efficacy.

Relying upon experimentation rather than process controls and expert feedback can feel dangerously risky to those used to ordered systems. No longer can risk be "controlled" through top-down processes. Not only that, but the need for continual experimentation necessitates that the working environment be both tolerant of failure and safe to fail in. Failure alone cannot be automatically viewed as an unacceptable hazard, let alone a sign of a shortfall in risk management.

However, there are a number of elements that people overlook when managing risk in a complex domain ecosystem. The first is that a tolerance for failure is not a license to experiment in ways that create unacceptable amounts of risk. No one succeeds by rashly throwing experimental changes into critical production services that will likely impact customers negatively. There needs to be enough situational awareness to allow people to mitigate any excessive risks that might otherwise make it unsafe for an experiment to fail.

This leads us into the second challenge. Despite being in an unordered system domain, it is still important to continually invest effort in creating order and transparency where you can. Good configuration management, packaging, and deployment practices are extremely valuable for reducing ecosystem noise that can make gaining situational awareness far more difficult than it needs to be.

Time and again, I encounter organizations that push code live and manually change configurations without bothering to capture the changes sufficiently to enable the organization to understand and easily re-create the changes in the future when needed. This not only creates fragile snowflake instances, their irreproducibility means that any destructive event (whether a failed drive, an accidental deletion or overwrite, or a ransomware encryption attack) can become dangerously unrecoverable.

The same goes for serverless architectures where insufficient care and consideration is spent understanding and mapping out their event-driven architecture. I have seen all sorts of race conditions and data mangling occur from unexpected event flows. Similarly, I have seen organizations that had so many production configuration switches and A/B testing combinations left live in production that no customer journey was definitively known or repeatable, making troubleshooting and dependency management nearly impossible.

One final area of concern comes from organizations that retain job and team silos. Above all, for experimentation to work well everyone needs to hold the same shared target outcomes. This helps to not only maintain cross-organizational alignment but also minimize the number of times an incorrect hypothesis needs to be disproven.

Silos make this difficult. They both unnecessarily fragment situational awareness and lead to the setting of localized targets that can easily become disjointed or compete with one another. This not only can make it difficult for solutions to emerge but can plunge the organization into an even more unordered contextual domain: the chaotic.

Chaotic: "The Domain of Rapid Response"

Figure 5.6
The chaotic domain, where everything feels out of control.

Problems in the chaotic domain tend to resemble a runaway freight train full of explosives engulfed in flame. The environment has ceased to function with any semblance of stability, making it the immediate priority to contain and establish order. It is the domain of the "unknowable," where everything is collapsing catastrophically with no clear sign of a root cause or how to fix it. In effect, this makes it the domain that delivery teams should rightly fight hard to prevent.

In chaos the relationships between cause and effect are impossible to determine because the dynamics shift constantly with no manageable pattern. Situational awareness has been lost, and with it the ability to make all but the most rudimentary decisions. Such crises require decisive action to immediately triage and address the most pressing issues. Success for those who find themselves in the chaotic domain requires the following:

- Identify and protect the most important areas in critical danger that can be saved.
- Quickly delineate zones of stability and crisis.
- Improve the flow of information wherever possible to improve awareness of and track the situation.
- Establish effective lines of communication to reduce confusion and help marshal resources to contain threats.
- Seek to stabilize and move the situation from chaos to complexity.

This all has to be done while quelling the desire for people within such an environment to panic.

The occasional foray into the chaotic domain can sometimes be therapeutic for organizations that have become ossified and need to be shaken up. These experiences create an opportunity to break with old concepts that are no longer fit for purpose and spur innovation and new ways of working. In fact, it is not uncommon for transformational leaders to nudge an organization into chaos in order to speed up the adoption of necessary changes.

However, the chaotic domain is not one that organizations can afford to remain in for any length of time. It is extremely stressful, and the lack of stability often drives away any sensible customers and staff alike. It is so dangerous that military strategists like Sun Tzu and Boyd encourage destabilizing the enemy by causing the dynamics of the battlefield to change faster than their decision process can handle. This is often referred to as "getting inside the enemy's decision loop."

There are some who thrive on the adrenaline rush and sense of heroism that can come with rushing into the crisis. They go to great lengths to seek it out, sometimes to the point of consciously or subconsciously creating the very conditions that push the organization into chaos themselves. They often crave the cult-like adoration that being seen as a hero can create. These groups can be thought of as the *dictators* and the *firefighter arsonists*.

Figure 5.7
The dictator.

Have you ever wondered why there are some people who seem to be content in, or even enjoy, environments that seem perpetually in chaos? You may even have gone further, wondering how dictators like Stalin, Mao, Saddam Hussain, and the Kims of North Korea were able to retain power despite having regularly purged their ranks in ways that seemingly weaken their nation's capabilities. Such dictators seem to intentionally perpetuate the very chaos that is destroying what they should be protecting.

Some look to placate personal insecurities, while others want to experience that ego high they get by playing the hero. Frequently, it is some dynamic in the way that recognition and rewards are given either in the current organization or from one in the past that causes both types of people to act in ways that instill organizational chaos. It is important to recognize their danger signs, as well as the structures that can circumscribe their impact in case you someday discover one in your midst.

Dictators are the more dangerous of the two groups. Rather than helping the organization in the pursuit of target outcomes, they are instead constantly looking for ways to destabilize others. Sometimes the targets are potential rivals they want to undermine in order to gain advantage over. Other times the goal is simply to make their own area look comparatively better than others. Some particularly sadistic ones simply want to feel some sense of power and control that is ordinarily out of reach, even at the expense of the larger organization. The fact that the instability they cause may be costly to the organization is irrelevant as long as they achieve their personal aims.

Contrary to popular belief, such people do not need to be in a high position within an organization or have a particularly vast scope of authority. In fact, the most formidable ones sit at key pinch points and gatekeeping roles within the ecosystem. I have encountered them in roles as vast as Finance and Vendor Management, Legal, Architecture, IT Operations, Project & Program Management, and even IT desktop support. This gives them undue influence far beyond their assigned responsibilities, thereby enabling them to potentially endanger the overall goals of the business and desired outcomes of customers.

Common dictator patterns include threatening to slow, stop, or even force an alternative decision in a seemingly arbitrary way under the umbrella of protecting the company from an unseen or imagined risk. One example I have seen is forcing the use of a particular technology or architecture, claiming that it is the "only approved and acceptable option," even when it is clearly inappropriate for the task at hand. Such behavior can force those having to navigate the gate to plead or make suboptimal choices in order to avoid missing deadlines or looking bad.

Another common example of a potential dictator is a developer or operations person who refuses to share with others on the team the intricacies of how to handle a particular subsystem. Their protected knowledge stunts the situational awareness, and thus overall decision-making abilities, of the entire organization. Intentionally or not, they use their knowledge to hold others in the organization hostage.

It is important to investigate the root cause for the behavior. Some who are lured into dictator-like behavior may be looking for control, whether to wield it over team members or to control the work itself and how it is prioritized. However, sometimes such behavior is caused by organizations that regularly act in ways that destroy trust. In such cases, the potential dictator may fear team members "messing things up" with no accountability, or that they themselves are not valued and are at risk of losing their job.

While dictators in leadership positions can use crises to drive needed change, some instead use them to quash such efforts, to reassert their control. They can commandeer resources and shut down viable alternatives under the banner of safety and security from perceived organizational threats. This is an effective means for crippling rivals and quashing ideas they find dangerous before the ideas can be proven to be viable and safe alternatives.

Figure 5.8
The firefighter arsonist at work.

Firefighter arsonists have entirely different motivations from dictators. They enjoy the thrill and label of heroism that comes with subduing chaos. They often seek out roles that allow them to rush to the rescue but are uninterested in any sort of crisis prevention.

Often you can tell that your organization is vulnerable to firefighter arsonists if individual heroes are regularly identified and celebrated. Public recognition for hard work can be extremely attractive, especially if other more healthy forms of recognition, such as shared pride in delivering products or services that really help others or the ability to regularly gain valuable career growth, are not readily attainable.

While there are some who crave the attention that comes with tackling crises, not all firefighter arsonists deliberately create a crisis. In fact, many people become unintentional arsonists by narrowly focusing on their immediate area of responsibility and not taking ownership for how their role and the work they do helps the organization achieve its objectives. This functional focus, which is often reinforced by the organization and the way it evaluates individual performance, causes some to ignore or not feel responsible for what is happening upstream or downstream. Others insist upon performing their role in accordance with some prescribed process or long-established practice, believing that they are working in an ordered domain even when there may be external signs that those processes and practices are negatively affecting the health of the larger ecosystem.

By maintaining this siloed view, such IT firefighter arsonists may add features that they know will earn them kudos without thinking of how they will be used, or how the health of the underlying code will be supported and maintained. They might ignore the value in unit testing, sensible repository structures, frequent check-ins, automated build systems, continuous integration, automated deployment, or environment hygiene. Often they will use the excuse that such activities are wasteful or are not conducive to their "more effective" way of working. In reality, the pushback typically is due to deep-seated concerns that no one of sufficient importance will recognize and give them credit for such efforts. Likewise, they will triage an outage and create workarounds for bugs out of expediency to get back to more interesting work without seeking to understand the root cause of the problem or how to prevent it from reoccurring.

One of the most effective ways to deal with dictators and arsonists is to look at what in the ecosystem might be causing them to act the way they do. Does the organization reward bad behavior? Is there little trust or transparency? Are roles and responsibilities laid out in a fragmented way that discourages people to see the whole? Is there an organizational culture that encourages following processes over delivering outcomes? Are there organizational bottlenecks managed by someone not accountable for helping deliver the target outcomes that matter to the customer? These are important places to investigate in order to minimize or eliminate the underlying root causes whenever possible.

Another strategy that helps flush out such dysfunction is to rotate duties. This can help widen people's feelings of responsibility and desire to collaborate, particularly if they believe that they might fall foul of suddenly being responsible for the unknown. Rotation forces people to investigate and learn.

The Domain of Confusion

Figure 5.9
Sally realizes that she just entered the land of confusion.

Much like being between gears in a car, *confusion* is a domain of transition that sits in the fifth quadrant in the middle between the systems and other domains. It is like being lost in a dense forest. The primary goal when you find yourself in confusion is to gather more information so that you can orient yourself and move into a known domain where you can then take the appropriate action. Few find themselves in confusion for long, if for no other reason than because it is the domain of decision paralysis.

Reimagining Risk Management

While understanding the complexity of the domain that you are operating in is important for helping you avoid approaching risk management the wrong way, there are several actions you can take that can help reduce risk and improve your ability to make effective decisions regardless of domain complexity. Each will likely sound fairly obvious at first glance, and all are elements that can be found throughout this book.

Let's take a look at each of the actions.

Have Clear and Understood Target Outcomes

Many of us in IT focus so much on the risk of failing to meet deadlines, service failures, missing service level commitments, and security breaches that we often forget the most important risk: the risk that our work will not achieve the needs and target outcomes of the customer.

One of the biggest causes for failing to meet target outcomes is simply not knowing or understanding well enough what they are. This can occur because no one bothers to mention them, or what is shared is either output-based or localized to individual silos and not aligned across the organization and with the needs of the customer. Similarly, few discuss fully the anti-goals, or what hazards and situations must be avoided and why. Chapter 11, "Mission Command," goes into great depth about both the causes for these common dysfunctions and ways to avoid or overcome them.

Knowing and understanding the target outcomes is important for everyone in every type of complexity domain. This even includes the Clear domain. While tasks might be so obvious in a Clear domain that management can script them, there is actually a lot of value in making sure the workers performing the tasks know what they are for and what outcomes they are trying to achieve.

This was a key part of the Job Instruction part of Training Within Industry, the program considered as one of the leading sources of many of the founding principles of Lean Manufacturing that the US military used to train new factory workers to help the war effort during World War II. While work was broken down into small pieces and scripted, workers were also told what outcome the work was trying to achieve. The idea was that by knowing the target outcome, workers could use that knowledge to find and suggest improvements that superiors might not have noticed that can better achieve the outcome. Having a clear purpose also has a great side benefit of being motivating to workers.

Make the Best Choice the Easiest Choice

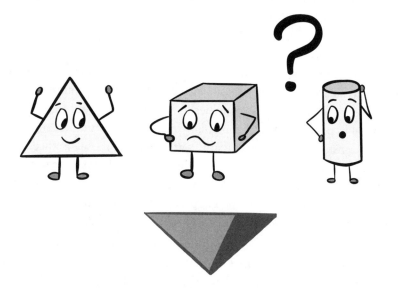

Figure 5.10
The best choice should
be the easiest to
execute.

Whether it is manually performing quick hacks to production or choosing a shortcut that reuses an unreliable or insecure piece of software, a lot of poor decisions are made because the chosen action is quicker or easier than the best choice. Choosing the shortcut simply because it is quick and easier might seem absurd due to the risks involved. Yet time, resource, and budgetary pressures themselves are often viewed as immediate risks that need to be mitigated. The more serious risks they create are not only distant, but those who ultimately have to deal with them are frequently different.

The best way to mitigate such risks is to make it far easier and obviously beneficial to choose the best, and ultimately less risky, choice for the organization and customer. One approach is to use an idea from Lean Manufacturing of making it so that parts can only be assembled the right way. Network RJ-45 jacks and USB cables are common physical examples. Software packaging and various forms of defined and managed access controls and versioning for service APIs can make it so that software can be installed only in the right place with the right dependencies, and that services can talk only to services with the right access and version details.

When it comes to minimizing manual hacks, the first step is to make the environment such that using traceable and reproducible approaches is faster, requires less effort, and is longer lasting than any alternatives. Automated hands-free build, deploy, and configuration management tools that reduce the effort and friction to make changes certainly help. I usually pair this with eliminating all need for any sort of shell or administrative access where manual changes can be put in place. I do this by putting in place tools that can perform those activities in a reproducible and trackable way. I also put in place a system that regularly polls for configuration and state of deployed instances. If any irregularities are detected, those instances can be either immediately and automatically shut down and quarantined for later examination, or automatically destroyed and rebuilt from the last known good configuration state. Such an approach makes it extremely difficult, if not nearly impossible, to make unknown out-of-band changes.

The next step is to find ways to make the total cost and risk profile of using a quick but poorly suited solution visible. It is important to note that the time and cost pressures that make suboptimal solutions appear attractive often ignore the total cost of ownership (TCO) in the form of support, maintenance, and risks to the organization's ability to satisfy its customers. Sometimes this is caused by a project team that is not responsible for the ongoing costs and success of a solution after delivery. Other times someone in the decision chain is suffering from a *sunk cost fallacy bias* (mentioned in Chapter 6, "Situational Awareness"), hoping to somehow recoup money already spent regardless of the solution's suitability for the task.

To capture the TCO, I use a combination of the data collected by the Queue Master and the data in the team's workflow board (as discussed in Chapter 12, "Workflow"), along with any instrumentation data (or lack thereof) showing how well the solution performs to meet customer outcomes. Such information can often be reshaped in a monetary (such as people and resource costs for support and maintenance, as well as risks to contractual commitment costs and lost customer revenue) or lost opportunity form (such as resources that must be committed to supporting and maintaining the solution instead of being used for other initiatives, as well as risk exposures to any known potential unrecoverable faults or security breaches).

I find that such cost information not only helps with rebalancing the consideration of near- and long-term costs, but also helps create a means for putting project teams on the hook for ongoing costs. This might not be easy to do yourself if you are an individual contributor. However, by creating the means for collecting and reporting cost-benefit data around the options being considered, management has a way of ensuring that project teams are aware that they must choose between committing resources to pick up excess costs or having their sponsors be charged back for them.

Continually Improve Ecosystem Observability

Figure 5.11
Improving ecosystem observability helps you understand what dynamics you are up against.

It is difficult to mitigate risks that you cannot find or know anything about. This is why it is critical to continually look for ways to improve the observability of the state and interactions of elements throughout your ecosystem.

It is easy to assume that everything is automatically observable by default in an ordered system domain and hidden in an unordered system domain. Neither is necessarily true.

In ordered systems everything might be visible but enough context is obscured that awareness degrades. This obscuring of problems is remarkably common. For manufacturers, tools and materials on a workbench can look both ordinary and expected yet be hiding a number of serious problems, from misplaced or broken tools to defective material. Lean Manufacturers use color coding for tools, carts, and workspaces to make it obvious when anything is out of place or to make it clear when an item is broken or defective. In IT, simple tasks like restarting a service, creating accounts, or even pushing an update to an environment can hide everything from defects and demands on team resources to potential security concerns. This is why such items are captured and tracked by the Queue Master, as mentioned in Chapter 13, "Queue Master," and reviewed regularly for improvement.

In unordered systems, not bothering to improve observability just makes it more difficult for context to emerge or activities to be directed to stabilize a chaotic situation. There are lots of ways throughout the service delivery lifecycle to greatly reduce the noise in an unordered system domain. The first is to organize your service ecosystem "workbench." This includes the following actions:

- Make sure all code, packages, configurations, and (if possible) tools and tests used to deliver and maintain the services are revision controlled and tracked throughout their lifecycle. The goal is to put in the key data needed to be able to re-create and "walk" the delivery and maintenance chain based on release, time, and deployment environment.
- Capture and track any changes to your ecosystem. Who updated the code/package/configuration/tool/test/deploy targets, when was it updated, what was changed, and why was it changed? This should allow you to trace back to when errors or vulnerabilities were introduced in order to help with troubleshooting, understanding the length and extent of any potential exposure, and ultimately fixing the problem.
- Capture and track your dependency chain. Are there third-party technologies or services you rely upon? If so, where are the touch points? How much visibility do you have into the stack to determine their stability and security? What are the effects to your delivery and production service capabilities if they fail or are compromised in some way?

Part of your service workbench also includes the environment that you use to build and run your services. Ensuring good environment hygiene is a good way to ensure that as much of the configuration of the delivery and operational environments are known and reproducible as possible. To do this, the team should aim to achieve the following:

- Put mechanisms in place so that every instance can be destroyed, and the entire stack confidently re-created identically from scratch from the component level. Along with what versions of components are deployed, I also like to track the last date each component was rebuilt from scratch. That allows you to spot potential blind spots that may need to be investigated.
- Implement mechanisms so that anyone authorized can, with a known level of confidence, generate a full configuration manifest of an instance without using "discovery tools." This allows you to track what you have, as well as spot potential vulnerability areas and their impacts quickly.
- Ensure that there are mechanisms in place that allow the team to confidently track and trace through component, instance, and environment changes over time without resorting to digging through change requests and guessing. They can use this date to confidently reproduce the configuration that was live at a given date.
- Understand the data stack and the flow of data across the service ecosystem. There are many aspects that are important to know, such as:
  - Where is the data located, where does it flow, and how does it move across your delivery ecosystem?
  - What is the security/protection/privacy profile of each data element, and how is it secured and verified?
  - How does that data profile affect where the data can be placed, who can use it, and how long it can be retained?
  - What data qualities impact the performance and availability of various services?
  - How are these data qualities captured, tracked, tested, and verified as part of delivery?
  - How would the ecosystem be restored, how long would it take to restore it, and are there any data synchronization or alignment issues that would need to be addressed (and, if so, how)?

Finally, there are other areas throughout your delivery lifecycle where data can and should be collected and regularly reviewed and analyzed as part of the delivery team's tactical and strategic review cycles that can help uncover potential risk areas. Many of these areas are covered in Chapter 11, "Instrumentation," and include the following:

- Code and build statistics
- Person, tool, and service access control lists and the mechanisms to track and audit access events and resulting activities
- Team stability and communication patterns
- Responsiveness and reliability of each external delivery and maintenance supply chain dependencies
- Code management efficacy
- Bug densities and integration issues
- Incident histories
- Production load and performance statistics
- Code instrumentation
- Customer usage patterns and journey flows across your service ecosystem
- Environment configuration management hygiene levels
- Customer tolerances for degraded performance and failure
- Security incidents and impact severities

Each of these is likely to produce some level of insight into the health and stability of various elements of your ecosystem.

Where they become particularly powerful is when these mechanisms are used together. For instance, someone can look at customer usage patterns that trace when and how they use a service. This data can be combined with incident and performance statistics to see if there are any interesting correlations that may indicate a problem. The results can then be matched with code instrumentation to determine which pieces of code and infrastructure are being exercised at those moments. From there, delivery teams can review the code and infrastructure that make up those exercised components to see if any are new or have a history of instability or brittleness.

Over time, such mechanisms can be used to help two useful patterns emerge. The first is an indication of potential risk areas that may need extra attention to better understand and ultimately mitigate. Secondly, the data from these mechanisms can provide clues of changing patterns that may indicate new emerging risks or even an unexpected shift in domain complexity. This information can be used to help the organization prepare and more proactively manage these risks.

Summary

As the service delivery ecosystem has become increasingly dynamic, interconnected, and important to customers, the flaws in the more traditional ways of managing risk in IT have become apparent. The move to DevOps is an opportunity to rethink how best to perform risk management. Understanding the dynamics and contextual domain of your delivery ecosystem can help you spot where the wrong policies and behaviors can expose you and your customer to problematic delivery and operational risks. By ensuring that everyone knows and shares the same target outcomes, all while putting in place mechanisms that improve observability as well as make it both easier and more likely that better and less risky decisions will be taken, you can both deliver more reliably and securely to meet your customer's needs.

Chapter 6

Situational Awareness

For want of a shoe the horse was lost. For want of a horse the rider was lost. For want of a rider the message was lost. For want of a message the battle was lost.

And all for want of a nail.

Unknown

Situational awareness is being aware of what is going on around us. We use it to orient ourselves, and it is a key ingredient of the decision-making process. To gain good situational awareness we need to understand the current conditions and capabilities in our ecosystem. Much as John Boyd predicted in his work on the OODA loop, how well we construct this awareness determines how quickly and accurately we can make decisions.

While information availability and observability is an important ingredient in creating situational awareness, there are other factors that are even more crucial in ensuring its accuracy. These span everything from our past experiences, relevant concepts that we were taught, and what we perceive as the purpose or outcome we are pursuing. Unbeknownst to many of us, situational awareness is also heavily influenced by various cultural elements we have been exposed to at home and work, as well as other habits and biases we have acquired over time. Together these not only shape how relevant we consider the information to what we are trying to achieve but can even interfere with our ability to notice it at all.

The topic of how we build and shape our situational awareness is deep enough to warrant its own book. This chapter is merely an introduction to these factors to help you spot important patterns that can negatively affect any decisions you and others in your team make. At the end of this chapter there are some tips that not only will help improve your situational awareness, but also strengthen the efficacy of other practices in this book.

Making Sense of Our Ecosystem

Gathering and assembling the information we need to build the situational awareness necessary to make accurate decisions can be surprisingly difficult and prone to mistakes. We have to identify what information is available to us. We then need to determine what elements are relevant, as well as whether what we have is both sufficient and accurate enough for our purposes. Then we need to figure out how best to access and understand it.

Despite being one of the largest and most powerful in the animal kingdom, the human brain struggles to reliably and accurately find, sort, and process all the information we need to make decisions. In fact, there is an abundance of research that suggests it is surprisingly easy to overwhelm the human brain. For instance, according to the US Federal Aviation Administration (FAA), at least 70 percent of commercial aircraft accidents and 88 percent of general aviation fatal accidents are attributed to human error primarily caused by the stress of deficient cockpit design.[1] Since the late 1960s, research performed by cockpit designers found that too many signals can actually make it *harder* for us to find the crucial information we need. Cockpits with too many gauges and indicators increased the stress levels of even the most experienced pilots, causing them to make far more mistakes.[2] Even today, pilots describe the experience of learning cockpit automation systems as "drinking from a fire hose."[3]

To overcome this limitation, our brains create clever shortcuts that filter and pre-process elements in our surroundings in order to lighten the load.

1. US Department of Transportation Research and Special Programs Administration. (1989). *Cockpit Human Factors Research Requirements*.
2. Wiener, E.L., & Nagel, D.C. (1988). *Human Factors in Aviation*. London, United Kingdom: Academic Press.
3. BASI. (1999). Advanced Technology Safety Survey Report.

We see these shortcuts in action when we effortlessly perform relatively complex tasks without thinking, like riding a bicycle or playing a favorite video game. These mechanisms are why experience can often lead to faster and more accurate decision making.

Why it is important to know about these shortcuts is that they come with some significant shortcomings. For one, they are far from perfect, and in their rapid handiness can themselves damage your decision-making abilities. Some of the more innocent side effects can be seen with our brains' over-eagerness to pattern match. We might see familiar objects in cloud shapes and ink blots that aren't really there. Unfortunately, this eagerness can also cause us to see nonexistent patterns in more consequential circumstances that can lead us to chase problems that are not there. We might, for instance, connect the coincidence of a service failure with activities being performed in a completely unrelated part of the ecosystem, leading to a large waste of time troubleshooting with nothing to show for it.

More problematically, our brains use these same shortcuts to filter out information that they deem superfluous to the task at hand. When our mental shortcut is flawed or our understanding of the situation is inaccurate, these same mechanisms can filter out the very information that we might need, causing us to completely miss the most obvious of facts even when they are jumping around right before our eyes.

This filtering problem was demonstrated many years ago in a short video called "Selective Attention Test," with the results later being published in a book called *The Invisible Gorilla*.[4] It depicted six people, three with black shirts and three with white ones, passing a basketball around in a hallway. The viewer was challenged to count how many passes were made between people wearing white shirts. During the 80-second video a guy in a gorilla suit strolled out into the middle of the action, faced the camera, thumped his chest, and then wandered off. Even though the gorilla was on screen for a whole nine seconds, over half of the people who watch it are so focused on counting the passes that they miss the gorilla entirely.

4. http://www.theinvisiblegorilla.com

Figure 6.1
"What gorilla?"

We have all at one point or another been convinced something must be happening that wasn't, all while missing the proverbial gorillas in our midst. They can come in the form of a faulty piece of code in a place we do not expect, a misconfiguration that detrimentally affected some dependency we missed, or even a misalignment between people that is wreaking havoc on our environment.

To improve our situational awareness, we need to first understand how our brain creates and maintains these mental shortcuts. Doing so can help us devise ways to avoid the shortcomings that can get in the way of accurately making sense of our ecosystem.

To start this journey, let's examine the two most important of these mental shortcuts, the *mental model* and *cognitive bias*. This will help us better understand how they work, how they go awry, and how we can catch when they fail us.

The Mental Model

Figure 6.2
The mental model.

A mental model is a pattern of predictable qualities and behaviors we have learned to expect when we encounter particular items and conditions in our ecosystem. Some are as simple as knowing that a rubber ball and an egg will act differently when dropped from a height, or that people will usually stop at a red traffic signal. Others can be more complex, like the behavior and likely output of a service journey when given a certain request type. Together they shape how we perceive the world and the probability of certain conditions occurring that we can use to make decisions and solve problems.

Mental models are typically constructed from data points we collect through a combination of first-hand experience and information gleaned from people, books, and other sources. These same data points become clues that we use to identify, verify, or predict ecosystem events. The more relevant data points we collect about a given situation, and the more first-hand experience we have encountering those data points, the greater the depth of situational awareness we can gain from them. Over time, continual contact with those data points not only dramatically reduces the cognitive load necessary to identify a given situation but also increases decision-making speed to become instantaneous and intuitive.

Gary Klein found when researching firefighters[5] that those with such tacit knowledge and expertise were able to decide and act quickly on important but minute signals others likely would easily miss. In one example a firefighter commander fighting what appeared to be a small kitchen fire in a house sensed that something was wrong when the temperature of the room did not match what he expected. In the unease, he immediately ordered his entire team to leave. Just as the last person left the building the floor collapsed. Had the men been in the house they would have plunged into the burning basement.[6]

In the previous example, the commander compared his mental model of a small fire (lower ambient room heat) with the data points he was observing (unusually high ambient room heat). The mismatch made him doubt not the accuracy of his mental model but whether his understanding of the situation was correct. This unease caused him to order his team to leave so that he could reassess the situation.

The Problems with Mental Models

When they are well constructed, mental models are an incredibly useful mechanism. The challenge is that their accuracy depends heavily upon the number, quality, and reliability of the data points used to construct them. Having too few can be just as dangerous as relying upon many irrelevant or unreliable ones. Take the example of the fire commander in the previous section. He would have received just as little situational awareness benefit from only knowing the fire was in a kitchen and was small as he would have knowing that the kitchen walls were painted blue or that the pots and pans in the kitchen had been wedding presents.

The mechanisms used to collect data also play an important role in how accurately our mental model is shaped. The most dangerous are those that are considered more trustworthy than they actually are.

---

5. https://www.researchgate.net/publication/254088491_Rapid_Decision_Making_on_
the_Fire_Ground_The_Original_Study_Plus_a_Postscript
6. https://www.fastcompany.com/40456/whats-your-intuition

One good example of this comes from the Three Mile Island nuclear power plant accident in March 1979. A series of minor faults led to a pressure relief value in the reactor cooling system becoming stuck, allowing cooling water levels in the reactor core to drop. A fault in an instrument in the control room led the plant staff to mistakenly believe that everything was okay. With no way to measure water levels in the reactor core, operators failed to realize that the plant was experiencing a loss-of-coolant accident even as alarms rang out that the core was overheating.[7] This resulted in a partial meltdown of the Unit 2 reactor, with radiation contaminating the containment building and the release of steam containing about 1 millirem of radiation, or about one-sixth the radiation exposure of a chest X-ray.

Figure 6.3
"Scary" nuclear power cooling towers.

Interestingly, the Three Mile Island accident created another set of flawed mental models. This time it was with the public. Despite the fact that the accident caused nearly no negative health effects, the public became convinced that nuclear power was far more dangerous than more conventional power sources such as coal. This is despite the fact that burning coal produces far more in the way of health-damaging toxins into the environment, often including aerosolized radioactive material. As a result, con-

7. https://www.nrc.gov/reading-rm/doc-collections/fact-sheets/3mile-isle.html

struction of new nuclear power plants fell precipitously while existing plants were pushed to close.

Data Interpretation Issues

Having accurate data sources does not mean that we are completely out of danger. The usefulness of a mental model also hinges on the accuracy of our *interpretation* of the data we use to construct them. Even when the data is factually correct, there are a lot of factors that can cause us to still misinterpret it in a way that is faulty. Timeliness, coverage, granularity, and suboptimal collection methods can leave us with a poor understanding of the current situation and the events leading up to them, as well as a flawed grasp of the effect of any actions taken.

Interpretation inaccuracy is a big problem in many industries. For instance, virologists long believed that anything larger than 200 nanometers in size could not possibly be a virus. This belief survived as techniques used to find viruses removed anything larger. It was only through some later filtering mistakes that they discovered the existence of entire classes of giant megaviruses, many with unique features that have altered many other ideas about viruses that researchers once believed. Similarly, many IT organizations suffer from monitoring that can be both too sensitive, producing so many false-positives that actual problems are lost in the noise, and not sensitive enough, where faults and race conditions that were not imagined are missed completely.

Mental Model Resilience

The longer a mental model is held, the more it begins to form the core of our understanding of the world. This makes it increasingly resilient. Such resiliency can be very useful for responding quickly and expertly to situations where the model is genuinely applicable but some of the details might differ in relatively unimportant ways from experiences in the past. For instance, driving a different brand or model of car is typically not that big of a deal if you are an experienced driver and the layout of its main controls are roughly where your mental model would expect them to be.

Unfortunately, when your mental model is flawed, an approach that is far superior is found, or your ecosystem has changed so much as to render your mental model obsolete, this same resiliency can still heavily influence your decision making. Old approaches can "just feel right" even when there is ample evidence of the problems they cause.

Such misalignments are also stressful for those who face them. To seek relief, those facing them can become good at explaining away any experiences that conflict with established ideas. At first it will be brushed away as a unique event or a stroke of bad luck. If the situation continues to deteriorate, they may even create an elaborate conspiracy theory to explain it. For some the stress can become so great as to cause cognitive dissonance. Such holding of two opposing ideas as simultaneously true inevitably causes considerable damages to the inflicted individual's decision efficacy.

To replace old models with new and more appropriate ones, people need time and support for them to properly embed. This is often hard in the modern workplace and is why culture changes and process transformations struggle to take hold. Many industries and occupations even have their own ingrained and dysfunctional models, making it even tougher to support such improvements. Without time and help to fix these misalignments, our brains will sometimes cause us to double down on the broken model. Our views harden further and we shut out or belittle any conflicts we encounter.

Cognitive Bias

Cognitive biases are a much deeper and often cruder form of mental model. They exist at a subconscious level, relying upon subtle environmental triggers that predispose us to filter, process, and make decisions quickly with little information input or analysis. Some arise from subtle cultural characteristics such as the perception of time and communication styles, or the level of tolerance for uncertainty and failure. However, the vast majority of biases are more innate and culturally independent. It is these that so often go unnoticed, affecting our ability to make sensible decisions.

There are many cognitive biases that plague us all. Table 6.1 includes a number of the more serious ones that I regularly encounter in service delivery environments.

Table 6.1

Common Cognitive Biases

Bias	Description	Impact
Confirmation bias	Tendency to pay attention to information that confirms existing beliefs, ignoring anything that does not	Inability to listen to opposing views, and the likelihood that people on two sides of an issue can listen to the same story and walk away with different interpretations
Hindsight bias	Tendency to see past events as more obvious and predictable than they are	Overestimate ability to predict and handle events, leading to taking unwise risks
Anchoring bias	Tendency to be overly influenced by the first piece of information received for decision making and using it as the baseline for making comparisons	Inability to fully consider other information leading to suboptimal decision making
Sunk cost fallacy	Justifying increased investment in a decision or endeavor because time, money, or effort has already been invested into it, regardless of whether the cumulative costs outweigh the benefits	Overinvesting resources that could be better spent elsewhere
Optimism bias	Tendency to underestimate the likelihood of failure scenarios	Poor preparation and defense against failure
Automation bias	Depending excessively on automated decision-making and support systems, ignoring contradictory information found without automation even when it is clearly correct	Increased risk from bad decision making, situational awareness, and learned carelessness (e.g., driving into a lake because Google Maps told you to)

This list is far from complete, and you will almost certainly encounter other cognitive biases in your own organization. What is important is ensuring that you and the rest of your team are aware of their existence and their effects, keeping a lookout for them as part of your decision-making process. Such awareness is itself crucial before taking the next step of finding ways to gain better situational awareness.

Gaining Better Situational Awareness

Now that you are aware of the failings of the shortcuts your brain uses to reduce cognitive load, you can begin the process to construct mechanisms to catch them in action, check their accuracy, and make any necessary course corrections to gain better situational awareness and improve your decision making.

The first step in any improvement activity is to start by getting a good idea of the current state. Fortunately, there are common patterns that every person and organization follows to organize and manage the information necessary for making decisions. These fall into the following categories:

- **Framing:** The purpose or intent that staff use to perform their tasks and responsibilities. Any alignment gaps between this framing and customer target outcomes can lead to errant mental models and information filtering.
- **Information flow:** The timeliness, quality, accuracy, coverage, and consistency of the information used for decision making as it flows across the organization. How is it used? Who uses it? Is information altered or transformed, and if so, why?
- **Analysis and improvement:** The mechanisms used to track situational awareness and decision quality and identify and rectify the root causes of any problems that occur. Who performs these activities, how often do they occur, and what are the criteria for triggering an analysis and improvement?

Let's take a look at each of these to understand what they are, why they matter, how they can become compromised or rendered ineffective, and how they can be improved.

Framing

Figure 6.4
Framing cannot be done
haphazardly.

Every activity you perform, responsibility you have, and decision you make has a purpose no matter how inconsequential. This purpose is your guide to know whether you are on track to successfully complete it, and the way that it is framed can heavily influence what information and mental models you use along the way.

Framing can take a number of forms, many that can interact and even interfere with one another. Some are the acceptance criteria of an individual task. There are also the overall objectives of the project or delivery itself. Then there are team and role responsibilities and priorities, as well as the performance evaluation measures used for raises, promotions, and bonuses.

Ideally, all of this framing should add context that better aligns work to deliver the target outcomes desired by the customer. However, it is extremely easy for gaps and misalignments to form when there are so many layers that people have to contend with.

Finding and Fixing Framing Problems

For better or worse, organizational framing problems tend to follow familiar patterns. Recognizing these patterns can help you find the misalignments in your organization that need to be fixed. Each of these patterns is described next in turn. I have included some details about how they often manifest themselves, as well as some ways to overcome them.

Pattern 1: Customer Engagement

Aligning work to a customer's desired outcomes is never easy. Customers aren't always willing to share, and even when they do it can be difficult to understand their desired outcomes in the same context they were derived. It also doesn't help that many delivery teams never get an opportunity to meet and build a relationship where that information and context can flow directly.

Few organizations do much to help matters. Many use product and project management, Sales, and even managers to effectively broker information between customers and those responsible for doing the actual delivery work. This is usually done under the flawed belief that intermediating can maintain better control over information flow, and thereby the work performed, to keep technical staff focused on what are deemed as the correct priorities while not unnecessarily scaring customers with out-of-context details of service delivery processes.

Such an "air gap" in the information flow creates a lot of opportunities for information loss and misframing. It makes it difficult to check and correct errant assumptions, creating awareness drift that can result in dangerously flawed mental models, just like the children's game of telephone where information increasingly gets lost or is distorted the longer the chain grows.

Figure 6.5

Information can become scrambled as it passes between people.

While the best way to solve this awareness drift is to actually try to engage with the customer, jumping straight into a conversation with one is not always possible or advisable. Even if you do, it is likely that it will take time and patience to dispel any flawed assumptions that you and others in your team have collected over time before you can start to really see what is going on.

> **"They are using it wrong!"**
>
> Trying to establish some form of customer contact can be extremely valuable. At one company I took my team to a customer site to see their tools and services in action. There were many, so after each review I pulled my team into a room to discuss what they saw. As with many of the other instances, one of the first pieces of feedback from my own team would be "They are using it wrong!" It always takes time and patience for them to realize the problem lies with their interpretation and not the customer's usage of their solution.

When beginning the journey to understand the customer, one of the best places to begin is to closely examine the ways they interact with your ecosystem. First, evaluate the services the customer uses directly. Capture and analyze their experience to spot potential problems and opportunities. This evaluation has the advantage of being both more familiar and accessible than an actual customer, and can also facilitate any conversation in cases where you do eventually have an opportunity to interact with the customer. It also has the benefit of revealing aspects of customer interactions that they might not realize themselves or might be unwilling to freely disclose.

Customers inevitably leave a long trail of clues behind. Much of this trail is discussed in Chapter 11, "Instrumentation," and includes everything from logging and service telemetry to monitoring transactions and service performance, as well as tracing customer and service journeys.

Customers also engage and impact with your organization directly in ways that can provide additional clues about both their needs and how your organization handles them. Sales, Customer Engagement, and Support functions can help provide a bridge to the customer, as well as some insight into their desires and concerns. You might discover places where service properties are misunderstood. I have prevented many potentially disastrous engagements by finding and correcting such misunderstandings in both the sales and contract negotiation phases, as well as in digging into the details behind customer complaints and feature requests.

I also, as discussed in Chapter 11, "go to the gemba" or where the work is being performed to see how customer interactions affect delivery and service supportability. Sometimes customers are more than happy to make adjustments to their own demands if they realize they are degrading the delivery or supportability of other functionality that is far more important to them. Capturing this information allows you to have more factual conversations that can help you better help them reach their target outcomes.

Pattern 2: Output Metrics

Measuring an output is generally easier than measuring an outcome. Outputs are also far less ambiguous. This is a big part of why managers have a natural preference to evaluate individual and team performance based upon meeting delivered output targets.

The problem is that customers measure their own success not on the outputs you generate but the outcomes they achieve. Customers do not care if your service has 99.999 percent uptime or extra features if none of it ensures that they are able to use it effectively to meet their needs at the very moment they need it. I have encountered this issue repeatedly, especially on trading floors where the customer can be extremely vocal. Such mismatch between targets and making sure the customer has what they need when they need it can be costly both financially and with customer trust.

While it is true that outputs have the potential to contribute to a customer achieving a customer outcome, having staff focus centered on delivering the output only guarantees that the output will be achieved, not the outcome. Information that is not needed for delivering the output can easily be missed, ignored, or even buried if it might detract from delivering it. This is especially true if delivering the metric is tied to performance evaluation metrics.

I actively seek out and try to eliminate output-based metrics whenever possible. In their place I work with individuals and teams to construct metrics that are meaningful for helping customers attain their target outcomes. One of the best places to start is to look at framing the acceptance criteria for tasks and responsibilities to help the customer reach them, and then search for ways that the contribution can be measured. For instance, in the case of uptime I look to measure the negative impacts toward the customer reaching their outcomes due to service loss, errors, and latency. For features, I look at how the feature fits into the customer journey, how often is it used, how easy is it for the customer to use, and how valuable is its usage to helping the customer achieve their target outcomes. All of this helps reorient you and your staff to reframe how you view the ecosystem around you and the decisions you make within it.

Pattern 3: Locally Focused Metrics

Metrics that are tightly framed around team or person-centric activities are another common distortion in organizations. Besides not being framed around customer outcomes, the tight focus often causes teams to lose sight of the rest of the organization as well.

There are a multitude of ways that this occurs in DevOps organizations. Sole focus on your own tasks can cause you to have long-lived branches with little thought of merging and integration issues that will likely crop up later. When specialty teams exist, there is a risk that they can concentrate only on their own areas rather than on those that achieve the target outcomes of the customer. Sometimes alignment is so poor that other teams put in workarounds that can make overall situational awareness worse.

Information flow also breaks down and becomes distorted. At best local framing results in ignoring any information immediately outside that tight scope, even if it is likely beneficial to another group. When the measures are used to compare and rate teams against each other, it not only discourages sharing and collaboration, it leads to information becoming a currency to hoard, hide, or selectively disclose to attain an advantage over others. The end result is information distortion and friction that degrade decision making throughout the organization.

I actively seek out locally focused metrics for removal whenever I can. In order to reverse the damage they cause, I often create performance metrics centered on helping others in the organization be successful. These may be other teammates, adjacent teams, or other teams delivering solutions across the same customer journey. I find that doing so helps refocus people to think about others, the whole organization, and ultimately the needs of the customer.

Information Flow

There is little chance that all information in an ecosystem can be made readily available with sufficient accuracy to everyone on demand at any time. Even if it were possible, it would likely be overwhelming. While accurate framing and valid mental models can narrow the scope of information needed, alone they provide little insight into the timeliness, quality, accuracy, coverage, and consistency that information must have to ensure you have sufficient situational awareness to make accurate decisions.

This is where the dynamics of your delivery ecosystem come in.

Why Ecosystem Dynamics Matter

As you learned in Chapter 5, "Risk," the dynamics of your operating ecosystem do play a fundamental role in determining which information characteristics are important for decision making. The reason for this is that the rate, predictability, and cause-and-effect of ecosystem change directly correlate to how often and to what extent mental models need to be checked to maintain an accurate awareness model for decision making.

In other words, it doesn't take much feedback to get to reach a "good enough" decision to reach a desired outcome in a relatively predictable and easily understood environment. Under such conditions you only need enough information to identify what mental models to use and when to use them as there is little risk of any dramatic or unforeseen change invalidating their accuracy.

As the dynamics of your environment increase and become more unpredictable and undiscoverable (or "unstructured," in the language of Cynefin, discussed in Chapter 5, "Risk"), the accuracy of your mental models begins to break down and the thresholds for what quality, coverage, type, and timeliness of feedback needed to both catch and correct any mental model problems as well as reach a "good enough" decision grow considerably.

To help to understand this better, let's consider the dynamism of the ecosystem of your commute to work. There is little need for lots of rapid, high-quality feedback if your commute consists of nothing more than logging into work from home on your computer. The process is well known and is unlikely to change much without considerable warning.

There is a little more variability if your commute consists of catching a train to the office. You will need to know train availability, departure and arrival times, possibly which platform the train will depart from, and whether you need to obtain a new ticket. While this is certainly more information than is needed when you work from home, most of it only augments existing mental models. Inaccuracies are not only rarely fatal, they can usually be easily corrected for along the way with at worst only mild inconveniences.

Figure 6.6
Commuting by train has low information flow requirements.

Commuting to work by driving a car, however, is a completely different story. Driving requires operating in a very dynamic ecosystem. Everything from traffic and traffic controls, other drivers, pedestrians and animals, weather, road conditions, and even unexpected objects can dramatically change a situation, and with it appropriateness of any decision, instantly. I have personally had to dodge to avoid everything from chickens and moose running around on the roadway, a barbeque flying off the car ahead, to flash flooding and police chases. With such dynamism, feedback needs to be instant, accurate, and with enough coverage to adjust for any new developments that if missed can detrimentally affect achieving the desired outcome of getting to work alive without injuring yourself or others. Unlike in the other two scenarios, mental models are more geared for helping facilitate information gathering and decision prioritization than acting as a step-by-step recipe for executing the activity to outcome.

Figure 6.7
Sam needs to stay situationally aware of his surroundings in order to safely commute by car.

Figuring out what characteristics and information you need takes knowing the dynamics of the delivery ecosystem. As you will see, you will need to consider the mental model friction and cognitive biases of people within your delivery ecosystem, what outcomes you are targeting, as well as the risk profile you are willing to accept to reach them.

Meeting Your Information Flow Needs

To be effective, each individual has different information needs. Some people are quick to spot a meaningful condition or discrepancy and investigate. Others can easily miss or happily ignore anything that does not precisely fit the expectations of their mental models. Most people fall somewhere in the middle of this spectrum, catching some information, missing other information, and force-fitting everything else in ways that filter or distort their understanding of what is actually happening.

Finding these variations can be challenging. This is why whenever I begin in an organization I find a variety of "tracers" (which are little more than information elements, tasks, and events) to effectively trace what information characteristics are used across different people and teams as information flows through the organization. A tracer is often little more than a set of information elements, tasks, or events that forms part of a decision and delivery item that is important to meet customer needs. Some examples include a deployment, an incident, a standard request, and work planning.

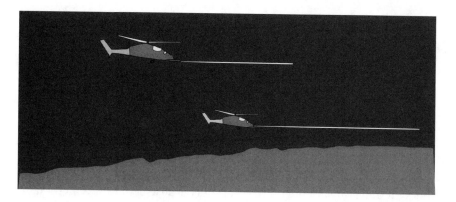

I find that tracers can help expose the level of predictability and preparedness for events, their likely range and rate, how and where they enter and are handled, how adequately they are managed and completed, and how this lifecycle impacts customers. Tracers also uncover the sources and consumers of the information needed for decision making, as well as its flow and how well its characteristics match the needs of decision makers. Together, all of this should expose efficacy gaps that can be investigated more deeply so that any problems and associated risks can be reduced or eliminated.

Examining tracers in an ecosystem that you have been long a part of can be difficult, if nothing more than because you have to contend with your own flawed mental models and cognitive biases along the way. Fortunately, there are some common patterns for information flow problems that you can look for that can help you get started.

Pattern 1: Information Transmission Mismatches

Figure 6.9
Despite Suzy's plan to add text messaging functionality to her phone, she still struggled to get the information she needed.

Transmitting information in a way that it is immediately understood with the correct context in an actionable way at the right time is surprisingly difficult. As we saw with the Three Mile Island incident, this is especially challenging if the information needs to invalidate any potential mental models in the process of trying to inform.

One of the most common problems in transmitting information comes from relying upon mechanisms that do not reliably possess characteristics that can get information to the people who need it in a way that can pierce through any flawed mental model to be employed to guide key decisions at the right time. Most of the time this occurs because people haven't thought clearly about what characteristics are important. Instead, they rely upon either whatever transmission methods are most readily available or whatever others typically use without giving any thought to their suitability.

Some common mismatches include the following:

- Monitoring systems that are configured to catch and relay events rather than relay the current conditions to provide effective decision-making support. As a result, information must be sifted out of noise and then cobbled together by staff using their past experiences, available documentation, and guesswork to find out what is going on. This high-risk, high-friction approach can fail spectacularly, as it did with Knight Capital when cryptic alerts about a critical misconfiguration that ultimately sank the company were missed, as they were sent by email in the early hours of the day.
- Sourcing data from systems to drive decisions without regard to its accuracy, context when it was generated, and its relevancy to other data it is processed and compared with. Such mismatches are common in AI/ML environments that must rely upon data from sources that were not originally designed with such purposes in mind. This might be harmless when it results in poorly targeted ads, but can be dangerous or even fatal when it involves medical or environmental data.
- The use of lengthy requirements documents, poorly laid-out user story tasks, long email chains, and numerous meetings to communicate task and role objectives, dependencies, and anti-goals.[8] Unlike

8. Anti-goals are events, situations, or outcomes that you want to avoid.

what was detailed in Chapter 3, "Mission Command," little is done to ensure that there is enough information regarding target outcomes, the current state, potential risks, or which risks are tolerable in pursuing those outcomes. Instead, most communication focuses primarily on *what* to deliver and ignores what outcome it is trying to deliver and *why* it is desired. This results in both frustration and the likelihood of unknowingly delivering without sufficient context of ecosystem dynamics and not achieving the target outcomes.

- The use of methods for cross-team and cross-organization communication that do not consider how much or at what speed and accuracy context needs to be communicated, nor sufficiently promote camaraderie and collaboration. This has become an especially pressing problem in the distributed working environment that so many of us now find ourselves in. Emails, task tracking tickets, chat rooms, and video meetings each are limited in their fidelity for communicating contextual information. They also struggle to flag disconnects and flawed mental models. This all results in a fracturing of ecosystem understanding, "us-vs.-them" conflicts, and siloed thinking. All of these make it extremely difficult to correct mental model flaws and effectively deliver target outcomes.

Transmission mismatches are endemic in IT. This is likely because most in the industry tend to think more about convenience, novelty, or following the same approach that others are using than about finding the method best suited for making timely and accurate decisions. However, IT is far from the only industry with such mismatches. I have encountered them in industries spanning from medicine and finance to energy and industrial supply chains. Many industries might not be as willing to use new or novel methods as quickly as IT, but even groups with names like "Business Intelligence" and "Decision Support" often still struggle to think about ensuring that information flows ensure intelligent and supportable decisions.

This is why it is so critical to regularly check the flows in your own ecosystem. Many of the practical methods mentioned in this book, from the Queue Master (Chapter 13) and Service Engineering Lead roles (Chapter 9) to instrumentation (Chapter 11) and the various sync point mechanisms (Chapter 14), are provided to help you and your team on your journey.

Disaster at Kasserine Pass

The US Army learned the hard way about the importance of information flow and familiarity between command and the troops at the Battle of Kasserine Pass in February 1943. The experience led to a complete overhaul of US battlefield tactics and command structure that still exists in part today.

Kasserine, in Tunisia, was the first proper engagement between US and German forces during the Second World War, and the first with American troops in joint action with the British. The initiative was to cut off German supply and retreat lines in the hopes of causing German General Erwin Rommel to surrender. US Commanding General Lloyd Fredendall proceeded to make a wide array of damaging errors. First, he built his headquarters 65 miles away from the front lines in a difficult-to-reach canyon far away from communication lines, where he stayed for the entire engagement.

Fredendall was a known micromanager who dictated where positions needed to be rather than leaving it to his subordinates to decide. This created confusion among units and destroyed trust with his subordinates. One observation from a GI on the field was "Never were so few commanded by so many from so far away!"[9]

If this weren't bad enough, Fredendall spread his troops thinly across the battlefield, never bothering to inspect what was going on. His troops, mostly ill-trained, dug shallow shell scrapes barely deep enough to lie in rather than proper foxholes, meaning that they were not only heavily exposed to enemy arms fire but could be (and were) run over by German tanks.

Thinking he was being clever, Fredendall issued orders over the radio using slang and obscure phrases. The idea was to baffle any enemy monitors, but all it did was confuse his own troops. Air, artillery, and infantry units were kept separate and forced to route everything through Fredendall, dramatically slowing down responsiveness. He was also an Anglophobe, which impaired his working relationship with the British.

All of this, of course, destroyed any shared situational awareness between Fredendall and his troops. In the face of this, the Germans were easily able to overrun the Allied positions, pushing them back over 50 miles and with the US losing 183 tanks, suffering 10,000 casualties, and having 1500 troops taken as prisoners. Eisenhower replaced Fredendall with General George Patton. Eisenhower also insisted going forward that commanders lead their units from the front

9. D'Este, Carlo. *Patton: A Genius for War*. New York: Harper Collins, 1995, p. 457.

and keep command posts well forward. Allied junior officers were given greater scope for initiative and were told to keep forces concentrated. There were also efforts to improve the integration of artillery and air support with infantry units, improving the communication flow and responsiveness between groups.

Pattern 2: Cultural Disconnects

Figure 6.10
Cultural differences often go far beyond language.

The differences in experiences that individuals, teams, and organizations have affect more than the mental models they hold. They also impact the characteristics and perceived value of the information itself. When experiences are shared within a group, they can become part of common cultural framework that can facilitate intra-group communication of information in the right context.

Just like any other culture, as these shared experiences grow and deepen over time, this framework can expand to include a wide array of jargon, rules, values, and even rituals. While all of this can further streamline group-centric communication, it does have some downsides. One is that shared mental models are even tougher to break than individually held ones. The other is that one group's communication streamlining can seem like impenetrable or nonsensical gibberish to outsiders.

Such cultural disconnects can create real problems for the information flow necessary to coordinate and align the decisions necessary to deliver the right outcomes.

IT organizations can hold any number of such cultures, each full of its own terminology and priorities. Development teams value the speed of delivering feature functionality or using new interesting technologies, while operational cultures tend to favor stability and risk mitigation. Database teams are interested in schema designs and data integrity, while network teams tend to pay close attention to throughput, resiliency, and security. The differing dispositions and motivations of each team alters what and how information is perceived. Without the right motivation and coordinated objectives, maintaining alignment to a jointly shared outcome can be difficult.

Being aware of these cultural differences can help you find ways to reduce frustration and conflict caused by faults and misalignments in the situational awareness between teams. This can aid in finding and correcting any misperceptions of the target outcome such misalignments may cause. There are a number of ways to do this. One is by building better communication bridges between groups that encourage trust and understanding, as discussed in Chapter 3, "Mission Command." You can also minimize the number of faults in your assumptions by being clearer about what is going on, as well as use the Mission Command techniques such as backbriefing and increased personal contact in order to improve information flow and catch any misalignments that might form along the way. These can make you and your team better decision makers.

Pattern 3: Lack of Trust

Trust is an underappreciated form of information filter in an organization. Your level of trust is the gauge you use to determine how much you need to protect yourself from the selfish self-interests of a person or organization. The less trust you have the more likely you are going to hide, filter, or distort information that the other party might use for decision making. This has the obvious effect of slowing the flow of information in a way that erodes situational awareness and decision effectiveness.

Trust can be squandered in a number of ways. Rarely is it due to personal or organizational sociopathy. Most of the time the cause starts out as a misunderstanding or mishandling of a situation where a person has been left feeling injured or taken advantage of. In IT, the following are the most common ways this occurs:

- Forced commitment: A person or team is forced to accept a commitment made by someone else, often with a careless disregard of its actual feasibility. This could be anything from aggressively set release deadlines to signing up to hard-to-deliver requirements. The crux of the problem is the mismatch between customer expectation and effort. With the commitment made, the customer expects that the risk of failure is lower than it actually is. Not only is the delivery team constantly under a sizeable threat of failure, any herculean efforts made to improve the odds for success go unrecognized.

- Unreasonable process inflexibility: A process that is supposed to improve situational awareness actually damages it through its stringent inflexibility and problematic process chains. Rather than working toward what ought to be the desired outcome of the process, people hide details and use political and social pressures to work around the rules and procedures. This, of course, opens up the risk of surprise and further distrust.

- Blame-based incident management: Incident management processes look for scapegoats either in the form of people or technology and assign blame rather than finding and eliminating the incident's root cause. This results in a game of "Incident Theatre" where investigative scope is severely narrowed to the event itself, details are obfuscated or omitted to minimize blame, and improvement steps are limited to either a confined list of identified symptoms or blown out into a list of poorly targeted improvements that are unlikely to tackle the root cause.

The most effective way to avoid losing trust is to build in a culture and supporting mechanisms that actively promote a strong sense of respect between the people in the organization. Respect is what creates a unified sense of purpose, sense of trust, and sense of safety that motivates people to break down barriers to work together to achieve success.

Teams and organizations that foster trust and respect regularly demonstrate the following:

- Creating a safe working environment: It is never enjoyable to work in an environment that is unnecessarily stressful. Often stress comes from the technology itself, such as having to handle/debug/develop on top of hazardous software that is poorly designed, overly complex, brittle, tightly coupled, full of defects, difficult/time consuming to build, integrate, and test, or simply was never meant to be used the way others now want to use it. Other times the supporting elements for building and supporting a safe working environment are a major source of stress, such as having unreliable infrastructure or tools that fail for no reason, or tools that are difficult to use or make it difficult to reliably and efficiently deploy, configure, or manage your services. Stress can also be working in an environment full of constant interruptions from noise, meetings, or activities that take away from the effort required to get the job done. Teams need to be allowed to have time actively set aside to identify and remove such stressful elements from their working environment. Doing so not only shows that the organization cares about their well-being, but also helps reduce the noise and stress that reduces situational awareness and decision making.

- Fostering a sense of feeling valued and belonging: People who feel they are a key part of what makes the team successful, and not just some interchangeable resource, are far less likely to hide or distort information. Help them take pride in their work by trying to create an atmosphere where they feel they have a part in the successes and accomplishments of the team, organization, and ultimately the customer achieving their target outcomes. One way to do this is by replacing person-specific performance targets with more customer-centric or organization-centric ones. Encourage the team to identify errors and mistakes not as points of blame but signs of some element in the ecosystem that has been found to be unsafe and needs to be improved and made safe. I also encourage teams to get to really know each other and not view others as resources or rivals.

- Creating a sense of progress: People can become demotivated and feel that work is less purposeful if they do not feel a sense of progress toward a goal. Establish frequent and regular quality feedback mechanisms that show how much progress is being made toward a set of outcomes or goals. Iterative mechanisms such as daily standups and visual workflow boards help with showing accomplishments. I also use retrospectives and strategic reviews, as covered in Chapter 14, "Cycles and Sync Points," to have the team reflect on the progress that they have made. This helps people see that there has been progress in improving, as well as can be motivational for finding ways to get even better.

Analysis and Improvement

With so many ways for our situational awareness to become fractured and distorted, it makes sense to have some means within your team to regularly check for, correct, and proactively look to prevent the future development of any flaws that might damage service delivery.

Most teams do have some means for checking and correcting for context and alignment issues. They usually take the form of checkpoint and review meetings geared for verifying that everyone has the same general understanding of a given situation and what needs to be done to move forward, as well as checklists to help ensure that steps are not accidentally missed along the way.

While such a strategy can work to catch and address misalignment and understanding mistakes, it counts on having everyone fully participating and paying attention. This is not a safe assumption to make in the best of times, and is one that usually fails spectacularly when people are under stress. It also does little to tell us the root causes that might be creating awareness gaps to form, let alone address them so that they no longer persist to cause damage again in the future.

One of the best ways to fix this is to recraft the way you and your team look at mistakes and failures. Rather than thinking of them as the fault of a person or misbehaving component, approach them as a faultless situational awareness failure. Finding why situational awareness was lost, whether it was from a flawed mental model of a situation, a misframing, or faulty information flow, can help you uncover why it occurred and put in mechanisms to reduce the chances it occurs in the future.

Such recrafting has an added benefit in that it makes it far easier to avoid blame. The mechanisms that support individual and team situational awareness have fallen short and need to be improved to ensure success. This reduces the risk of finger-pointing and other behaviors that do little more than further erode team effectiveness.

It is also important to proactively search for potential hazards that can cause situational awareness to degrade before they have a chance to harm. Many of the techniques covered in this book, whether in the form of roles like Queue Master and Service Engineering Lead, sync points like retrospectives and strategic reviews, work alignment mechanisms like workflow boards and backbriefings, or instrumentation and automation approaches, are designed with elements that try to expose any drift between the way that people understand their surroundings and their actual state.

Another mechanism that I regularly use is to war-game various scenarios with the team. To do this I will ask about a particular service, interaction, flow, or some other element to see how they construct and update their situational awareness. Seeing how much people rely upon their mental models, how strong those mental models are, and what information they feel can help guide them to the right decisions and can help uncover gaps that can be quickly rectified. Often gaps can be found in simple roundtable discussions, though sometimes these are followed up with actual or simulated scenarios to double-check that details are correct.

Summary

Our situational awareness is how we understand our ecosystem and orient ourselves to make sensible decisions within it to reach our target outcomes. There are a lot of ways that our situational awareness can go awry, from flawed mental models and poor communication methods to cultural differences, badly calibrated work evaluation approaches, unclear or locally focused objectives, to a lack of trust and sense of progress. Understanding these dynamics within your ecosystem and constantly improving them can help improve the sorts of misalignments and disappointments that damage delivering the right services optimally.

Chapter 7

Learning

Learning is not compulsory… neither is survival.

W. Edwards Deming

In 2006, product design guru Peter Skillman gave a TED talk about some surprising discoveries he made in his design and learning experiments. In them he challenged people to work in teams for 18 minutes to build the tallest structure they could using only spaghetti, marshmallows, tape, and string. Astonishingly, he found kindergarten-aged children consistently scored better than everyone else. Even more interestingly, business school graduates somehow always fared the worst.

Why is this?

The secret lies in the difference in how each approached the challenge. Adults start by organizing themselves into roles and build a plan of action. We do this because our traditional education and business management systems have trained us to look at ways to divide up tasks aligned to a centrally coordinated plan. Having clear roles and assigned sets of responsibilities for everyone feels more organized and more efficient.

This structured approach fits well with many of the management ideals that came from the days of mass production, when tasks were known and there was low variation in work. Its problems become more apparent when trying to solve new challenges, whether building a tower out of food or delivering complex IT services. It ignores the fact that we rarely know enough about the problem we are trying to solve and the ecosystem it lives in to build a workable plan and optimize work up front. Not only is all the time and effort spent on organization and optimization wasteful, but it can actually slow down what progress is made through unnecessary fragmentation, missteps, and rework. Worst of all, it also hinders our ability to learn and adapt.

Kindergarteners do not have these problems for the simple reason that they haven't been taught any of it yet. Instead, they plunge straight in with a target rather than a plan. Unlike us adults, they aren't hindered with the "right" way of doing things. Instead, they simply try things and quickly learn what does and doesn't work. With no plan or sacred cows in the way, they can toss away dead-end ideas and incorporate shared discoveries more quickly. Through this, they collectively hone and improve upon the knowledge they gain, then deploy it more effectively than their fragmented elders can. This results in structures that are not just more creative but also better than those of the adults.

Breaking these entrained habits is extremely difficult. They are ingrained so deeply as to make the path to recovery seem nonintuitive if not just wrong. To understand why they came to be, it is best to start with understanding their seemingly innocuous origins. Only then can we once again learn how to learn.

The Emergence of Skills Attainment Learning

Figure 7.1

The rise of public education.

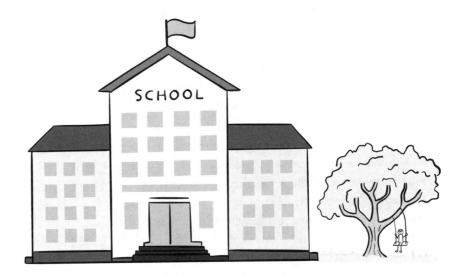

We are born with an innate ability to learn. We look at, touch, taste, listen to, and try out various things to understand the properties of the world around us and how items behave within it. The challenge with learning is that without structure it can lead to intellectual drift and meandering into dead ends that can slow the improvement process and lead to inconsistent skills and knowledge across the team and population.

To bring consistency and structure to the learning process, educators from the 19th century until today have been encouraged to develop and hone an education model focused on building a collection of knowledge and skills that, like a toolbox full of tools, can be employed to solve a given problem. Students would then demonstrate what they learned through a series of graded assessments.

This model has been compelling for both governments and employers alike. Governments can assure citizenry had both foundational literacy and numeracy skills needed for tradesmen and professionals at all levels, as well as gain a sense of community and civic responsibility through civics and history lessons. Employers gain access to a skilled workforce that is likely to need less training and be more productive sooner.

Having a useful set of skills is undeniably a good thing. It is hard to imagine being able to work as a developer or DBA without some previous knowledge of the subject. However, determining a person's mastery level at a given skill can be difficult to gauge if the mechanisms used to assess those skills vary from educator to educator. While standalone assessments can help a teacher find any gaps individual students may have, they do not provide much insight into how well the student performs against their peers in other classes or schools. This lack of insight makes it difficult for employers to easily gauge someone's suitability for a job and hinders government officials from having a good way to measure the effectiveness of schools and educators.

To solve this, organizations from schools and universities, along with the authorities who support them, to businesses desiring to know the skills of prospective employees have turned to having students take the same standardized tests. While the idea is sound, it is also where the bad habits begin.

The Rise of the One Right Way

Figure 7.2

Some insist there is only one right way regardless of the consequences.

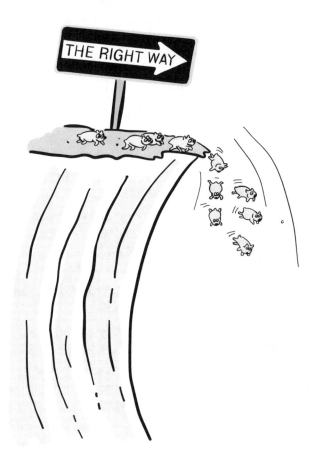

The first problem that standardized testing posed was the creation of the tests themselves. Determining someone's knowledge level is difficult if questions are answered in vastly different ways. To make grading easier and limit debate, tests intentionally limit the number of answers and approaches considered acceptable to receive full marks.

This decision has had a number of unintended consequences.

The first of these is that it incentivizes teachers to "teach the test." Knowing that their professional success will be assessed on their students' test scores, they have little incentive to allow anything that does not closely adhere to the narrow set of acceptable answers and approaches.

Teaching to the test favors covering particular testing tricks over ensuring a firm understanding of the subject being taught. Even when teaching the subject, educators can find themselves bound to teaching particular methods that might be less conducive for helping students grasp key underlying concepts, all to keep students aligned to preferred exam approaches. Not only can this cause students to struggle, but by neglecting to develop an understanding of the underlying concepts, students might begin to find the topic, and ultimately schooling, pointless and tune out.

Another consequence of teaching to the test is that students become trained to believe that there is only one right approach for everything, and that following it will always lead to success. This encourages rule following over innovating to improve beyond the status quo. People become entrained to use whatever "best practices," tools, and technologies they have been told are the right ones to use rather than finding the ones that in their ecosystem are more effective at helping them achieve the desired outcome. Many will even go so far as to prevent others from seeking out to make improvements solely on the grounds that they are not the "standard" or "best practice." This often results in long-obsolete processes and technology lingering far beyond their usefulness.

Perhaps the most frustrating part of all of this is that it encourages people to focus on completing tasks and being assessed on how well they were performed rather than whether their efforts contributed to achieving the desired outcome. This limits the scope of what can actually be learned and improved, as failure can occur just as easily by choosing the wrong task to perform as performing the right task badly.

In order to correct this bias, organizations need to change the focus of learning and improvement from tasks and other localized measures to ones centered on the target outcome desired.

Institutionalized Non-Learning

One of the things that annoys me the most are review processes that fail to ensure learning and improvement. I regularly encounter teams that have implemented Agile retrospectives, ITIL continual service improvement processes, or project post-implementation reviews or incident postmortems. Many of these review processes result in useful problems being exposed, sometimes even with recommendations for further exploration of each problem, proposed steps to prevent the problem from happening in the future, and other "lessons learned" from the experience.

However, although notes or documents are typically generated on the findings, they are often filed away and ignored along with any real action to improve. Such processes are both depressing and a waste of time. But what is interesting is that many of the teams I encounter feel more guilty about not regularly running them as prescribed than concerned they are failing to improve.

I firmly believe that processes that do not serve their intended purpose should be analyzed and either fixed or replaced by ones that do, as it is that purpose and not the process itself that is important. Still, when I get teams to do this there is almost always a mix of skepticism and a belief that the process police are going to scold them. Relief only comes once improvements are made and are allowed to take hold.

Outcome-Directed Learning

Another approach is what I call outcome-directed learning. The idea is that learning is guided by a stated desired outcome or set of conditions, with the learner exploring and experimenting to build knowledge and skills to eventually reach the desired outcome. This approach is at the core of continual improvement processes such as Lean. While practitioners rarely completely eschew skills attainment learning, the emphasis on the outcome moves the focus away from individual acts to the purpose of the activities.

There are a number of critical pieces to this approach that need to be in place for it to work effectively. The first is that it is not enough to simply state the outcome. The practitioner also needs to know the reasons why the outcome or condition is desired. This not only gives some purpose to the journey, but also can provide some clues to the best measures to use to know you are progressing toward the target outcome.

The next important element is for the practitioner to have a good idea of the current state. The current state is the reference point that you will ultimately be measuring from to determine whether any actions taken, knowledge acquired, or skills learned are closing the gap toward the outcome.

While you do not need to have exhaustive knowledge of the current state to get started, you will find that you need to gain enough detail along the way to discern the size of the gap between where you are and where you need to be in order to successfully close it.

With outcome-driven learning, the gap between the current state and target outcome is where learning and improvement take place. Closing the gap requires a series of investigative, experimental, and (importantly) analysis steps to find, make, and determine if your actions result in progress in the right direction. As Figure 7.3 illustrates, progress can be quick but is not always linear. What is important is that you learn with each step taken.

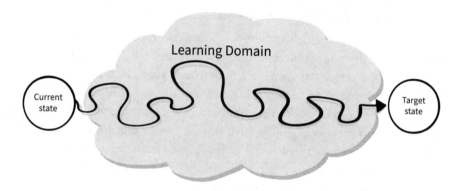

Figure 7.3
A typical nonlinear delivery journey full of missteps.

What is powerful about this approach is that it can be used for building new products and features, as well as for fixing problems and streamlining delivery and operations. To see how this might work in practice, let's quickly walk through a common example of wanting a continuous delivery capability.

In the traditional model there would likely be an architect or engineering manager who would have one group for an automated build and integration setup, another group for automated testing, another for environment setup and management, and maybe a fourth group for deployment automation and orchestration. Each team would think about performing their piece, occasionally talking with other teams to help fit it altogether. However, with no real shared understanding of the outcome or how it differs from the current state, the entire initiative would count on the efforts of the solitary manager or architect to ensure that the outcome is delivered.

This is very unlikely. Automated tests might not be properly focused or comprehensive, some environment management might be missed, orchestration edge cases might not be considered, and even build ordering and packaging might not be sufficiently thought through. In fact, the approach would likely perform only marginally better than blindly dropping in place an off-the-shelf continuous delivery tool.

Unfortunately, I regularly encounter teams that have followed this very path. This lack of a shared outcome inevitably results in fragile pipelines, code and service quality being suspect, and authoritative knowledge of the state and configuration of environments being so low as to make it difficult for anyone to catch or even understand the effects of inconsistencies within and between environments that can cause service quality issues.

Taking an outcome delivery approach turns the problem around by putting forward the target outcome and why it is desired. This might still be led by an architect or manager, but the approach would be done in the Mission Command style of stating the intent and the reasons behind it. This allows those doing the work to ask questions and explore some ideas to better understand the purpose of the goal and the factors that are important to measure to assess progress toward it. For instance, an organization might want to improve the quality of service delivery if they have far too high of a rate of failed deployments and rework, or too much friction promoting builds through the delivery process.

From there, the teams would then look at what is currently in place to understand what is going on. Is the build system manual or does it produce unpredictable results? Are there coverage gaps in automated testing, or are the testing tools too difficult to trigger automatedly? What is missing from having environment management fully automated and authoritative? How automated and reproducible is the deployment and configuration process? What other risk points exist that could cause problems along the way.

Any gaps then become the target areas to experiment, propose, and ultimately deliver solutions to improve. Along the way, people discover new problems and solutions for them that they use themselves and share with others on the journey. As the outcome is shared, there is far less danger that localized improvements that prevent the rest of the organization from reaching it will be tolerated, much less seen as wins for its implementers.

Creating a Learning Culture

While changing the way that you and your organization approach learning and improvement can make a big difference, maintaining its efficacy over time can still be a little challenging. People get busy, fall out of the habit of seeking to learn and improve, and generally grow to accept the status quo as unavoidable.

Lean tackles this by creating a *kata*, or a structure of regular practice, around learning and improvement. The idea is that regular practice can make learning and improvement a continual and natural part of your day to day.

There are three parts to consider when trying to make learning and improvement a continuous pursuit in your team: the day-to-day practices; the way you structure improvement and problem-solving activities done as part of deeper retrospectives and strategic reviews; and coaching to guide and teach people how to approach learning and improvement holistically.

Let's quickly review each to better understand.

Day-to-Day Kata

The first part of a Lean learning kata is looking at the tasks you perform every day to see whether you can make any changes that will improve your ability to meet their intended outcome. The idea of improving your methods of work comes directly from the Job Methods approach of Training Within Industry (introduced in Chapter 4, "Friction").

Building in a culture that challenges everyone on the team to regularly look for ways to improve the day-to-day job means getting everyone comfortable with challenging the status quo. As a team leader, I do this by constantly challenging staff to find even small improvements that can lower their workload and reduce errors and rework. The following are some of the questions that I pose to them:

- Can a solution be delivered more simply or elegantly with a small change of your approach? If you think it can be, try it and share what you found.

- Can manual work be automated without coding in dysfunction? Try hacking something together quickly and share it with your colleagues, or if it might take more effort, talk with the Tools & Automation Engineering team to see if it makes sense to do.
- Can a small change to the way a service is instrumented or data is captured improve situational awareness for you or the team so that you can deliver and operate services more effectively? Test it out and see if it helps.

One of the key aspects of making this work is for the improvements to also benefit the team members who come up with them. If someone comes up with a way of reducing their workload by 30 percent, giving them that much more work in return does little good. One of the ways I handle this is by giving them more time or flexibility to go after another improvement that they really care about or explore another area that is mutually interesting to them and the future of the team. Doing that makes work far more motivating.

Improvement and Problem-Solving Kata

Not all improvements are small or obvious enough that they can be found and handled by one person in their day-to-day job. Sometimes demand for improvements can even arise from growing customer or management needs. Whatever their source, making progress on those larger challenges requires layering on a structure to the outcome-directed learning approach.

In Lean the journey usually starts in an organized way, either through a regular kaizen event (an organized event where individuals and teams have time set aside, much like a hackathon, to try to make improvements) or a more directed problem-solving initiative. In the DevOps world teams can use retrospectives or Strategic Reviews, as discussed in Chapter 14, "Cycles and Sync Points," in a similar fashion. This ensures that such problem-solving events dedicate enough time at frequent enough intervals to allow for everyone to step back and reflect on the situation in order to understand what is happening, correct any problems, and learn from the experience.

The way that I structure retrospectives and Strategic Reviews follows the outcome-directed learning approach. Problems, along with the desired outcome or target conditions, are presented and discussed. This is followed by either a review of the current state or an agreement on next steps before suggesting improvements, which are then chosen, acted upon, and then later reviewed.

As there are a lot of steps where problems can occur, Lean practitioners use a number of problem-solving tools to maintain focus and progress. One is the A3 template. I have provided a copy of an example template in the appendix. This is a simple sheet of A3-sized paper (hence the name), which is very roughly equivalent to two US Letter pages side by side. The template frames the problem, the current condition, as well as the target outcome. It also includes a number of spaces to document additional analysis, proposed solutions to the problem, an agreed implementation plan, as well as a review and follow-up once it has been executed. It is a living document and not necessarily a one-shot plan. I have seen teams cycle through and build upon initial options until they reach a satisfactory state, constantly sharing lessons learned along the way.

Sometimes teams still need help to solve seemingly intractable problems. For this, teams can reach out to a coach to help them.

The Coaching Practice

Figure 7.4
Coaches are an important part of the improvement process.

Managers are far from passive participants. They provide the purpose and direction to prevent teams from pursuing unimportant factors. However, team members often need more than just a direction. They often need guidance to break entrained habits and learn how to use techniques that help them understand underlying problems and come up with sensible solutions to them. This is where the coaching practice comes in.

Establishing a coaching practice is a big part of what brings the learning process together. Even though managers and team leaders are often mentor coaches, they are not the only ones. I have seen some organizations draw from internal coaching "tiger teams," as well as external consultants, who can help break unhealthy command and control dynamics and get teams and their leaders on the right track.

The coaching practice works a lot like a mentor/mentee relationship. The mentor-coach provides active guidance to the mentee to help them overcome obstacles and constraints, and to support the learning process with the goal of reaching the target condition. The intention is to provide just enough guidance to help the mentee to build effective habits for reaching out, exploring, and learning how to find a path forward to reach both the target outcomes and any target conditions that can enable them.

The coaching process starts similarly to a military directive, in the form of an assignment, need, or challenge. These typically arise from the team as part of a strategic review, with some potential clean-up from the coach in order to make sure that the overall intent is clear. The mentee then comes back with a short proposal, much like a backbriefing. Being succinct and brief is key as the first pass is simply the starting point. The first round is closer to an interactive ideation session to give the mentee enough personal insight into the target outcome and/or condition to shape a more meaningful and actionable set of next steps.

Once the mentee has pulled together a sensible backbrief they can begin the learning process. At this point it is extremely important that the mentor not tell the mentee what to do or how to go about the activity, which would take away from the learning. However, the mentor can point the mentee toward appropriate Lean problem-solving tools such as an A3 to help organize their approach.

The mentor is there to help keep the mentee structured and progressing toward the target outcome. While the mentor may understand the target outcome better than the mentee and be more proficient using problem-solving tools, their job is to help others learn those skills. By helping others become more proficient, the organization's ability to improve grows. It is also a great way for promising mentees to grow and feel valued.

Another important part of the coaching practice is for the mentor and mentee to be comfortable with small mistakes and missteps along the way. Making mistakes is part of the learning process. The coaching practice makes it even safer to make them. This is a big variation from the traditional way that managers evaluate workers based upon how they perform a task.

It is worthwhile to note that there can be more than one mentee. I personally prefer, and even encourage, people to work in small informal groups. This is especially beneficial early on when the learning process is still new and hasn't had time to become firmly established. The reason for this is that people will tend to get caught up worrying more about organizing group dynamics than actually learning. In these cases, the coach will find themselves working both individually and collectively with the group to discourage and show the suboptimization caused when people inevitably fall into such behavior.

Summary

Learning is incredibly important to help us improve our decision making and ability to deliver more effectively. Even though we are born with an innate ability to learn, the structure of modern education causes us to pick up many bad habits that damage it and lead us astray.

Building a learning culture that uses elements of outcome-based learning and is supported with dedicated time, problem-solving tools, strong coaching practices, and management encouragement to constantly improve upon the status quo can make work feel more rewarding, both to individual contributors and to managers and team leads.

Chapter 8

Embarking on the DevOps Journey

> *Organizations which design systems ... are constrained to produce designs which are copies of the communication structures of these organizations.*

Melvin Conway

The IT industry is full of people with strong opinions about how best to organize IT service delivery teams. Some insist that separate development and operations teams are necessary to maintain team focus and attract people with the right skills, as well as to meet any separation of duties requirements. Others believe that modern cloud and service delivery tools are good enough that there is no need for special operations skills, let alone having a dedicated team to handle operations work. Then there are those who believe that delivering services is so unique that it necessitates creating a dedicated service-focused "DevOps" team separate from any others to handle it.

Despite your personal preference, the factors that really determine the optimal delivery and support team structure for your organization are the dynamics and constraints of your delivery ecosystem. This is why blindly adopting an organizational structure used by another company probably won't meet your needs. Not only that, as ecosystem conditions change, so might the factors that affect the friction and risk you and your team encounter as the effectiveness of the mechanisms used to maintain situational awareness, learning, and improvement start to break down.

This deterioration in effectiveness can sometimes be so dramatic as to require adjustments to team structures and ways of working to remain effective. Such complexity is why the topic of organizational structures is weighty enough to deserve its own book.[1]

Responding to change by constantly reorganizing teams also doesn't work. Not only is it disruptive, team member stress, along with their misreading of ecosystem conditions, can cause teams to become *less* effective.

A better approach is to understand the conditions that affect team effectiveness. From there, team members and management can work together to build in stable mechanisms that regularly measure their health. This allows deterioration to be spotted, its root cause to be found, and countermeasures to be put in place to restore and even improve team effectiveness.

You know from the earlier chapters that effectiveness counts on striking the right balance between friction, risk, situational awareness, and learning so that you can make and execute the best set of decisions at the right time to make progress toward the customer's target outcome. While the importance of each factor can vary over time, fortunately the conditions that determine that balance stay relatively consistent.

The first of these factors is the flow of information necessary for team members to make the most appropriate decisions at the right time to meet customer needs. What makes this tricky is that not all information is "necessary." To be necessary, information needs to be accurate, available, and relevant enough to ensure the best decision to help the organization's customers in their pursuit of their target outcomes. It also needs to enable the decision to be made in a manner that leads to timely action. No one benefits from a perfect decision that is performed well after it is necessary or relevant.

Secondly, there needs to be enough information flow across the organization to maintain sufficient cross-organizational alignment. What makes this different from the first factor is that the information needed for alignment can differ between teams and even team members. Success means

---

1. For those interested in such a book, I highly recommend *Team Topologies: Organizing Business and Technology Teams for Fast Flow* by Manuel Pais and Matthew Skelton (IT Revolution Press; September 17, 2019), which does an excellent job in analyzing the suitability of various DevOps organizational structures.

ensuring there is sufficient shared situational awareness of any activities being performed to troubleshoot, change, or improve ecosystem conditions and capabilities to avoid potentially dangerous "decision collisions" between teams and team members.

Finding that right balance of what information needs to flow where at what rate and time takes more than measuring information flow rates and coverage and adjusting to close any gaps that form. In fact, it is better to approach the challenge from the bottom up by designing the organizational structure and any incentive models in a way that fosters a strong sense of ownership and pride among team members for the whole of the services and capabilities they are delivering rather than just the piece they work on. Feeling a sense of ownership and pride not only makes work more fulfilling, it encourages team members to use their knowledge and skills to collaboratively deliver a whole set of healthy and well-maintained services that sustainably achieve the conditions necessary to achieve the target outcomes.

Achieving these conditions is far more involved than acquiring a bunch of tools, moving to the cloud, or placing operational responsibilities with a team and calling it "DevOps" or "Service Reliability Engineering" (SRE). In order to build a sense of ownership and pride, the team first needs to know and share in the value of the intent behind what you are trying to accomplish. This is why it is important that the structure aids in communicating a clear and consistent business vision that details the problems the target outcomes are trying to solve, along with any constraints that need to be considered when delivering the services. Mechanisms within the structure also need to regularly measure the amount of ordered "knowability" of your delivery domain. This helps everyone understand the areas and levels of "fog" that might hinder information flow.

These next few chapters are meant to be a practical high-level overview of these challenges, with some tips and models of ways of working that you might find helpful as you embark on your DevOps journey. They are based on my experience and are patterns that I have personally found helpful, and integrate much of the thinking espoused in Chapters 3 through 7.

The Tale of Two Businesses

BigCo had long been a successful provider of commercial shrink-wrapped software. Their success had grown into large product lines with many talented engineering teams. As Software-as-a-Service (SaaS) became popular, an increasing number of customers began clamoring for BigCo to come up with a SaaS offering of their products. At first, BigCo ignored all of this, thinking that it was a fad that would never catch on. However, after a couple of start-ups began stealing away their customer base with competing hosted offerings, BigCo decided that they had no choice but to make the plunge.

Figure 8.1
BigCo.

BigCo started by hiring some of the top Operations staff they could find, many of whom had years of experience in the field managing large operational infrastructure. On their advice BigCo quickly built some of the most advanced datacenters out there, full of the latest in automation and cloud technologies. At the same time, the development teams set out to convert their applications into hosted offerings.

At first things seemed to be going well. The services being developed by the development teams looked great. They were at least as easy to use as BigCo's traditional products, yet didn't require anything to be installed by the client. Similarly, the datacenters were beautiful. It was easy to deploy thousands of instances of anything with a simple push of a button; however, problems quickly surfaced.

While the datacenters were advanced, much of the operational plan had been left to the Operations staff working in conjunction with the incumbent IT organization. They had adopted many of the request, support, and change control processes that they had long used internally. These processes were not just cumbersome, but much of the advantage of the infrastructure automation was lost along the way. This resulted in such frustratingly slow response and turnaround times for both incident and request handling that even the most loyal customers were threatening to go elsewhere.

Not all was well on the development side either. Developers were accustomed to creating software, leaving the operational responsibilities to someone else. Few had any real experience delivering live production services, let alone those at the scale BigCo was attempting. Interactions between Development and Operations were slow and error-prone, making deploying new releases and bug fixes cumbersome and taxing on everyone involved. These interactions left a large expectation gap that no one was sure how to fill.

Around the same time that BigCo was struggling with their transition, one of the upstart competitors, FastCo, was going through their own challenges. Unlike BigCo, FastCo was a pure on-demand software services company with no legacy shrink-wrap product. They started small, but over time became extremely popular. They quickly grew, with millions across the globe relying upon their services every day.

FastCo prided themselves on delivery speed. They never felt much need for a separate Operations team. Instead, they relied upon developers and their cloud provider to run the service.

Everything seemed to be going well for FastCo until the day they faced a rather unexpected problem. Their success had begun to catch the attention of big customers in their space. One Fortune 500 company was so impressed that they struck a particularly lucrative multiyear deal with FastCo to provide their services.

For FastCo this was a big win. It not only guaranteed the business a steady revenue stream in the tens of millions of dollars a year, but it also upended the argument competitors like BigCo used stating that no major business would buy such important software as a service. The downside to this big win, however, was that FastCo agreed to a contract where they had to deliver their services with a 99.9% service level guarantee.

Figure 8.2
FastCo.

Service level agreements (SLAs) were entirely new to FastCo. While they knew that service uptime and reliability were important and took great effort to keep everything running, nobody was sure what the uptime really was as no one had bothered to measure it before. With very specific contract measures now in place, FastCo had to figure out how to measure and meet them, fast.

There was also the problem of their cloud provider. Not only were the SLAs with them very different than the ones they had just signed up to, they knew there were times when momentary lag and drops in those cloud services created errors and unpredictable behavior in their own services. No one was sure if it was even possible that they could protect themselves from these.

These SLA commitments also got some at FastCo thinking about business continuity. If something really bad happened, such as a production environment suddenly disappearing, could they recover in a timely fashion? They knew that they could deploy service instances quickly, which certainly helps. They even had a number of handy tools from their cloud provider that could allow them to turn up any requisite infrastructure elements as needed.

But anyone who has done business continuity planning can tell you that deployment of infrastructure and software is only a small part of the puzzle. Maintaining current and accurate environment configurations is even more important. Small and seemingly unimportant differences can have hugely important behavioral and performance consequences. Upgrades, manual troubleshooting, and newer fresh instances can all create subtle but consequential drift that can go undetected until it is too late. Similarly, configuration friction such as hard-coded IP addresses and pathing can also creep in throughout the service side as well as even on the client. This can make it difficult to move or re-create services elsewhere.

There is also the whole data resilience and recovery problem. Customers need their data to be both available and accurate. While the means available for storing and replicating data are vast, few service providers spend the time to really understand the nature of the data generated, stored, and manipulated enough to ensure that the right mechanisms for storing and handling it are in place and configured optimally. How can service data be handled so that loss and corruption can always be kept to a minimum acceptable level?

As FastCo's staff began to look at the situation, they were shocked. Not only would recovery be difficult and time consuming, but no one was confident that anyone could reliably restore everything they had. Even though engineering skills and experience on the team were deep, the fact that no one had been formally tasked with ensuring any of those things at any meaningful level meant they were often overlooked or ignored.

How would these two very different companies overcome such challenges?

The Service Delivery Challenge

It might not be apparent at first, but both BigCo and FastCo face much the same problem. Both have failed to establish the level of situational awareness within their delivery ecosystems necessary to ensure their services efficiently and effectively meet their customers' needs. What is more interesting is that the root causes of this failure arise from shared origins.

Despite having very different models, both organizations still manage to retain many old habits and outdated mental models inherited from traditional IT. Rather than trying to determine how best to help the customer reach their target outcomes within the overall business vision, this mental framing causes those delivering and operating the services to focus on aspects of delivery that more closely align with their areas of expertise.

At first glance this narrowing of focus might seem to be a great way of avoiding unnecessary distraction. It was also one that could work when software was handed to a customer to run on their own infrastructure.

The split in roles created enough plausible deniability that anything beyond one side's immediate area of responsibility could easily be deflected.

On-demand IT service delivery invalidates plausible deniability by eliminating this division. Customers rightly believe the entire ownership of the service lies with the service provider. From the customer's perspective it is the service provider's responsibility to make sure not only that everything works as expected but that the provider does whatever it takes to know what those customer expectations are.

With the obligation to build and operate the service entirely in the service provider's remit, there simply is no room for the sort of ambiguity and finger-pointing that can cover for poor communication flow across the service ecosystem. As a result, service providers must find ways to understand what customers need from the services and then establish strong feedback, reflection, and improvement mechanisms necessary to deliver them to meet those obligations.

Traditional Delivery Fog in the Service World

Figure 8.4
Delivery fog.

Let's look back at BigCo and FastCo to see what exactly is causing them to both fail to establish the necessary situational awareness and improvement loops that are essential to succeed.

There are few surprises in the failures at BigCo. They have simply replaced the customer's IT operations with their own. Despite possibly having more advanced datacenters, tools, and dedicated staff, all the old split-responsibility habits that shaped team ways of thinking over so many years as a traditional software company still linger. Many of the same organizational structures remain in place, fragmenting situational awareness and any chance of developing shared responsibility for ensuring the service stays attuned to what the customer desires.

If this is not bad enough, the fragmentation caused by the organizational structure encourages teams to assess and reward teams based upon more traditional and locally focused metrics. This creates little incentive to close any awareness gaps, let alone collaborate on work outside the immediate remit of the team that is unlikely to be rewarded by the team performance assessment mechanism.

While FastCo has no legacy organizational structures to disrupt information flow, there are still signs that some traditional mental models endure. For starters, developers are often assessed on delivery speed and output, not on understanding and achieving customer outcomes. Nobody intentionally tries to build anything to meet outcomes they are not incentivized to achieve.

The problems do not end there. Few developers are motivated to learn how to manage the operational side of a service environment any more than the minimum absolutely necessary. What many fail to realize is that knowing your own code and having significant technical knowledge does not automatically make you the best person to both operationalize and operate it. This lack of operational knowledge and available expert guidance can lead to poorly crafted or dangerously unsuitable software being released with little more than a view that it seemed to work fine in the development environment.

The lack of operational awareness not only creates challenges with service design and coding but also can have a real impact on the effectiveness of service hosting configuration design, instrumentation, and operational management mechanisms. Many mistakenly believe that operational details, and even the whole of Technical Operations, can be easily made to go away by pulling in enough operational tools and solutions from outside cloud platform and infrastructure providers. But such thinking is as flawed as believing that you can become as talented as a famous basketball player by wearing the same brand of shoes as them.

For starters, having great tools does not necessarily mean you know how to use them effectively. In fact, the increased depth of complexity and potential lack of transparency they can create in the service stack can make it harder to understand the nuances and interactions within and across the stack, even when you are actively trying to look for them. This increases the risk that some element critical for service health will be missed.

You can also introduce otherwise avoidable problems by simply trusting that external providers who deliver operational functions will automatically match the service quality levels your customer expects. FastCo discovered this the hard way by committing to service level guarantees far higher than those of their upstream provider with little forethought on how to close the gap.

Uptime and reliability are far from the only potential mismatches. There can also be others in the performance, scalability, defect remediation, and security offered by upstream providers that, without sufficient operational awareness, can remain hidden until it is painfully expensive, disruptive, or time consuming to mitigate. This can lead to unexpected behavior and embarrassing incidents that can put your relationship with your customer base at risk.

To deliver services that meet the objectives and expectations of your customer, you not only need to overcome the various obstacles that can get in the way of your awareness of service ecosystem dynamics, but you also need to be sure your service aligns with the "ilities" customers require.

The Challenge of the "ilities"

It is far too easy for service delivery teams to become unclear about or pay too little attention to the specific service qualities that the customer expects to be in place to help them achieve their target outcomes. Customers often do not help matters. Some focus on the solution or functional/procedural details for how it is delivered (as discussed in Chapter 2, "How We Make Decisions") rather than on how various service qualities might affect them. Still, it doesn't take a genius to know that not delivering what the customer expects is not a strategy for success.

There can be a lot of service qualities that a customer might find important. As most of these qualities end in "ility," I prefer to refer to them in the same shorthand way as Tom Gilb, a well-known systems engineer and early Agilist, by the term *ilities*. Ilities tend to fall into two categories:

- Service *performance* requirements (such as availability, reliability, and scalability) to meet customer needs.
- *Risk mitigation* (things like securability, recoverability, data integrity, upgradability, auditability and any other necessary legal compliance capabilities) to meet customer, legal and regulatory requirements.

Ilities are often overlooked for a number of reasons. One of the larger challenges is that when they do surface, they are often labeled as "nonfunctional requirements." The problem with this term is that it is easy to believe that developers deliver functional requirements, and that any "nonfunctional" ones are either already naturally present or are delivered by someone else. Proving that a non-functional requirement is not present is often left to the testing team, who must then prove unequivocally that it is both missing and that remedying the situation requires otherwise unplanned work. Not only is it tough to prove something doesn't exist, especially when there can be enough differences between test and production environments to create plausible deniability, but also convincing others that work must be done to satisfy the non-functional requirement for delivery must also fight the bias against creating unplanned work that can delay the overall release.

Delivering the ilities that your customers need also faces the problem that their importance and how they are perceived can differ depending on the nature of the domain where the customer uses the service.

Just as air requirements differ between a runner and a deep sea diver, the ilities needed for a service used by an investment bank trading desk are very different from those needed for a free consumer email service, and both are entirely different from those required for a service that manages hospital medical records. Even within a service type, the ilities might vary widely depending upon service hosting and consumption locations (United States vs. Europe vs. China) and customer type (consumer vs. business vs. government).

Such variables can make what is suitable for one customer (like a US hospital group) completely unfit for another (such as a Chinese government-run hospital). As a result, service providers who know little about an industry, market, or customer can easily either fall foul of customer needs or find themselves limited in what/where/how they can deliver or otherwise uneconomically exposed.

Another challenge with ilities is that they require understanding what delivering them effectively means within your service ecosystem. What elements contribute to delivering them? Are they built into the service or require specific actions to maintain? What is your ability to track how well you are delivering them and counteract any events or conditions that might put their suitability at risk? Do the means required to deliver them limit your ability or options available to respond to new problems or opportunities?

All of these can be surprisingly difficult to do, even in less complex, ordered operational domains. Ilities like availability, scalability, security, and data integrity usually depend upon multiple delivery aspects working together in a known and complementary way. Any one problem or misunderstanding, whether from a technical limitation, broken interaction, or even an environmental hygiene issue, can create a cascade of failures that can both hide the cause and obfuscate the severity of the real and damaging impact on the customer.

With all this lack of poor information flow, missing skills, and poorly understood ilities, how can an organization build up enough ecosystem and operational awareness to confidently deliver services that will meet the needs and expectations of customers?

The Path to Eliminating Service Delivery Fog

Figure 8.5
Eliminating service delivery fog takes more than having a fan.

Eliminating service delivery fog begins with first knowing the outcomes you are trying to achieve and the intent behind trying to attain them. This allows you to then identify the service ilities that contribute to achieving those outcomes. With that information, you can then start the journey to identify the relative importance of various sources of information, where it needs to flow, and at what rate.

There are a number of ways teams can try to close this awareness gap, from reaching out to customers to instrumenting services and the dynamics of the surrounding ecosystem to better understand how they are used and align to customer expectations.

However, in order to cut through any customer biases and ensure various teams come to the same aligned conclusions, teams first need manager-level leadership to convey an overall business vision. Rather than telling team members what to do, managers need to instead work with each one to help them identify how their work ought to contribute to that vision. As you will soon see, such an approach helps team members find the right signal in the noise and take ownership of delivering the right solution.

The Role of Managers in Eliminating Service Delivery Fog

Many mistake the role of manager as one geared toward telling people what to do. Some even go so far as thinking it is the manager's responsibility to tell staff how to perform their work.

Anyone who has been effective at management knows the reality is necessarily quite a bit different. For one, managers are not all-knowing entities. Unless the delivery ecosystem is in the predictably ordered Cynefin *Clear* domain (as described in Chapter 5, "Risk"), they are far less likely to have both more-detailed subject matter expertise and more-up-to-date details of the service technology stack than their staff. Even if they somehow managed to have both the awareness breadth and expertise depth, not only would the manager be incapable of scaling sufficiently to handle a team of a reasonable size and set of responsibilities, they would create an unstimulating working environment that needlessly wasted the capabilities of their own staff while simultaneously limiting everyone's ability to grow and improve.

Such a combination is, at best, a recipe for unhappiness and failure.

While managers might not know everything, their position does provide them with three important and unique capabilities:

- They are part of the organization's leadership structure, which gives them a seat at the table that can be used as a conduit to capture, convey, and provide clarity around the intent of the business vision.
- They act as a chief advocate for their team that can help articulate any capability gaps or obstacles that the team needs leadership help to overcome.
- They can help leadership map delivery work to customer ilities, and communicate any important team findings that might affect the larger strategy.

There are a number of great ways that managers can perform this, one of which is the *commander's intent* pattern, as detailed in Chapter 3, "Mission Command."

Another unique capability a manager has is that they have the ability to get the attention of and interact with peers across the organization. This enables the manager to see across the organization, facilitating information flow by helping remove communication barriers that might distort context or limit team members' ability to learn. The manager can also provide outreach and foster collaboration between teams.

Finally, managers are well placed to see the overall dynamics of their own team. This allows them to act as a mentor and coach to help the team and its members learn and improve. Mentoring is one important way, some of which is discussed in the "Coaching Practice" section in Chapter 7, "Learning." Part of this mentoring also includes providing team members a space and air cover to step back from the dynamics of the delivery ecosystem from time to time to experiment and fail in a safe and informative way.

Allowing for failure may sound anathema to management. That might be true if carelessly high risks are allowed. But managers can help define and defend experimentation boundaries that allow teams to safely try new technologies and approaches and allow team members to better understand the delivery ecosystem, innovate, and ultimately to improve. By allowing failures to be tolerated, everyone can openly discuss what happened and why something did not work so that they can come up with a potentially better approach in the future.

Frustration and Data Engineering

Helping to reduce service delivery fog is an important part of being a manager. It also isn't particularly hard if you regularly focus on ways that you can help your team improve their delivery effectiveness.

To demonstrate this, let me give an example of a situation I encountered a few years back when I was asked to step in to manage a group of data engineering teams. The company's strategic business intelligence (BI) program was going badly. The technical teams were consistently missing their deadlines, and what deliveries they had made were seen as poor quality. The myriad of business customers the company had were rightfully angry, causing some in the company to question whether the program's budget might be better spent on other initiatives.

When I met with them, the teams were clearly demoralized. They had all been working long hours and had little to show for it. They were defensive when they would hear that there were concerns they were insufficiently skilled or not working hard enough. If anything, they felt resource constrained and could not understand why the company was reluctant to deploy more engineers to the project.

At first glance, the situation seemed intractable. However, as I started to dig into the situation, it started to become clear that the real problem was excessive delivery fog.

There were three causes for this fog. The first was that it was incredibly difficult to see what progress, if any, was being made. The teams all worked using Scrum-style sprints that were two weeks in length. Each team would bring in one business component at a time, with the first group of sprints being dedicated to identifying and then verifying the various data feeds, along with their sources and structures. The second group of sprints were dedicated to writing the code that would then handle the ongoing processing of those feeds for the BI system.

This all sounds fairly sensible. However, the teams never bothered to expose any details about what work was being done at any given time, who was doing it, the amount of effort that was being put into it, when the work might be complete, or what problems were being encountered along the way. All anyone outside the team could see was that a single business component was being worked on. As a result, a component would typically sit *In Progress* on the scrumban board from two to six sprints, a four to twelve week period during which there was little visibility beyond the engineers working on the feed itself having much grasp of the amount of progress that was being made.

Another challenge was that there was little shared understanding, let alone agreement, between business teams, engineers, and data scientists of the relative importance of each data feed. This affected both prioritization and the accuracy in the way data was handled, cleaned up, and ultimately interpreted.

With no visibility of the work in progress and an inconsistent view of the value of the BI program, business units felt free to change around the data structures in their data feeds to handle new business requirements. Of course, changes were rarely communicated to the data engineering teams even though each data change meant any work on the affected feed had to be thrown out and redone.

Establishing transparency and communication flow was critical. The first step was to improve the visibility of the work being performed by the team. To do this, the engineering teams were asked to break up their work into sensible-sized chunks that were no more than two man-days' worth of effort. Any artifacts created along the way would then be linked to the given task so that anyone interested could take a look to better understand what was going on.

Breaking up work and linking artifacts had several benefits. One was that the business could get a sense of the progress being made. The engineers doing the work could also both see that they were making steady progress and build up useful information for those times they encountered a problem and needed help.

This building up of artifacts had another benefit in that other engineers could use this newfound transparency to see if there were common feed types that could be generalized into more robust and reusable libraries. This ultimately sped up and industrialized the BI feed onboarding process, while also encouraging business customers toward shared standards.

The next piece was improving engagement and collaboration between the business customers, data engineers, and data scientists. Before onboarding a customer, everyone needed to agree to the relative priority of each feed and target outcomes desired from it. This helped with ordering and direction of work as it hit the engineering teams. Business customers also agreed to share their technical roadmaps, and work toward minimizing changes that would disrupt BI work. If for some reason a feed needed to be changed while it was being worked on, it was agreed that work would stop and the feed would be put to the back of the priority list.

As a result of these actions, the rate feeds were onboarded sped up dramatically. Tensions began to drop and morale improved. The quality of the resulting BI work also improved significantly, helping business customers better achieve the outcomes they were looking for.

Identifying What You Can or Cannot Know

Even though they play an important role in the process, managers obviously cannot singlehandedly eliminate all service delivery fog. The key elements in your service delivery ecosystem that contribute to those ilities that are meaningful or important to your customer not only will span systems, software, people, skills, and suppliers, they also will be affected by the interplay between them. Some, from the software and systems themselves to configuration, access control subsystems, network services, and the data itself, contribute directly. Others, from troubleshooting and recovery tools, skilled staff, and instrumentation systems, are supporting mechanisms that aid finding and fixing ilities that start to drift outside acceptable parameters.

Understanding what these elements are, the relative importance of the ilities they deliver, and how they contribute to them will help you build a map that you can use to learn and improve your ability to deliver them. What is particularly important about building this map is that you will soon realize how much control you have with managing the ilities these elements provide. Elements will fall into the following three distinct categories: the *known "manageables,"* the *known "unmanageables,"* and the *unknown*.

Let's look at how each category can help you and your team gauge and ultimately shape your organization to best manage your operational risk.

What You Know and Can Manage

Known "manageables" consist of all the elements in your service ecosystem that you know you can demonstrably control that directly contribute to the operational ilities of your service. This is the category where, in a perfect world, all the elements necessary for all critical or important ilities would optimally live.

Figure 8.6
The operational ilities of
an On/Off switch should
all be known and
manageable.

However, being known and "manageable" is only useful if you are able to monitor, respond to, and recover from any events that jeopardize the delivery of those ilities in a timely and effective way. Let's take the example of transaction responsiveness. Most customers will have expectations regarding what length of delay is acceptable for a transaction. Having known "manageable" elements that you can adjust or change to shorten growing delays is not terribly useful if you are not able to make those adjustments at a speed or in a way customers can tolerate.

Similarly, it is not enough to simply have the element that is directly and knowingly "manageable." You also need the supporting mechanisms that find any ility delivery problems with that element and correct them to also be responsive enough. This is one of the most common ways that organizations that try to manage ilities fail. Some will put in place elaborate tools and technologies for managing such ilities as scalability and recoverability. Yet I have seen where they will either not have sufficient in-house skills to use them effectively, or split responsibilities across the organization and include teams that are unable or unwilling to contribute effectively to meet customer needs.

It is important to know such elements and how they contribute to the success of the service, know and test their thresholds, track their current state in production, and ensure that any groups that must act when thresholds are approached are capable of doing so in an acceptable timeframe with an acceptable level of accuracy.

The Known Unmanageables

Figure 8.7

It took a while, but Sam's team finally found a way of demonstrating a known unmanageable to him.

Known "unmanageables" are all the elements in your service ecosystem that you know contribute to the operational ilities of your service but are not under your direct control. The most common of these today are cloud and PaaS services, such as AWS and Azure, that are relied upon for critical infrastructure and platform services. Just as common as these services but often overlooked are components delivered by commercial hardware (such as a provider of network, compute, or storage equipment) or software (such as database, payment, or security COTS packages) providers, smaller but often just as important caching and gateway service providers, as well as providers of externally run build, test, and deployment services.

Knowing their importance and what they contribute is extremely helpful. But the big thing with known "unmanageables" is to minimize their risk to your ecosystem. With systems and software, this might involve building robust monitoring, troubleshooting, and recovery procedures, along with using more standard or proven versions and configurations in places where they provide critical capabilities.

Another even more effective approach is to engineer and operate your services in a way that is intentionally resilient to any ilities issues those "unmanageables" might create. This is very much the thinking behind Netflix's Simian Army and Chaos Engineering. For Netflix, they knew that hosting significant components of a streaming service on AWS instances could expose them to unpredictable performance characteristics that might cause lags and frame drops that could hurt the customer's viewing experience. They also knew that engineers have a tendency to ignore or downplay the threat of ecosystem problems, creating software that struggles to deal with the unexpected.

By using tools like Chaos Monkey and Latency Monkey, engineers knew that "once in a blue moon" sorts of problems would definitely occur, forcing them to engineer their software to resiliently deal with them. This results in lower risks to the business and ultimately the more predictable delivery of the ilities the customer expects.

The Unknowns

Figure 8.8
Billy could never be sure what, if any, dangerous unknowns were out there.

Even if you have the ability to manage an ility, it is going to be of little help if you do not know its constituent elements, their state, or how to best operate them to deliver what the customer needs. Ilities of this sort are the *unknowns*.

These unknowns introduce a level of unmanaged risk that can damage or even destroy your business.

Unfortunately, with all the lack of information flow and suboptimal grasp on the service part of delivery, being an unknown is the default state for most ilities. It is also where most service delivery organizations find themselves at the beginning of their service engineering journey. Even if you solve the problem with determining what the customers need, you know that you still have a lot of work to do to close the awareness gap within your delivery ecosystem to deliver it.

You Don't Know What You Don't Know

I regularly encounter BigCo- and FastCo-style companies that might seem successful on the outside but inside have managed to get themselves in a big mess. Both models have their own challenges. Surprisingly, even with far less in the way of organizational politics complicating things, I often find that FastCo-types, in their drive to be agile, have somehow managed to build spectacularly deeper ility voids.

One very well-known and often celebrated FastCo-style online service company unexpectedly found themselves in a rather nasty problem of their own making. They had proudly taken continuous delivery to the extreme. The organization consisted of many teams who frequently released new feature functionality into the area they were responsible for. To try out new ideas while still managing risk, they heavily used configuration switches, canary, Blue/Green, and A/B rollouts. These were done so that only a percentage of the user base was exposed to the new code until they were comfortable rolling it out more widely.

This all sounds very sensible. However, there was one important issue that the company had not thought about. Even though they saw themselves as a confederation of different services, customers experienced them all collectively as one product. Teams rolled out independently of one another, often with long A/B rollout cycles. While teams did talk often to each other and coordinate, their lack of thinking of the services as one product meant that they did not think sufficiently about the whole picture.

What this meant was as follows. Each new switch had the possibility of creating a whole new process flow, and with it a new user experience. As the number of different switches grew, the number of potential user experiences multiplied exponentially. Teams were trying out new ideas all the time. They eventually found themselves with tens of thousands of live switches splitting traffic across many millions of potentially different journeys. In fact, there were so many journeys that it was not only quite possible that no user had the same journey twice, but that two users sitting side by side consuming the service at the same time would have very different experiences.

This had many obvious faults. For one, it created both a nondeterministic user experience problem and a service engineering nightmare. It made it difficult to understand what the user community was experiencing. The seemingly infinite number of potential combinations a user could traverse also multiplied the number of edge cases they could hit. Such variability also messed with the one thing they were trying to achieve: gaining insight into their work. How can you ensure you understand what is going on if you cannot definitively know what paths a user took to your code?

Ways the Team Can Eliminate Service Delivery Fog

There are several other ways that teams can, regardless of your organizational structure, enhance their shared situational awareness, all while continuing to learn and improve. Organizing work to make it clearer of what is going on (covered in Chapter 12, "Workflow"), having regular good but lightweight ways of sharing information and ideas (covered in Chapter 14, "Cycles and Sync Points"), and having intelligent and ility-meaningful instrumentation (covered in Chapter 11, "Instrumentation") are obvious ways to help. There are also ways to restructure governance processes (covered in Chapter 15, "Governance") and automation practices (covered in Chapter 10, "Automation") so that they enhance rather than hinder awareness.

Before getting into specific patterns and practices, it is good for you and your team to capture and close any maturity gaps that can hinder information flow and delivering effectively. This is discussed in the next chapter, along with the first of the "duty" roles that a team can use to facilitate operational information flow and spot improvement areas within and between teams. I have used the pattern myself in a number of organizations and have found it a great way of breaking down silos while simultaneously improving cross-team technical coordination and expertise.

The second "duty" role, the Queue Master, is far more critical. It is covered in Chapter 13, "Queue Master," and is a means to allow each team member a chance to step back from their normal work to improve team situational awareness and spot learning and improvement areas by monitoring the work flowing through the team.

Summary

Effective service delivery requires that teams have the right amount of information flow to know the intent of what is trying to be accomplished, the ilities that customers need to be present, and the elements within the ecosystem that can contribute to delivering them. By restructuring how people look at their roles and larger ecosystem, teams can reduce the service delivery fog that so often obscures their path to success.

Chapter 9

Service Delivery Maturity and the Service Engineering Lead

If you cannot see where you are going, ask someone who has been there before.

JJ Loren Norris

Delivering services effectively can be difficult. Many service delivery teams focus on the challenge of having to figure out how to deliver what the customer wants seamlessly and cost effectively. But customers need more than just a bunch of features. They also need services to have the "ilities" (described in the previous chapter) they need to meet their outcomes. A lot of service delivery teams struggle to build the maturity to consistently and confidently provide those "ilities." Growing ecosystem complexity only increases the difficulty to achieve it. As the size and number of teams, instances, and services grow, even seemingly great teams can struggle to maintain shared awareness and cross-organizational alignment.

Unfortunately, emerging tools and delivery approaches have mostly continued to focus on removing delivery friction. As a result, they often contribute little to ensuring that the information flow needed to stay aware of the ecosystem interactions that shape service "ilities" is sufficient.

This means that small gaps and misalignments are free to spread around the ecosystem, often silently warping our mental model of service dynamics in ways that ultimately undermine the effectiveness of our decision making.

The best way for you and your team to overcome this challenge is to start assessing the maturity of the practices and behaviors you rely upon that impact information flow and situational awareness. Doing so can provide clues to your exposure to awareness problems and their likely sources so that you can begin the process of escaping the awareness fog that damages your decision making, and ultimately your customer's service experience.

This chapter will introduce you to some approaches that I have found that can help you begin your process of discovery and get you on the right path to improvement. The first is a maturity model framework that can help you discern how well you know, and can effectively manage, the parts of your service ecosystem that affect your ability to deliver your services with the "ilities" that are expected. The framework relies on the knowability concepts from the previous chapter, and adheres to many sensible hygiene, architecture, and collaboration approaches that allow teams to better understand and improve their ability to deliver successfully within the means under their control.

As you progress, you will likely find that solving your awareness fog takes more than a handful of process and tool tweaks. Sometimes team members have such demanding workloads that they are constantly under the risk of developing tunnel vision that obscures critical relationships between their area and the larger ecosystem. Other times the need for up-to-date deeply technical information is so high due to rapid and complex ecosystem dynamics that it cannot be fully satisfied by even the most-engaged and well-intentioned manager, architect, or project/program manager.

Such challenges is where the second piece fits in. It is a rotating mechanism that can more directly help boost team awareness and alignment. Depending upon how complex and fragmented your ecosystem is, as well as what capacity and ability your team has to improve, it can be used on either a temporary or more continual rolling basis. I like to call this mechanism the *Service Engineering Lead*, or *SE Lead* for short.

This chapter will cover what these mechanisms are, how they work, and some ideas for how they can be rolled out in your organization.

Modeling Service Delivery Maturity

Our industry is festooned by all sorts of maturity models. So many of them are little more than gimmicks to sell consulting services that even mentioning the concept can evoke groans from team members. However, there are some places where a well-structured model can be an effective way to measure and guide an organization toward more predictably, reliably, and efficiently delivering the capabilities and services necessary to satisfy their customers.

It might sound obvious, but one of the best ways to determine whether a given maturity model is likely to help is to look at what is being measured. A helpful model should teach you how to spot and then either mitigate or remove the root causes of any unpredictability and risk plaguing your organization. This differs from more-flawed maturity models, which tend to focus on counting outputs that, at best, only expose symptoms rather than their root causes.

The beauty of a maturity model is that, unlike a school assessment grade, you do not have to have a perfect score across every dimension to have the maturity level that is most practical for you. You may encounter situations, as I have, where some immaturity and variability in an area is perfectly acceptable as long as its causes and range are known and never affect the "ilities" customers depend upon.

In fact, any maturity model that insists success only comes when every score is perfect is inherently flawed. I regularly encounter organizations that seem to aim for high levels in a number of areas that not only are unnecessary but damage their ability to deliver the "ilities" that the customer actually needs. This is why your maturity model needs to be implemented in a way that is attuned to your customer outcomes and "ilities."

One such example are those measures that aid service availability, such as supportability and coupling. Even without a maturity model in the way, availability measures often do not match what the customer actually needs. I have teams strain to meet some mythical 99.999% uptime number, not realizing that customers only need the services to be up during a predictable window during the business day. Customers generally do not care if a service is available when there is no chance they will need to use it. In fact, they likely would prefer a much simpler and cheaper service that is available when they need it over a dangerously over-engineered and always available service that is expensive and slow to adapt to their needs.

To avoid such issues, I try to encourage teams to avoid treating maturity measures as an assessment, and instead use them as a guide to help improve their situational awareness of their service delivery ecosystem to meet the needs of their organization and customer base. Sometimes a maturity measure will expose ility shortfalls that need to be closed, or gaps in skills or information flow that the team might need help to address. Occasionally, teams need management or focused expert help, such as the Service Engineering Lead discussed later, to see and progress. By removing the fear of judgment, teams feel safe to share and ask for help to ultimately deliver effectively.

The Example of Measuring Code Quality

When measuring service delivery maturity, it is important to ensure that you are measuring an area in a way that will sensibly help you meet customer needs. You get what you measure, and it is easy to measure even an important area in a way in which resulting behaviors drift away from your intended goal. A good way to illustrate this is by taking a look at a common metric like code quality.

Code quality can tell you a lot about the likely stability of a given area and a team's ability to change, extend, and support it. A common assumption is that code quality can be measured by counting and tracking the number of defects that have been registered against it. For this reason, there are entire industries devoted to counting, tracking, and graphing the trends for how defect numbers rise and fall over the lifecycle of various bits of code.

The problem with this metric is that the number of registered defects only captures those that were found and deemed important enough to record. There can be hundreds or even thousands of undiscovered defects. Some might live in unexplored but easily encounterable edge cases. Others might only express themselves with mundane symptoms that cause the team to discount counting them. There might also be defects where interactions between components or services cross the responsibility boundary between teams.

Another problem with this metric is that teams are often rewarded or punished on defect counts rather than the overall success or failure of the service. As you can only count what has been registered as an open defect, team members are encouraged to hide or claim something is a "feature and not a bug" instead of striving to achieve what is actually desired: having higher levels of code quality in the ecosystem in order to build customer confidence in your ability to deliver and support the services with the "ilities" they need to reach their target outcomes.

Instead of counting defects, a good maturity model should look at what ways you and your team proactively mitigate the creation of defects. One such metric is how frequently and extensively teams refactor code. Not only does regular refactoring of legacy code allow the team to reduce the number of bugs in the code base, it also helps members of the team to maintain a current and accurate understanding of the various pieces of code that you rely upon. This reduces the likelihood of erroneous assumptions about a particular code element causing defects to creep in. Factors like having team members rotate around the code base further improves everyone's shared awareness.

Service Delivery Maturity Model Levels

An optimal service delivery maturity model works on the concept of maturity levels against capability areas of interest. I typically use a set of six levels going from 0 to 5. Besides conveniently aligning with the level count of most other maturity models, the number fits neatly with step changes in the span of shared awareness, learning, and friction management across the delivery ecosystem.

Here is the general outline of each of the levels:

- **Level 0:** Pre-evidence starting point. This is a temporary designation where everyone starts out at the very beginning of onboarding the model before any details have been captured. At Level 0 the maturity model is explained and a plan is put together to find out and capture the level for each capability area of interest. It is not uncommon for a team to immediately leap to Level 2 or 3 from this designation.
- **Level 1:** Emerging Best Practices. This is the where the information for a capability area of interest has been captured and found to be immature or in a poor state. At this level a "Get Well" plan with a timeline and sensible owners for each action should be assembled to help put in place improvements to get the area to at least Level 2.

- **Level 2:** Local or Component-Level Maturity. This is the level a team reaches when they know the state of a capability area of interest at a local or component level. They can track its state, understand what customer ilities it contributes or affects, understand how health and performance are monitored, and understand what can go wrong. There is a set of practices for managing activities around the capability that the team has adopted and can continually improve. Information and coordination beyond the local level is limited or immature.
- **Level 3:** Cross-Component Continuous Practices. At this level the team has a firm understanding of what components, services, data elements, and teams the components and services they deliver depend upon that is tracked and kept up to date. There is a demonstrably good set of coordination practices and regular clear communication channels with the teams and organizations that provide and support dependencies. For software and services, any APIs are clean and well defined, data models are clear and agreed upon, data flows are known and tracked, testing and monitoring is stable and reliable, coupling between components is well managed and loosened wherever sensible, deployment models are considered and aligned, and monitoring and troubleshooting practices are clear with roles and escalations known and agreed upon to mitigate any coordination problems during major events.
- **Level 4:** Cross-Journey Continuous Practices. At this level all meaningful service journeys traversed that include components and services of the delivery team are known end-to-end. This includes components and services that are outside the direct remit of the delivery team. There are few areas that are not either "known" or "known unknown" and dealt with accordingly. There is a clear understanding and tracking of the dependencies and level of coupling across all journeys, all cross-journey flows are monitored, failure types are documented and understood along with their effect on the customer and their desired outcomes, and troubleshooting, repair, and escalation are known, documented, and demonstrable. Communication and coordination with teams across the service journey are clear and regular. Instrumentation is in place to capture, understand, and improve customer service experience and usage patterns across the

journey. Teams often find themselves helping each other, rallying others across the business to help and invest in weak areas that may not fall under their direct remit. This level is essential for smooth service delivery in ecosystems with either multiple service delivery teams or outside service dependencies.

- **Level 5:** Continuously Optimized Service Delivery Practices. When delivery teams reach this level, everything works seamlessly. The delivery team can and does release on demand in close alignment whenever necessary with other teams and the customer. Continuous improvement measures are everywhere, and the team regularly challenges the business to improve and take on new challenges that actively help current customers and attract new customers to meet their target outcomes with the delivered services.

Maturity is typically measured across a number of dimensions, as the example in Figure 9.1 demonstrates. Measuring different dimensions, or areas of interest, rather than just having one maturity number is a great way to help teams expose potential risks and highlight the areas where they might need time and help to improve. Sometimes it might show that there is value in investing in architecture work to build in resiliency or loosen coupling with problematic dependencies. Other times it might expose places where a lot of effort is being spent that is not contributing to customer outcomes.

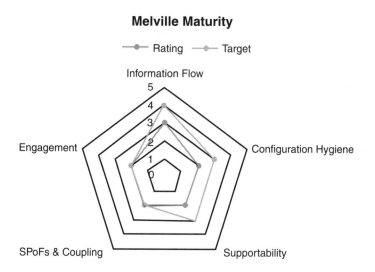

Figure 9.1
Maturity "spider" diagram representing current and target states.

One feature of this model is that each maturity level is cumulative. While it is possible to move up and down between maturity levels, most movement is caused by improving maturity through having a better understanding of what you have or by genuinely putting improvements in place, or reducing maturity when introducing new components, solutions, or teams to the service ecosystem.

Another benefit of this approach is that it provides a subtle yet effective nudge to improve communication flow and collaboration between teams and even other important parties outside the organization. This can be useful encouragement for more insular or combative teams. It also might highlight an unhealthy vendor relationship or, in the case of FastCo illustrated in Chapter 8, a problematic supplier service level mismatch that needs to be addressed.

To pull all of this together, the team usually works with the manager or a knowledgeable person from outside the team to collect, review, and track the evidence behind each capability measure. This makes it easier to audit the data from time to time, particularly in the unlikely chance some event occurs that does not seem to reflect the maturity level. This can help the team understand the root cause that has pulled maturity levels downward. I often encourage teams to build charts as well, like the example shown in Figure 9.1, to help track where they are, as well as where they are targeting to reach in their next improvement cycle.

One item to note is that it is generally rare for teams to confidently get to Level 5 on all measures. Level 5 is hard. It means that everything just works. Service delivery ecosystems are rarely so static that there is no longer a need to remediate arising problems and improve. Even at Level 5, the objective is for everyone to continually find new ways to more effectively meet target outcomes together.

Service Delivery Maturity Areas of Interest

Now that you have a good idea of a workable measuring mechanism, it is worthwhile to discuss the dimensions of what is likely meaningful to measure and track in your ecosystem.

All ecosystems are different. However, there are a number of common useful areas to look to in order to measure service delivery maturity. Software-, data-, and systems-level hygiene are certainly one set, as are the ways the team approaches various architectural practices like coupling, redundancy, and failure management challenges. All of these are traditional technical areas where any lack of awareness can create a large and potentially destructive risk of failure.

There are other areas that are less obvious but have an important impact on a service delivery team's awareness and ability to respond and improve effectively in the face of arising challenges. The list of interesting areas that I have found generally applicable to capturing the maturity of delivery capabilities in most organizations includes the following:

- Information flow and instrumentation
- Configuration management and delivery hygiene
- Supportability
- Single point of failure (SPoF) mitigation and coupling management
- Engagement

Why this list? Let's go into some detail on each to understand more.

Information Flow and Instrumentation

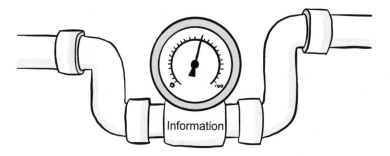

Figure 9.2
There is a lot of value in knowing how well data is flowing.

Effective and timely information flow across the ecosystem is critical for maintaining situational awareness. Information comes from people, the code and services delivered, as well as any platforms and mechanisms that support the creation, delivery, and operation of the code and services.

The intent of this measure is to capture how well situational awareness across the delivery and operational teams is maintained. This includes finding the answers to questions like:

- What is the balance of proactive and reactive instrumentation in place to help the right people become aware of a development that requires attention. How many of those measures are necessarily reactive, and why are there no reasonable proactive alternatives?
- How long are any potential time lags between a development occurring and the right people knowing about it?
- What is the quality of information flowing?
- How much expertise is needed to assess and understand a situation, and how widely available is that expertise in the team?
- How well-known are team and service capabilities and weaknesses?

Measuring information flow starts small with capturing simple and obvious things like how inclusive team meetings and discussions are to the observations, ideas, and concerns of members of the team. It also includes identifying information and knowledge sources throughout the ecosystem.

The team's ability to know who knows what, who has the knowledge to perform certain tasks, and how that knowledge can be shared and grown can tell you where there might be bottlenecks, single points of failure, or places where context can become distorted or lost. For instance, information that heavily counts on a manager or a subject matter expert to act as a bridge between a situation and the people needing to handle it can create unnecessary friction and information loss. Likewise, using chatrooms can be a great way of helping information flow. However, they can fall short if their membership is fragmented, there is too much extraneous channel noise, or if the information is not captured in some way for future reference.

Measuring the flow and quality of information coming from ecosystem instrumentation is just as important. Inconsistent logging practices, little to no code and service instrumentation, noisy or unreliable monitoring, poorly tracked instance configuration state, missing or out-of-date documentation, and erratic incident tracking can limit the team's ability to understand everything from service health and code interactions to customer usage patterns and journeys across the ecosystem. I regularly encounter teams that rely upon external service providers for key platform services like message queues, networking, and data services that do not really understand the usage patterns of those services and end up getting caught out exceeding provider caps. The resulting provider throttling, service cutoffs, and blown budgets are both embarrassing and can detrimentally affect the customer.

The value of metrics from the delivery process itself is also commonly overlooked. Having data about everything from amount of code churn, distribution of code changes by developers across the team within components, build/integration/testing statistics, versioning, packaging atomicity, deployment configuration tracking, to the restorability of an environment and its data all can reveal risk areas and friction points that can hinder the team's ability to respond to events and to learn.

It is also important to examine how, if at all, the team acquires information about customers and their needs and expectations. The way the team captures and learns about customer usage patterns, what "ilities" are important to them, and what outcomes they are trying to achieve can expose potential lags, gaps, and misdirection that can degrade vital situational awareness needed for decision making.

Many teams find gauging information flow maturity to be difficult. A big part of the reason is that information flow maturity is less about the amount of information flowing and more about its ability to provide enough context to align teams and improve decision efficacy.

Trying to answer the questions outlined earlier can provide a good start to help you and your team start on the road to information flow maturity. I often supplement those with a number of experiments that are geared toward testing how, and how quickly, information flows across the organization. Sometimes it can be as simple as asking the same questions to different teams and team members and then looking for clues in any differences in their answers. Other times I use what I call "tracers" (as mentioned in Chapter 6, "Situational Awareness") to look for any flow friction, bottlenecks, and distortions as the information and resulting actions move across the team.

Over time, everyone on the team should be able to check the quality of the flow themselves, even if it is only to improve their own awareness and decision efficacy. Checking what information is flowing, where it is going to, and its overall accuracy should be done in such a way that the team clearly understands that it is intended to help support the team, not to judge them. Gaps, bottlenecks, and single points of failure form with the best of teams. Value comes from catching them quickly, understanding how they formed, and then seeking to prevent them from appearing in the future.

Configuration Management and Delivery Hygiene

Figure 9.3

Hygiene is important in your delivery ecosystem.

As anyone who has had to deal with a messy teenager or roommate can attest, a disorganized room makes it difficult to know with any certainty what is in it, what condition those items might be in, and what dependencies they might need in order to work as needed. This not only slows down the process of finding and using any items, it can also result in lost items, rework, and other costly mistakes. It might be a minor annoyance if it is their bedroom. However, it can be outright dangerous to your health if the disorder extends to the kitchen where hidden joys like rancid food and contaminated utensils can sicken or kill.

This works the same for delivery ecosystems. Just like cooking a meal, any missing or damaged element, wrong version or type, or incorrectly used or configured part of the technology stack can result in all sorts of unpleasant surprises that cause services to behave differently than the customer needs.

Like having an organized kitchen, putting in place good ecosystem hygiene practices makes it possible to understand the state of your service components in a way that will provide clues to how well they and the mechanisms you use to assemble and deliver them will contribute to customer ilities. For instance, you should be able to look at build and test metrics to spot potentially brittle code. These will be those places where things seemingly go wrong every time they are touched.

Similarly, being able to get a sense of how much and where change will likely take place within the environment can help you ascertain the level of potential risk in rolling out that change. This includes determining what ilities might be impacted by the change, as well as how reversible the change might be if something does go awry.

To measure the level of ecosystem hygiene, I typically look to have the team try to answer the following questions:

- How does the delivery team manage their code and delivery environments? Is it done in a more mature way with good version control, atomic packaging, and tools that build and track configuration changes that can be easily audited for accuracy? Is it instead done in a less mature way with documentation that people might follow but where there is limited visibility in ensuring the final and current state?
- Are continuous build and integration techniques in place, and if so, how continuously are they providing insight into the state of the code? How often is this checked and used to understand code health and its ability to meet customer ilities?
- Does the development team do top-of-trunk development where all code gets checked into the same trunk and conflicts are dealt with immediately, or does the team have elaborate branching and patching/merging that means everyone's work isn't being integrated together all the time? It is easy for awareness details to be missed when sorting out merge conflicts.

- Is software packaged, and if so, are packages atomic so that they can be easily uninstalled without leaving residue like hanging files, orphaned backups, or potentially mangled configurations?
- Is all software and are all packages versioned and are changes tracked over time? If so, is it possible to determine what configuration was in place in an environment at a given time, as well as what changes were made, and when, in order to trace down a bug or an unexpected behavioral change?
- Is it possible to know who changed what, when they changed it, and why they changed it?
- Is version compatibility known, tracked, and managed across components, and if so, how?

The same needs to be done for environments:

- Are all of their elements known and tracked or otherwise dealt with?
- Does this include the hosting infrastructure?
- How much variance is allowable in the hosting infrastructure without causing problems, and why?
- Are variances known and tracked? If so, by whom and how often are they audited?
- Is the stack reproducible, and if so, how much time and effort are required to reproduce it?
- Does anyone authorized to build an environment have the ability to do it themselves?
- How long does it take someone to come up to speed on how to build and configure an environment, deploy and configure a release?
- Are the differences between development, test, and production environments known, and if so, where are the differences tracked, where are the risk areas caused by differences between the environments, and how are they dealt with?

Good configuration management and delivery hygiene is what enables continuous delivery tools and mechanisms to really shine. For this reason, it is the capability measure that can be most exploited by complementary operational tools and mechanisms.

Supportability

The level of supportability of a service is dependent on two important factors:

- The extensiveness and usability of capabilities in the delivery ecosystem necessary to install, manage, and support the service effectively.

- The amount of knowledge and awareness required by those operationally supporting the service. This includes understanding what might cause the service to degrade or fail and how it might behave when it starts to occur, how to troubleshoot and recover from problems when they occur, and how to scale the service both for growth and to handle occasional traffic bursts.

Supportability is an often misunderstood and neglected capability. For one, having a service ecosystem that has supportability mechanisms in place and some team members who potentially have the ability to use them does not necessarily mean that the capability is deployed effectively. Knowledge and awareness are often heavily fragmented across the team, with lower-tier operational support seeing what is going on but only having basic infrastructure and troubleshooting knowledge, while deeper skills sit in specialized silos such as front-end, back-end, and database teams. As you might expect, this slows down responsiveness while simultaneously making it difficult to see relationship patterns between disparate ecosystem elements.

Another challenge is that the concept of supportability can easily be misconstrued as the number of prepared processes and plans for handling incidents. I regularly encounter runbooks that expect their step-by-step processes to be mindlessly followed to contain a problem rather than encouraging staff to understand the problem so that they can find ways of proactively reducing the chances of such problems occurring in the future. On the other end of the spectrum are disaster recovery and business continuity plans that try to pre-plan the steps for handling specific catastrophic disasters. While documenting approaches for troubleshooting likely problems and executing recovery and business continuity procedures is sensible, counting on having captured and documented all failure and recovery paths in a way that they can be executed by anyone technical, regardless of the depth of their knowledge of the ecosystem they run in, is often dangerous. Not only is it unlikely that all paths will be captured, but they often do not account for an unforeseen combination of events, such as a couple of components degrading or a data corruption event, which are both more likely to occur and require deep ecosystem awareness to resolve.

Anyone who has spent a number of years in their career has likely been caught out by a cascade of seemingly little problems that snowballed into a disaster. Some, such as Facebook/Meta's BGP mishap in October 2021,[1] the 365 Main datacenter power failure in 2007,[2] or the Azure Leap Year outage in February 2012,[3] were all big enough to shake thousands of affected customers out of their catastrophically passive reliance on poorly understood dependencies. However, you do not have to be a large service provider to be lulled into such traps. I have personally witnessed hundreds of lesser-known but no less destructive failure cascades, many of which I had been repeatedly assured beforehand would never happen. By encouraging staff to understand the service ecosystem and the outcomes it is attempting to deliver, you can greatly reduce the potential outage length and the damage it can cause.

There are a number of good ways to track supportability. One place to start is to measure how quickly someone can come up to speed on installing and supporting a component or service. I have done this in the past by instituting an onboarding exercise for new staff where they were given the task to install various key service components. This includes finding out how to install various components, then performing the installations and documenting what they experienced. This is followed by a debrief with the new starter so that they can suggest what should be fixed, and describe what value they believe their proposed fixes would bring.

At one company this exercise began by placing a new server fresh out of the box on the person's desk. They then had to figure out not only how to install the service, but also how to get the server in a rack and networked,

1. More details about the October 4 outage, Meta: https://engineering.fb.com/2021/10/05/networking-traffic/outage-details/
2. 365 Main's credibility outage, Gawker: https://www.gawker.com/282257/365-mains-credibility-outage
3. Summary of Windows Azure Service Disruption on February 29, 2012, Microsoft: https://azure.microsoft.com/en-us/blog/summary-of-windows-azure-service-disruption-on-feb-29th-2012/

get the right operating system on it, and determine all the other configuration and support details. This was an impressively effective way of improving installation and configuration of services. Everyone who went through it could recall all the pain they went through, and were motivated to find ways to continually simplify it.

It is easy to run similar exercises when services are delivered in the cloud, including guiding code through a delivery pipeline or trying to determine how to spin up new service instances. I know several companies do this by having new hires perform pushes to production as part of the onboarding process in order to help them become familiar with the delivery and push process, as well as to gain insight into ways they can be improved.

There is also value in putting in place similar processes that measure how quickly current team members can come fully up to speed on any parts of the ecosystem they have not previously worked on. This is especially beneficial in larger organizations that have a plethora of service components scattered across many areas. This not only can be eye opening, but it is a great way to encourage everyone to openly share and collaborate across team boundaries.

Tracking incidents can be another great window into the supportability of parts of your ecosystem. Like code quality, the value does not come from the number of incidents, but what is happening in and around them. For instance, at one company we managed to find a major fault in the bearings inside a particular model of hard drive this way. As we had thousands of these drives, our proactive tracking saved us from lots of potential data loss and headache.

A good starting point to gauge team maturity is to have them try to answer the following questions:

- Do certain incidents coincide with a change? This might indicate a situational awareness problem in your delivery ecosystem that needs to be remedied.
- Do certain types of incidents seem to always be handled by the same small subset of the total team that handles incidents? This might indicate dangerous knowledge gaps, over-specialization, or single points of failure.
- Are incidents so common in a particular area that team members have created a tool, or want to, that cleans up and restarts the process rather than fix the underlying problem? This can dangerously hide customer-effecting problems that can degrade your service delivery ilities.

- Are there patterns of failures in or between one or more particular components or infrastructure types? This might provide clues of ecosystem brittleness or loss of information flow that need to be addressed.

As in the case of installation, one way of proactively finding such awareness weaknesses during troubleshooting is by simulating failures in testing, then dropping in various people from the team to try to troubleshoot, stabilize, and recover. When done well, such activities can improve responsiveness and spark innovative new ways of resolving future problems.

Single Point of Failure Mitigation and Coupling Management

Figure 9.5
It was at that moment that Bill realized being a SPoF was no fun.

Single points of failure (SPoFs) are terrible. They happen in code, services, infrastructure, and people. These choke points limit the flexibility of the organization to respond to unfolding events. The desire with this measure is to capture where SPoFs might exist, why, and how they formed, so that you can then put in mechanisms to remove them and prevent them from occurring in the future.

People are arguably the most dangerous form of SPoF. They trap knowledge, awareness, and capabilities in a place the organization has the least ability to control. People can die, leave, or forget, leaving everyone exposed. SPoFs usually manifest themselves in individuals that the organization continually relies upon to solve the most troubling problems. These people not only are helpful, but often work long hours going out of their way to save the day. For those of you who have read the book *The Phoenix Project*,[4] the character Brent Geller is a great example of one. When we encounter them in the wild, we often joke that they may have saved the day, but they did so by turning the ordinary into superhero mysteries.

Getting your Brent to do a task they've always done before feels safe. Who wants to risk a problem when you know that Brent can confidently do the task himself? That logic works until the day eventually comes when there is no Brent to ask.

People SPoFs can happen on both the development side and the operational side. Avoiding SPoFs is one of many reasons that I am a strong proponent of rotating team members around to different areas. Rotating duty roles like Queue Master and the SE Lead also helps reduce SPoFs. They not only are great mechanisms to help team members take a step back and spot dysfunction or discover some key detail that hasn't yet been captured and shared adequately, but they are also a great way of reminding everyone to constantly share knowledge widely throughout the team. The practice of rotating roles and the sharing necessary to make them work also reinforces the value of regularly rotating all work around the team. Nothing is more annoying than getting stuck doing the same work time and again because you are the only person who knows how to do it, or risk suffering from constantly getting bothered with questions about some detail no one else knows that you forgot to document on some past work.

4. Gene Kim, Kevin Behr, and George Spafford (IT Revolution Press, 2014).

Code, service, and infrastructure SPoFs are also dangerous. These include places where components are tightly coupled. Tight coupling, where one component cannot be changed or removed without having serious or catastrophic consequences on another component, limits flexibility and responsiveness. Changes, maintenance, and upgrades often need to be carefully handled and closely tracked. Closely coupled components frequently have to be upgraded together or tested for backward compatibility.

Capturing and tracking these problems is important for highlighting the risks that they pose to the team so that the team can target and eliminate them. This can be done in a number of ways. I have had teams create rosters of tightly coupled components and ordering dependencies and their effects that are then highlighted every time they are touched.

For people SPoFs, I have team members trade roles and then document every case where they were unsure of something or needed to reach out to the other person for help. When someone is particularly possessive about an area, sometimes it is good to have the manager or the team recommend that the individual be sent away on training or vacation to expose the extent of the problem. The information gaps that can be identified and then closed while the person is away can be a great way to help people understand the value of reducing the SPoF risk.

Engagement

Knowing what is going on within the team does not always help your overall awareness across the rest of your delivery ecosystem. It is important to measure who the team engages with, how and how often they engage, as well as how consistent and collaborative those engagements are in order to find and eliminate any barriers that might reduce shared awareness and knowledge sharing. It is especially important to monitor and support engagement between the team and entities that they depend on. Examples may be another team that their components or services are closely coupled with or a supplier of critical services. It also includes operational teams that might be running and supporting your services, as well as one or more customers you and your team know are important parts of the user community you are ultimately delivering for.

The engagement metric is a means to measure the health of these engagements. Are collaboration and feedback regular and bidirectional? Are engagements more proactive or reactive? Are interactions friendly and structured well with clear objectives and dependencies or do they happen haphazardly or in an accusatory way?

How well do delivery and support teams work collaboratively with counterparts in nontechnical teams to coordinate activities with each other and with the customer? Do they happen smoothly, or does there seem to be a lot of haphazardness and finger-pointing?

If development and operations are in different groups, do the two teams think about, share, and collaboratively plan the work they do together or do they only consider their own silo? This can often be measured by the amount of resistance there is for change and the number of complaints about changes being "tossed over the wall at the last minute."

Engagement with the customer in some form is also very important. Delivery teams do not necessarily have to directly engage with customers, but they should know enough about customers that they can craft and tune their work to at least try to fit customer needs. This includes understanding what actions and events might seriously impact customers, and if there are particular time periods when it is particularly disruptive for them to occur. Are there solutions in place that can minimize problems? Are there known times when maintenance activities can be done with minimal customer impact? How are these known, and how are these checked?

Maturing the team's ability to engage is important for everyone's success. It is also probably the area that, under the constant pressure of delivery, teams often neglect the most.

To help with engagement, I have looked for opportunities where beneficial information can be shared. For instance, I look to see if team members can go on a "ride-along" with Sales to a friendly customer to see their product in action. If there is a User Experience team, I look to have team members go to see UX studies in action. To encourage cross-team sharing, I encourage teams to invite other teams to brown-bag sessions where they discuss some task or component from their area. I also look for ways that people from different teams can work together on a particular problem so that they can build connections.

Sometimes, cross-team engagement needs more than informal engagement. This is one of the many places that the Service Engineering Lead pattern might be able to help.

The Service Engineering Lead

Figure 9.6
The Service Engineering Lead.

A lot of teams find it hard to balance the need to maintain situational awareness and improve their ability to deliver all while handling the flood of work coming in. Part of the reason for this is that many of us have long been conditioned to think about our jobs within the confines of the traditional roles and responsibilities of someone holding our title. We all also have a tendency to lose sight of the bigger picture when we are busy focusing on the tasks we need to complete.

Countering all of this often takes focused effort. This focus becomes even more critical when trying to improve delivery maturity and fill knowledge gaps. For these reasons, I have found it useful to put in place what I call the Service Engineering Lead.

The Service Engineering Lead (or SE Lead) is a duty role (meaning one that rotates around the team) that is tasked with facilitating ecosystem transparency throughout the service delivery lifecycle. One of its missions is to have someone who is for a time focused on some aspect of the team's service delivery maturity to help it find, track, and close any gaps that are hindering the team's ability to deliver effectively. This is particularly important for teams that get busy or tend to specialize into silos and need help to ensure enough effort gets set aside to help the team help themselves improve.

Another important area where a Service Engineering Lead can be a big help is when there is a need to improve engagement, information flow, and shared ownership across teams and specialist silos. This is particularly useful when such silos run deep in tightly interconnected ways, such as in a more traditional configuration of separate development and operations teams.

Why Have a Separate Rotating Role?

Some teams are fortunate to have a manager, architect, or project/product manager person or function who not only has all the time, skills, technical and operational prowess, team trust, and desire necessary to take on SE Lead responsibilities but already performs much of that role. If that is the case, creating the rotating SE Lead role might not be necessary.

However, few organizations are so fortunately blessed. If you think your organization might be, you should check for two important conditions before deciding to forego an SE Lead rotation. The first is whether you have one particular person in mind. This, of course, risks creating a whole new single point of failure. Decide if you can cope or easily pivot to having an SE Lead if that person leaves.

The second check is whether the person or function is close enough to the details to have the situational awareness necessary to really help the rest of the team both maintain their situational awareness and learn and improve.

Some unfortunately mistake the SE Lead as being another name for a number of roles that fall far short of meeting these requirements. The most common include

- Another name for a project manager or coordinator. While the SE Lead does help, the whole team is responsible for improving service delivery maturity.

- Another name for a helpdesk function. While an SE Lead will often pick up activities focused on improving information and workflow, they are not another name for a capture and routing function.
- In the case of separate development and operations teams, another name for a delivery team's dedicated IT Ops support person. The SE Lead might pick up and perform some of the operational tasks when doing so makes sense and does not distract from their primary focus of providing operational guidance and cross-team alignment.

There are a number of reasons why I prefer having the SE Lead rotating among technical peers who are well versed in both coding and service operations. The first is that by being part of the team, even if they are from an operations team and are rotating in as the SE Lead for a development team, they will already have intimate knowledge of their area. This can help bridge any potential knowledge gaps when building and delivering software, tooling, service infrastructure, and support capabilities. Having someone who is familiar with both code and service operations can ensure sensible design, deployment, and operational support choices that help deliver the service ilities needed.

Being part of the team also means the SE Lead has the necessary relationships with the team members to improve awareness and information flow. Knowing team members and their areas also increases the chances that the SE Lead will know who needs to be looped into conversations to understand or guide incoming changes or decisions.

Finally, having the SE Lead rotate among technical peers also increases the "skin in the game" necessary to improve the chances of success. They will have a chance to step back and look at what is going on within the team or with a particular delivery and know that any improvements they are able to help put in place will ultimately help them as well.

Rotating the role as a temporary "tour of duty" can also really open people's eyes to challenges and the cause and effect of certain challenges they might not have otherwise been aware of or fully appreciated. For this reason, it is important to find the right balance between stability in context and minimizing the chances of creating a new single point of failure when deciding on the rotation rate.

Under normal conditions, I usually rotate the SE Lead at a sensible boundary roughly a month in from when they start. A sensible boundary is usually after the end of a particular sprint, at a lull or change in focus point in the delivery, or simply at the end of week 4 or 5. The only time I might extend the length of the SE Lead period is at the initial discovery phase when onboarding the maturity model. At this time the team will need a lot of help. The Lead for that phase will need to be very knowledgeable about the model so that the team knows what the model is for and why it is important for helping them. For that reason, I usually handpick the Lead and have them work full time on the onboarding for double the normal length, or typically two months.

SE Leads can be a useful addition to guide more than just code and service deliveries. They are also useful in operational, business intelligence, data science, as well artificial intelligence and machine learning activities. The nature of responsibilities might differ for SE Leads depending upon the type of delivery. What remains important throughout is that they actively work to improve awareness and alignment to ensure the delivery of the "ilities" expected from the service.

How the SE Lead Improves Awareness

In order to try to improve information flow and situational awareness, the SE Lead needs to be fully embedded in the team. This includes, whenever possible, attending all the meetings, standups, and other team sync points. This allows the SE Lead to stay attuned to the delivery, the "ilities" that the delivery team needs to deliver with the service, along with any dependencies and coordination points that might ultimately affect the successful delivery and operation of the service.

To do this, the SE Lead will work with the team to answer the following questions and identify what evidence the delivery team will likely need to collect to ensure that any required conditions are met:

- What services and "ilities" are part of or might be affected by the delivery?
- Which customers are likely to be involved and/or affected?
- What are the minimum acceptable levels for affected "ilities," and will the products of this delivery meet them?
- How many of the required conditions are in place to meet stated and agreed upon contractual commitments?

- Are there any infrastructural elements that might be required or affected by the change? If so, what "ilities" will they impact?
- Are any new infrastructure, software, or service components being added that need to be acquired from outside vendors?
- Are there any lead times that need to be considered for ordering and receiving external dependencies?
- What configuration elements are going to be touched, and how are changes captured and tracked across the ecosystem?
- Are there any specialist skills that might be needed for delivery that have to be drawn from outside the delivery team? If so, how will coordination and information flow be handled so that team awareness doesn't degrade?
- Is the delivery creating any notable changes to the way that the service will be operationally managed (new services, old ones going away, new things to monitor and track, new "ilities," new or different troubleshooting steps, new or different management methods, etc.)? If so, how will they be captured and tracked?
- Are there any legal, regulatory, or governance requirements that need to be considered or might require additional work to be done, processes followed, parties notified, and/or artifacts generated?
- What are the security implications of the delivery? Are any elements improved or degraded, and if so, how and to what effect?
- Are there any changes to data elements, data flow, data architecture or any classification and treatment adjustments that need to be made? If so, what are those data changes? Who is responsible for implementing them? How will they be managed and tracked?
- Are there any known manageable "ilities" that need to be tested and documented?
- Are there any known unmanageable "ilities" that the team needs to be aware of and defend against?
- Are there any unknown "ilities" that might cause problems?
- Are there any activities or changes that are being made by teams or organizations outside that might affect the team's ability to deliver?
  - If so, what are they, who is delivering them, and how might they affect the team?
  - Who is coordinating those changes with the team, tracking them, and informing the team of their effects?

- Are there any platform tools or technologies that might help the team deliver more effectively that could be integrated into the delivery? These are generally tools and technologies that can facilitate delivery and overall ecosystem hygiene.
  - If so, what are they, and who can help with educating the team about them and their use?
  - Can they be used in the delivery without either impacting the overall design and architecture of the service or unnecessarily derailing the delivery?

It might be difficult to get clear answers to many of these questions, particularly when you first start out and service engineering is not very mature within the organization. But having answers to them helps the SE Lead and others start the process of exposing the problem areas and building a roadmap for how to start to eliminate them.

Organizational Configurations with the SE Lead

Figure 9.7
Traditional team configuration.

Everything from history and internal politics to legal and regulatory rules can affect the layout of organizational structures and responsibilities. While these differences do not prevent you from having an SE Lead, they will likely affect the overall shape of the activities that make sense for a Lead to engage with.

To illustrate this, and to better understand what areas the SE Lead is likely to be able to help with within your organizational structure, let's walk through the two most likely configurations.

Separate Development and IT Operations Teams

It is still quite common to have the responsibility of service operations handled by a team that is organizationally separate from development. Some organizations are legally or regulatorily required to have such a separation of duties. More often, the configuration has grown out of the different ways that organizations look at the responsibilities of development and operations, and the differences in skill sets those responsibilities require team members to have.

In such a configuration, it makes the most sense to draw the SE Lead from the IT Operations team, and then have each Lead rotate through the development team.

Having an Operations SE Lead in the development team has a number of distinct advantages. For one, it is far more likely that Leads will have the sorts of deep operational knowledge so often missing in the development team. Being part of the delivery team, the SE Lead can guide developers to design and implement decisions that are more likely to meet the outcomes and ilities that the customer wants.

Operational SE Leads are also a great way to ensure ecosystem information flow. Their experience with the service ecosystem can guide developers through the details that are important and need to be considered in order to make better technical design and implementation decisions. This allows developers to understand whether an easier-to-implement choice now will introduce extra risks or friction that may prove too costly in the long run.

Most IT Operations teams are also familiar with, if not actively engaging, any other development teams or suppliers who are delivering components or services that the development team might depend upon or otherwise be affected by. This creates a new conduit for the development team to obtain insights into existing or upcoming conditions they might need to consider or flag as potential risks for their own delivery. I have personally seen this happen a number of times, spurring conversations and proactive adjustments that prevented later headaches.

Likewise, SE Leads can help the rest of the Operations team get earlier and likely deeper insight into the nuances of an upcoming delivery. This reduces the likelihood of surprises, allowing the Operations team to more proactively prepare for installing and supporting any changes, and thus increasing their chances of operational success.

Importantly, IT Operations team members are far more likely to be familiar with the various cloud and DevOps tools and technologies. They should understand which ones are present or make the most sense to use within your service delivery ecosystem, and be able to help developers to take maximum advantage of them. If the Operations team has a Tools & Automation Engineering function (as described in Chapter 10, "Automation"), the SE Lead can help coordinate between the two.

Lastly, having the SE Lead participate as part of the delivery team is also far more likely to foster a feeling of shared ownership for service delivery success between the two organizations. By becoming part of the delivery team, the SE Lead can build relationships that help break down silo walls that so often disconnect teams from the shared outcomes that come from their decisions.

Challenges to Watch Out For

Placing a person from an external team in such an important role as SE Lead does have a number of challenges.

The first is that there will likely be some significant cultural differences between developers and IT Operations staff. Developers have long been encouraged to deliver quickly, while Operations staff have been pushed to minimize risk. Often these conflicting views have soured relationships between the two groups. To resolve this, managers on both sides should look to change incentive structures so that each side benefits from collaboratively delivering what actually matters: the target outcomes and ilities that the customer desires.

Another challenge is that traditionally few IT Operations staff have much experience with code and the software development end of the delivery lifecycle. Likewise, developers rarely have a full grasp of the entire service stack they are delivering into. Many are prone to feel embarrassed or try to hide these knowledge gaps, or worse be convinced that they do not exist or do not matter.

Both sides should look for opportunities to educate each other. While Operations Service Engineers do not necessarily need to become full coders, it is extremely beneficial for them to know basic scripting and understand some rudimentary coding and software delivery concepts like dependencies, coupling, inheritance, consistency, and version control. Not only will this help them engage more effectively with developers, it can alter how they think about troubleshooting and operating the production environment. Knowing how to script is useful in that it gets a person to think of ways to automate away boring repetitive tasks. Even if they do not end up coding up anything, thinking about places to do it is important to help the team find bandwidth to do the more valuable work.

Getting developers to better understand the service stack helps reduce the chances that they will hold flawed assumptions about it. They are also far more likely to design their software in ways that can use cloud and DevOps tools in more effective ways. Finally, seeing the operational side up close can encourage developers to think about how to instrument the services they produce to help everyone understand what is happening when they are deployed. Developers often are so used to being able to probe a development instance that they forget how difficult it is to do the same thing when there might be hundreds or thousands of instances of it deployed in production.

Incentivizing Collaboration and Improvement

Talented managers know that the most important measure of team success is how well they can deliver the outcomes that matter to the customer. This is where the maturity model can help. By incentivizing teams across the delivery lifecycle to improve the organization's ability to deliver those outcomes and the ilities being sought, it can encourage team members to find ways to remove team barriers and collaborate.

One of the most compelling ways to do this is to look for sensible pairings of organizational activities that together improve delivery. One of the best examples is pairing improving packaging and configuration management with automated deployment and environment configuration management tools.

Developers and testers are always looking for good places to try out new code, but the options they have for doing so are far from ideal. The sandbox where most developers code rarely reflects production conditions. Even if one gets over infrastructure sizing differences, the sandbox is littered with extraneous cruft and usually lacks all the necessary dependencies. Test environments are typically only marginally better, and are often limited in number and in high demand. With the wide availability of cloud providers, building out infrastructure elements can be as easy as using a credit card. However, the means for deploying the rest of the service stack are far more troublesome. Some people try using shortcuts like snapshots of preconfigured containers and virtual machines that, without sufficient care, can themselves grow outdated and filled with extraneous code and configuration data that, as with Knight Capital, can cause problems.

An automated deployment and configuration system, particularly one that heavily encourages cleaner and more atomic software packaging, tokenized configurations, and audit functions, can dramatically reduce installation friction while making it far easier to find and track otherwise untraceable changes. This type of automated system can be combined with dashboards to show configurations of various environments and flag any differences or drift, making it far easier to spot potential risk areas and ultimately help manage environments more effectively.

Another great pairing is improving code instrumentation and service instrumentation hooks with production monitoring, telemetry, and troubleshooting tools. Many developers and testers either are unaware of what can be collected and presented with modern IT Operations monitoring and telemetry tools or do not see much personal benefit in extending the richness of information exposed to them. Expanding the availability of such tools can help build shared awareness across the delivery lifecycle, leading to more-educated ways of matching up conditions in the various environments to produce better services. If done well it can also help SE Leads better spot potentially problematic discrepancies earlier in the delivery lifecycle that can be investigated and either tackled or prepared for.

Developers Running Production Services

Figure 9.8
Trying to do it all.

An increasingly common configuration is to do away with IT Operations entirely and instead overlay service operations duties on top of the developers building the product. Some view this as true DevOps, or even NoOps. With no team boundary between service operation and development, there is not the issue of those two teams having conflicting priorities, nor is there the risk of information flow breakages between the two functions.

There are a couple of ways that you could implement the Service Engineering Lead in such a model. The most common would be to rotate the duty among members of the delivery team. This has the distinct advantage of eliminating any potential incentive conflicts and trust issues between teams. It also ensures that there is still someone who is looking out for maturity improvements to more effectively deliver the service ilities that the customer needs.

There are, however, some challenges that can potentially limit the value that having an SE Lead might bring. The first is that much of the value an SE Lead brings is being that person who can deliver that extra bit of focus to ensure information flow and situational awareness in order to deliver the service ilities the customer needs more effectively. Unless your team is working alongside other delivery teams where an SE Lead might be able to help improve coordination and alignment, most of the SE Lead's attention will likely instead need to focus on the operational aspects of the service.

The problem with this is that few developers have sufficient operational experience to accurately translate operational service ilities into service design and delivery. This can be especially problematic when it comes to operational tools and the configuration and use of the infrastructure stack. A lack of knowledge in either of these areas often results in them not being used effectively, if at all.

I have personally encountered a large number of different teams in recent years that have suffered greatly from this problem. By the time I am asked in, they usually have managed to twist their production environment into unmanageable knots by misusing everything from Kubernetes and containers to AWS infrastructure services. In most cases this had real effects on not just the organization's ability to release changes, but also on what the customer experienced. Sometimes customer sessions were dropped, orders lost or doubled unexpectedly, or worse.

This is obviously not a great way to meet customer target outcomes.

Larger organizations that have many delivery teams might find it advantageous to build the SE Lead capability into a central platform team, particularly one that is already providing core operational tooling. This configuration has the advantage of encouraging information sharing between teams while also promoting platform tool adoption.

Overcoming the Operational Experience Gap

While some delivery teams are fortunate enough to have one or more strong senior developers who have spent a significant amount of time in operational roles and can help frame up an SE Lead discipline, most are not so fortunate. To overcome this operational experience gap, teams might want to consider hiring one or more people with a solid service operations and operational tooling background to seed your organization. This would not be a wasted hire. Once your team either learns how to perform the SE Lead tasks effectively or grows out of the need for an SE Lead, this operational tooling person can rotate into a Tools & Automation Engineering position where they can enhance your operational tooling capabilities.

Once you have identified some people to help you begin your journey, those people should help the team devise a backlog of operational items that the team needs to put in place in order to build up the team's maturity. These items might include such improvements as clean atomic packaging and automated deployment, identifying the key metrics and thresholds for service health, determining what instrumentation is needed to help with troubleshooting and understanding ecosystem dynamics, minimizing manual changes, capturing and proactively managing configurations and versioning of deployments, tracking what service versions are deployed and which are in use, having methods to ensure knowledge sharing and staying attuned to customer outcomes, and the like.

From there, the team needs to come up with a means of rotating the SE Lead duties around. Just as in the IT Operations model, the duties the team member takes on during their rotation should be reduced to allow them to step back and assume the role. This is where building in experience and a maturity backlog or checklist early on is extremely helpful. This allows for maturity improvements to be shared across the team, as well as for those who are inexperienced or uncomfortable with the operational side to have enough guidance and people to lean on to still be successful.

Another challenge that such double-duty teams also tend to have is with managing reactive unplanned work. Having reactive work in the team will likely require a number of adjustments to the team's way of working. The biggest of these is making the flow of work visible to everyone, particularly those within the team (see Chapter 12, "Operations Workflow"). There also needs to be a mechanism to minimize the amount of reactive work that hits the whole team (see Chapter 13, "Queue Master").

Finally, as with all service delivery configurations, the team will ultimately benefit from having a small team of one or more people who are dedicated to building, acquiring, and improving the operational tools and automation the team uses (as discussed in Chapter 10, "Automation"). This allows the team to have capacity that can focus on making the tooling improvements that will be necessary to take full advantage of maturity improvements like atomic packaging and configuration management.

Summary

Putting in place a maturity model that measures and creates targets to help your team improve its ability to cut through the service delivery fog is an effective way to help ensure that you can deliver the outcomes and ilities that the customer desires. Creating a Service Engineering Lead rotation can further bolster progress by allowing the delivery team to have someone who can take a step back to look for awareness disconnects and inefficiencies that can form and get in the way.

To further bolster this journey, teams should look at how they manage and track their workloads. This is where workflow management and the Queue Master can help.

Chapter 10

Automation

*Automation applied to an inefficient operation will magnify the
inefficiency.*

Bill Gates

The ability to deploy, configure, and troubleshoot production services
quickly and easily through tools and automation is compelling. For the
business side it promises the ability to rapidly experiment with different
market offerings while also improving the organization's ability to respond
quickly to new or changing customer demands. For the technical side it can
help increase the amount of work the team can complete while simultaneously making that work far less complex to perform and its results more
predictable.

However, what many organizations miss is that really gaining the benefits of automation takes far more than simply installing a bunch of tools.
For one, the best automation approach for one organization is likely to be
considerably different from the best approach for another. In fact, ignoring these differences by using tools that do not match the conditions of
your ecosystem can actually lead to *more* work and *less* delivery predictability.

Finding the optimal automation approach for your organization starts
with first understanding the dynamics and conditions within your delivery
ecosystem, then crafting tooling decisions that best fit them. As you will
see, through this process you can build a positive feedback loop that both
improves your ecosystem awareness and makes it more predictable and less
labor intensive.

• 257 •

This chapter begins with an overview of the ways environmental conditions can impact automation effectiveness. From there, we explore how concepts such as 5S from Lean can improve awareness while reducing unnecessary variability. We also introduce the role of Tools & Automation Engineering and how such a group can dramatically improve your automation strategy, and ultimately expand the capabilities of your organization.

Tooling and Ecosystem Conditions

Companies want to automate for a variety of reasons. Some want to deliver and scale faster. Others want to reduce costs. There are even companies that really don't care about any of it but want to be seen as having some sort of automation/cloud/DevOps strategy.

Those organizations that have some passion for automation often describe what they want as some mix of the cloud capabilities of Amazon, the service capabilities of Netflix, the resource fluidity of Spotify, the data mining capabilities of Google, and the continuous delivery capabilities of Etsy. They might not always be clear on all the details, but they usually want automation now, think that it is straightforward to get, and want to know what tools they can buy or download to make it happen immediately.

Companies that desire such automation sophistication are usually well intentioned but misguided in where to start. The biggest problem lies in the chasm between the conditions we see and those that need to be in place to deploy tools with any chance of achieving the desired objectives.

Mismatching tooling with ecosystem conditions is like using the wrong type of race car for a race. For example, a Formula 1 series race is designed as a contest of speed and agility. Cars that are driven in it are optimized for those dynamics, but as a result require impeccable track hygiene. One stray piece of garbage or a poorly surfaced track and someone is likely to get hurt. On the other end of the spectrum is off-road racing. While it is still a car race, it is a contest of endurance through rough and unpredictable conditions. Off-road vehicles have to balance ruggedness and speed, making them far slower but more durable than their Formula 1 counterparts.

Automation works in much the same way. Some of the time the mismatch means that, like the off-road racer in a Formula 1 race, the tool ends up not being particularly useful. This happens, for example, when build and code repository practices aren't aligned to installed automated build and continuous integration (CI) setups. Putting automation around a clunky, slow, or fragile build process tends to only add complication. The same is true for CI if developers check in code infrequently, there is excessive code branching, you are only building and integrating small parts instead of everything together, or the delivery process is heavily phase-gate. The automation is supposed to provide rapid feedback into the state of the entire code base. This is difficult to do if you are only occasionally getting feedback from a small percentage of this process.

Mismatches can likewise cause frustration or even additional wasted effort. One of the most common places this occurs is with monitoring and data analytics tools, where it takes little for a mismatch to have an outsized effect. On the service side, mismatches tend to take the form of inconsistent, inadequately documented, or poorly maintained interfaces and data, any of which can make it difficult to correlate and understand what is happening within and across systems. Heavy reliance on proprietary vendor-supplied software and services can be so impenetrable as to create a large analytic black hole in your ecosystem.

Often, mismatches happen because the software or services themselves were simply not designed with analytics or instrumentation in mind, leaving poor-quality data artifacts that contain far too much noise to use for surveillance and understanding. Other times, the problem is actually with the choice of monitoring or analytics tools and their configuration. I regularly see such tools become blind or errantly spew garbage because either they have been deployed in an environment they were not designed for or there has been some subtle change to the inner workings of a process that causes the metrics or data the tools once looked for to no longer be relevant.

The dangers of mismatches can be extremely hazardous. Just as Formula 1 cars need heavily controlled track conditions, some tools likewise are extremely sensitive to mismatches. But unlike Formula 1, it is usually the ecosystem that suffers.

This is particularly the case with automated deployment tools. The challenge of overly tight service or data coupling can make automated deployment difficult. However, the bigger problem comes from simply not having a clear and sufficiently consistent model of your deployment ecosystem. If deployment targets aren't organized with high configuration hygiene and minimal unknown or unmanaged state drift, automating deployment greatly increases the chances for unforeseeable or uncontrollable deployment and configuration problems that are irreversible.

Not all mismatches are necessarily technical in nature. Some of the most difficult mismatches to deal with affect what and how people go about their work. Automated deployment and public cloud solutions can deeply affect established procedures and have very real legal and regulatory consequences. Adapting people and processes to new delivery approaches can cause real business headaches for organizations. If the new technologies and processes lack sufficiently clear and trackable governance controls and protections, any perceived shortfall can even limit what markets and customers can become customers. If automation choices are not made carefully, they also can make the jobs of staff far more cumbersome and error-prone, leading to pushback that can undermine the viability and effectiveness of the automation initiative itself.

Building Sustainable Conditions

So how do you go about finding and eliminating mismatches? Your first instinct might be to get an idea of what the conditions are within your ecosystem. But to do that you first need to know where to look.

Chapter 6, "Situational Awareness," discusses how gaining sufficient context takes far more than just looking around. Everything from mental model biases to poor or misleading information flows can lead you astray. A much more effective way is to take a page out of Lean Manufacturing. Lean relies upon two desires that are commonly held by staff. The first is to be proud of your workplace and accomplishments within it. The second is that the work ecosystem is set up such that performing work the correct way is easier than performing work the wrong way.

How Lean accomplishes this is through an approach called 5S.

5S

Like IT automation, factory tools and automation only work well when the ecosystem is known and clean and the tools match what workers need to turn materials into the desired end product. The Lean method for organizing and maintaining an orderly workplace is called *5S*. The traditional 5S pillars are sort (*seiri*), set in order (*seiton*), shine or clean (*seiso*), standardize (*seiketsu*), and sustain (*shitsuke*). They fit together like Russian matryoshka nesting dolls, with each subsequent pillar building upon and reinforcing those before it.

On the surface the names of these pillars might sound like irrelevant janitorial tasks to many in IT. What on earth gets "shined" in IT anyway? Don't concern yourself with the terms themselves, as they are no more than a mere shorthand for something much bigger. Even manufacturers who only focus on the terms see little benefit. For both manufacturing and IT alike, it is the intent behind each term that is relevant. Table 10.1 provides a guide to help.

Table 10.1
The 5S Pillars

Pillar	Meaning	IT Equivalent
Seiri	Sort	Know and classify the artifacts within your ecosystem and remove those that are unnecessary
Seiton	Set in Order	Organize artifacts and workspace sensibly to maximize effectiveness and minimize uncapturable change

Pillar	Meaning	IT Equivalent
Seiso	Shine/Clean	Maintain/improve artifacts, tools, and workspace to ensure their utility
Seiketsu	Standardize	Build/maintain/improve common shared frameworks and processes that support end-to-end maintenance and transparency across eco-system while encouraging continuous improvement
Shitsuke	Sustain	Build/maintain structural and managerial support to sustain continuous improvement

Let's take an in-depth look at each of these 5S pillars to see how they can help us on our journey.

Seiri: Know What Is There

 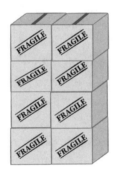 

The first and most central pillar of 5S is sort (*seiri*). The purpose of seiri is to get a handle on all the bits that make up your environment, from the code, infrastructure, and other building blocks of the service stack to the tools and processes within it. It is not a simple inventory audit or discovery exercise. Those only provide a snapshot of what you might have in your environment. Seiri is necessarily continuous to maintain awareness of what you actually need and why you need it.

Finding which components exist in your ecosystem, what they do, who uses them, who owns them, where they live, as well as how they enter, move around, and leave the ecosystem is obviously useful. It improves your awareness of what is going on, helping you spot risks and potential mismatches that could cause problems that might complicate automation efforts.

Trying to identify the purpose of everything also helps you to spot those things that are unnecessary, no longer needed, or really shouldn't be where they are. In manufacturing, seiri is seen as a useful mechanism to tackle waste. Organizations habitually collect all sorts of clutter. Often little time is devoted to removing it because either people are too busy or the effort simply doesn't seem worthwhile. Some might even think they are being clever by leaving it around. Seiri emphasizes why ignoring or keeping "clutter" is the wrong approach.

By getting rid of everything that is not directly needed for delivery, you eliminate many of the places where things can hide as well as the noise that obscures your understanding of what is going on. A good analogy is clearing your yard of leaves or dry brush. Clearing a yard makes it easier to avoid tripping on your garden hose or stepping on a snake that has decided to take residence in your yard. Removal also has the added benefit of eliminating something like a piece of code or errant configuration that can cause catastrophic problems.

Seiri is a good way to get everyone thinking about the purpose of everything in the ecosystem, which not only improves everyone's understanding but also inevitably encourages people to think of ways to improve. Seiri also greatly reduces the number of ownerless orphans that can lead to potentially disastrous surprises down the line.

Knight Capital

If seiri doesn't make much sense or seems unnecessary to you, it might be worthwhile to walk through a rather famous example of how not doing it can lead to disaster.

Knight Capital was once a high-flying financial services broker-dealer in the United States. Like many such firms, Knight Capital had invested heavily in building their own high-speed algorithmic share-trading system. These systems are designed to find and exploit subtle price differences, or "inefficiencies," within and between markets. There are lots of reasons that these differences can appear. Probably one of the more notorious reasons is the existence of "dark pools." These are private exchanges that were originally established to allow for large institutional investors to anonymously buy and sell large blocks of securities (typically to rebalance their portfolios) without impacting the market. Later, dark pools became a pathway for trading firms to avoid exchanges and market makers entirely, sometimes even to profit at their customers' expense.

In June 2012, the New York Stock Exchange (NYSE) received permission to create their own "dark pool" called the Retail Liquidity Program (RLP). Knight quickly acted to modify their internal trade router software, called SMARS, to change its order-handling process to integrate into RLP for its opening day on August 1.

The job of SMARS was to receive parent orders from the top-level trading platform and then figure out, based upon available liquidity, the best way to divvy up the orders to external pools and markets for execution.

Like many companies in the financial industry, Knight Capital favored new functionality over maintaining what already existed. This is especially true for front office functions like trading desks, where traders are constantly in search of any new feature that might give them a market advantage. This meant that there was a lot of old, dormant code lying all around. SMARS was no different. One of these was a piece of deprecated functionality called "Power Peg." It had been designed to track cumulatively how shares were being fulfilled across markets to know when to stop trying to send out orders. Power Peg had been discontinued in 2003, with the tracking piece eventually being moved out of the Power Peg routine and into another function. But while this particular routine had been discontinued, the code not only was left in but was also still callable.

As you might imagine, leaving dormant code around that is still callable is incredibly dangerous. It is the software equivalent of leaving the safety off on a loaded gun left carelessly in a pile of stuff in the back of your closet. Any number of unassuming things could accidentally reanimate it, wreaking havoc in your environment. This is exactly what happened at Knight.

Knight developers were aware of this proverbial gun but clearly didn't appreciate the full extent of the danger they faced. As part of the RLP work, they had decided to remove the Power Peg code so that they could reuse the flag that activated it for the new RLP code.

While removing callable code is always a good idea, doing it at the same time that you are going to be reusing a flag that activates it is like grasping around in the back of a dark closet for the loaded gun. Unfortunately for

Knight, they had some other clutter-creating issues that left the barrel of the gun pointed right at them. One of these was that, like so many companies, Knight weren't particularly good at keeping deployment configurations in a known and aligned state.

On July 27, shortly before the RLP launch, the new RLP SMARS code was scheduled to be slowly rolled out to the eight SMARS production servers to minimize disruptions. Unfortunately, one of the eight servers was missed and not upgraded with the new code, leaving a server where the Power Peg software had not been removed.

The fact that this server configuration discrepancy happened meant that there were no sufficiently effective mechanisms in place to prevent it. Lack of discovery suggests that any checks in place were either not thorough enough or not visible enough to bring this anomalous situation to anyone's attention. This is hardly a deficiency developers want, especially when they are too busy or sloppy to remove dormant code.

One and a half hours before market open on August 1, Knight received orders from customers who were eligible to use RLP with the repurposed flag. While the seven servers that received the new code processed the orders correctly, the orders activated the Power Peg code still present on the eighth server.

At this point Knight still could have recovered. The conditions on the eighth server triggered a series of 97 alert errors notifying that there was a problem. As this was still before market open, there was a possibility that the alert could have triggered a response to investigate, find, and potentially even fix the problem before the markets opened. Unfortunately, the alerts were missed, exposing yet another likely issue of clutter obstructing awareness and action.

Instrumentation is incredibly important. If done well, it can help considerably by giving you a much greater understanding of what is going on in your environment. Missing an early alert of a potential problem is never good. Missing 97 of them over the course of 90 minutes and then still being in the dark as to the cause well after disaster strikes hints at massive amounts of dysfunction with the way that instrumentation was set up, how it was used, and how it was interpreted. While it is possible that alerts were not going to the right place, more likely there was so much noise that context, and thus value, were lost. Anyone who has been on the receiving end of a noisy monitoring system knows that after a while you simply ignore everything.

At market open the Power Peg code proceeded to wreak havoc. As the dormant code was no longer able to track whether orders were filled, it continued to replicate the orders millions of times. The administrators, still unaware of the configuration discrepancy, responded (as many would who want to stop the bleeding without knowing what is going on) by rolling back the code on the other production servers. This, of course, made the problem worse. The flag was in the orders, so rolling back resulted in all eight servers having the problem. This hints that there was either limited understanding of how the code worked or little assessment of the risks involved in the approach taken.

By the time the errant code was stopped 45 minutes later, it had executed over 4 million orders in 154 stocks for more than 397 million shares, leaving it net long in 80 stocks with a position of $3.5 billion and short in 74 stocks for about $3.15 billion. In the end, Knight Capital lost over $460 million in unwanted positions.

This knowledge breakdown ultimately crippled Knight, leading to not just the $460 million loss, but ultimately its demise as an independent entity.

Seiton: Organize So It Is Useful

Figure 10.3

Mary found that keeping her work environment organized sparked joy.

Knowing what you have and getting rid of what you do not need is a great way to avoid becoming the next Knight Capital. But knowing you have something is only useful if you know where it is and that it is available to use when you need it. That is where the second pillar of 5S (*seiton*) comes in. Seiton is about organizing the various parts of your ecosystem in a sensible order. In a factory this means creating a well-laid-out workbench with each item easily locatable in the most sensible and convenient place for it. Organizing everything logically improves flow and accuracy and keeps users of these resources aware when something is amiss.

For those who have never spent any significant time in a well-organized environment, this probably seems more like a nice-to-have than an important requirement. It might be a little frustrating to have to hunt for things from time to time, but organizing takes time away from other, more important tasks you might make money from.

The reason these beliefs endure is that this same lack of organization obscures its actual cost. A useful way to demonstrate this is by shifting this disorganization and lack of care to something where the dangers are far more obvious.

Imagine for a moment that you have to go to the hospital for minor surgery. You are directed to a room and told to get up on the operating table. As you enter the room, you find it strange that there is a pile of surgical tools in various states of repair heaped in a pile on the floor in the corner of the room. A short time later the doctor comes in with a nurse behind him. The doctor asks you to lie down as he starts to pick through the pile.

After some time, the doctor reaches into his pockets, pulls out a couple of old spoons and a steak knife, and says "I'm glad it was soup and steak day in the cafeteria! I can't find the right surgical equipment, but these should be good enough for the job." During this time the nurse has been filling a syringe from one of the many vials on the cart. As he sticks it in your arm he says "All the drugs look the same. This one is closest to me so it will just have to do!"

Such a scenario would likely have you desperately trying to run out the door. The risk to your well-being is both high and obvious, and one you would likely only tolerate in a disaster situation where your life was on the line and there were no other options.

Yet hospital environments do not naturally organize themselves. While you might not find surgical equipment on the floor, keeping equipment and medicines organized in a way that minimizes mistakes is still an ongoing challenge. In fact, the Institute of Medicine's first Quality Chasm report stated that medication-related errors accounted for 1 out of every 131 outpatient deaths and 1 of 854 inpatient deaths, amounting to more than 7,000 deaths annually.[1]

Organizational problems are one of the most common causes of medical errors in hospitals. Many medications have look-alike/sound-alike names and are stored in hospital pharmacies in identical containers. This is why hospitals increasingly use seiton and other 5S techniques like differing the color and shape of medication containers; organizing medical carts and cabinets for separation to reduce the likelihood of mistakes; and using barcodes and other secondary checks to flag errors before they cause life-threatening problems.

While not always so obviously life-threatening, disorganization in IT can be just as dangerous. When under pressure to deliver and code is difficult to work with, tools are new or cumbersome, or establishing a working environment takes too long, people will inevitably cut corners. Just like the doctor using cafeteria utensils, the sloppily copied code, poorly managed dependencies, or repurposing of some random or less suitable deployment target might seem "good enough" to do the job.

While seeming carelessly reckless to outsiders, this mentality exposes the organization to unnecessary variability and risk. This makes code harder to read and work with and problems harder to troubleshoot, often wasting more time and effort than is saved through the original shortcuts. For automation, such variability creates additional edge cases that those deploying automation tools will inevitably need to uncover and deal with to ensure their efforts are both useful and work reliably. When tools or even large sections of the supply chain are of unknown quality or provenance, as occurred in the SolarWinds and codecov2 security breaches, these unknowns can even introduce outright dangers to your business.

Just like hospitals, seiton efforts in IT should be designed to make it both easier and more worthwhile to do things the right way than to use short-

---

1. Institute of Medicine. *To Err Is Human: Building a Safer Health System*. Washington, DC: National Academy Press; 1999, p. 27.

cuts. Often this means exposing and fixing the root causes for dysfunction. For instance, poorly laid out code repositories and excessive branching often lead to check-in mistakes and painful merges that increase mistakes and consume time to sort out. These problems are often caused by unfamiliarity with version control tools and their best practices; poorly designed and implemented code; and inadequately defined and managed work. Sloppy coding and poor dependency management are often a result of a combination of misperceptions about the problem space; unrealistic time and resource constraints; and hidden or insufficiently understood existing technical debt.

This is the same case on the operational side. Slow and cumbersome provisioning processes, poor software packaging, and inconsistent or manual installation and configuration not only are frustrating but encourage people to develop workarounds that create yet more variability that must be dealt with. You can break the loop that causes the problems in the first place by organizing your ecosystem through improved packaging, configuration, and provisioning, along with measures that reduce the need to log into deployed instances.

Disorganized Dependency Management

Few IT professionals would doubt the importance of dependency management. Yet, there are even fewer who actually spend the time to ensure that dependencies are being managed adequately.

This disparity between importance and execution ultimately took center stage at one large global company. They had decided to rewrite one of their core services. It had grown organically over the years into a difficult-to-support mix of several languages and technologies. The desire was that cleaning up the stack and rewriting it in a single language (Java) would make the stack more supportable, extensible, and reliable.

Like many large projects at big companies, it quickly grew to contain hundreds of software developers in over 20 teams scattered around the world. This might not seem terrible at first. The problem was that they were all working on the same overall service, and many of the parts coming from different teams were closely coupled, if not outright tight dependencies, with each other. What made this worse was that each team had decided to use their own Maven instance. This meant that there were over 20 different project object models (POMs), which meant over 20 different versions of dependencies.

The problem with how Maven figures out library dependencies, especially at the time, made this problem worse. When there were references to two different versions of a library, unless you explicitly told it otherwise, Maven tended to pick the one closest to the root of the dependency tree. This was tricky to always get right even when you knew everything that you were pulling in from both public and private repositories was backward compatible, as library versions could still shift from build to build, opening up the possibility of all sorts of new variability.

Add 20 teams not talking to each other and with no certainty of backward compatibility? At integration time you have the equivalent of a 100-car crash. Nothing could consistently build, let alone work, and as a result the project ground to a halt.

A dedicated team was put together to unravel the problem. What made the situation especially bad is that there were many cases where conflicts cascaded, involving multiple conflicting versions across tens or hundreds of components and multiple teams. At times it felt like searching for a needle in a haystack.

Teams were up in arms as many months of work had to be rewritten or thrown away to overcome the conflicts. In some cases, teams had to be dissolved or work shifted around to minimize further problems. In the end, the project never totally recovered and was declared a massive failure.

Seiso: Ensure and Maintain Utility

Figure 10.4
Proactive maintenance keeps everything in optimal working order.

The third pillar of 5S, *seiso*, is about creating mechanisms and a culture that maintains and improves the organization, health, and utility of the artifacts and processes in the ecosystem. Seiso reinforces seiri by helping build the mechanisms that keep unnecessary clutter away, and reinforces seiton by keeping those organization efforts effective.

Maintaining the health of your delivery ecosystem seems like a reasonable thing to want to do. We know that everything from our car, our computer, our house, and even our own body needs some care and attention from time to time to stay in reasonable working order. Sadly, this is hardly the case in IT. Everything from code and systems to the processes that deliver and operate them are habitually neglected. Bugs and outdated or suboptimal processes are frequently deprioritized or ignored, allowing them to linger until they cause a major event that makes addressing them absolutely necessary. The same goes for systems. Once they are in place, they tend to be rebuilt from the ground up only when they absolutely have to be, and then often grudgingly.

Some argue that the main culprit is the sense that maintaining and improving is throwing more money away on what should be an already solved problem. It is easy to blame managers and modern business practices like zero-based budgeting that tend to favor new features and products with seemingly clear yet unproven returns on investment over trying to tackle existing buggy or unreliable setups with far more opaque benefits. But as anyone who has had to argue to prioritize a bug fix or tried to encourage team members to proactively refactor code or rebuild systems knows, development and operational teams are just as likely to prefer working on the new and shiny over caring for what is already there.

The rapid and continuous evolution of IT ecosystems makes it particularly important to tune and maintain the systems, software, and processes that they are composed of. This is true even in relatively stable and simple environments with few changes in requirements. Technology shifts still regularly make technology stacks obsolete. Hardware and software alike become increasingly expensive to maintain as vendors declare older versions to be end-of-life (EoL). But that is hardly the toughest problem. Many banks and large businesses with legacy IT systems can tell you of the high expense and difficulty involved in finding people who both know and are willing to support long-obsolete technologies. No one likes to try to take on supporting a system that is old and cumbersome, especially when those who built it are long gone and the organization has no interest in improving or modernizing what is there.

There is also the problem that long-lived legacy systems tend to collect so much clutter that staying sufficiently aware of what's on the systems and how it all works becomes extremely difficult. This creates the worst of all scenarios, which is a progressively more difficult to support component that becomes increasingly difficult to improve or replace without unknowingly breaking something important.

Implementing seiso doesn't mean constantly chasing the flavor of the month, but it does require staying within the mainstream by establishing a culture that takes ownership and pride in the health and well-being of the ecosystem. Encourage people to point out problems and try to improve the ecosystem in a way that both tackles the problems and is aligned with the outcomes the organization is trying to achieve. This is where the learning kata and kaizen concepts (introduced in Chapter 7, "Learning") come in handy. They help people look at problems and, rather than take on and solve a huge problem all at once, try to incrementally improve and learn in a more sustainable way.

To get there, however, you need more than excited people and a process. This is where the last two 5S pillars come in.

The Mystery System

There are lots of stories of various banks, airlines, and telecommunications companies with long-obsolete systems causing hugely embarrassing outages. Some of the more well-known ones include the RBS stable of banks (RBS, NatWest, Ulster Bank, etc.) incident in which people lost access to their accounts for days;[2] the crash of the Sabre flight reservation and booking system used by various airlines;[3] and the many British Airways flight operations IT crashes.[4] While those companies were very unlucky, they are far from the only ones that find themselves carrying such legacy risks.

2. https://publications.parliament.uk/pa/cm201213/cmselect/cmtreasy/640/640.pdf
3. https://techcrunch.com/2019/03/26/us-airlines-computer-issues/?guccounter=1
4. https://edition.cnn.com/2019/08/07/business/british-airways-london-flights-canceled/index.html

Early in my career I worked for a company that built trading systems for investment banks. Not only did we have our own proprietary core technology, we also deeply integrated our products into the various trading, compliance, back-office, and reporting systems of our customers. It was a great learning experience. It also exposed me to all sorts of lessons of what not to do.

I found myself in a very odd situation several years after I had moved away from working in the financial industry. I was invited to visit a well-known investment bank to discuss some distributed software development challenges they were having. The office that I was visiting had once been that of another investment firm that I had spent some time with. What I didn't realize was how much of a stroll through memory lane it would end up being.

On our way to the conference room, my hosts took me through the trading floor. Trading floors are often pretty impressive, with lots of monitors and technology all around and fast-paced action. As we were walking through, I recognized a couple of aging HP 9000 servers that I had once worked on. I commented that I was surprised that they were still there.

That was enough for everyone to stop. One of my hosts asked what I knew about them. I found that they had tried a couple of times to extract them, but found that each time various critical back-office jobs would fail in unexpected ways. It was such a mess that they simply left them in place.

Fortunately, I was able to explain what they did while my hosts took copious notes. I was so amused by the situation that I asked for the console. From there I typed in my old login credentials and, sure enough, I still had access.

Seiketsu: Transparency and Improvement Through Standardization

Even though the entire ecosystem benefits from the first three 5S pillars, their primary focus tends to be on organizing and improving things at the function level. Seiketsu's primary purpose is to remove the variability that gets in the way of understanding the state of the ecosystem well enough to be able to confidently deliver predictable and reliable results. This improves cross-ecosystem transparency, while also building up a level of complexity-cutting awareness and familiarity to help different functions work more effectively with each other.

It is important to note that these standards are not the traditional "best practice" rules that are created and enforced from the top down. Instead, they are developed and agreed upon by those in the trenches to reduce the amount of variability and "noise" that makes it more difficult to deliver the target outcomes.

There are many excellent places to implement seiketsu in the delivery ecosystem. On the development side, seiketsu usually is implemented in tools that enable any developer to work effectively on any piece of code and in any project or team with little ramp-up time. These tools include such things as coding style standards, standard logging and data structure formats, observability instrumentation, and build and development environment standards. While not always implemented perfectly, these are fairly common in very experienced enterprise software development organizations.

On the delivery and operational side, the most important places to implement seiketsu are in software packaging, deployment, and environment configuration management. Having clean and predictable configurations and flows that are authoritatively known and easily reproducible eliminates many of the variability problems that delivery and support teams face. Clean configuration management also makes it far clearer when and where problems crop up by eliminating the noise where they can otherwise hide.

More controversially, development and operational teams should also try to use the same repository and task management tools, if not the same repositories and task queues (with, of course, the appropriate permissions scheme in place to manage who can do what where), when it makes sense to do so. When there are vastly diverging needs between teams, this might not be possible. However, often teams choose different tools and repositories out of personal preference rather than out of any real need, often unknowingly introducing unnecessary friction and risk into the delivery ecosystem as a result. Such teams inevitably begin to struggle to manage work or collaborate whenever code and tasks need to move back and forth between teams and their different systems. Not only does it take more effort to keep the systems in sync, it also increases the risk that tasks and code might be mishandled or distorted in ways where situational awareness becomes damaged.

The alignment that seiketsu creates can streamline work considerably, providing two benefits:

- It discourages doing something the wrong way because it takes more effort than doing it the right way. For instance, creating a deployment-ready atomic software package means less effort to manually install, troubleshoot, and remove the software on its target than a more irreversible "spray and pray" approach.

- Streamlined standardization can enable locally specific elements, such as new automated test harnesses and business intelligence tools, to be easily added to preexisting pipelines across the delivery lifecycle.

Processes can also follow this approach. Teams can agree to provide standard interfaces to improve information/code sharing, collaboration, and timing in ways that still allow internal flexibility. This is the intent of both the Queue Master and Service Engineering Lead positions. In both cases, this approach improves predictability and reduces friction in the flow.

It only takes a little bit of forethought to start to standardize in such a way as to allow you to start linking the more critical tools and processes together. Linkages also do not all need to happen at once, or everywhere. They should happen in those places where they can provide a lot of value, in the form of either new insights or smoother and less error-prone delivery.

The Problem with "All-in-One" Tool Suites

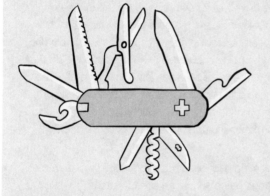

Figure 10.5
Like a Swiss Army knife, all-in-one tools often have to trade features for effectiveness.

A key to making standardization work is that it feels sensible and "right" for those using it to do it that way. One of the big challenges I repeatedly encounter are tools and processes that fail dreadfully in this regard. Sometimes people simply lack sufficient training or otherwise find themselves struggling. When this happens it is unfortunate, but it is fairly easy to catch and correct. More frequently, the enforced "standard" is the problem.

A common reason why attempts to standardize fail is that vendors try to lock customers into their tooling ecosystem by selling them a whole suite of tools, along with "best practice" processes that try to commandeer the entire service lifecycle. Usually, the journey begins when the customer is attracted to one or a handful of genuinely useful tools. When they engage the vendor, the customer soon finds themselves being pushed into purchasing a whole suite of tools and processes for their desired tools to work "optimally." More often than not, the additional tools and processes are weak, cumbersome, or simply do not match the needs of the customer. What is worse is that many times the suite extends far beyond the scope of the purchasing organization, forcing others to choose to use a bad tool or use a parallel set of tools and "double key" as necessary.

Application Lifecycle Management (ALM) and IT Service Management (ITSM) vendors are the most egregious users of such bundling techniques. Their solutions often try to assume control of all aspects of the ecosystem by tightly integrating ticketing, repository, configuration management (CMDB), deployment and environment management, automation, monitoring, and reporting tools and the processes around them into a single end-to-end bundle.

From an outsider's perspective, having one nice out-of-the box solution that takes care of all aspects of the delivery lifecycle may sound appealing; however, rarely do such solutions work well for everyone. Even though teams across an organization need to coordinate and pass work between each other, they often have very different needs. Often these variations go beyond role distinctions and arise from unique challenges the organization might face. The tools and best practices in all-in-one solutions inevitably generalize team needs in ways that ignore these differences. Often this adds unnecessary delivery friction for no reason other than to fit the solution or, worse, distorts or strips out ecosystem information that teams need for effective decision making.

In one such case, an organization had rolled out a tool suite that attempted to impose unnecessary change gates across an already streamlined CI/CD pipeline. In another, the tooling forced the organization to choose between replacing a fully automated delivery pipeline with one that required manual manipulation of the tooling suite every time code needed to be launched or breaking the configuration management database (CMDB), and with it, the monitoring and ticketing systems.

For that reason, I usually strongly dissuade organizations from going "all in" on one suite. I have seen many teams fix seemingly intractable dysfunction by moving away from fancy tools that didn't work for them to either "dumb" ones like Bugzilla or sticky task cards on a wall that did.

This problem is not unique to IT. Manufacturing shops that try to adopt Lean techniques often find that they produce better products faster and cheaper with simpler tools than with slicker but far more inflexible "all-in-one" tools.

Shitsuke: Building a Support System to Ensure Success

Shitsuke, the final pillar of 5S, focuses on building a culture that maintains the structural and managerial support needed to sustain the previous four pillars. Shitsuke is the recognition that work and improvement initiatives are not sustainable when done in total isolation. They need a structure that encourages awareness, cross-organizational cooperation, a sense of progress and belonging, and learning. While everyone plays some role, it is management's commitment that is most crucial. By understanding and supporting each of the 5S pillars, management can create the conditions that allow those on the ground to sustainably communicate, collaborate, and continuously strive toward ever better ways of delivering the goals of organization.

Managers are uniquely positioned to shape how information flows, is understood, and is acted upon. Through their peers and superiors they have the potential to see and help with the coordination of activities across several teams. Management can facilitate information flow and cross-organizational alignment, which helps with everything from knowing the state of the ecosystem to organizing, improving, and creating sensible standards to help meet target outcomes.

Managers also tend to either be part of or have more access to executive leadership, enabling them to play a role in shaping strategies that define organizational objectives and target outcomes. They can do this by improving executive awareness of conditions on the ground, as well as by ensuring that they convey the intent behind outcomes accurately to those in the trenches.

All of this works if these same managers create and nurture the conditions that encourage people to set up the mechanisms that allow information to flow. This means cultivating a culture of safety and trust. People at all levels need to feel comfortable speaking up without fear of retribution, be willing to challenge assumptions, and try new things in the pursuit of the target outcome. This is true even if they later prove to be wrong, as long as the lessons learned from the experience are shared and accepted.

Micromanaging how work needs to be performed, encouraging zero-sum rivalries between teams, and punishing failure can certainly quickly destroy any sense of safety and trust. But so can more-innocent actions like rolling out a new tool, technology, or process without at least trying to include those who have to use it in the decision process somehow. This isn't to say that everyone needs to agree. However, if you are unable to convince many who are affected (skeptical or otherwise) how this 5S approach creates conditions that help them better achieve organizational target outcomes in some demonstrable way, trust will break and the solution will never achieve its potential.

Seeing Automation 5S in Action

Now that we have walked through each element that makes up 5S, how does it all come together to help with IT automation? There are lots of examples from every part of the service delivery lifecycle that can be drawn upon. I have chosen two examples from my own experience. One is an on-demand service start-up. The other is a large Internet services company.

The Start-up

Start-ups can rarely afford the luxury of hiring large numbers of staff before they have proven their offerings have found a profitable market where they are in demand. This is especially true when you are an on-demand online service start-up, where demand can rise and fall quickly. Such companies are often the perfect place for all sorts of automation. Not only does automation reduce the need for large numbers of staff to deliver and scale services up and down quickly, but when they're done well, customers are unlikely to worry about service failures from provider staff burnout.

It is relatively easy for a new business starting from scratch to automate everything from the start. However, without taking the care of implementing 5S principles, it is easy to damage your ability to remain quick and lean once services are live and in use with active customers.

I was brought in to run a major part of the delivery and operations at a start-up that had managed to work itself into a situation that made service delivery automation difficult to maintain and grow. Not only had the software become extremely complex, with tight coupling between components throughout the service stack, in the pursuit of new business, customers had been allowed to heavily customize their instances. For some, this customization went all the way down to the hardware and operating system. The software customizations also went deep into the code, to the point where some customers had their own code branches.

All of this customization was made worse by the fact that customer software stack versions were not kept in a tight, consistent band. A new customer would often get the latest version of the software stack, while older ones would have to wait until there was both agreement from the customer and capacity by the delivery team to perform an upgrade.

Delivering upgrades was also difficult. The complexity and variability meant that there was little possibility for consistency between development/test and production environments. This was so bad that the software rarely would work as expected, if it worked at all, when deployed. This led to constant firefighting and manual hacking in production. This made it nearly impossible to know how anything was configured, let alone reproducible.

Putting in tooling that would be useable and deliver predictable results meant straightening out all this mess. The only way to make such a clean-up both work and stick was to somehow in the process make it far easier for everyone to take the same organized approach than to continue the free-wheeling approach they were currently using.

To find a path out of the situation the start-up had found itself in, my team and I decided first to compile a generic stack configuration that could be used as the most basic starting recipe (a form of seiton). If we were clever, we could change the way we organized our environment, separating out elements into generic, consistent building blocks. Any customer-specific differences would then be added as needed in a trackable way at assembly time. For instance, we knew that a web server was made up of a Linux OS instance, an Apache web server, and some modules. The modules might differ depending upon the specific customer, but these could be added or subtracted from the build manifest at install time. Configurations were also typically files that could be templated with customer- or instance-specific differences being defined and added as necessary.

We then built standardized versioned packages of that generic base and automated the deployment and configuration of it. Because we did this before such tools as Terraform, Puppet, Ansible, or Chef were available, we used a souped-up version of Kickstart that pulled from repositories that held the packages and configuration details.

We then set about to convince the rest of the engineering team to organize and standardize their ecosystem.

We started small by building an automated continuous integration system with which we regularly built and packaged some of our tools. One of our early tools was the ability for a developer or tester to "check out" a fresh base instance built from our automated deployment tool.

Up to this point building and refreshing an instance to work with was slow and laborious. A tool that could build out a standard instance quickly and reliably was a huge timesaver. Developers quickly wanted to have more of the stack included in the build in order to further speed things up. What we demanded in return was the following:

- All the software needed to be cleanly packaged so that it could be installed, configured, and removed atomically (seiso).
- Each software configuration file that was to be automatically installed had to have any customizable values tokenized so that the tool could fill in at install time.
- All customized values would be generated based upon the rules of the roles that instance was a member of. So, a development Linux web server instance in Denver would be a member of a development role, a Linux role, a web server role, and a Denver role and would acquire the software and have configurations generated from the rules associated with those roles.

It did not take long for most of the stack to be onboarded. As developers were also very keen to quickly reproduce customer configurations, developers and managers soon became willing to spend the time cleaning up and standardizing those configurations as well.

As customer instances were steadily cleaned up and standardized, we onboarded them into our management tooling. Difficult hardware and software configurations steadily melted away. In most cases customers were eager to make the trade for the benefit of being on instances that could be built, upgraded, and scaled up seamlessly in little time. Occasionally, a customer resistant to being onboarded might be ditched if company leadership decided that it was more cost-effective to do so.

As we had built the automation the way we did, the configuration repository was, in effect, an authoritative source of truth for the configuration of anything that it managed. This meant that we could run a "diff" and see the configuration differences between environments. We could also trace dependencies, and use this information to drive monitoring and other supporting mechanisms. Being versioned also allowed us to look at who made what changes to what configurations when and for what reason. This could be used for everything from auditing to troubleshooting to find the causes of perceived performance or behavior changes to services over time.

The power of having an organized representation of our ecosystem soon became obvious, as did the problems with any sloppiness in definitions or packaging. Once we were able to describe everything in the ecosystem as a member of so many roles, it was like a curtain had been pulled back. We could suddenly see and understand the state of everything. We started to eliminate unnecessary customizations and configuration drift. We could also use the repository to drive the entire service delivery lifecycle.

The Large Internet Services Company

A couple of us who had worked at the start-up later moved to a much larger established Internet services company. While the company had been extremely successful, for years they had organically grown, adding services by hand. There were various automation tools around, and even a centralized tooling team responsible for building out additional ones. Because there were so many unknowns and lots of disorganization, however, the company found automation to be difficult coupled with unpredictable results.

Shortly after we joined, the company faced a crisis. They had signed some large deals with stringent service level agreements that they had little idea how to meet. We saw this as an opportunity and got to work.

Our earlier experience had taught us that we needed to get a handle on what was there (seiri), organize (seiton), and standardize (seiketsu) where we could. Helper mechanisms like the development environment building tool we had put in at the start-up, along with encouragement from management (shitsuke), would help attract people to use, maintain, and improve upon the mechanisms we were putting in place (seiso), allowing us to not just improve our ability to meet service levels but also to offer better automation tools.

Even though there was a lot of pressure to progress, we still knew that we needed to start out small to succeed. We picked some services from one business unit to begin with. One person looked at ways of incorporating the learning we had from the start-up to build a workable configuration repository that could drive automated operating system installations and software deployments, while another looked at retrofitting existing automated installation and deployment tools, as well as making improvements to software packaging.

While this was happening, a second group sought to identify what was in place. This included more-knowable information, such as what hardware was in place, as well as useful but less accurate information, like what software and services were on the hardware, how they were configured, and who used them. Interestingly, it was this last part that proved to be the most difficult. There were times that we had to disable network ports and wait for someone to complain before we knew what something was.

Once we had some ability to build, deploy, and track in a far more organized way, we moved all new deployments to the new setup. With the information that we had collected, we also could begin to look for opportunities to rebuild what was in place. While there was some initial resistance, much of this faded when development and support teams saw the benefits that were gained by putting in some additional effort.

Once we had a demonstrably working model in one business unit, we started to reach out to others to transform. This continued until we had brought over most of the organization. Along the way we added new automation tools and capabilities such as full CI setups, automated deployment and test frameworks, and continuous delivery pipelines and reporting tools. All the while, any remaining legacy unknown became increasingly isolated from systems and services that had been brought into the new management framework.

Even with all this success, we still encountered some teams that simply refused to use the tool no matter what the benefits were or how much help was offered to make the transition. This was recognized as far from ideal by those at the highest levels of the organization. Eventually, the company decided to make adopting the tool a requirement for being in a production datacenter. They did this by opening new datacenters and allowing only those who were using the tool to migrate there. They then announced one by one the closure of the old datacenters and gave the resistant teams one last chance. It did not take long after the first one closed before the remaining teams onboarded.

Tools & Automation Engineering

Building sustainable conditions is critical for establishing a sufficiently sound foundation for any automation to both remain useful and have predictable results. As in our previous examples, making conditions sustainable might even form much of the initial direction for any automation efforts. But getting automation that is optimally fit for helping the organization both build sufficiently sustainable conditions and successfully pursue its target objectives does not come magically on its own. It needs someone sufficiently skilled to deliver it. That is where the role of *Tools & Automation Engineering* comes in.

Figure 10.6
As a Tools & Automation Engineer, Dan is dedicated to making the tools that are critical for helping the rest of the organization.

The concept of Tools & Automation Engineering comes out of the recognition that even when people have both the desire and all the requisite technical skills to deliver automation, they might not always have enough time or objective mental distance to do it. Having one or more people dedicated to crafting and maintaining the right tools for the organization helps overcome this challenge. Unless you have a relatively large organization, particularly one that is also geographically distributed, the number of people required for this role is never very high. Even one or two people is often sufficient for most organizations.

The best Tools & Automation Engineers tend to talented scripters and programmers with sizeable exposure to the operations world, including operating systems, networking challenges, and troubleshooting live services. These are often the same sorts of people who naturally believe in the concept of "delivery as code." They do not necessarily have to be pure operations people. A fair number have a release engineering, backend engineering, or whitebox testing background that has straddled the development and operational world through their work.

This deep exposure to the operational side is very important. It not only enables Tools & Automation Engineers to grasp the concepts necessary to understand and automate the service ecosystem effectively, it also positions them to create solutions that integrate with operational and infrastructure tooling in ways that are more resilient to operational failure conditions than more conventional programmers.

Organizational Details

Tools & Automation Engineers are often the most effective when they are organizationally situated with those responsible for operationally maintaining the "ilities" of the service stack. The reason for this is that the operational environment forms the foundation of the customer's service experience. By staying intimately aware of operational service conditions, Tools & Automation Engineers can build in the mechanisms that support the 5S pillars at the point where they matter most, and then work backward through the delivery lifecycle to improve the delivery team's ability to build and maintain the desired service "ilities."

In organizations that separate development and operations, having Tools & Automation Engineering within the operations team helps Tools & Automation Engineers stay attuned to operational conditions. It also gives operations staff a means to get help to create capabilities they need to automate and support the production ecosystem but either do not have the skills or the time to deliver themselves. Being both aware of operational conditions and well versed in software development, Tools & Automation Engineers can also aid Service Engineering Leads in communicating and bridging between development and operations.

In organizations where delivery teams build and run software, Tools & Automation Engineers provide cloud and CI/CD expertise for the delivery team and ensure that there is dedicated capacity to build and support delivery and operational automation. This is important for preventing tooling designed to support 5S pillars from being deprioritized in favor of new service feature functionality.

Workflow and Sync Points

While Tools & Automation Engineers participate as part of the team responsible for the production service, they are intentionally not part of any on-call, Queue Master, or Service Engineering Lead rotation. This is done to ensure that they can respond to any threats to the 5S pillars in the delivery ecosystem. However, despite this difference, they are still an integral part of team workflow and sync point mechanisms.

As you will see in Chapter 14, "Cycles and Sync Points," being an important part of helping improve and stabilize Service Engineering maturity means using the delivery team's workflow and participating in its synchronization and improvement mechanisms. This might seem a bit odd at first, especially as tools and automation work tends to look a lot more like typical development work than operational work; however, besides improving shared awareness, Tools & Automation Engineering plays a very important role in energizing improvement efforts.

Most of the tools that Tools & Automation Engineering end up building are heavily influenced by improvement needs that arise from the team's retrospectives and strategic review sessions. The reasons for this quickly become apparent. For instance, it doesn't make sense to automate the deployment of more services if the ones that you have already automated aren't working reliably. The same goes for instrumentation and troubleshooting tools, build frameworks, and repositories. If any of these is too brittle or unreliable, then creating more of the same will only make things worse.

By participating in retrospectives and strategic review sessions, Tools & Automation Engineers can learn more about the pain points experienced in the operational environment with much deeper context. They can use the sessions to ask questions and propose further exploratory work to surface root causes and come up with tooling solutions to help the team overcome them.

Being part of retrospectives and the workflow also allows Tools & Automation Engineers to spot friction and risk points in work the team is receiving and performing that might be reducible through new or augmented tooling. For instance, a developer or operational person might get used to the packaging and deployment of a particular service being slow and cumbersome. A tooling person can look at the problem with a fresh set of eyes and potentially find a way to fix its root cause.

For Tools & Automation Engineering, work tends to behave quite similarly to a development Kanban. Most work is usually known going into the planning meeting, where it can be prioritized and ordered in the Ready column for tools engineers to pick up throughout the week. Work items can come into the workflow in an expedited way for tooling engineers, though just like expedited Service Engineering work, the same general post-expedited reviews should still take place to see if there are ways to minimize the need for such actions in the future.

While there is some flexibility to allow work items to be somewhat larger in size than is allowed for other Service Engineering work, in general most of it should still be sized to be no more than one or two days' worth of effort. This both helps improve exposure of what is actually going on and keeps items moving across the board.

Summary

Delivering effective automation is an increasingly critical element needed to ensure the success of modern IT organizations. If done well and in collaboration with the delivery organization and management, it can help improve the organization and maintainability of the infrastructure, software, and services within it. But simply putting tools in place is neither a safe nor sustainable approach. The 5S pillars from Lean of seiri (sort), seiton (set in order), seiso (maintain), seiketsu (standardize), and shitsuke (sustain) allow you to build the situational awareness and predictable structures that successful automation efforts require.

As the delivery team improves their knowledge and management of the delivery ecosystem, they should consider creating a dedicated Tools & Automation Engineering function that sits within the operationally oriented Service Engineering area in order to provide tooling and automation solutions that help the organization meet the target outcomes of customers with an operational context.

Chapter 11

Instrumentation and Observability

We are doomed to failure without a daily destruction of our various preconceptions.

Taiichi Ohno

It is increasingly popular for businesses to claim to be data driven. Business intelligence and Big Data initiatives try to pull together the growing piles of data that are created across the delivery ecosystem to improve awareness and to learn. This combination can seem powerful, especially when paired with methodologies like Lean Startup and Agile that are designed to exploit such feedback in ever faster and effective ways. Yet, in practice, delivering on the promise of ever better and more secure solutions for customers more quickly and seamlessly still seems elusive.

What is going wrong, and how can this shortfall be resolved?

Delivering effectively takes more than building and deploying service capabilities quickly and then collecting any data generated. For a delivery to be effective it also must deliver solutions that customers feel are important for them to achieve their target outcomes. Collecting data is only useful if it provides feedback that improves decision making and your ability to meet those goals.

Obtaining this sort of high-quality information is actually much harder than it sounds. You need to first have a good idea of what sorts of information would be useful. Most who gather and analyze ecosystem information tend to collect the sort that agrees with what is believed to be true. This leads to confirmation bias that can damage the quality of the very decisions needed to deliver effectively.

To avoid such bias-driven flaws, it is far better to search for evidence that refutes rather than agrees with your beliefs. Such an approach reduces the chances of being lulled into flawed mental models that will steadily degrade your decision making. Capturing and analyzing unexpected results creates opportunities to learn and improve.

Determining the best mechanisms to capture the information you need is the second step. They must do so accurately and in a timely manner with enough context that the information can effectively guide decision making. In fact, it can be dangerous to simply apply off-the-shelf tools to capture and process existing ecosystem data. Doing so risks capturing and analyzing data outside of its intended context. Not only might the data be devoid of useful insights, the tools used might process and mix unrelated information in ways that can create false correlations that can actually damage your understanding of what is transpiring in your ecosystem.

Finally, the information you do capture needs to be visible and understandable enough to the decision makers it is designed to inform that they can actually put the information to maximum use.

This chapter attempts to take you on this journey while providing some answers to help you accomplish this pragmatically. It draws on many of the concepts discussed throughout this book to help you overcome the many challenges in determining the "right" data. Also, as the technical landscape is ever-shifting with new and innovative approaches arising every day, I have tried to remain tooling agnostic. Any references to specific tools should be taken as useful examples rather than specific mandates.

Determining the "Right" Data

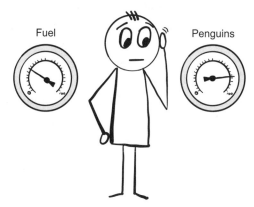

Some time ago I attended a dinner meeting with a number of luminaries from the DevOps movement. As often happens, one of the topics that came up was around monitoring and analytics. I started talking about some of the interesting service instrumentation that we had put in place at one of the companies I had worked for. Much of the instrumentation was aimed at allowing us to trace everything from user and task journeys to related events and their effects on the service ecosystem.

At one point several people challenged me. Some of these challenges really stuck with me, in part because what I took for granted as obvious was clearly not. They revolved around the following:

- "Even if I had a way of obtaining the information, why would I want to have it?"
- "Collecting data has become a fetish. I am already swimming in too much of it. Adding more would only make it more difficult to get anything done."

In their pushback they were highlighting a very real problem. A shockingly large percentage of data collection and analytics efforts are put in place for no other reason than someone thinking that, with the growth of "data driven" buzzwords, everyone must have to do it.

It is true that the explosion of interest in data science and analytics has for many organizations been as productive as digging through a random hoarder's garage. While there *could* be something useful in the mountains of random stuff, without knowing the quality of what was collected, where it was collected from, or how relevant the original reasons for why it was collected match your needs, the chance any of it *will* be useful are low. In fact, collecting and sifting through lots of random data often buries or distorts useful information that might exist, making finding it in a timely fashion to be put to constructive use nearly impossible.

For those at the dinner meeting who were pushing back, my description of collecting and analyzing data sounded like more of the same. However, this case was different. The company in question had learned that the key principles for ensuring effective instrumentation and analytics were as follows:

- All collected data has to have a known purpose. No data should ever be collected if there is no identifiable purpose or value to collecting it. It also must not be collected if its sole purpose is to only agree with what is believed to be true.
- All collected data has to have a known audience. Collection and presentation instrumentation need to ensure that the intended audience understands what the data represents well enough to be able to derive value from it.
- The source of the data must be known to be sufficiently trustworthy, consistent, and timely for the purposes the data will be used for.

The company did not only enforce these rules for new data and instrumentation. Existing data, the sources of that data, those relying upon it, and the documentation supporting it all were also checked regularly to make sure they were still valid. When this was no longer the case, the reasons would be investigated, with the result being the replacement or retirement of the instrumentation and data.

For anyone who has been in an environment with lots of unknown or obsolete data and systems around, the listed criteria prove to be extremely useful for both reducing clutter and retaining instrumentation and analytics focus. For those who want to know more, let's walk through each rule to better understand its importance.

Know the Purpose and Value

Just because data can be collected does not mean it should be. Not only does collecting lots of superfluous data waste a lot of resources, it can actually make it much harder to find the information you need and build the necessary context to put it to good use.

This is why there needs to be a clear purpose behind what you collect. The purpose will typically revolve around one or more of the following:

- Uncovering or clarifying the target outcomes that need to be pursued
- Aiding any decision making required to pursue the target outcomes
- Aiding your understanding and awareness of the delivery ecosystem in order to improve any relevant capabilities needed to execute more effectively within it
- Providing evidence necessary to meet legal or regulatory requirements

One of the biggest challenges with service delivery is not having a clear idea of the target outcomes. Sometimes this is due to not having direct access to the customer to find out. Other times there might be inaccurate assumptions or biases that have hidden or distorted the problem that needs to be solved. Occasionally, as happened with companies like Slack and Flickr, you might stumble on a completely different customer need that is far more valuable than your initial target to pursue and satisfy.

In order to make certain you have the right understanding of the target outcomes, you need to start by putting some instrumentation in place to capture and present the dynamics of the current situation that would impact attaining them. This process is necessarily iterative, as you will likely discover that a number of your initial measures are irrelevant or have gaps that reduce their utility.

As you learn more and begin to experiment with solutions to try and progress toward the target outcomes, you will want to build more detailed and targeted measures that can tell you more about not only the outcomes themselves but also how well your improvements are closing the gap to help the customer reach them. It will also start to become clearer what sorts of instrumentation can capture the dynamics of your ecosystem and the efficacy of your capabilities within it that you can then use to learn and make improvements to your capabilities and approach.

Let's look at two very different examples to show how determining the purpose of data works.

Buying Furniture Online

Figure 11.2

How do you know the experience is meeting your customer's needs?

A customer who is considering buying furniture online is usually looking for ideas of various furnishings available that meet their needs and desired aesthetic and that they can afford to purchase. Success typically means finding and purchasing exactly what they were looking for (possibly along with some other items they didn't know they wanted but now cannot live without). To achieve success, the customer must be able to locate the online store, search for and find the furniture they want to purchase, order and pay for the furniture, and then receive and happily keep it. Anything that hinders any part of that journey is not only damaging to the store's relationship with that particular customer, but likely to dissuade others from becoming potential customers as well.

The metrics for measuring the success of an online store are fairly straightforward. They usually follow the following rough outline at the start:

- The ratio between the number of searches and the number of items that were placed in the shopping cart

- The number of abandoned shopping carts and where they were abandoned in the order flow
- The ratio of successful and failed payments, with any reasons for the failures
- The ratio of returned items to total number delivered, with any reasons for the returns
- The ratio of satisfied and return customers to unsatisfied customers

Each of these provides a starting place to then explore and build upon. For instance, the search information can be extended to learn about how many searches were needed before an item was found, how many searches came back with no results, and how many unconverted searches were category-based versus characteristic- or named-based. Most importantly, you might start to look for ways to capture clues as to why.

Another important aspect of the instrumentation for observability journey are cases where key parts of your delivery ecosystem are delivered by other parties. This would likely be the case for the payments processor as well as the furniture delivery logistics fulfillment provider. Even though you might not be able to instrument them directly, their performance is still an important part of whether the customer will achieve their target outcome. Finding ways to instrument, even indirectly, for the conditions that would likely impact the customer negatively is valuable. For instance, capturing and looking for patterns like payment validation errors, return rates, and complaints can provide useful clues that can indicate value in investigating the situation further.

Getting Successfully Treated at the Hospital

There are instances where the purpose for data collection and analysis might seem abundantly clear, yet the instrumentation and data available are so fragmented and dysfunctional that making it useful for effective decision making is far from straightforward. This is certainly the case with hospitals.

People go to hospitals for a wide variety of reasons, mostly for injuries, sickness, or some problem that is affecting the patient's quality of life. Few go with the expectation that they are putting themselves at additional risk of dying. Yet going to the hospital is arguably one of the most life-threatening activities you can do.

In 2006 the UK's Chief Medical Officer, Sir Liam Donaldson, stated that the risk of death due to hospital medical error was 1 in 300, or 33,000 times more likely than dying in a plane crash. If medical error doesn't kill you, then an infection you acquire from visiting the hospital might. According to the US Centers for Disease Control and Prevention, nearly 1.7 million hospitalized patients annually acquire an infection, killing more than 98,000 of them.[1]

Figure 11.3

How do you ensure good patient outcomes?

In a medical environment, the overall purpose for any hospital visit is to diagnose and then treat a patient's medical condition. The target outcome is typically not only to stabilize the patient but also to put them on a path that

1. "Health care-associated infections – an overview," US National Library of Medicine, US National Institutes of Health, 2018; https://www.ncbi.nlm.nih.gov/pmc/articles/PMC6245375/

improves their overall health. Achieving this outcome with limited or faulty data that can lead to mistakes or exposure to any dangerous pathogens that might be around is incredibly difficult. This makes it critical for hospital staff to acquire and analyze the contextual data necessary to make sound decisions that help patients achieve good outcomes.

There are a number of areas where acquiring and presenting contextual data in a timely fashion would help with achieving the right patient outcomes, including:

- Data about classification and routing accuracy rates at triage and admission
- Causes and incidence of problems with accuracy, availability, and completeness of patient medical records
- Treatment delays and mistake rates, types, and causes
- Location and usage patterns of equipment, medicines, materials, and staff
- Location and movement patterns of patients and admission types, and their exposure to equipment, medicines, materials, and staff

Much like the online furniture store, each of these areas is merely a starting point to build upon. For instance, medical record issues could be a sign of a fragmented records system, or a system that is cumbersome and error-prone for doctors to use, or a sign of larger records management problems. Likewise, usage patterns of medical equipment can be paired with cleaning and maintenance records to see if cross-contamination has occurred for some reason. Each of these areas can then be explored for further learning and improvement to help improve patients' chances of receiving safe and accurate treatment.

Know the Audience

Knowing the purpose of the information you are collecting is certainly valuable in identifying the best information to collect and the best way to collect it; however, the purpose doesn't always reveal the best information to collect, or the optimal way to collect and present it. You also need to understand who is going to consume it.

Figure 11.4
Knowing your audience can avoid embarrassment and failure.

Audiences tend to naturally break out into several overlapping groups:

- The technical teams that use information to troubleshoot, design, and improve technical solutions
- Nontechnical teams that are part of the overall product or service delivery, such as the warehouse and inventory team at the furniture store or doctors and medical staff at the hospital in the earlier examples
- Staff and partners supporting more business-oriented functions such as customer and market targeting, planning, upselling, operational and financial reporting, and compliance
- The customers themselves, who are often trying to understand and optimize their activities toward meeting their target outcomes

Not everyone consumes information the same way, with the same context, or with the same motivations. This means that what might appear to be the right data for you might not be optimal for those who need it. Being able to spot and fix potential mismatches can go a long way in ensuring that the intended audience is able to do something with the information that ultimately helps them achieve their target outcomes.

Let's explore some of the more common information mismatches and the problems that they can cause.

Language Mismatches

One of the more common mismatches is caused by presenting data in a way that is not aligned with the audience consuming it. This prevents them from understanding the information and what it means to them, causing them to ignore it or make faulty decisions.

Figure 11.5
"We're running in the sandbox?"

There are many things that can cause this disconnect. Sometimes it can be caused by using language that might have a very different meaning to the audience receiving it. A simple example is not realizing that "dropped tables" means something different to the furniture store than to your DBA. People can also get confused by acronyms that can stand for different things in different contexts, such as "ATM" for "Asynchronous Transfer Mode" or "Automated Teller Machine."

Another common form of disconnect occurs when the audience has learned what a term or statistic is but is not sufficiently informed about the underlying information to use the term or statistic effectively. I have seen both technical and nontechnical teams struggle with this issue. This can be particularly painful when instrumentation is geared to satisfy a legal or regulatory requirement. Misalignments in language, such as access and change information for Sarbanes-Oxley (SOX), can create false alarms that cause huge compliance headaches for fast-moving delivery teams.

Perhaps the most frustrating situation is one in which the instrumentation is positioned in an area where those who should be using it either do not use it or lack the expertise to interpret its output. This happens regularly with software statistics like build and code metrics, as well as infrastructure and service utilization rates. I have encountered teams who had excellent metrics that showed instances where brittle code was suffering high defect rates due to heavy code churn late in a development cycle, but the teams could not interpret the metrics effectively themselves. Likewise, I have seen instances of obvious bottlenecks where a small increase in load or a change in usage patterns would cause a cascade of damaging service failures, yet decisions to cause service behavior to change were blindly being implemented.

Such mismatches can be extremely frustrating for all involved. To improve the chances of getting your message across, try to hunt down any language that may cause problems and replace it with plainer language. To help find such language, as well as metrics that might be misunderstood, take advantage of new team members. New team members are unlikely to know the meaning of any unusual terms or metrics used internally. Capturing any problems they encounter that lengthen the time it takes for them to ramp up and reach their full potential can help you find and address areas where disconnects and misalignments are likely to happen. These may come in the form of terms or processes that are unclear that they can document and feed back. They may also encounter areas where existing staff have different interpretations for a metric or process that needs to be realigned to help the team be more effective.

For legal and regulatory compliance, I always recommend spending time with the Legal and Compliance teams. That way you can check that you understand what information the organization requires for compliance, as well as get a good understanding of the underlying intent behind why it is needed and what it will be used for. That way you can make sure that the information that is captured is the right information, that it is clear and complete, and that it can be easily understood by the parties who will be consuming it. You might also find communication challenges in the request for compliance information as well. I have personally had several instances where what was actually needed was far easier to provide than what was requested, thus eliminating a lot of headache while in the process building up useful confidence with the compliance team.

Capture and Presentation Distortions

Sometimes the problem with the data is not the language used but how its context and meaning are lost or distorted by the way it is captured or presented. When this happens, the result can be worse than having no data at all.

I've regularly encountered situations where the instrumentation and data distortions were so great that the audience for the information had developed a false sense of awareness and understanding of the delivery ecosystem. There were those who were blissfully unaware of performance, reliability, security, and even usage patterns. Others misinterpreted the data and ended up chasing after phantom issues, often coming up with elaborate and entirely unnecessary solutions to deal with them.

Much like language mismatches, the best way to solve such errors is to spend time with the audience of the information. What data do they need to meet the purpose behind the data, and in what format can they best understand its nuances? For instance, presenting trending information often requires knowing the scale and scope to ensure that important details are not hidden or averaged out.

Where the information is presented might also be important. For example, in the Knight Capital fiasco detailed in Chapter 10, "Automation," in the hours leading up to the failure, the SMARS system issued 97 alerts of the dangerous issue that ultimately destroyed the company. However, the alerts were both vague and sent to an email account where the urgency of the issue was missed by the support team.

Likewise, the information might also need to be presented in a way that gives it far more context. An example of this is presenting everything from monitoring and services to production data flows through the lens of their dependency trees. Such presentations improve tracking and troubleshooting as well as planning, coordination, and verification of service changes.

Know the Source

Figure 11.6

"I am sure this was mountain spring water at some point!".

Getting the "right" data does not depend only on *who* consumes it and *why* they need it. The source of *where* it comes from and *how* it gets to where it is needed are also important.

Most of us know implicitly that not all data sources produce information of the same value. For instance, a battery of service probes is likely to provide a clearer picture of the nature of a service response problem than a complaint of service slowness from a single user. The probes are likely to provide a lot more context about what is slower, by how much, under which conditions, and what its effect is on the service ecosystem. This provides a great deal more factual focus that can be acted upon.

Unfortunately, the most optimal source for the information needed at a given time is not always so clear-cut. How can you systematically determine those sources that, if not the best, are at least sufficient to achieve the target outcomes?

There are a number of aspects of any given source that can help you determine its suitability in helping the intended audience meet its intended objectives. These include the following:

- How trustworthy and consistent is the data source?
- How timely is the data gathered, processed, and communicated to meaningfully inform and improve the audience's decision-making ability?

Let's take a look at how each aspect affects your source's suitability.

Trustworthiness and Consistency

Trustworthiness and consistency are fascinating and often misunderstood aspects of data analytics and information management. For one, many of us confuse trustworthiness and consistency with accuracy. Data can actually be accurate and considered neither trustworthy nor consistent. A customer complaining of slow service responsiveness is certainly one example of this, and for good reason. A customer complaint often comes randomly and does not consistently direct us to a cause that can be fixed and solved.

The problem is that few of us spend much time thinking about the trustworthiness and consistency of the sources of our data, let alone bother to understand how those qualities can distort the decision process itself. This challenge is most apparent when you rely upon data that has been generated or manipulated by instrumentation that might not match your situation or the intent you are using it for.

I encounter this most frequently with off-the-shelf tools and solutions. Mismatches tend to fall into three categories. The first is mining the default log data without first understanding the purpose, accuracy, or context for which entries are generated. I have seen situations where organizations tried to intelligently mine data from the logs from across their service journey only to find themselves struggling in a haze of confusion due to the fact that the thinking behind what and how information was captured and logged was different across various externally developed or delivered solutions. Some of the mined data had large and unexplainable gaps, while other sources for the data used cryptic language with the idea that only the authoring organization would look at it.

Then there are the mismatches that occur when the off-the-shelf tool is the instrumentation. One form is caused by a mismatch between what the instrumentation is designed to capture and how it is interpreted. Sometimes the issue is with biases that are built into how the solution approaches the ecosystem it is in. This can be everything from taking the approach that no explicit problem means that everything is fine, to viewing a customer journey in fragments (such as separating the finding and buying part from the processing and receiving end in our online store example, or separating staff, patient, and equipment streams in the hospital example) rather than looking at the full end-to-end journey.

This is a common issue with synthetic transaction monitoring solutions. They are typically designed to tell you whether certain defined flows are working as expected. This is useful when service flows are made up of many moving parts, as well as when customer journeys take consistent and well-known paths.

However, it is common for synthetics to be accepted as fully representative of the customer experience, even when customer usage patterns are neither consistent nor even well known. Synthetics often miss important aspects of the delivery ecosystem that have a real impact on what the customer experiences. These include differences in client environment configurations (such as what systems and software clients they are using to access the service, where they are accessing it from, etc.), client caching strategies, and user characteristics that might alter the way they navigate and use the system. At times these differences can be so extreme as to render the metrics gathered from synthetics useless.

One common pattern I have seen with many companies is to track login transaction times, even though their users almost always stay logged in. I have also seen transactions that were tracked without taking into account the fact that the response time always directly correlated with the size, structure, or permission level of the user or the amount of information cached on the client side. There are also times where the user must run a series of actions not because the actions themselves are useful but because that is the only way they can glean a particular piece of data or achieve the service state they desire. This meant that opportunities to restructure or otherwise optimize transactions were repeatedly missed.

INSTRUMENTATION AND OBSERVABILITY

The third mismatch happens when off-the-shelf instrumentation is applied in an ecosystem that it was not designed for. This is common for various generic resource utilization and performance trackers that are applied to virtual and cloud environments. Hypervisor, container, and virtually provided services can distort resource availability and process timing. Sometimes resources can seem to be available when they are not (a common virtual machine issue), or appear that they are not available even when they are. Docker for a long time had stat bugs that made it look like there were resource shortages when there were none.

Likewise, there are situations where instrumentation is unable to interpret a problem it was not designed to see. For instance, I have seen instrumentation designed to find responsiveness and corruption problems that could not see dropped frames or data errors from streamed sources.

Dealing with such challenges means taking a step back and assessing how much you know about the trustworthiness and consistency of the instrumentation and data sources. If the instrumentation is important and you cannot be completely confident that it meets your needs, you will likely need to change your approach.

Timeliness

Figure 11.7
Sometimes arriving late is worse than not attempting to arrive at all.

How many times have you found a key piece of information you needed only after you needed it? Obtaining and being meaningfully informed by data in a timely fashion is increasingly important in our information-hungry age.

Investment bankers pay millions to get and turn around information milliseconds before anyone else, while other businesses look at being data driven as a key differentiator for success.

Likewise, the timeliness of feedback determines how quickly we can make decisions to respond to changing dynamics in our delivery ecosystem. Timely feedback is needed not only to give organizations an edge over their competitors. Customers expect service providers to quickly be alerted to, respond to, and solve any service problems they encounter. Customers feel aggrieved when they have to notify a provider of a problem under the belief that they are somehow doing the provider's work for them.

Instrumentation needs to capture and present the full context when it is needed. This means that everything from how long it takes to acquire and present contextual information to when and how it is used needs to be considered in the design of the instrumentation itself. This also includes ensuring that instrumentation that relies upon multiple data sources is able to reconcile any time lags and fragmentation of those sources. Such reconciliation can be daunting. It usually means that the data is at best only as timely as the most lagging data source.

For instrumentation that is already in place, it is important to regularly keep track of its acquisition and presentation cycle to ensure that it is only used for decisions that match the accepted time window of its underlying purpose. If there is so much lag that it goes outside this window, the organization using the instrumentation must determine whether lower information and context is acceptable until a more timely way to acquire the data is found.

I have seen many businesses make the mistake of doing this backwards. They come up with elaborate plans for data analytics to drive near-real-time decision making that can be done in, say, one to five minutes, only to find that it takes three to seven *days* to acquire and process the data necessary to drive the target decision.

Making the Ecosystem Observable

Having a way to think about the usefulness of data is an important first step. However, delivering effectively and securely takes more than instrumenting and collecting production data. You also need to have some confidence in your understanding of the rest of the ecosystem that creates and delivers the services as well. To do that, you need to think how to make the delivery ecosystem observable.

This journey begins by taking a step back and looking at your delivery ecosystem across the lifecycle. In Lean Manufacturing, they do this by performing what they call "walking the gemba," which means "walking the floor" or place of work in Japanese. In manufacturing, they walk through all the steps of the delivery process to observe what is going on and build context across the whole ecosystem.

The one key detail is that they do not start this "gemba walk" at the beginning of the delivery process and walk to the end. Instead, they start at the very last step and go backward through the lifecycle to the beginning.

Figure 11.8
Walking the gemba back to front.

There are many reasons to start at the last step. One is that by starting with the result and walking backward you can far more easily trace its qualities back to their causes. For instance, if you see damage in the same place on the door of a few completed cars fresh off the assembly line, you will start to look for potential causes earlier on in the manufacturing process.

Similarly, you will look for the reasons that a defect found in a production was *not* found earlier in the delivery cycle. In one company I found that the reason many production defects were never found earlier was that the software packages put into production were never tested beforehand. Instead they were built and packaged right beforehand. As there were certain libraries that were only included in the production packages, there was simply no way that any problems that cropped up between those libraries and the new byte code could be found anywhere but production.

Another reason for walking backward through the process is that it makes it far more difficult for your brain to make assumptions that risk glossing over important details. Most people are wired to skip over details that seem boring or irrelevant unless there is an obvious problem occurring right at that instant. If a problem does become noticeable later, you would then have to backtrack to figure out the cause.

In a service delivery ecosystem I usually begin the gemba walk with any customer engagement and support function to look for what sorts of requests and complaints are flowing in. This can provide some clues as to where the current solution is falling short in meeting customer expectations and their ability to meet their outcomes.

I then go to production itself and the people who are managing it. I look at their demeanor, what they are complaining about, what work they are performing, and what instrumentation and data sources they use to guide it and how that information flows. I then look at how proactive versus reactive their work is and how effectively their labor improves the service. It is not unusual to encounter highly reactive production operations work that fights hard to maintain the status quo, or for information to silo or become distorted in ways that lead different members of the team to have different levels of awareness and views of ecosystem dynamics.

From there, I continue the journey up the lifecycle, looking at the difference between release and bugfix deployments, the dynamics and information flow in testing, build, and code/package repository processes, and the instrumentation around them. I then look at the development process itself, including how the teams are organized, how well they know the code and the ecosystem, how familiar they are with what customers and users want, and the dynamics between them and any product and architecture functions.

I also look at information and artifact flows, the instrumentation around them, who uses it, and how it is used.

The journey continues through Product and Architecture, Marketing and Sales, and sometimes includes one or more customers and perhaps senior management. At this point, I look for the level of awareness each of these groups has of the rest of the lifecycle to determine if there are any significant disconnects, and if so what their potential causes might be.

All of this should help you generate the roughest of outlines of your operating ecosystem. It shouldn't take long to perform. Depending upon the size of the problem space, it usually takes me between two and six weeks end-to-end to coordinate, see, meet, test hypotheses, and document. You might find it a bit challenging to do, but it is important to timebox the first pass to something relatively short.

What you produce in the end is the very beginning of what you will use to shape a roadmap for making the ecosystem observable. It won't be complete. Some of it may not even make sense at the beginning, or even create more questions than answers. It also might not feel prioritizable or actionable yet. All of that is okay. You are only at the very beginning of the journey.

You will also almost certainly see problems that you think need to be addressed urgently. You may even have quick fixes to tackle them. Unless not addressing the problem immediately will cause major irreparable damage to the organization, *don't do it*. Not yet. It is still very possible that you are missing a key detail that may change how, if at all, you may address the situation. Instead, it is best to quickly record the problems first. That way you can avoid inadvertently starting your own tire/dumpster fire.

Before moving on to the next phase, you need to test some of your hypotheses by running traces through the ecosystem. These traces are usually run to observe the dynamics of key activities, or ones that you didn't observe in action or have questions about. These activities might be something like following a small piece of work through to production, troubleshooting an outage, fixing a bug and deploying its fix, installing new capacity, and the like. This should help cover anything that you missed in your first pass through or answer some questions you might have. Often they can be done simultaneously as opportunities open up.

From there, you can start to look for opportunities to make the ecosystem observable.

Instrumenting for Observability

The next step in the journey is to start to identify the types and potential sources of data with acceptable trustworthiness, consistency, and timeliness needed to stitch together the information required to both build your contextual information ecosystem and, ultimately, meet the purposes behind the objectives of your audiences.

Your initial survey should give you an idea of what already exists and how suitable it might be for providing useful insight. Some of the instrumentation, such as the monitoring system and ticketing system, might seem like a good jumping-off point. However, before you start with the cleanup work, you should first identify places across the ecosystem where there are breaks, gaps, and misdirection in information flow. These are indications of the ecosystem *unknowns*.

Making as much of your ecosystem a known known or controlled known unknown as possible is important. This helps you minimize the unseeable impacts that unknowns might cause, not only to your information objectives but also in your journey to meet the target outcomes.

The sections that follow address the delivery ecosystem, along with some of the ways to approach instrumenting them. While the order begins with what most would view as the beginning of the technical lifecycle, do not take that as the spot you necessarily need to begin. I have started journeys at just about every spot in an organization, and in many cases kicked them off in several places in parallel because it made sense.

Instrumenting Development

Outside of perhaps production, the development environment is arguably one of the most information-rich parts of the delivery ecosystem. It is often overlooked, or is used to manage people instead of the fitness of the delivery and delivery ecosystem. Tasks and task workflows, code, build statistics, and other useful information can provide great insights into delivery dynamics. All of this data is even more useful when you are able to connect it to tell you *how* everything works together.

To do this, I usually start with small measures, some of which developers do already. First, I put identifiers on all work items. These identifiers are extremely common and come as a natural matter of course if you are using a ticketing system like Jira, Bugzilla, or GitLab/GitHub to track your work. As work items are the tasks that someone deemed worthy to document and perform, these are some of the first traceable elements that can be used to tie together the "whys," "hows," and other important relationship qualities between artifacts across your ecosystem. Sometimes they live in a specification or requirements document. Other times they will simply be contained in the work item themselves. Having an ID allows you to mark those artifacts with the work item created.

Next comes the work itself. The vast majority of development work involves code. Make sure that everything possible gets checked into a version control repository and is marked with the task ID in the check-in comments. This creates traceability to allow others to understand which artifacts were touched in what ways to complete what sorts of tasks. This procedure is so powerful that many organizations I have worked with have configured their repositories so that check-ins are accepted only if they have a task ID associated with them.

All of this data begins making your delivery pipelines observable, with the purpose of improving the overall awareness of the people within the delivery ecosystem of its dynamics.

Code metrics (changes, churn, dead/dormant code, distribution of developers) can help give you a reasonable understanding of everything from potentially brittle areas, to interactions that might need to be tested and who actually knows your code. Capturing code metrics and regularly reviewing them as part of the delivery lifecycle can help you better target testing, as well as find and minimize single points of failure. Amazingly, this sort of information is rarely captured and scrutinized, leaving a huge and easily fixable set of unknowns directly in the heart of the delivery process.

The next step is to automate and report on build and integration results. Automated build and CI systems can provide useful metrics about build and integration problems. When such systems already exist, there is value to ensure that build reporting is structured and displayed in a way that can improve the visibility of any patterns of problems or failures that are tied to particular pieces of code. Having the task IDs as part of any code commit should enable you to also see if there are problems with certain types of work items, as well as expose any potential coordination issues between individuals and/or teams. This allows you to spot where there might be problematic code, friction, or information flow problems.

Actively try to roll up all of this information into dashboards that allow you to start at any part of the journey, dig down, and trace all the relationships. You can do this with everything from heavily customized Jenkins configurations to custom top-level dashboards that track, graph, and allow you to drill down into the various areas.

Technical teams are the biggest consumers of this information. It helps them avoid overlooking problems that they should be able to see themselves. Instrumenting development might not seem terribly useful outside of build statistics. I regularly get pushback from teams about the need to put task IDs on check-ins and tracking work. This is especially the case in low-trust environments where people think they will be judged on their "efficiency." There are ways to work around some of that pushback, though it is important to find mechanisms to expose the dysfunction it causes. As you will see in the sidebar story, however, the data can also prove to be very useful for the business as well. With guidance, it can allow discovery of otherwise unknown risks and single points of failure that have gone undetected and could prove damaging.

Heikkovision

I encountered a unique example of the power of development awareness at a start-up that was in the process of being acquired. While the organization appeared to be thriving, the executive management team was nervous. Despite having seen huge improvements in delivery speed and service quality by moving to Agile development techniques and deploying CI tooling, there was unpredictability around quality and release timeframes for feature functionality. Slippage and poor-quality features created an obvious risk to the attractiveness of the company. There were also real risks caused by the acquisition itself. Acquisitions are resource intensive and distracting. They may also entice key people to leave. There was little understanding of who these people might be, what the impact might be if they did leave, or how to mitigate any damage.

I was asked if I could help.

While there is no way that you can always definitively know who will leave an organization or what problems might get in the way of delivering a release, you can do a lot to identify those places where risks are high. To do this I kicked off two initiatives. In the first I wanted to map how releases moved through the organization.

It didn't take long to find the source of release unpredictability.

The first problem was that while teams were working in short sprints, little had been done to minimize the number of tight dependencies between teams. This created situations where dependencies created long, serialized release chains. In these chains a feature might require work from one team, say on an important code library, that would then be passed and incorporated into the sprint of another team, and so on, as depicted in Figure 11.9. Some of these chains were six or eight teams in length, meaning that even in the most optimal scenario it would take upwards of 16 weeks (the number of teams times the number of weeks per sprint) for a feature to be released.

Release!

Figure 11.9
Serialized dependency chains.

The problem was that few features took the optimal path. Often a downstream team would find a bug that required a fix from an upstream team. It was common for this to occur several teams down the chain, requiring traversing each upstream team again. There were also times when multiple sprints were required to complete a piece of work, or something happened that caused the serialized work to be deprioritized by a team midstream, leaving everything stuck.

Identifying both the cause and the feature functionality likely to require serialized release chains meant that everyone could now see where the problems lived and what caused them. People could decide to live with them and set expectations accordingly, remove or loosen dependencies, reorganize work, or simply avoid taking on those sorts of activities altogether. In most cases the choice ultimately ended up being a mix, usually resulting in shorter and more predictable chains.

The second initiative focused on making risks more visible. Some of the work done to expose dependencies also allowed us to see some risk areas, whether in the form of clusters of important work, dependencies, or defect hot spots. This was somewhat helpful. However, one of the most important risks that needed to be captured and understood were places where there were human single points of failure (SPoFs).

To understand this risk, we started mining code statistics to understand which developers had worked on each piece of code, when and how often the code had been touched, and how much code churn there had been. That data was then fed into dashboards that allowed us to see places where few people in the organization knew the code, who they were, and code brittleness. This made it obvious what code areas were exposed to human SPoF risk, as well as where code refactoring would be most valuable.

The dashboards were extremely powerful, and they quickly gained the nickname "Heikkovision" after the developer who helped pull them together. It felt like x-ray vision that could cut through the noise to help see what was going on throughout the company. It helped the business size up their risks and improve resource management, release prioritization, and planning. It also gave the technical side the evidence they could then use to show the potential benefit in investments to make their lives easier.

Instrumenting Packaging and Dependencies

The next pieces of the flow are the build artifacts themselves. Again, like development instrumentation, the information gained is mostly helpful for technical teams. Interestingly, relatively few people spend much time looking at the shape of these artifacts, how they are used, and the details behind their dependencies. Most just put them on a server or storage landing zone somewhere in an untrackable manner.

I personally prefer placing the artifacts in a repository where they can be versioned more cleanly and where task IDs, build information, and other notes can be left. This is also where I like to notify various automation tools of any updates that can be used to trigger the next steps in a given delivery pipeline. Many pipeline and orchestration tools are designed to be configurable to look for such information. This allows you to have additional traceability from the artifact both upstream through the build to code and task IDs, as well as downstream through deployment. Tag rolling is also a useful signal to tell automated deployment systems to trigger an update of a deployment target environment. When you also manage all of the software and configurations of your build environments in a fully tracked and automated way, you can also track the packages with those conditions.

When done well, all of this should be capable of being queried and placed on a dashboard at some later point.

Beyond what you capture that is specific to an individual version of artifact, there are a number of important factors that are worth capturing and reporting:

- **How atomic are my packages?** Having atomic packages means that you can apply and remove them in any environment with little concern that they will leave detritus or otherwise alter the environment in a way that is not or cannot be reverted automatically.
- **How environment independent are my packages?** A lot of organizations get in the habit of building different packages for development, test, and production. This isn't a great habit as it creates potential "unknowns" lurking about that might cause problems. These differences should be turned into configuration parameters or flags that can be set at install or run. If there is a reason this cannot be done and such differences are truly unavoidable, make sure that environment-dependent packages are reported along with their reasons, potential risks they might cause, and ways to test for and mitigate them.
- **What dependencies do these packages require?** Dependencies are nasty things that get a lot less attention than they should. This is especially true when they are external or, worse, are pulled in by something like NPM or Maven. These dependencies need to be captured and reported, with mitigations in place wherever possible, such as having local copies to avoid them disappearing or causing hidden problems.

Each of these factors is targeted to find and track your level of exposure to potential unknowns. I usually put these questions up on a dashboard or wiki so that everyone can be aware of their state and how well they are currently being managed. The goal should be to minimize these risks, either by eliminating them or highlighting their danger.

Instrumenting Tooling

Increasing reliance on tooling and automation is generally a good thing. When done well, it reduces variability and makes us think about ways of making our ecosystem more repeatable. But how many of us instrument our tooling to capture and track what has been done with it, how it performed, and what the end results were? How many of us create traceable links between tooling actions, the artifacts they used or interacted with, and any tasks behind their initiation?

Capturing this information is very useful, particularly to those who are heavily reliant on the expected tooling performance. This information provides visibility of the overall health of the tooling and how well it is performing its job. If you have been unfortunate enough to have had tooling die or misbehave and leave your ecosystem a mess, you probably know how useful any records of what happened and why are for cleaning up from the wreckage and preventing it from happening in the future. I have seen many cases where monitoring systems get overloaded and do not report in a timely way. I have also discovered build tools, backup jobs, and other maintenance activities that broke in silent ways that were not discovered until disaster struck.

Instrumentation can help you spot inconsistencies before they become problems. Instrumentation can also help you spot potential improvements and even size up their likely value. A good habit to get teams into is scheduling a regular instrumentation and reporting review to get teams in the habit of reviewing how well they understand what is going on with tooling, as well as to find any areas where instrumentation missed or was not sufficiently effective to proactively spot deteriorating conditions. Often this can help the team discover inconsistencies within or between various tools, or places where it was misinterpreted, that can be improved.

Instrumenting Environment Change and Configuration Management

An extremely common and generally good practice in IT is to create change tickets whenever you make an environment change in production. It forms a good record to know when changes were made, who made them, what changed, and why.

But how many of us actually capture in any great detail what was actually done, how exactly it was done, and the differences between the original and new states? How many of us go back to change records with any regularity to compare current or past ecosystem dynamics with changes that have been made?

As the deliverer of services, the changes that you make are arguably the most notable and important activity you do that affects the dynamics of the ecosystem. This is why it is important to capture the changes you make, as well as the differences between the existing and new configuration state. Doing this is very important for building shared awareness, as well as aiding in troubleshooting any subsequent incidents a change causes in a way that the root cause can be understood. Documenting changes in this way is so important that I always encourage teams to put up links to the details of the last five to ten changes on the front page of any incident reporting tool. I have found time and again that this not only helps whomever is fiddling an incident to reduce the time to recover, but also helps those involved in the change to address any of the root causes in a much more succinct way.

Unfortunately, most delivery teams do a terrible job of capturing the full details of any change in a way that can both maintain shared awareness of ecosystem state and be used as a complete audit trail. It is often done so poorly that many operational teams are resistant to frequent production changes.

The most common way that change information is missed occurs when changes are performed manually. Such untracked manual changes sometimes happen when people have to jump in to troubleshoot a problem to get things to work. Other times there is some commercial software being used that forces changes to be made by hand through admin consoles or other difficult-to-script mechanisms. Both of these result in details often being missed and should be minimized or tracked wherever possible. I have seen teams save shell histories or use scripted test tools that can manipulate GUIs to have a more repeatable and trackable record.

Another surprisingly common challenge occurs when work is automated but the tools performing the change do not capture the prior configuration state, what transpired when the change was performed. Some fail to check the end result of the change to see that it matches what was expected. I have personally seen deployment tools that shuffled around files or symbolic links, appended things to configuration files and the like, or shuffled around some containers, and then declared victory without actually seeing that the actions resulted in what was expected. In some cases, the tools ignored errors, from permissions conflicts to files either not being where they were supposed to be or not being complete, and moved on to the next step. Other times service APIs failed to come up properly or responded in unexpected ways. Even when the errors are captured, few bother to look at them until something blows up, if at all.

Perhaps the biggest and most common issue is that while we might track changes made to production services, very few of us do the same for test and development environments, or for changes made to supporting services such as monitoring or backup services. In fact, it is extremely common for changes to be made by an untracked hand in all of them.

The other challenge is that few of us actually capture and compare the configurations that exist in development, test, and production to analyze their differences and understand how these differences might create different dynamics in each. Did the package going to production pass through the development and test environments? If not, was it installed in them afterward? This does not mean that development and test environments need to have exactly the same configurations as production, or even that they need to have the same configuration as each other. Most of the time it is nearly impossible for that to be the case. However, accepting that there are differences doesn't mean that you shouldn't bother to know what those differences are, or check and take into account how they might alter behavior. Overlooking or ignoring these differences creates yet more unnecessary and often problematic unknowns.

Capturing, reporting, and analyzing such information allows you to have a much better grasp on what you have within your environment. Creating links between all the artifacts and activities, from task tickets to the change tickets at the end of the cycle, allows you to walk your ecosystem, beginning at any point, to understand and build context into what is happening in it.

Instrumenting Testing

When done well, testing will contain a treasure trove of useful information. It can provide all sorts of insights, many that go beyond exposing potential risks caused by defects in the code. One of the most important ways that testing instrumentation can help improve shared ecosystem awareness is to use it to capture how service changes will likely behave in the target operational ecosystem.

Using automated testing tools and testing instrumentation in this way might sound unremarkable at first, or even a restatement of what most believe testing teams do. The difference is that it is not aimed at "quality assurance." For one, the premise of quality assurance is broken. QA does not really assure much of anything. It mostly tells you what bugs were encountered during testing. Others likely exist that were simply not encountered.

This doesn't mean that such testing shouldn't be done. Instead, testing should be oriented in a way that tries to improve your understanding of how services will behave under different scenarios and conditions in order to improve your ability to respond effectively to various service behaviors. Testing should also help you more easily figure out what conditions are likely occurring when certain service behaviors are seen.

I also like to use testing to better expose the service hazards created by brittle code found through development instrumentation. This helps expose more details of the "size of the prize" by investing in refactoring or a more thorough overhaul of a problematic area.

To make testing instrumentation maximally useful, I try to augment it with production instrumentation tooling whenever possible (and vice versa). Monitoring and service instrumentation, log analysis tools, nondestructive test tools, synthetic transaction tools, and so forth can provide a quick way of being able to compare like-for-like results. Exposing test cases and test case results in a way that can be compared with what is experienced in the production environment also allows for both test and operational instrumentation to be retuned in order to make sure that the right dynamics are looked at and compared in the future.

Another useful item to capture is the deployment configuration difference between test environments and production environments. Doing this in a way that can also capture and denote the various behavior and performance differences that the configuration differences between the environments create allows you to verify your understandings of potential points of friction and bottlenecks caused by deployment configuration differences. This allows you to have more confidence in what levers can be changed when such conditions are triggered in production.

Instrumenting Production

Few IT professionals would argue that instrumenting production is not sensible. Learning the best way to do so is probably the main reason you decided to read this chapter in the first place. The production environment is an extremely target-rich environment for making your ecosystem observable. It is where your users meet your services, and thus is the place where you should look to understand how those services are helping customers meet their target outcomes. Many organizations have realized this, which has given birth to a great deal of interest and investment in Big Data analytics solutions.

What is often missed is that building an accurate level of understanding of this dynamic in the most holistic and efficient manner requires more than what can be done using more traditional monitoring and logging approaches. This is true even when supported by fancy Big Data analytical tools.

If your goal is to improve your understanding of your production ecosystem in order to make more effective decisions, there are a number of instrumentation areas that are worth considering that are often overlooked, as described in the following sections.

Queryable/Reportable Live Code and Services

One of the biggest problems with serverless services and the like is that instrumenting and tracking them in traditional ways isn't all that straightforward. One of the best ways to overcome this is by placing queryable hooks in your services directly that can give you an idea of what is going on.

You do not need to have particularly advanced hooks to start. Even something as simple as a hook that responds to a flag asking "Are you alive?" is a useful start. This can easily be expanded to "What are your health vitals?" all the way to more debugging-like information such as "What is happening with these users/sessions/data as it traverses the service?" Other ways to instrument and track what is happening is to use capabilities like Java Management Extensions (JMX), or having services register themselves and push out regular metrics in a pub/sub sort of way to a central bus or point where they can be collected and analyzed.

None of these approaches are particularly difficult to implement. What makes such capabilities worthwhile is that implementing and using them can reduce a lot of the complexity and time lag that occurs with trying to do the same thing through a more traditional logging mechanism. The values they return can be made to conform to a usable standard, which allows the values to be quickly put up on a dashboard for analysis to find any disparities across service instances.

When done well, instrumenting services and user interfaces can enable you to observe users and user sessions in near real time as they move across the service ecosystem. This is a particularly handy capability to have when analyzing problems being experienced by one or a small subset of users.

Presenting Task, Change, Incident, and Problem Records Together

A lot of service management tool vendors talk about the power of using their tooling ecosystems being in how everything connects together. They will include ticketing systems with workflows, configuration management databases (CMDBs), and even monitoring. The problem is that the vast majority of the data is either buried in its own silo or isn't particularly easy to put together in views that are useful to you and others who need it.

I have found that it is often extremely useful to present all of this information together. This is especially true with change information, which should be immediately viewable to anyone who is fielding an incident. To do this, I generally favor using a simple web page or some other equally uncomplicated mechanism that is easily viewable whether you are on the go or sitting at your desk.

While keeping change and incident records together is extremely important, I also like to look for ways of easily tracing the chain of relationships from any point in my ecosystem. Having the ability to start, for example, with a package or configuration and walk both back to the series of tasks that created it and forward to *where* it was deployed and *how* is extremely powerful. This approach allows you to pull together information you might need in the right context at the right time. The cross-seeding, as mentioned earlier, is critical to this; however, making it easy to use also means that it will be used much more heavily. Creating a simple system that allows you to easily walk the ecosystem is key to this.

Another useful thing to do is to present the data and trends that might be interesting to technical and nontechnical audiences regularly. This can be everything from failed changes and aspects of changes that created unexpected service behavior to incidents that took far longer than normal to handle. This presentation needs to be done in a way that can spur improvement, not in a way that gets turned into a blame game. Blaming, as we know, encourages people to hide data and disconnect relationships. I tend to focus most reporting to those closer to the action but allow it to be packaged up in a blameless way for delivery to upper management when help and support are needed.

Environment Configuration

We talked about configuration management and deployments earlier. But are you aware of everything that is in your delivery ecosystem? Do you know how quickly and consistently you can rebuild and redeploy each part of your delivery ecosystem from scratch?

Knowing what you have in your delivery ecosystem is more than knowing the versions of the software installed or very basic elements like network addresses. It is about knowing and regularly reviewing exactly what the ecosystem is composed of. I have found the best way to discern this information is by rebuilding as much of your ecosystem as you can regularly. By "rebuilding" I mean more than moving a bunch of containers or Virtual Machine Disk (VMDK) files around. I mean being able to reinstall the full stack, configure it, and put it into production. Knowing how quickly and consistently you can do this enables you to know how long it might take to rebuild any component in an emergency.

Rebuilding also acts as a catalyst for flagging situations where there are single points of failure in the rebuild process. Being able to rebuild this way also means that you do not have to count on some discovery tool to try to learn and monitor what you might have, if it can figure it out at all. It also means that if you fall foul of a security breach such as a ransomware attack, you can have some confidence regarding how much of the stack you can burn to the ground and rebuild rather than lose.

Another important part of tracking the environment configuration is that you can build a way to capture and understand what is changing in your environment and how it is changing. It also allows you to spot suspicious or unauthorized changes quickly.

I try to look for opportunities to regularly do rebuilds, as well as build dashboards that record friction points and other danger hot spots that the team can try to remove. These should be reviewed at very regular intervals, at least as often as strategic reviews, where goals can be set and actions can be taken to improve the situation.

Logging

Logging is a traditional and important part of every ecosystem; however, how often do we actually examine those logs? How trustworthy are they in telling us what we want to know? How structured and readable are they?

I approach logging in two streams:

- **Operational usefulness:** Logs that are not trustworthy, that are difficult to parse, or that simply do not provide any value should be highlighted. What about them is not useful, trustworthy, or easy to parse? What is the effect on operational support? Capturing and reviewing this information allows you to address the situation. You sometimes might find that there are better ways of obtaining the same information, or that there is so much spurious noise that much of what is currently logged should be shut off or tuned way down. Logging is definitely one of those places where you can have too much, too little, and too irrelevant.
- **Longer-term utility:** What do the logs convey, and who can use that information? Are there any legal or regulatory rules that might affect their handling or storage? Are they easy to obtain and process? How long do they take to process into a useable form, and why? What is their accuracy? Highlighting and tracking such logs and log data entries, especially those that are important or may diverge from the needs of those looking to consume the information, helps identify potential awareness lags that might reduce the efficacy of decision making.

Monitoring

Monitoring is one of those things that we all do. It makes sense. But much like the concerns about service instrumentation that my DevOps friends expressed, how useful is all of the monitoring to you? Does it always tell you what you need to know in a timely way with enough context to act?

Even though much of the monitoring data organizations collect is sub-par at best, many of us tend to feel that more is better. We will often collect alerts and statistics that we almost never look at, let alone use, leaving monitoring systems looking like the digital equivalent of a hoarder's garage full of old newspapers.

The best way to approach monitoring is by going through it to determine not only its accuracy but also who will consume the data, for what reason, and what decisions they are likely to make based on it. If there are better, more accurate, or more timely ways that information can easily be obtained, then the old method should be replaced with the newer, better one. If monitoring triggers alerts that do not get looked at until several pile up or something else occurs, that issue should be addressed. Getting too much useless information is sometimes worse than not receiving anything, as it desensitizes you to the information.

Monitoring tuning should be part of regular tactical review. This should be done especially after incidents where it was not sufficiently effective in helping proactively catch problems before they caused problems. There is also value to look at how to improve the overall efficacy of monitoring at strategic reviews. Monitoring needs to be continuously tuned and improved as dynamics change. Staff should also be encouraged to not grow to accept the buildup of noisy or useless monitoring.

Security Tracking and Analysis

Security tends to be the source of policies that create inconveniences that often seem far larger than the security value they provide. However, in the services world security is necessary to protect both your organization and, ultimately, your customer; however, security also has a side benefit that is often overlooked. Security can provide an even stronger impetus to capture and track what is in your ecosystem. This can be used to better understand ecosystem behavior caused by various states and user activities that can improve your overall awareness.

Many security techniques and instrumentation tend to either sit on top of other tracking mechanisms, like logs, environment configuration tracking, and the like, or have their own specialized tools to monitor such things as peculiar traffic and threats. These mechanisms are looking for things that look odd or abnormal, which can be done in two ways.

You can use these mechanisms to look for a list of activities and states that reflect known security threats and violations. This is the way that most organizations go about it, as it is fairly straightforward to do, but it is not the best approach to count on entirely as it assumes by default that there has been no unauthorized access. This is not the best stance for most organizations, especially those that are a big or interesting enough target. This approach also does not account for the fact that a lot of the more nefarious security violations begin from the inside, either from an internal bad actor or someone who has had their credentials compromised in some way.

The other way to approach security is to try to capture and track the state and activities of as much of your operating ecosystem as possible. This includes tracking configuration and data changes, network traffic, and the like, leaving tempting honeypots around to try to lure bad actors to learn more about them so that you can better protect the more sensitive parts of your ecosystem.

To be able to track this information, capture and track the configuration and changes that you make so you can easily query and check for any unknown differences. This should capture both potential security threats and behaviors (whether from errant tools or unfollowed processes) that aren't being tracked.

Highlights of such data should be made visible to help teams and the organization improve.

Service Data

The last area that you should consider consists of the structure, storage, and accessibility of service data. This includes both customer data and other forms of data used to drive your services.

Even though most Big Data programs look to heavily mine service data, relatively few organizations spend much time thinking about the overall architecture and structure of the data they have beyond what is absolutely necessary to drive services. Such data inevitably grows organically into various piles scattered about the ecosystem. This results in duplication and mismatches that make the data far more difficult to piece together and understand than what it represents. It also makes it more difficult to obtain the information to analyze.

To reduce these sorts of problems, it is best to put two mechanisms in place as part of your delivery process:

- Have a rotating role that builds and owns the architectural map of what data is stored where, in what way, and by which applications and services it used. Duplicates and mismatches should be found and eliminated wherever possible.
- Have data architecture and design be considered as part of the delivery process to begin with. Where should data live? What should access it? Have duplicates been accounted for and minimized wherever possible? How might data be extracted, to where, and for what purpose? This process does not have to be particularly heavyweight. In fact, it is far easier to manage smaller changes than bigger ones.

Pulling It All Together

Putting in place the right instrumentation to deliver the right information to the right audience to meet their objectives can sound really difficult. Where do you start? How do you keep it going? How do you improve?

Sometimes it is difficult to see the best path forward, especially when you are very close to the problem and used to the ways you have always done things.

Fortunately, IT is far from the only industry that faces this sort of instrumentation problem. Many other industries require instrumentation because they also have high availability requirements, highly unpredictable demand, and unforgiving high sensitivity to failure. Looking at how someone in a very different context copes can often help you step back and more objectively look at your own world.

The industry that I personally like to walk through is one that most of us interact with almost every day but think little about: *the wastewater management industry.*

Instrumenting a Wastewater Ecosystem

Figure 11.10
Instrumenting a waste-
water ecosystem is more
than a simple gauge.

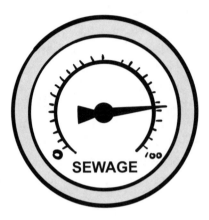

Few would argue that a service that both takes care of your waste and keeps your neighbor's out of your home is not important. Yet how many people think about the complexities of building and managing such a system?

I had the opportunity to see one such system run by the City of Los Angeles up close. The smells were predictably nasty, as were the daily safety hazards employees were exposed to working around a live network of sewers, wet wells, digesters, and holding ponds. But what most would assume would be a very pedestrian and often forgotten-about service soon proved to be anything but.

Like most cities, LA provides water and sewerage services to residents and businesses through a network of pipes and tunnels running throughout the city. People not only expect their water to be safe and whatever goes down the drain to not come back up, but also expect the streets to be free of waste. Sewers are also places where, without active monitoring and dispersion, harmful gases can build up, creating hazardous clouds and at times explosive conditions.

Los Angeles, however, faces far more challenges than the average municipality. The greater metropolitan area covers over 4800 square miles of arid and semi-arid terrain crossing a complex topology of mountains and valleys. The area is prone to both drought and flash flooding. Both are bad for sewage systems. The former can leave waste building up in the pipes. The latter can overwhelm the waste and runoff systems, leaving hazards filling the streets, and sometimes even people's homes. To add to the complexity, LA also has to contend with additional natural hazards like earthquakes, landslides, and wildfires. If that isn't difficult enough, the water, sewage, and storm systems crisscross a maze of local authorities that often do not see eye to eye, let alone have both the desire and means to cooperate.

Despite these challenges, I witnessed a dynamic system in action that has become one of the most advanced in the world. Not only is sewage in the streets exceedingly rare, but runoff and waste discharges have over the years been reduced by over 95%. What is more, the system has improved water quality and delivery capabilities, dropped total water consumption in real terms, and reduced the amount of coastline fouling and other environmental problems. This has been accomplished despite continued population growth and change across the region.

How does the LA Sanitation department do it?

For one, they realized there was no way the ecosystem would survive if the city took the approach of building a static design of a network of pipes in the ground. A single storm or a rogue factory illegally dumping hazardous materials into the system could destroy large sections of the region. They needed to actively learn about the ecosystem and the changes going on within it, all while constantly trying to find new ways to improve.

The department stayed focused on the target outcomes: keep wastewater out of people's homes and the streets, and minimize health hazards and pollution, all while looking for opportunities to recycle and reuse water along the way. They began by trying to understand more about the environment they were operating in. They scattered sensors and ran tests throughout the network and across the region. These help them understand how water flows on the surface, underground, as well as through the drainage and sewerage networks. These check not only capacity and flow rates, but also monitor for hazardous concentrations of everything from explosive and poisonous gases to problematic materials flowing through the system.

They also look at how the entire system is performing, from the sewers, pump stations, and treatment plants to the behaviors of the people who use and operate them.

This monitoring and tracking is fundamentally different than traditional IT monitoring and service workflow management. Unlike IT, they were not focused primarily on spotting anomalies to react to. It can take months or even years to change a storm channel or add sewer capacity, making even the most backward IT procurement process seem lightning fast. Instead, they go beyond IT by seeking to actively understand and shape the ecosystem itself. Information is constantly analyzed and used to continually improve the efficacy of everyone's understanding of the network.

This approach and mindset does more than improve responsiveness to potential failure scenarios. It allows for friction points and risk areas to stand out and be better understood. Anything from a new factory to a reformulation of a commonly used bath gel can easily change the dynamics of the entire network. They also look at local and regional hydrology and surface drainage patterns to understand and predict potential runoff hazards. Active harvesting of information helps build an ever more accurate understanding of the operating environment and any relevant patterns it might contain. This improves the targeting of everything from high-value infrastructure improvement to local policy and ordinance changes. They even go so far as to engage in planning and permitting to understand how proposed changes might affect the system, proposing solutions that help keep the ecosystem healthy.

As sophistication has increased, so have the public demands that have been placed on the service. If water is so scarce, can runoff and wastewater be harvested and made reusable, or even potable? Can waste be somehow recycled and put toward a useful cause that reduces its negative environmental impact?

The district tries to stay attuned to these demands. They constantly look at revamping storm drainage, sewage, and water delivery methods to maximize water reuse. Not only has wastewater treatment improved, but the district has learned that they can take advantage of some unique features of the LA basin to improve water reuse. Much of Los Angeles sits on top of alternating aquifers and oil. They realized that they can confidently inject recycled gray water into the ground at strategic locations where the soil composition will further treat the water while simultaneously recharging underground aquifers that are already used as potable water sources. This maintains local water sources while stabilizing the ground to reduce the risks of subsistence and saltwater intrusion, as well as minimizing underground movements that may potentially activate an earthquake fault. These efforts have been so successful that not only have waste levels been lowered, but actual water usage has been reduced in real terms even as the population has grown

Recovery does not end with water. Methane from the network is captured and used to generate power, all while efforts are put in place to recycle as much of the rest of the waste as possible. This is an immensely challenging task, particularly as there is no real way to force users across the ecosystem to report on what they flush down the drains, let alone how and when they use the network.

The result of all of these efforts is that those running the ecosystem feel as if they understand the heartbeat of the city. They can see the patterns of usage every day, from a steady increase in flow from residential districts as people get up in the morning, to a shift to office and retail parks and industrial districts as people go to work, and back to residential districts in the evening. Similarly, market trends and seasonal patterns of factories and offices become apparent as flows and the makeup of their contents change. Even the impacts of public events and weather patterns can be identified and understood within the signal noise of other events occurring throughout the network.

All of these observations allow for better targeting and more proactive response to change, helping surprises become increasingly rare. This knowledge can then be fed back into city planning, zoning, and permitting, uncovering potential problems before they have a chance to damage this otherwise hidden-away ecosystem.

Instrumenting an IT Ecosystem

You can use the same sort of thinking described in the previous section to build a similarly powerful understanding of your IT ecosystem.

Later in my career, I worked for a company that provided a wide variety of web and Internet-based services. Performance and usability expectations differed considerably. For instance, users were far more sensitive to response and quality issues with streaming media than, say, an RSS feed. However, there were also important differences between markets. Not meeting these expectations had a significant detrimental effect on both market reputation and the bottom line.

Being heavily consumer-facing, many of our services were also vulnerable to extreme "Slashdot-effect" style traffic spikes. There were times when traffic would suddenly grow by 1000–100,000 times the normal flow. Without sufficient available infrastructure and a quick response, everything could quickly collapse. However, the business case for acquiring all the extra capacity was not always clear-cut. It was prohibitively expensive to have so much excess remain idle most of the time, and as service performance characteristics change over time, it was not even clear that capacity acquired now would work effectively in the future.

With so many shifting variables, we needed to find ways to instrument to better understand the dynamics of our ecosystem.

On the service side, we started to build in hooks that allowed us to peer into the health and performance characteristics of the services themselves. We matched these with other operational instrumentation such as logs and monitoring information to provide additional clues of how various events would affect the dynamics of the operating ecosystem.

We also put the same sorts of instrumentation in place in the development and test environments, where we looked for the sorts of events and load profiles that might create performance problems. This allowed us to then work out various options we might have for handling such challenges, from more traditional capacity scaling to disabling various features and making certain elements static or cached.

We then began to instrument up the amount of time and variability involved in responding to changing events. This included turnaround time and accuracy for responding to an event, the time and potential risks involved in changing the capacity of various service elements, time and complexity involved in disabling or changing features, time and potential problems with moving and restoring data, and the like. This gave us some indication of our costs of delay that could be used to guide investments.

Another element that was important to all of this instrumentation was understanding customer expectations and usage patterns. While it was never easy to spot coming load spikes or gauge customer satisfaction with a service, we did find a number of useful clues that helped. For instance, we noticed clear time windows during the day when some services were used more heavily than others. We could also see a number of clues of customers becoming frustrated with service performance.

With all of this information, we started finding places to optimize. We began to heavily automate our ability to deploy and reconfigure service instances to improve our response speed and flexibility. We used customer usage patterns to dynamically rebalance the capacity of various services throughout the day. For elements that had higher friction profiles like data, we looked to opportunistically replicate and reposition data to improve our responsiveness to potential events.

We also regularly reviewed the quality and timeliness of our instrumentation data. This allowed us to continually tune what we had, find new places to instrument, and build reasonably accurate indications of the likely return on investment (RoI) for such work.

In the end, we became far more responsive to ecosystem changes. We also managed to improve our overall utilization rates to maximize the value of our infrastructure and development investments. Being more proactive also greatly improved team morale and creativity.

Summary

Instrumenting your delivery ecosystem to make its dynamics observable is critical to establish the situational awareness necessary for decision making. But to do it effectively you need to understand what the right data is for the audience consuming it, and what they are consuming it for. We in IT do a lot of things that make this difficult, from hoarding the wrong data to picking up data that is distorted by insufficient accuracy, timeliness, and biases. By building the right instrumentation and review mechanisms in your ecosystem, you can find and minimize these distortions to get you on the right track.

Chapter 12
Workflow

Learn how to see. Realize that everything connects to everything else.

Leonardo da Vinci

Workload unpredictability is one of the most frustrating things that service teams face. Service breakages often come out of nowhere, forcing team members to drop everything to respond. These can lead to newly discovered problems that inevitably lead to yet more unplanned work, all of which then must be prioritized against current commitments. Any work that gets delayed as a result predictably leads to disappointment by the customer and frustration within the delivery team. Who wouldn't become commitment-shy when faced with that?

IT teams with reactive service commitments do what any sensible person would under such circumstances: make as few hard commitments as possible, leave plenty of slack to accommodate for the unforeseen, and make change requests as painful as possible. This usually results in behavior like padding out project commitments and using governance processes to minimize the frequency and scope of any changes, particularly those that might lead to service breakages that can exponentially expand the volume of unplanned work.

Unfortunately, with the increasing demands of customers that push developers to release service changes at an ever faster rate, these strategies are no longer tenable. Instead, teams need to find better ways to understand the root causes that drive change requests and unplanned work. They also need to learn where potential hazards and friction points exist that might lead to effort and scheduling variability as well as rework. One of the best ways to do this is by looking at the flow of work itself.

In this chapter we will explore the best ways to structure your team's workflow to better understand what work is moving through your ecosystem, how and where it flows, and how to better structure these flows so that your team can be better positioned to deliver production services that meet the needs of the customer.

Workflow and Situational Awareness

Figure 12.1
Workflow boards are only part of the situational awareness journey.

A work item is more than something that someone has to perform. It symbolizes a believed need that must be fulfilled in order to meet one or more of the customer's target outcomes. Understanding the way that work is created and defined and the route work takes as it flows through an organization can tell you a lot about the delivery capabilities of the organization's teams and their overall health. This includes each of the larger themes in this book, such as:

- How well the target outcomes are understood
- The level of situational awareness to determine everything from where any gaps between the current conditions and the target

outcome exist to the level and sources of risk in any proposed actions that might close them

- Where delivery friction occurs, how much is encountered, and how well its causes are understood
- How and how well any learning opportunities are captured and exploited

There are a number of useful patterns that can reveal far more about the deeper dynamics of each of these themes and how they affect the overall dynamics of the team. Some of the more obvious measures include the ratio of proactive to reactive work, the number of people and teams a work item needs to move through to reach completion, and even who can declare an item "done." Some may even explore the common forms of dysfunction teams face, such as the number of rework cycles a work item goes through, the amount and types of unplanned work that the team encounters through a given cycle, and inaccuracies in work estimation.

However, while many IT organizations might be aware of these sorts of problems in their ecosystem, few bother to investigate deeply enough to uncover the underlying root causes. Most will, at best, put in place some superficial changes that address some of the symptoms.

One of the reasons for this breakdown comes from the way that most IT organizations think about and approach the problem of managing work. Let's take a quick look at the two most common patterns to see what is happening and why.

Managing Work Through Process

Arguably the most common approach for organizations to manage the work that flows into teams is through formalized processes. Often these align to some official project or IT Service Management (ITSM) methodology, which provides extensive amounts of supporting materials for a wide range of processes, along with professional communities that can help with implementation details.

Figure 12.2

"Why does the release process require collecting garden gnomes?".

While the ready-made processes and supporting materials of these methodologies are nice and convenient, they do come with a number of limitations. For one, they tend to focus people more on the processes and how to follow them than on how well the work moving through them helps customers achieve their target outcomes. I regularly encounter teams with extensively detailed change management processes that do little to effectively manage and track change, or heavily structured incident management processes that seem to do little to prevent future incidents or improve how they are handled. I see these backed by complex ticketing tools with detailed workflows that capture and move work through the team all while building extensive management reports. Yet every time, I find that it seems nearly impossible to dig deep enough to see and understand any useful workflow patterns and their causes.

Traditional process management is not the only place that suffers this process focus. Increasingly, I see Agile teams that have standups that do not coordinate work and retrospectives where nothing is learned or improved upon.

What makes all of this worse is that when real problems occur, the solution with a process-focused approach is to follow the process harder. So the result of an incident caused by a change usually will focus more on increasing the scrutiny and compliance to the change process and less on the dynamics behind the root cause for the incident.

This way of thinking aligns with the traditional assumption that all ecosystems are ordered systems where cause and effect are always clear and observable. In such a world, any failure is caused not by a breakdown of situational awareness but by poor execution rooted in insufficient compliance to process. Unfortunately, not all ecosystems are ordered systems. The reasons for this are discussed in depth in Chapter 5, "Risk."

Managing Work Organically

Figure 12.3
"I manage work as organically as this service architecture!"

Another increasingly common pattern is to take the other extreme and avoid imposing any processes whatsoever. In this model the team is considered to be in the best position with their firsthand experience to structure their work. If they are left to self-organize in whatever way lets them get the job done, they will inevitably find the best structure for the situation.

For those accustomed to method-driven management, this model sounds like a scary recipe for failure. The primary problem with this approach is not the absence of a process, but that it is really easy for teams to forget to have a clear feedback mechanism to ensure information flow and cross-functional alignment.

Those who usually go down this path start in a small environment. Process can often get in the way of getting the job done. As context and situational awareness are within easy reach of everyone, this approach can work rather well to start, given the right interpersonal relationships.

As an environment becomes larger or more dynamic, however, it becomes exponentially more difficult to stay on top of every aspect of every activity across the ecosystem. As a result, context and situational awareness degrade.

Without some active mechanism to ensure cross-functional alignment, team members often start to form a view inwardly focused on the part of the ecosystem they are most familiar with. This myopia fragments context and degrades the efficacy of decision making. With fewer obvious opportunities to share knowledge, knowledge islands start to form and workloads start to become uneven across the team.

The Tyranny of Dark Matter

Having the wrong focus when managing work is not the only way that situational awareness can break down. In fact, some of the most destructive ways that decision and delivery effectiveness can degrade often arise from those seemingly innocuous patterns that so often go ignored, creating what I like to call *Dark Matter*.

Figure 12.4
As Dark Matter grows,
so does its
dangerousness.

Dark Matter arises from two types of common conditions that occur in teams responsible for maintenance activities. The first are those tasks that only a small number of people have enough context and experience to know how to perform. The tasks might be relatively simple and might not even require much skill. However, they might prove impossible to perform without enough of the right context.

The second set of conditions is even more nefarious. These are the various pieces of work that no one bothers to capture and track. These tasks could be one-off individual events or something that unexpectedly crops up while performing another, larger activity. However, the most common are those activities that seem so small and mindless that they hardly seem worthwhile to record, let alone track. They include such things as service restarts, password resets, log rotations, small configuration tweaks, and various code and environment build and cleanup activities needed to keep things humming along. If it takes longer to fill out a ticket than to do the actual job, filling out the ticket might seem pointless to bother with, particularly when the team is busy.

However, these poorly known or rarely captured tasks introduce a layer of Dark Matter that is corrosive to situational awareness. That small or uninteresting task might be a clue to an important problematic pattern or a need for some improvement that has yet to be fully understood. Being hidden, there isn't an opportunity to determine what triggers the need for the activity, let alone the benefit of performing it. As such, it can hide dangerous problems and bottlenecks. With no record of the source or number of these tasks, the quality and availability of information on hand to investigate subtly degrades with the passage of time.

Dark Matter leaches capabilities away from the team. Even if these tasks are individually small, they take time to do and can be disruptive to other, more challenging work. As a byproduct, these distractions often increase task switching that can introduce mistakes, accidentally lose context, and cause team members to fall into the trap of taking on too many things at the same time.

Dark Matter inevitably lurks in most service environments, particularly those where recording friction is high, such as organizations with rigid processes or difficult-to-use ticketing systems. The more difficult a system is to deal with, the more likely people are to work around it. This feeds a vicious loop that encourages the creation of ever more Dark Matter, all while creating a façade of capture and control.

The same is true with teams that cover multiple roles, such as development and operations. It is easy to miss the importance of capturing the task and its context while juggling work, particularly if it is one task of a large string and its importance may not be clearly apparent due to one's own context shifting or personal viewpoint.

Another potential source of Dark Matter has to do with the tools themselves. As an increasing number of delivery and operations tasks become buried in stacks of tools, important information can be missed. This is especially true where the system of tools is cobbled together with little time invested in working out an effective way of capturing and reporting what the tools are doing in meaningfully contextual ways.

Learning to See the Disconnects in Action

Even if you are convinced that you and your team have any Dark Matter problem well under control, how easy is it for you to check the level of shared situational awareness in your environment? Would anything change if suddenly you had the power to see everything as it flowed through?

Let's take a moment to try and visualize what is usually happening to a typical IT team. Even if you have complex processes and many layers of support, in the end work ends up hitting the team roughly, as illustrated in Figure 12.5.

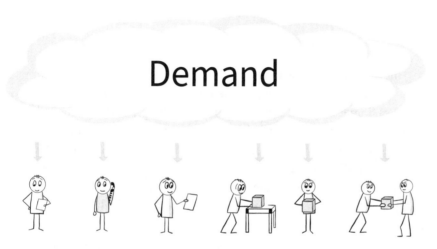

Figure 12.5
The happy delivery team in action.

When all is well, work drops down as a steady stream from a cloud of demand. Tasks might be coming through as an assigned ticket, a suddenly noticed issue, a drive-by request, or a system alert. Like most delivery teams they have only limited reach to pierce through the demand cloud, and this is only if they have both the time and management buy-in to do so. The urgency of the request and the real possibility of being interrupted by another, more urgent item encourage them to complete the task as quickly as possible, sometimes alone and other times in collaboration with others.

Figure 12.6
The unexpected
interruption.

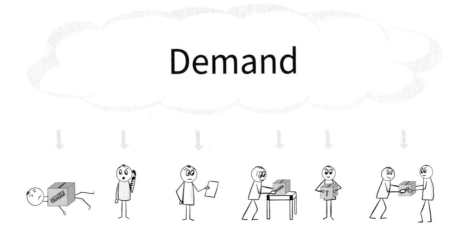

Demand

Inevitably, there are times when something happens that takes out a team member. We have all had something like this happen at one point or another. Sometimes it is a particularly difficult or poorly articulated task. Other times it might be one of those "boomerang" rework activities that bounce back and forth between the team member and someone else, or a task that is far larger than initially anticipated. Regardless of the cause, there is now a work item that is consuming at least one person's time and effort that just won't go away. It is as if a crate were to suddenly fall on you and prevent you from moving.

In a warehouse, often people will rush to help you. Unfortunately, in IT this sort of thing is rarely so visible. Even if someone happens to notice, many times the trapped team member will signal that they are okay. As IT professionals, our tendency is to indicate that it is just a bad day, and we'll just power through this one like all the others. We even fool ourselves, often squirming under the crate thinking "I can do this!" Figure 12.7 illustrates how problems can begin to spiral out of control.

The problem with this approach, as we all know, is that work keeps coming. If we are particularly unlucky, it will start stacking up on the pinned-down team member. Sometimes this is caused by a lack of visibility of the problem, or tasks that make sense for only that person to do. Conditions continue to quietly deteriorate as long as the person remains stuck.

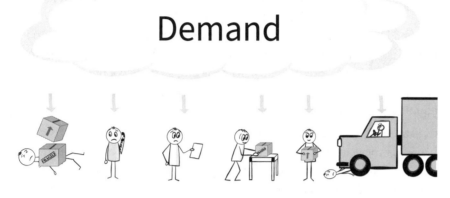

Figure 12.7
The chaos begins.

From the management perspective there might not appear to be any problem. The rest of the team might continue to get through work quickly enough, even if a sizeable percentage of them happen to become similarly stuck. The problem occurs when a far more visible constraint hits, such as a big incident or release that fully occupies the bandwidth of one or more team members. If the team is particularly unlucky, the event is more significant, such as an accident, illness, vacation, or even someone leaving the company.

Figure 12.8
The chaos spirals out of control.

With capacity already constrained, the team can find itself fighting to stay afloat. If a team member does depart, any unshared knowledge may be permanently lost. This is particularly hazardous if they were quietly performing Dark Matter tasks that didn't happen to be captured or understood by others. This can leave a gaping hole in the team where work becomes lost or neglected. Many often refer to this as having a "truck count of zero."

Work still continues to stream in. The work of the now buried worker is long overdue. With deadlines missed, activities dependent upon them begin to cause ripple effects that might make customers upset enough to complain. As these escalate through the management chain, a manager might decide to pull someone else off of their work to expedite the late work. That, of course, further reduces capacity, causing further disruptions to both work and the remaining workers who will have to rush around juggling tasks just to keep up.

Work that was being silently handled by the now departed worker will start to pile up. Anyone who has been in this situation knows that these work items will ultimately end up going in one of two directions. If the team is lucky, the work will be something others know how to do and someone will quietly request another person directly to perform it. The other route is the one that leads to the black hole.

Being effectively invisible, work items that go into the black hole will fester, quietly eroding the operational service. Inevitably, a failure or escalation will lead to their discovery, creating more expedited work. Those work items that someone manages to prevent from falling into the abyss are tossed onto the remaining team members. Without sufficient understanding of the amount of work and its value, there are few, if any, expectation changes. The increased load leads to more stress, long nights, heroics, inevitable mistakes, and disappointed customers. Unless demand shrinks or capacity increases considerably, morale will worsen as the team steadily becomes overwhelmed by problems.

While the graphics might be funny, the reality isn't. These sorts of things happen all the time, even under the most ordinary of circumstances. Unfortunately, IT work by its nature is rarely so visual. Managers and team members alike seldom can see the dynamics on the ground effectively, let alone use such insight to better manage work, improve prioritization, or invest effectively.

Resolving Disconnects by Building Context

Figure 12.9
Lucy resolves the disconnect to illuminate the situation.

If situational awareness is so important, how can we find better ways to capture, visualize, and understand what is going on in our workflow?

The first step is to look at how contextual information flows across your organization. Effective information flow is necessary to ensure that the right level of context is available to maintain the situational awareness necessary to make accurate decisions that are needed to perform work effectively.

One useful place to start is by looking at how quickly and accurately information moves between people and teams that work and rely upon one another across the delivery lifecycle. Common ways that information flows slow or loses context include the need to involve managers or single individuals to communicate and align teams and work. Another occurs when teams rely upon different communication mediums. For instance, teams using different ticketing systems or fundamentally different ticketing flows that split related activities into separate buckets that are not clearly interlinked or exposed to other teams across the lifecycle can be particularly dangerous.

Poor communication flow between people or teams that have little to no regular in-person informal engagement can make it particularly tricky to build and maintain any sort of shared context. Anyone who worked remotely during the COVID-19 pandemic probably experienced some of these problems. A lot of incidental communication, whether it is in the hallways or over lunch, can help individuals not only share information but also surreptitiously pick up important context by observing how the other person responds to various situations. As familiarity increases, teams begin to "entangle" and build a detailed shared context that allows individuals to work effectively with one another with low communication overhead.

Communication methods are also important. They can take many forms, from emails and verbal conversations to issue-tracking tickets, slide decks, documents, and videos. The function of each communication method is to capture and convey information and context. Each method has its own advantages and downsides. The trick is to not only understand the pros and cons of each, but also find a means to bolster the way that information flows by favoring the methods whose downsides can be minimized in some way.

For instance, to avoid the ephemeral and untraceable nature of teleconferencing, teams often move verbal communication to chatrooms like IRC, Slack, or Teams, where not only can everyone catch what is going on, but communication can be captured and saved easily. Likewise, email suffers from being easily lost, misinterpreted, or unintentionally omitting people. Such context loss can lead to confusion or misalignment. More effective teams tend to favor a combination of interlinked chat, wikis, and tickets. Even things such as presentations and meetings can be recorded and put up online internally for reference in the future.

There are also a number of ways to link and cross-reference information across communication mediums in order to maintain context. For instance, chatbots can capture and relay build, test, and production health information, as well as capture and post chat conversations to wikis. Linking issue-tracking IDs into code repository check-ins, builds, test runs, and deployments facilitates easy cross-referencing of any activity with related artifacts and events throughout the activity's lifecycle.

Spending the time to put the right methods in place to ensure information flow and context can prevent a great deal of confusion not only across teams, but also between new, remote, and vacationing members and their peers.

Visualizing the Flow

As previously discussed, the IT industry is hardly alone in having the problem of figuring out how to successfully coordinate activities among a group of people in a dynamically changing environment. Manufacturers have struggled with aligning people, raw materials, suppliers, and machines for decades. They are plagued with everything from broken machines, design defects, resource bottlenecks, supplier issues, all the way to customer demands for customized solutions. Top-down management through command and control processes in manufacturing these days can destroy a business through high defect counts and the creation of a lot of scrap.

To overcome these challenges, Lean manufacturers have come up with a system of visual signals across the manufacturing process to allow those on the floor to share situational awareness quickly and noninvasively. Tools and parts are engineered to ensure it is clear when they are not being put together correctly (poka-yoke), while stations, tool boards, machines, and carts are organized to not just make it easy for the worker to do the job but to make it obvious when something is not quite right. Lean manufacturers also came up with a very useful logistical control technique to ensure just the right number of parts are in just the right place at just the right time. It is called *kanban*.

Kanban means "signboard" in Japanese. Just like the "refill me" cards you might have seen at the back of displays in supermarkets, it provides a signal to notify an upstream supplier when additional material or work is ready to be brought over, or "pulled," to a workstation. The signal might be anything from a physical card that sits in the material supplied to the work station to a specially colored container. It is positioned at a point that gives the upstream supplier enough time to resupply the station before all remaining material is exhausted.

The best way to think of kanban is as a chain being pulled from the end of the line as illustrated in Figure 12.10. In manufacturing that is usually where the customer is, as it is the customer who creates the demand.

Figure 12.10
Simple chain workflow.

The card triggers the station upstream to begin work. As it exhausts its supply of parts, a card signaling the need for replenishment appears and is sent to the supplier upstream to generate and send the next batch of parts, and so on as Figure 12.11 illustrates.

Figure 12.11
Walking up the chain.

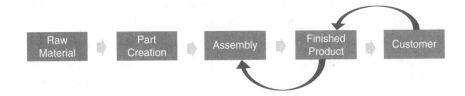

Each station keeps just enough resources on hand to both satisfy demand and allow enough time for the station it depends on for supply to respond.

Although this sounds deceptively simple, when used in conjunction with Andon (a signal used to alert that something at a workstation is awry), this technique provides a rather sophisticated form of telemetry. This greatly improves the flow of communication needed to ensure there is enough effective shared situational awareness to maintain a sustainable flow across the entire manufacturing process. With this technique, no station begins until its immediate downstream customer makes a demand. The card or signal demand tells the provider exactly what the downstream "customer" needs, and is timed to arrive just at the moment that the customer requires it. This means that the placement of the card in the supply should be able to tell us the cycle time for each step, not only indicating throughput but pointing out potential bottlenecks across the delivery chain.

A variation on this technique has been adapted for software development by David Anderson. Anderson's technique uses cards to represent work items and a simple board where the cards are posted to denote the state of each work item. Its simplicity and visual nature make it a very effective way to see the state and flow of work as it moves through to delivery. This helps both worker and interested party alike to see for themselves what is really going on. With no initially required significant changes to the way that people work, there are fewer potential barriers to thwart implementation.

These qualities have meant that interrupt-driven support and operationally focused organizations have increasingly adopted kanban-style boards to improve task and delivery workflow management. This technique has proven successful across a wide range of industries.

Unfortunately, as the technique is so simple, many try to create unnecessarily complicated flows and rules, and in the process lose track of its actual visual purpose. To help you avoid putting yourself in the same situation, the next section provides some important basics for you to consider when using a kanban-style workflow board.

Workflow Board Basics

The most important rule for creating a successful kanban-style workflow board is to keep everything about the board as simple as you can for as long as you can. Complexity, whether it is in building sophisticated state columns and swim lanes or investing in what you think is the ultimate workflow software tool before really understanding how work flows, will only add unnecessary noise that gets in the way of establishing the situational awareness you are trying to attain.

Begin with the following:

- A whiteboard, wall, or large piece of white butcher paper on which you can draw or mark out lines with a pen or colored tape for use as the board
- Cards or Post-it Notes/sticky notes to stick on the board

The size of the board needs to be big enough to fit all the cards in a way where they are all visible. Unless your team is large or has many hundreds of tasks going at any given time, something roughly a couple of meters long by a meter wide should be sufficient to start. You can easily adjust the size as needed, which is the beauty of starting with a simple physical board. Figure 12.12 illustrates the simple starting board.

Ready
Doing
Done
T16
T34
T19
T9

Figure 12.12
The starting kanban board.

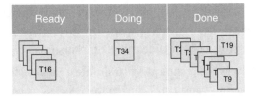

State Columns

Workflow boards are typically laid out with a series of columns, as illustrated in Figure 12.13. Each column represents the current state of the task.

Ready
Doing
Done

Figure 12.13
The state columns.

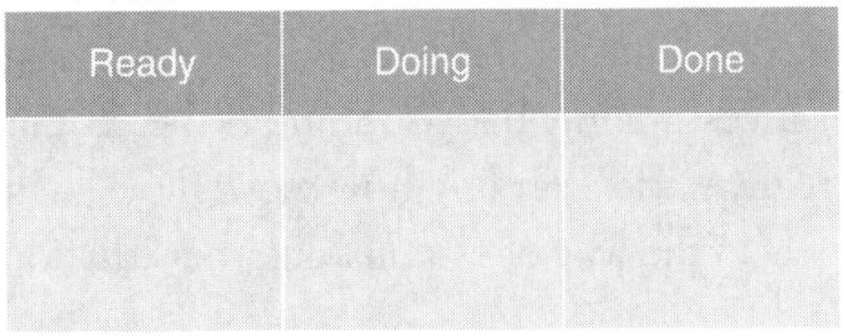

The rule with columns is to start with as few as possible. People have a tendency to think of all kinds of corner cases where additional columns could be useful. Remember that in the beginning, complexity is your enemy. It can obfuscate patterns that cause you to lose visibility of what is really going on. You should include additional columns only if you can show that they will be regularly used by most, if not all, people using the board, *and* that they demonstrate significant tangible value over the added cost of board complexity.

Most boards start with *Ready*, *Doing*, and *Done* columns, going from left to right. This simple layout works for the vast majority of cases, with little variation. The *Ready* column holds those items waiting to be worked on, the *Doing* column contains the work currently in progress, and the *Done* column consists of those items that have been completed.

Boards that include the full delivery cycle work similarly. They have a *Doing* column named for each phase. The main differences are with the *Ready* and *Done* columns. There is only one *Done* column at the end. Work that is completed in the middle of the board simply moves from the *Doing* state to the *Ready* state of the next required phase, such as *Dev* to *Ready for Test*. Figure 12.14 demonstrates this workflow board (where *Dev*, *Test*, and *Deploy* are *Doing* columns).

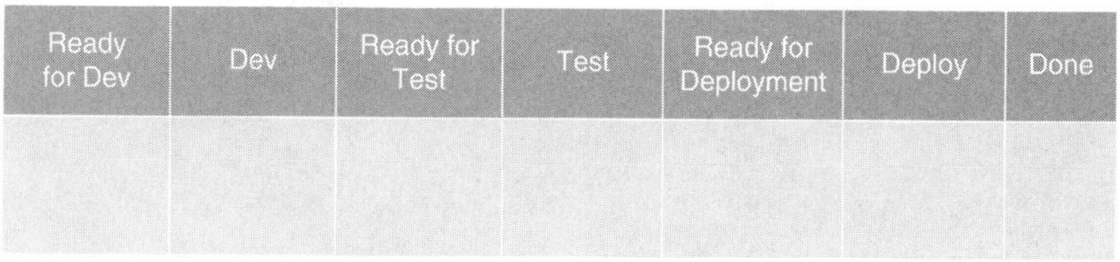

Ready for Dev	Dev	Ready for Test	Test	Ready for Deployment	Deploy	Done

Figure 12.14
Full delivery cycle board.

State Columns for Operations

Operational work often entails a few phases that are fundamentally different than typical software delivery work and thus affect the layout of the board. Operational-specific boards sometimes need a couple of additions. The first is a *Prequalified* column, placed at the very left before *Ready*.

The *Prequalified* column is to deal with many of the common quality problems associated with tasks that hit teams with operational responsibilities. For instance, tasks that say things like "move datacenter" are too large and opaque to be helpful. Such items need to be broken down into smaller, more manageable chunks before they can make their way to the *Ready* column. Similarly, a task that says "fix service" does not tell you what is wrong, whether it is urgent, or even if it is a production issue. The *Prequalified* column not only helps keep out of *Ready* the sort of garbage that might damage flow but also provides a spot to break work into reasonably sized pieces while gathering enough information to understand its priority and what needs to be done.

Having a *Prequalified* column can also provide a useful indication of how severe your task quality issues are. A high number of rejected tasks that hit it, or items that seem to take weeks to sort out, could mean there are disconnects upstream that need to be investigated. As you manage to tackle their root causes, you might find that you can eventually retire this column. Figure 12.15 demonstrates a workflow board with a *Prequalified* state column.

Figure 12.15
Operational workflow board.

Prequalified	Ready	Scheduled	In Progress	Done

As indicated in Figure 12.15, the second potential addition is a *Scheduled* column. This is used for work, such as maintenance events, that require a predetermined start date to coordinate resources and align with business and change requirements. The *Scheduled* column typically contains a master item with a date and/or time flag, with all the associated subtasks that need to be completed at that time. A good rule for this column is that all the work has been reviewed and is in sufficient shape to execute.

The *Scheduled* column is useful for resource scheduling. It can also be handy for spotting large peaks of work proactively, giving the team an opportunity to shuffle work around to reduce load.

If scheduled events are few and far between, or include only a small number of tasks with few required resources and little coordination, it is possible to do away with the *Scheduled* column and instead use color-coded task cards (covered in the upcoming "Task Cards" section) to indicate the special nature of the events. Practices such as automation, dark launching, and feature toggles can also help do away with much of the need for a *Scheduled* column.

Swim Lanes

Another configuration option for the board is to introduce horizontal rows, sometimes referred to as "swim lanes," as illustrated in Figure 12.16.

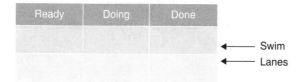

Figure 12.16
Swim lanes.

Swim lanes are typically used to divide work into different service classes. This is done so that very special types of work can be visually separated from everything else through a dedicated lane. The best way to think of a swim lane is as a visual representation of a team's bottlenecks. Each swim lane reduces both the capacity and flexibility within the team, creating resource islands that not only allow for misalignment across the team, but do so in a way that obscures the whole of what is trying to be accomplished. The more swim lanes, the more bottlenecks, and the more likely important work will get stuck behind a bottleneck.

For this reason, it is beneficial to keep the number of swim lanes to an absolute minimum. Most teams find that they can get by with no more than two swim lanes, one for normal work and the other for items that need to be expedited. The *Expedite* lane is for work that is so important that everything else needs to be dropped to take care of it. These work items hit suddenly without notice and, if not immediately jumped on and resolved, can severely damage the business. Few items should ever be placed in *Expedite*, and when something does, it should not be for very long The *Expedite* lane is organizationally costly and disruptive, and as such should only be used sparingly.

An expedited item should immediately include a "kaizen" (or improvement) retrospective review that occurs after the item has been handled. This acts as a good way to find out why the item was expedited, and figure out if there is any way to prevent it from happening again in the future. If the same event happens more than once, the problem needs to be escalated. The escalation of a task that happens more than once not only deters others from abusing the column to prioritize their work over everyone else's but also ensures that senior management is aware of the problem to help support any remediation that needs to be put in place. Such rigor not only helps find solutions that eliminate the need for anything to be expedited, but also helps everyone appreciate the impact that an item has on interrupting flow.

Avoid Building Swim Lane Superhighways

A common temptation of teams is to build lots of swim lanes. Some of the most common reasons teams do this is to divide work types into separate categories—for instance, splitting web server and backend work, or database and networking tasks. This is particularly appealing to inflexible specialist roles. Other times teams will create one swim lane for each person in the team. Building lots of swim lanes should be fiercely resisted, as they have a nasty tendency to create internal bottlenecks and dysfunction for very little gain.

Consider the following real-world example to better understand the problem. Suppose that you need to deliver to a customer a new application or service that requires infrastructure services such as network, storage, and a database to be set up for it to run on. Many would be tempted to break each of those tasks up across a board that looks like Figure 12.17.

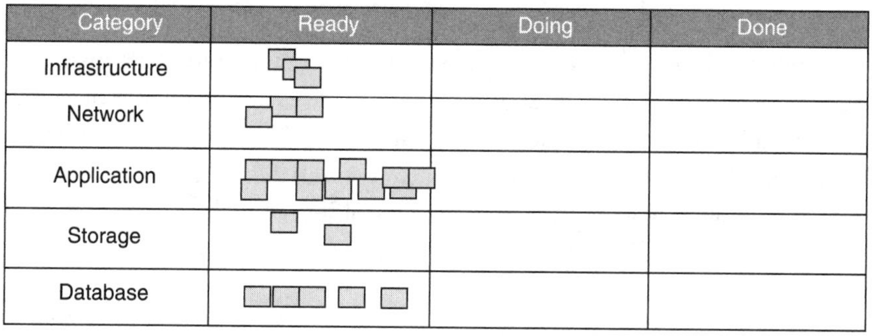

Category	Ready	Doing	Done
Infrastructure			
Network			
Application			
Storage			
Database			

Figure 12.17
Team swim lane example.

This layout might seem sensible, but there are two very obvious problems:

- **Work isn't balanced across the columns:** If there are separate people tied to each column, the ones stuck handling the application work may find themselves overwhelmed, all while the storage team sits around with nothing to do. Even if the storage team does go to help the application team, should they drop their application work whenever something appears in their swim lane?
- **How do you deal with dependencies across swim lanes?** This issue is far more challenging. For instance, everyone might be dependent upon an infrastructure ticket being completed before they can start working. There might be even more complicated flows between application, database, and storage where the interdependencies move back and forth between swim lanes. Not only is all of that lost, but so is clarity of the priorities and ordering of tickets across the swim lanes. Not only does managing that become a nightmare, but the value of the board itself becomes severely limited.

If work categories are important to you, you might be better off starting with a simple traditional board with two swim lanes and using colored tickets. That way, ordering and dependencies can be placed in the same swim lane, reducing confusion. Also, putting everyone in one swim lane reduces the potential for an "us vs. them" mentality within the team.

This isn't to say that you should never add a swim lane. Although doing so seldom makes sense, if you do introduce an additional swim lane, you must be vigilant in monitoring the overall flow of work across the board to see whether the swim lane accomplishes your goals without introducing dysfunction. If you do add another swim lane, you should accompany the addition with an action plan to try to change the conditions that require the added lane. This might include such things as cross-training, automation, or simply eliminating the work. This can give you the flexibility in the future to remove the swim lane in case it is causing problems.

Task Cards

The final piece of the board is the task card, which is typically a 3×5 paper card or sticky note used to write a task on. The task card should contain some sort of identifying information, a creation date to help with tracking cycle time, and potentially a short description of the task. Color coding the cards based on what type of a task each represents can be very helpful. Categorizing the task card can be done any number of ways, from specific product or project streams to work or skill types. One successful configuration is color coding by types such as "projects," "maintenance," "production changes," and "requests."

As mentioned earlier, tasks should be broken down into reasonably sized and logical chunks. Optimally, these tasks should be reduced down to that which can be done in no more than a day. Why a day? The cadence of activity within the operational world is fast and ever changing. Items that can't be done in a day tend to get interrupted and put aside for more urgent tasks, creating delays to that task and leaving partially done work lying around. Also, larger tasks tend to get stuck on the board, which reduces the sense that progress is being made, frustrating people and causing people to ask for status updates on the stuck item, a very common and nasty form of interrupt.

You'll likely find that the majority of operational tasks tend to be small enough that any one person can handle several in a day. If you find this is not the case, however, you should dig in to understand why. At times you might find that your environment has become so complex and difficult to work in that it is in danger of becoming completely unresponsive to the business. Under these circumstances, it is imperative to find ways to reduce environment and task complexity. This might include accompanying technical or organizational friction that needs to be streamlined or removed.

Another important thing to think about when creating tasks is to ensure that there is some ability to learn from the activity by answering the following questions:

- Why did we have to do it?
- Are there ways to improve it or make it go away?
- Is it clear what the target condition is behind it?
- Did it uncover some problem that we need to investigate further.

You shouldn't put any of this sort of information in the ticket unless it is particularly valuable. It is intended more to prime review and improvement activities later.

Preventing Dark Matter

Having to create a ticket for tiny tasks is still an issue with a workflow board. Most teams will find the friction to be far too high, even if they somehow overcome the challenge of being convinced of the value of capturing something so miniscule.

To reduce this friction, you should consider creating simple tally boards where each completed (*Done*) task becomes a simple mark on the board, as illustrated in Figure 12.18. You might have one board for restarts, another for password resets, another for simple cleanup jobs, and so on. The board can be as simple as a piece of paper on the wall next to the workflow board that anyone can add to. If you use a software tool, you can create a simple web page with a button that instantly creates and closes a ticket of that specific task type.

Figure 12.18

Example tally boards.

At the end of the week the tallies can be collected and added up. Numbers can help support further investigation or investment cases. Growth trends can provide an early indication of coming trouble. The most common result is that the team and management alike are surprised at the sheer size and scale of how often they have to deal with little tasks.

The Board of Many Problems

I frequently encounter teams that manage to get themselves into a mess when trying to roll out a workflow board. It is usually caused by the same mix of problems, whether it is too many columns, too many swim lanes, poor-quality tasks, poor board visibility, or poor management of work in progress (WIP). One team, however, memorably outdid themselves by having them all.

This team developed, tested, and operated internally built software. They decided to create a board that would capture all of the work that the team performed, from design, through development, test, and release, as well as operational support activities. Even though the team members were all co-located in the same office, they purchased an electronic tool under the guise that it made it easier to allow people to work at home. We were brought in when management became concerned that this "kanban thing" had been going for a while but seemed to be making little difference.

What I found was startling. While some team members wore multiple hats, each person tended to focus on a particular type of task. They decided to create a board where each team member had their own swim lane. They then created lots and lots of columns, including several for design tasks, one for development, one for building, one for each type of testing, and several different ones for various operational tasks. Tasks would be pushed onto the board by a manager into some random column, where they would then travel in various directions between different columns. It was not uncommon for a task to re-enter the same column several times or get stuck and sit in one place for weeks on end with no apparent progress. Work would bounce between swim lanes whenever tasks needed to be handed off to another person. While the team tried to institute WIP limits per column in each swim lane, most swim lanes had lots of WIP scattered across several columns. The worst part was that all of this was happening in the darkness allowed by the electronic tool.

While it was tempting to set fire to the whole thing and start again from scratch, I needed to make sure that the team first understood what a mess they had gotten themselves into. I first found a way to show them their board, in all 19 columns and 15 swim lanes of its glory. This was even more difficult to do than it sounds, and the software was only one of the many problems we faced.

Figure 12.19 illustrates the workflow board before attempting to simplify it.

Figure 12.19
The "before" workflow
board.

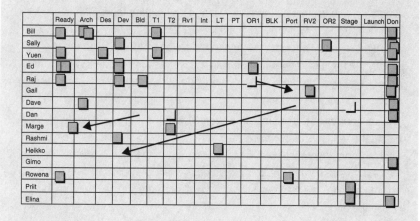

Figure 12.20 shows the workflow board after simplifying it.

Figure 2.20
The "after" workflow board.

Ready	Doing	Done

Once that objective had been accomplished, the team moved to a very simple physical board with three columns and two swim lanes. Anytime that anyone wanted to add a column or swim lane, they had to write up a proposal that detailed the advantages the addition would give the whole team. The advantages had to be clear and measurable. Penalties were introduced for any time that work cycled back and forth between the additional column or lane. This proposal would be voted on, and had to achieve unanimous approval. It would then be reviewed and voted on monthly.

A better mechanism was then put in place for creating tasks. We agreed upon a maximum working size that allowed for work to flow through the board more easily without introducing too much overhead. We also created a rule that all work had to start at the left of the board, and that no task could be moved into any column by anyone other than the person it had been assigned to.

These changes had an immediate effect. The full amount and types of work hitting the team suddenly became much more obvious. The team began to take far more ownership of the tasks assigned to them, and a sense of flow was established. While the team did occasionally play around with adding a column here and there, they still kept the board very simple, helping everyone in the end

Using the Board

The way that the board itself works is simple. Each team member grabs a work item that is in the *Ready* column that they are ready to work on and moves it into the *Doing* column. They then perform the task. When the task is complete, they move the work item to the *Done* column, marking on the task card the date that the work was completed. They then grab the next item in the *Ready* column to work on and start the process all over again.

It is that simple.

There might be some occasions where tasks come in and go straight to the *Doing* column. These are usually important activities that are either being expedited or, more likely, an additional related and unforeseen item a person handling a task has noticed and wants to quickly record and take care of. While important activities should not have to wait for a long time in the *Ready* column, it is important for tasks to not be pushed into *Doing* by someone other than the person who is taking on the task. Pushed tasks can cause interruptions and work in progress to build unnecessarily.

Watching tasks moving across a board is surprisingly satisfying. Seeing the completed work building up in the *Done* column both gives a sense that work is being done and allows the team to get a visual indication of the sheer amount of work that they are doing. As many operational tasks end up being small, expect it to be a sizeable pile. The board also works as a great public relations tool that helps others see what and how much is happening. It allows the team to improve their perceived responsiveness to their customers as well as spot and defuse moments when the team is being overwhelmed. As most IT work is often invisible, seeing lots of items moving across the board provides a great visual representation of what is really happening.

Seeing the Problems

It is inevitable that work will get stuck in the *Doing* column. There can be all sorts of reasons for it. Sometimes work will get blocked by an external dependency. Other times items will be far more complicated than they first appear, consuming far more time than was expected. People can also get interrupted by other work or life matters, causing tasks to get held up. Then there occasionally is an expedited item that flies by that forces work to be momentarily dropped. The power of the board is that all of these eventualities should create a visible effect that everyone can see.

I have employed some tips to handle these eventualities to keep the board moving. The first is to track task cycle time. Often this will be obvious, with one or more cards sitting stuck in one place. However, if you have a lot of work flying through, you might want to consider marking when the work items entered into the *Doing* column. By timestamping tasks as they move into the *Doing* column and again when they are moved to *Done*, even just at the granularity of date, you can start to spot those that took longer than normal to make their way through the workflow. This can provide clues to help diagnose and solve problems that exist in your environment. You may also find value in noting when items first arrive in the *Ready* column as well if you suspect certain tasks are sitting without any activity being performed on them for too long.

Another common challenge comes from tasks that become blocked. Blocked work happens all the time within Operations. There will often be tasks with external dependencies, including waiting for a new software build, data to be loaded, or a supplier to deliver hardware. Blocked work creates subtle yet important disruption in flow. Understanding when blockages happen, as well as their causes, is very important. Work that is blocked can be tagged with a bright-colored marker, such as a neon-colored Post-it Note stuck on top of a physical board or a visible highlight for an electronic one. These make blockages stand out, bringing attention that can help with removing impediments.

Some people may be tempted to move the task to a "Blocked" holding column in order to declutter the *Doing* column. They often feel this makes blocked tasks more obvious and searchable. This may even be inevitable with an electronic tool.

The problem with having this extra column is that it adds visual complexity to the board. While it makes it easy to see the number of blocked tasks, you might miss important details regarding their state. Are they partway done or yet to be started? Blocked tasks can easily happen in either or both situations, such as in the previous example regarding application, storage, and database work. What is worse, you will inevitably see blocked tasks getting shuffled back and forth between columns. This breaks a common board rule that tasks should rarely move backward across a board.

Tasks moving up and down the board in loops can give a false impression that more work is being completed than is actually the case. It also can break the continuity of tasks as they fit in the bigger picture of activities. This can make it more difficult to find the true nature of dependency chains and misordering of work pulled into the board. Figure 12.21 illustrates this scenario.

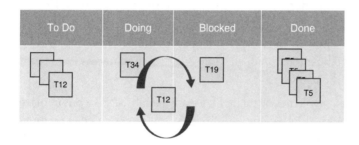

Figure 12.21
Blocked column state confusion.

If you are using a tool that makes it otherwise impossible to add a blocked state tag to a task, the holding column will need to be highly visible and carefully monitored. This is to ensure that everyone is aware of the situation to prevent tasks from being accidentally lost or left languishing, and to get help to remove any obstructions quickly.

Limiting Work in Progress

Busy teams that suffer from reactive work often face large piles of partially done work. Workflow boards will capture these piles, making them visible to everyone. In Lean circles this is referred to as *work in progress*, or *WIP*.

As many of us know WIP can build up for any number of reasons. The most common reason is task switching caused by reactive or poorly specified work coming in. Often teams get interrupted midstream through an activity, causing one to be dropped for another. Other times team members will try to multitask either when work items are being passed back and forth between teams or while waiting for a job to complete. If work is specified particularly badly, someone might even find that they have started a task only to have to kick it back so that it can be clarified or a raft of dependencies can be cleared before it can be picked up again.

Small amounts of WIP are inevitable. It is when WIP grows uncontrolled that it can wreck the flow of work in the team. Not only does work end up sitting around for a lot longer than it should, completion dates for WIP start to become increasingly unpredictable. As the pile of WIP gets larger, seeing and understanding what is going on becomes ever harder. All of this can make customers nervous, creating escalations that end up causing even more work to be interrupted, all while creating an unnecessary amount of extra stress on the team.

To thwart this problem, one tactic that many teams use is to put in place limits to the amount of work that can be in a progress, or *Doing*, column at any given time. These WIP limits are used to reduce task switching and work items from languishing partially done. Some teams go so far as to limit work items to one per person, eliminating the possibility of multitasking altogether.

Monitoring the amount of WIP is important. You may even find that conditions in your environment may favor establishing limits both to help protect the flow of work and to prevent team members from switching between several tasks. This can help shield the team from having to take on more work than they can sensibly complete.

Having overly strict WIP limits does introduce some significant dangers, however, especially in very dynamic operational environments. Many operational tasks are small by nature. It is not uncommon for someone to handle tens of 5 to 10 minute tasks while they are simultaneously monitoring a long-running task without encountering any problems. Enforcing strict WIP limits without first understanding the dynamics in the ecosystem could force more of the sorts of dysfunction that you are trying to avoid in the first place, whether it is in not recording work being done or creating yet another team division to shed everyday tasks to. Other problems such stringent WIP limits can create include having work repeatedly change state or be broken down into unnecessarily small pieces, all to work around the limit.

Maintaining situational awareness in an operational environment is far more valuable than limiting WIP. I tend to institute WIP limits only after we have noticed problematic patterns developing. More often than not I have found that they need to be enforced upon individuals with the propensity to take on far more than they can sensibly handle rather than seek help for the entire team. In those cases such tools can protect wannabe superheroes, often saving teams and careers.

The Limits of a Workflow Board

The board is a very important tool to put in place, but in fast-paced, dynamic environments it is not enough on its own. Without additional help, structure, and mechanisms to collectively better understand what is going on, work will continue to fly all over the place and chaos will continue. You will also need to work through other considerations, including how to keep everyone across the lifecycle aligned and improving in step with one another, as well as how best to handle the differences between delivery and operational work. Ignoring these considerations will result in only marginal improvements.

Managing the Board

The first important challenge to overcome is finding a way to keep the board and workflow maintained. While the board appears simple, it still requires some sort of oversight to ensure tasks enter the workflow correctly and do not get stuck for too long along the way. This includes not just stopping misprioritized work from jumping the queue, but also making sure tasks are an appropriate size and clarity. Without this, boards can become messy or inaccurately reflect what is going on.

Someone should also be regularly looking at the board holistically end-to-end to ensure that contextual information and subtle but important activity patterns are being captured and understood across the team. While managers can help, it is preferable to push this activity down into the team as a rotating duty as the *Queue Master*. Not only can the Queue Master accomplish these things far more effectively than a manager, but they can help prevent workflow from reverting to a push model while simultaneously strengthening the managerial escalation path for problems. Chapter 13, "Queue Master," explains this Queue Master role structure in more detail.

Managing Flow and Improvement

The team needs a natural cadence of sync points to fix any alignment issues, learn from each other, and improve. The workflow board itself does not do this alone. It must be supported by establishing a regular cycle of sync points dedicated to this purpose. Without it team members inevitably begin to drift, creating conflict, confusion, and rework.

Another related issue is that workflow boards focus on flow, making it unclear for how project-related activities might fit alongside the everyday flow. While such items can be put into the boards like any other set of tasks, scheduling and dependency management are not completely straightforward. This is especially the case for larger teams that handle multiple projects and releases simultaneously.

Fortunately, there are some effective ways for overcoming each of these limitations that I have worked out over many years of experimentation. The first we will cover are around the cycle itself. From there we will work through the various roles that hold it all together.

Summary

The best way to manage work flowing in and through a delivery team is to optimize for shared situational awareness and team learning. And the best way to do that is to use visual workflow boards that expose the work moving through the system. This enables the team to see trends that might create bottlenecks or overload the team. Watch out for work management approaches that focus on generic processes and "best practice" as they have a tendency to create distortions that hide information, curtail learning, and cause process friction that encourages people to work outside the process to accomplish their goals. Small tasks, or "dark matter," are also dangerous. These are tasks that require less effort to complete than what it takes to create a ticket to track it. The urge to not capture the task can hide problems and demand that consume team resources in ways that make it difficult to fix.

Workflow techniques such as kanban can help improve work visibility and awareness. It is also a great way to spot and remove bottlenecks and single points of failure, as well as to learn and improve.

Chapter 13
Queue Master

The only people who see the big picture are the ones who step outside the frame.

Salman Rushdie

Anyone who has worked in an active technical environment knows how difficult it can be to stay on top of everything that is going on. Work comes in from different directions, tasks are often fragmented or out of order, and objectives can be unknown or unclear. The reactive nature of the environment amplifies all of this confusion, obfuscating what is happening across the ecosystem.

Having a visual workflow can help. But if you have spent any significant time with a kanban board or other workflow mechanisms, you likely know that tasks require more than just being slotted into a task board or tracking tool. They need to be added in with sufficient context to help the team avoid errors, conflicts, and rework.

Some people might think that managers are a natural solution for this issue. However, they are usually not close enough to the actual day-to-day work to have enough context. If that is not challenging enough, routing all the work coming in through them can dangerously limit how much time managers are able to spend on important activities such as advocating for the team and bridging with the rest of the organization. Concerns about managerial work overload can lead to deeper management hierarchies to compensate, further increasing the sorts of handoffs that can damage or restrict information flow.

A far better approach is to have someone in the trenches manage the workflow entry point. Such an approach both overcomes the context, information flow, and learning problems that managers would face and limits the number of team members who are being interrupted. However, this approach must be implemented in a way that doesn't just create a context and learning problem somewhere else. It must also keep work flowing in a way that handles unpredictable events, maintains priorities, and spots dependencies that can block progress.

Fortunately, there is a strategy to do all of this and still help everyone retain their hands-on situational awareness. If executed well, it can create a means of uncovering useful patterns and help the team learn. Implementing this strategy requires creating a duty (rotating) role called the *Queue Master*.

An Introduction to the Queue Master

The Queue Master is perhaps one of the most essential and misunderstood roles for any dynamic technical environment. It is not a first-tier helpdesk function or a people management role. When it is working well, it can actually reduce the cycle time between when a request comes in and is completed.

The Queue Master arose in various incarnations in the early service delivery organizations that were trying to balance the need to maintain both high uptimes and respond rapidly to change. Ensuring all the work coming in was properly sorted and prioritized was a huge challenge, especially as an increasing number of tasks were reactive or unplanned. Most of the companies were also start-ups that could not afford to hire lots of staff. Instead, they needed some way of aligning priorities and identifying hidden blockers, bottlenecks, and dependencies, all while minimizing the number of interruptions hitting the larger team.

As described in Chapter 12, "Workflow," many delivery teams saw how work randomly entering the team was creating huge numbers of problems. Work duplication and collisions were common. Often team members felt so overloaded that they burned out and were unable to share what they were doing, let alone keep sight of the big picture of what was going on. As time went on, this began to detrimentally affect the ability to attract and retain talent, and with it service quality started to suffer.

Even those organizations that could afford staff often found that traditional approaches like establishing helpdesks, putting in place a tiered support model, or having a manager coordinator/project manager all seemed insufficient. They always struggled to be sufficiently responsive while also minimizing information loss.

I have found that tight and timely coordination requires the sort of immediate deeper context that can only be achieved by someone who also regularly performs the work. However, at the same time the person needed to not be so bogged down with work themselves that they could not maintain sufficient awareness across the service ecosystem. This combination was the only way that someone could effectively recalibrate priorities rapidly as necessary and readjust expectations smoothly to keep everything flowing.

Eventually, the team's continued experimentation resulted in establishing the Queue Master.

Role Mechanics

Figure 13.2
Role mechanics.

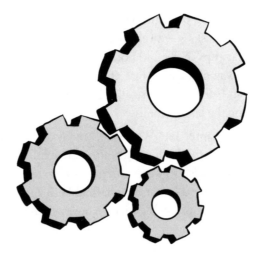

There are a number of role mechanics that are key to the success of the Queue Master. You may find some important additions that you need for your organization's circumstances. However, you need to be careful when making any material variations away from those covered in this section. It is easy for such changes to unintentionally damage the underlying intent of maintaining situational awareness and flow within the team.

Let's walk through each of the role mechanics to understand them a bit better, as well as why they are important.

Rotation

Perhaps the rule that is most important to the success of the Queue Master is that the duties *must* rotate across members of the team performing the work. Optimally this is done with a weekly cadence.

While at first many team members might find taking on a duty role to be disruptive to their own work, rotating the role at the natural cadence of a working week has a number of distinct benefits. The first is that it ensures the Queue Master maintains sufficient context with the work and team performing it. Active team members are exposed to the inner workings of the infrastructure, the software and services, and the people who manage them.

Figure 13.3
Regularly rotating the
Queue Master role is
important.

This exposure provides a level of insight that managers or anyone else not directly immersed in it lacks.

Rotating at a natural cadence also gives everyone a chance to step out of their day-to-day work and properly see what is occurring across the ecosystem. I cannot state strongly enough how eye-opening this can be. Most of us forget how easy it is to lose sight of the big picture when we are buried in our work. Stepping back from it to see what is going on across a typical work cycle not only helps us to see what is happening, but helps the team understand and resolve problems that damage team effectiveness.

Every time I have put in place the Queue Master rotation, I have had at least one of the team who was most skeptical of the idea come to me on day three or four of their first rotation exclaiming how they now understood why the role was so important, detailing how much crazy stuff they never realized was going on that needed to be fixed.

Rotating the role also helps everyone on the team start to see and really appreciate the knowledge and effort other team members are contributing. They will often see team members struggling with some problem or dysfunction that they can help with. They will also remember and appreciate when they are helped by another team member who takes on Queue Master duty. Together, this builds team unity and fosters further collaboration.

Rotation also brings value to the Queue Master role itself. The differing perspectives that each person brings to the role can uncover hidden problems and solutions. Rotation also reduces the likelihood that those in the role will get inured to the sorts of dysfunction that can so often damage team effectiveness. If nothing else, the shift in exposure to another perspective of the ecosystem is likely to spur people to question the status quo.

Rotation greatly reduces the chance of Queue Master specialization taking root in the team. The last thing any technical team needs is yet another specialization that reduces the flexibility of the larger team.

Entry Management

Figure 13.4
Entry management.

To be effective, the Queue Master must sit at the point where all non-incident work officially enters the team. This includes all work, from requests coming in from other teams to work internally generated by the team. The dual intent of this entry management is to ensure the clarity and priority of the work and to capture cross-organizational nuances that might otherwise be missed.

Entry management achieves a number of objectives. For one, it makes all work trackable and eliminates the chances of any assumptions cropping up that can be missed along the way. It also prevents people from misrouting tasks to any random person in the team, thus reducing interrupts and misprioritization of work. Another benefit of routing everything through the Queue Master is that they can act as a quick filter that helps limit garbage from entering the workflow. This reduces the chances of team members getting partial or incorrect information, or a misprioritized task hitting the team directly.

This does not mean that routing should be a heavyweight process, or that it is the Queue Master's job to write up all the tasks themselves. Routing should be extremely light touch whenever possible. In some cases, particularly for internal team work, routing might be as simple as someone mentioning that they are adding a task to help clarify or add some important missing piece of work. As for writing tasks, the one requesting the work should write and submit the task whenever possible. The Queue Master can, if necessary, then follow up to add any missing information. This reduces any information loss.

All of this helps prevent the clogging up of the workflow. Most people might feel that their request is both important and obvious, even when it is not. This checking and sorting ensures that everything goes in the right place with enough information that it doesn't get lost, misprioritized, or lead to unnecessary confusion. Critically urgent tasks will still always go into the *Expedite* column. The Queue Master can and should provide background and some queue reordering for anything else that might still be important or is a dependency to something that is yet not worthy of being expedited.

The best way to prevent unnecessary task rejection is for the team to proactively create and tune templates and examples of what a requester minimally needs to include in a ticket for it to be acceptable. This will go a long way in reducing both frustration and rework. Training and outreach should also be available to educate others across the organization. This will help stop the inevitable unhelpful tickets such as "The service is broken. Please fix," "Need some software installed," or the all-time favorite "Is the thingy backed up?"

Sorting and Dependency Discovery

As unplanned work tends to be a regular occurrence for service delivery teams, chances are good that work will come in that bypasses people like managers, project/program managers, and architects who can call out any hidden dependencies or ordering conflicts. To solve this, the Queue Master regularly goes through the queues in search of such problems to proactively help the team avoid any unnecessary blocks or rework that they might cause.

Having someone with intimate knowledge of the ecosystem do this has the added benefit of also catching any conflicts that might have been unknown or unclear to managers and architects. Sometimes this can be done in a lightweight way, such as simply flagging a conflict to the rest of the team to be aware of. In the case that the conflict is more serious, the Queue Master can send the task back to the requester for clarification or escalate to management for help.

To deal with all of this sorting, the default state of any work coming into the team is typically considered *Unqualified*, at least until the Queue Master has a chance to take a quick look at it to determine whether or not it is suitable for the board. Most of the time the Queue Master will determine the work item is fine and move it into the *Ready* column on the board. If, however, a task is just plain wrong or misdirected, the Queue Master can reject it and hand it back to the requester with an explanation.

Likewise, if a task is unclear, too big, or open-ended, the Queue Master has an opportunity to send the item back to the requester to clarify and improve the request before it has a chance to cause any problems with the team. One method for doing this is to alert the requester, then flag the task and place it in a *Clarification* queue in the workflow.

I have found that tracking both clarifications and rejections can help the team remain aware of what is going on while also helping them spot and understand if there are patterns or sources that are causing such problems that need to be addressed. This helps the team to focus only on the sorts of template, education, and process improvements that will make a difference in reducing problem occurrence over time. This improves their cycle time, but also reduces the frustration and workloads on the requester and Queue Master. It helps minimize any problems or misunderstandings that somehow make their way down to those performing the work, and does so without throwing in excessive processes for no real reason.

Improved entry management by the Queue Master also has the benefit of reducing the chances of work unevenly flowing across the team. Lean practitioners know that uneven flow creates waste. By ensuring that tasks enter in only through the Queue Master, team members avoid being put in a position where they have to choose between creating conflict with requesters and taking on too much work. This reduces team pressure.

Dark Matter Handling

Figure 13.5
Getting Dark Matter under control is a critical role of the QM.

One of the powerful benefits of insisting that all noncritical work must go through the Queue Master is that it becomes a single point to receive and handle all Dark Matter requests. This ensures that they are captured and tracked to aid in understanding their sources and occurrence.

Redirecting Dark Matter to one central place can be tough to do at first for both the organization and the team. However, doing so is worth all the grumbling and minor inconvenience. Not only is recording the tasks important for understanding the source of and sizing the demand for various activities, but offloading trivial tasks to one place reduces the number of interrupts that otherwise would pepper the team. *This reduces errors and helps improve responsiveness and flow.*

Maintaining Flow

The role of Queue Master does not end with work entering the workflow. In fact, many of the most valuable Queue Master contributions occur by keeping the focus on the bigger picture. One of these contributions is maintaining the flow of work.

For instance, not all tasks that reach the *Ready* column in the workflow board necessarily deserve the same treatment. While management, the product owner, or even individual engineers often do most of the prioritization work, there are some cases where the Queue Master may need to do some reordering. This is usually due to either sudden shifts in priorities or to ensure that one or more key prerequisites get completed to avoid workflow blockages. When a Queue Master does this, they will usually alert the team of the situation, either in the daily standup or via chat, to make sure that any priorities or dependencies are clear and understood.

If a task requires special handling because the work item requires either specific skills or specific context, the Queue Master can make sure that these handling requirements are clearly marked. This will aid in informing the team when the task is ready to be pulled in, and can help with tracking as it moves across the workflow. As a team matures and the Service Engineering Lead role (covered in Chapter 9, "Service Delivery Maturity and the Service Engineering Lead") becomes better established, the team itself frequently becomes the biggest source of such tasks. They are usually related to delivery tasks created and marked by the SE Lead to help with tracking.

While everyone is responsible for the board, there are times when there are items that can languish in a column. The Queue Master actively monitors the board to spot them and remove any blocks or potential problems that might be preventing them from progressing. The Queue Master also looks for large build-ups of work in progress, especially those caused by unexpected problems that develop.

The Queue Master uses the daily standup, as well as the team's retrospective, as a way to bring up issues the team members encounter. The Queue Master can ask team members for details, as well as help to remove the issues and restore flow. The Queue Master can also work with the team to understand the issues' root causes and find ways to prevent them from happening again in the future. Together, these ensure that work does not languish unnecessarily and that team members become overwhelmed with work.

Pattern Recognition

Figure 13.6
Patterns are useful for quick recognition.

One of the major advantages of having a Queue Master tasked with actively surveying the workflow from the entry point through to completion is that they will start to see patterns emerge that can go a long way toward helping the team improve.

Such patterns begin with the demand coming in itself. There is always subtle yet important interplay between the types of tasks coming in, those asking for them to be performed, and larger developments taking place across the ecosystem. This context is valuable, especially in environments where a significant segment of demand is not otherwise easy to plan for in advance. If you can understand the source of the demand, its frequency, and what might drive it, you can begin to predict when it might occur again in the future. It also gives insight into similar requests, and similar requesters, that helps you establish larger patterns of demand. This can aid in resource planning, as well as sizing investment return from standardizing and automating the task, or eliminating its root cause.

Similarly, you can also start to understand and track dependency patterns between tasks. If a particular task enters the flow, you know that there is a good possibility that those same dependent tasks might follow. Understanding these dependency patterns can help preempt additional requests and improve team responsiveness and understanding. This reduces workflow noise and provides useful automation targets. It also aids coordination.

Being able to uncover demand patterns also provides useful clues about what the requester is trying to accomplish with the request. This is important because not everyone shares or is clear about the outcome they are trying to attain. It is not uncommon for people to make requests that, due to solution bias or some other misunderstanding, will not achieve what they are after. The Queue Master is uniquely positioned to notice such discrepancies and flag them for further investigation.

Patterns also exist in the workflow itself. There might be tasks that take far longer than they should, require rework, or have a large number of handoffs. There are also times when the Queue Master might notice that certain tasks can only be done by one person or a small subset of the team, creating a dangerous bottleneck that indicates knowledge and awareness might not be flowing evenly across the team.

Each of these patterns should be noted by the Queue Master and discussed with the rest of the team through the various syncing and improvement mechanisms discussed in Chapter 14, "Cycles and Sync Points." Queue Masters who are great at pattern matching can make a big difference for a team. As more people take on the role, people start to share and find patterns based on their experiences. This strengthens the collective mind, providing fertile ground for innovative solutions to challenging issues.

Office Hours

It is important to point out that, unlike a typical on-call rotation, the Queue Master generally is not a role that must be available 24 hours a day. Nothing the role does is so urgent that it must always be attended to. Even if there happen to be off-hours requests that are so critical that they need immediate attention, they can easily be routed to on-call.

Figure 13.7
The Queue Master role
needs to be available for
daily demand peaks.

For that reason, it is worthwhile to set the expectation that the Queue Master will be around and available at a set time period during the business day. Usually Queue Master work begins after the daily standup and ends at a reasonable set time each day that corresponds to the lull of task requests at the end of the workday.

Besides preventing burnout, establishing office hours also makes it obvious when work hits the team at unreasonable times. This doesn't mean that there shouldn't be a mechanism for extremely critical work that happens in the off-hours. In fact, if something so urgent comes in that addressing it cannot wait until the next day, it should be treated as a production incident. This does several things. It ensures that it will get immediate attention. It also ensures that the request is subsequently reviewed to see if there is a genuine need that has been missed that requires a change or even a new tool in order to address it.

Finally, and most importantly, raising an off-hours request as an incident can help requesters consider the urgency of their request. This allows for true problems to be accounted for and addressed in more sustainable ways.

"Follow the Sun" Queue Mastering

Figure 13.8
For distributed orgs, the QM might need to rotate between offices during the day.

The one challenge to office hours is if your organization has technical teams six or more time zones away. Optimally, you should divide service responsibilities into self-contained parts that can all be handled locally. However, there are some cases where either this is unrealistic or cross-team coordination and awareness are so important that there is a daily need to ensure alignment.

In such cases you may have to consider having a "follow the sun" Queue Master setup. In this model, there would be at best two and no more than three Queue Masters, each separated by at least six time zones, to handle work during the core hours of their geographically distant location.

While I have successfully used the "follow the sun" model at several organizations, it is far from easy. A lot of context needs to be shared between each regional Queue Master to maintain alignment. I have found that this can be done by having the larger team try to do the following:

- Think carefully about how work is organized across the delivery team. Often you can keep certain closely coupled work types together over a given cycle. This reduces the number of handoffs, and thus context overhead, required to maintain alignment and minimize rework. I still recommend rotating these "type" clusters from time to time to avoid creating bottlenecks, but doing so at natural cycle breakpoint.

- Have as much communication as possible go over a globally shared chat channel. The transcript will add a lot more context than what can sensibly be put into a ticket.
- Have one of the Queue Masters for the cycle take the "lead" or primary position to help with coordination. Try to rotate which location's Queue Master takes the lead so that everyone feels included.
- The Queue Masters need to synchronize at least daily over voice/video chat with each other. They should also share notes in a shared document. These are particularly important if you must have three Queue Masters. Even if time zones are far apart, you will likely need to get all of them together at least twice (usually toward the beginning and then at the very end) to synchronize and avoid too much regional drift.

Sync Point Management

Maintaining situational awareness, learning, and improvement all require there to be a certain amount of alignment of the team. There are lots of mechanisms that you can use to do this, from wikis and document repositories to chat rooms, standups, pairing, demos, meetings, and just working in the same location and chatting from time to time. Each has its advantages and disadvantages, which is why I have dedicated an entire chapter (Chapter 14, "Cycles and Sync Points") to talk through patterns that have worked well in organizations I have worked. In them, the one common thread that I have found is that it is extremely helpful to have one person making sure that they happen. The best-placed person for that is the Queue Master.

The Queue Master will be exposed to the chaos at a high level, meaning that they should be better placed to see problems that others are living with but might be too close to see. By being the one in charge of the sync points, the Queue Master can help draw out the deeper details from others. This helps people get a better perspective and understanding of what is going on, helps build situational awareness, helps improve team collaboration, and even helps those in the heat of a situation to step back and look more objectively.

Other Work When on Duty

One challenge of a busy Queue Master cycle is that it might not give the person holding the role enough time to handle their normal day-to-day and project responsibilities. Like being on-call for production support, Queue Master responsibilities take precedence over just about everything else. This means that any other activities that the person has must either be transferred to someone else during the cycle or wait until that person has available capacity to continue.

This approach might seem extremely disruptive at first. However, as the Queue Master starts to make things visible enough that they can be worked on and improved, most can find a good balance between their rotation and their existing work.

One important thing that everyone should keep in mind is that the ability of the Queue Master to reduce the noise that otherwise would interrupt the team is of immense value. It means that the team members can complete their work without interruption, improving overall team flow throughput. Team members are also far more likely to share details about the work they are doing if they might need others to jump in to pick up the slack from time to time. This further builds team situational awareness and flexibility.

The cyclic rotation of the Queue Master role means the period is temporary and that activities can be planned to work around it. Over time as the workflow begins to settle, even this disruption will greatly lessen.

Typical Day in the Life of a Queue Master

Let's take the look at the typical day in the life of a Queue Master to better understand what the job entails and how it is expected to interact with the team.

It was Ed's week to assume the Queue Master role. He was glad that Simon had been on rotation the previous week. Simon was good at making sure all the work in the board was clear enough for everyone and that there were no nasty WIP jams to sort out. Simon was also the best at keeping the board free from the giant and ill-defined tasks like "Scale the Service" that sometimes came from the Product team. Simon was great at finding out what the underlying concerns were so that the team could effectively respond.

Ed's day began by taking a good look at the workflow board to see if there were any issues that had cropped up over the evening. He could see that Dave was still struggling with a couple of pieces of project work. It was worthwhile to ask about it in the standup. There was also a high-priority, time-sensitive task that the Business Intelligence team mentioned they would need soon that the team should be aware of.

After scanning the board, Ed checked the team's chat transcript to see if there was anything interesting before the standup. The standup always was held at 9:45 a.m. to help the team get in, organized, and caffeinated before kicking off the day. Besides the normal chatter there had been a bit of an issue with one of the feed services overnight. Sally had already dropped him a note that she and Simon might have some cleanup work to do that she would make sure to cover in the standup.

Dave then came around to chat quickly about his project. He noted that he was going to load up the board with a few more items, some that he needed to perform and a couple of others that other team members could do if they coordinated with him first to make sure there were no conflicts. They agreed that Dave would note them using a big orange D.

When 9:45 came around, just about everyone was huddled around the board. Because Sally worked late the previous night, she videoed in so that she could catch a little bit more sleep before the day got rolling. Ed started.

"OK, folks. Remember that to keep things quick we only talk through stuff that either happened yesterday or is going to happen soon that you think everyone ought to know about, along with a quick blurb on any problems you are having. Let's go around. I will be last."

After they were finished going around, Ed went through the workboard quickly, noting which of the new tasks in the *Ready* column were high priority. Despite Dave's and Sally's problems, there didn't seem to be any reason to be concerned about the flow becoming a problem, so they ended the standup.

When Ed returned to his desk, there were already a handful of Dark Matter items and a couple of new work items waiting for him. Seeing that the work items weren't urgent, Ed quickly knocked out the Dark Matter and added to the tallies. The automation that they had put in for self-service environment rebuilds and restarts was already a huge help. From the counts it was starting to look like there were some access management corner cases that needed to be more deeply investigated. He knew that Elise was already looking at the wider problem as part of her Tools & Automation role, but the team needed to make sure any solution wouldn't create an even bigger problem that caused them to lose control or awareness of what was going on.

Ed noticed that one of the items was a request for an SE Lead for a new initiative. He needed to reach out to the lead of the initiative to get a better understanding of what was needed. Was a new delivery team being built, new operational functionality that needed to be built, someone to take a deeper cross-coordination role, or something else? Most teams already had their embedded leads and no one was due to rotate teams yet. He pinged the lead and they agreed to chat later in the afternoon.

The day was relatively calm so far, so Ed pulled in a task from the Ready column and started working on it. Then, just as he was completing it there was another big production incident. Seeing that Sally needed help, Ed reached out to some of the relevant development teams to help make sure they were aware and able to engage quickly. As Simon was also dragged into the incident, Ed alerted the team he was working with about what was happening. He looked at the board and noticed that some of the upcoming work that Dave was going to be pulling in was in the affected area. He knew that Dave was aware of the problem, but made a quick note on the items to remind him. He then went back to keep track of the progress of the incident, offering to lend a hand whenever needed.

As the end of office hours approached, Ed finished a few more Dark Matter items and reviewed some additional work items that had come in. One was from the Product team that just said "more service instances." Sighing, Ed rejected it and noted that he would reach out to the requester on making sure there was a good understanding of what was driving the request so that the right things happened.

Ed reviewed the board again, making some notes on what he had seen. Dave had managed to clear his issue, but it was clear that the problem that Sally was encountering was likely going to turn into a much bigger problem. There were already a bunch of items that were put on the board from it, including some significant configuration changes that would likely impact other initiatives going on. Seeing that, Ed reached out to Sally and they determined that it was too big to be covered in tomorrow's standup and needed a longer discussion before the weekly Retrospective. Sally agreed to arrange the deeper discussion with the right people. She would loop Ed in both so that he was aware and so that he might be able to cover for her if there was another incident.

When the clock hit 4:45 p.m, Ed alerted everyone that they had 15 minutes remaining to submit Queue Master requests for the day. There was always a flurry of requests as people tried to get in beforehand, most of which could wait until tomorrow to tackle. Ed knew that tomorrow was going to be an even busier day, especially if the production problems continued. Some of the folks with their Service Engineering Lead hats on wanted to do some deeper coordination work on upcoming tasks. Hopefully they would know enough from Sally by tomorrow to know how likely things might need to shift around.

Queue Master Rollout Challenges

While the value of the Queue Master becomes increasingly obvious over time, it often seems like a struggle to get it established. The challenges always seem to follow a familiar pattern. This section describes some of the main challenges along with some strategies to work through them.

Team Members Don't See the Value

The first pushback most teams see is that most team members at first simply do not see the value of the Queue Master. Everyone is already extremely busy, so the idea of messing around with the way that work is handled sounds like another set of useless and cumbersome steps that will further strain the team.

The main intent of the Queue Master role is to build a better understanding of the patterns of work hitting the team so that the team can find faster, easier, and ultimately more effective ways of delivering the outcomes that matter. Team members often think that they already know what is going on and simply need more resources. Yet their awareness naturally narrows to their own work and the parts of the ecosystem that directly impact it.

This narrowing, along with not consistently having enough time to assemble enough of the right compelling evidence to convince others to invest and try out new things, can slow the speed of improvements. This can become increasingly frustrating and demoralizing.

Team members will often give the role a chance if they can be shown and convinced that the Queue Master is a faster and more effective way to capture and articulate the problems the team faces in a way that can help them get the support they need for improvements. Fortunately, it does not usually take too many cycles to open everyone's eyes to all sorts of ways the role can facilitate huge improvement gains.

More Traditionally Minded Managers Thwarting Rollout

Sometimes the team is more than happy to try something different, but there is resistance to do so from a more traditionally minded manager who feels that they are somehow losing control. They might feel uncomfortable with delegating many of the responsibilities they see as under their purview. These managers might be particularly concerned with some of their more junior team members handling the role.

For those managers, the positioning needs to be turned around to show that the Queue Master and workflow are there to make their lives easier. Unless the working ecosystem is in the Obvious realm (as discussed in detail in Chapter 5, "Risk"), it is highly likely that they already feel like their world is somewhat out of control. The workflow and Queue Master put the job of indicating what is going on in the hands of the people who are most likely to know. As the workflow is for the team, it and the Queue Master can help the manager see where there might be problems that need to be addressed, and help them build cases for a change in direction or more resources from the business. As the team becomes more successful, the manager can be more outward facing, further helping the team and their own careers.

One way to overcome this obstacle is by not trying to introduce the Queue Master role with everyone in the rotation all at once. Instead, begin with some of the more experienced team members, possibly with some experienced coaching help, to ease in the role. This not only helps everyone, including managers, get the most out of workflow and its learning and feedback mechanisms but also provides them with a better understanding of the role, why it is being implemented, and what everyone can do to improve it.

The case for project managers is similar. They are one of the key links to make sure that cross-team coordination is happening, and that work being performed is moving the organization toward the target outcomes of the project or program they are running. The Queue Master helps them to spot potential conflicts, problematic ambiguity, as well as resource constraints and general problems before they blow up the project.

Pushy Queue Masters

I have seen instances where Queue Masters see themselves as a sort of "boss for the week." When this happens they try to push work onto team members and *push* it through the workflow. This goes explicitly against the intent of both the role and the workflow mechanism. Work needs to get *pulled* through the workflow. The Queue Master's role is to help ensure that the priorities, ordering, and needs of the work items are clear. They can point out problems and help unblock work, but outside of keeping people within the rules of the workflow, they are *not* there to tell people what to do or how to do it.

Junior Team Members as Queue Masters

Most people are at least a little uncomfortable with the Queue Master role at first. It is a new role to them, and they still need to become familiar with its ins and outs. This is especially the case with less experienced junior team members. They are going to be put into a situation where they need to qualify incoming work, lead sync points, and ask more senior staff for guidance. This role can be tough and far more prone to mistakes. Sometimes junior team members might feel like they are facing a fire hose-like flow of work hitting the team that seems impossible to overcome.

For this reason, the more experienced people on the team should initiate the Queue Master role first. As everyone becomes more familiar with the role, junior people can shadow a Queue Master rotation, then flip it and have the more experienced person shadow the junior person as they take a turn at it. Once there has been a successful rotation, the junior person is included in the rotation. A buddy system (regardless of seniority level) is also helpful to help sort out questions. Eventually, everyone should be onboarded and helping everyone else.

The Timid Queue Master

The team struggled at first with the Queue Master role. They had been fighting a long time against the constant rain of work that was being pushed their way. It took them a while to stop allowing people to grab any ops person who happened to be around. That was tough, and a lot of developers and business people complained about having to always go to the Queue Master at first. But over time perseverance prevailed. The steady reduction of interrupts certainly helped the team get through more work faster. It also reduced the number of mistakes they made.

Some team members were initially skeptical of the value of capturing all the work coming in. Many thought that little tasks only came from little problems. The environment was so frenetic that there would be little chance of catching a potential problem before it became big and explosive. But the Queue Master had already managed to catch a couple of problematic items. One was from a new service that increasingly needed to be restarted. The Queue Master found that there was a bug that caused the service to stop under heavy load. Had it not been caught, it would have crashed the primary production service when the new marketing campaign went live.

It had been a bit rough for those who had taken on the QM hat. They had smartly started by rotating the role across some of the more senior members of the team. Eliza, who had been at the company for years, felt overwhelmed at first by the sheer number of tasks coming in. It took her a couple of days to realize that she wasn't expected to handle them all herself. She just had to make sure that they were clear, reasonably sized, prioritized correctly, and didn't conflict with anything else on the board before entering the workflow. This took almost no time now as everyone figured out how to use the new task template. Any problems were either kicked back to the requester or sorted by the team and Sally, the manager. This allowed Eliza to spend most of her rotation handling Dark Matter tasks and looking out for interesting patterns.

Eventually, the team got into the rhythm and started to widen the rotation out to the more junior members. One of these was Matt, who had originally been brought in for his great Unix knowledge. Even though he was comfortable enough to crack jokes and be the life of the party in the team chat room, he was extremely shy and quiet in person. He struggled to look anyone in the eye and was known to hide behind boxes in the hallway to avoid face-to-face conversation with anyone.

When it became Matt's turn for Queue Master, everyone was concerned. Could he handle the constant barrage of tasks? Would he hide under his desk to avoid the inevitable person coming by to ask for a service restart? Was his limited familiarity with the web frontend going to cause problems with the workflow?

The team never left anyone to sink or swim all alone. They knew letting one person fail could crush the rest of the team. Rashmi, one of the other senior team members with whom Matt had frequently played video games, offered to help Matt out. She shadowed him at first and let him know she was always there to answer any questions if he got stuck. Sally reminded Matt that she was always just a few steps away in case he needed help pushing back on a misprioritized or unclear task.

The cycle came, and Matt took on the role. He was terrified at first, but Rashmi and the team helped him through the rough patches. He spotted an interesting pattern of requests to change a particular server configuration that he was able to incorporate in the new operating system builds. He also learned a lot more about the web frontend. In the end, while the weeks he was made Queue Master were by far his least favorite, he knew it helped the team. It also gave him a new appreciation for the way that things worked around him. He even learned a few neat things as well.

Queue Masters Who Struggle to Lead Sync Points

Some people are shy, introverted, or just generally uncomfortable with bringing attention to themselves. Some simply do not want to be put in a position where they feel responsible for the success of the team. That is certainly understandable. Yet, it is important for everyone to have their turn at the Queue Master role, both to take part in helping the team and to get a chance to take a step back and see firsthand the dynamics across the service ecosystem. It is also critical that someone act as the lead to help bring the rest of the team together for the various sync points that occur during the Queue Master cycle, and the Queue Master is the best placed to do so.

As with junior team members, it is worthwhile for the team to help those uncomfortable Queue Mastering to build confidence. There are a number of ways to help the uncomfortable run sync points. There can be some shadowing by a senior member, much like Rashmi did with Matt in the sidebar story. The team can construct some simple templates for running the various meetings. There are some details in Chapter 7, "Cycles and Sync Points," that can help here. The team can also provide some constructive feedback and encouragement along the way. As the team should be participating in all the sync points, this should be fairly easy to do.

Above all, it should never be forgotten that the team is only successful if everyone is able to pitch in and give their best.

Summary

Like the Service Engineering Lead, the Queue Master is a critical role for helping improve situational awareness across the delivery organization, and everyone in the team should rotate through the role. It ensures that the workflow works well and helps the team learn and improve.

Chapter 14

Cycles and Sync Points

If we do not hang together, we shall surely hang separately.

Thomas Paine

Those of us delivering and managing services in increasingly complex and dynamic ecosystems have likely discovered that conditions can change without warning, swiftly rendering our best-laid plans obsolete. This is bad enough when it happens to one person. It can be catastrophic when it affects the awareness and alignment across the entire team.

Having a visual workflow, along with the Queue Master and Service Engineering Lead, does help expose emerging changes and events. However, without some mechanisms in place to make sure that everyone becomes aware of a changed condition so they can adjust, reflect, and improve, inevitably someone will miss out and be left behind.

The best way to establish this shared awareness is to do so with a set of communication mechanisms that brings everyone together. In order to minimize disruptiveness, the mechanisms should align with the rhythms of life. Following these natural flows and cycles goes a long way toward turning them into natural habits that reduce the level of interruption and misalignment that more traditional mechanisms cause.

This chapter will walk through the mechanisms I've found work well in the service delivery space. They not only augment those mechanisms that we have already covered, but also provide the investigation and learning space necessary for implementing and improving the instrumentation, automation, and governance mechanisms covered in subsequent chapters.

Inform, Align, Reflect, and Improve

Unless your ecosystem is full of arsonists bent on seeking glory through disorder, chances are that you and your team want to know two things:

- Are you making the right decisions to achieve the target outcomes?
- How can you improve to make both your decision making and actions more effective?

Making effective decisions can be surprisingly difficult. It isn't enough to know something. To guide action toward a desired result, you need to have just enough context about the dynamics of the situation at hand (your *informed* situational awareness) to match with relevant knowledge, either in the form of experience or knowledge resources that are easily accessible.

Improving your decision-making abilities requires a further step that involves taking the end result of any decision you made and comparing it to what was expected. If these do not align, you have to figure out (or *reflect* upon) what caused the misalignment.

Any number of events can cause misalignments that can degrade decision making, including:

- Having material flaws in your understanding of your experience
- Having outdated or incorrect situational awareness at the time of the decision
- Not having timely access to appropriate knowledge resources
- Lacking availability of sufficiently suitable execution resources
- Using process or execution mechanisms that contain too much friction (in the form of speed, variability, or reliability)

Avoiding these problems becomes more complicated with other actors in the ecosystem. Whether you are depending upon their actions or merely affected by them, any shortfall in shared awareness or alignment can cause collisions or muddy any understanding of the actual effects and accuracy of your decisions.

To counter such tendencies and maintain alignment, organizations have tried a number of different strategies. These span from trying to control alignment through a top-down process to leaving it to the team to self-organize and figure it out themselves. Each has some limitations that are worthwhile to quickly explore.

Top-Down Alignment Control Approach

The most commonly used is the top-down control approach. It relies upon direct orchestration of the work that staff performs using a mix of scheduling methods, along with process and method controls that are managed by some sort of project, program, or staff manager.

People rely on the top-down control approach because it is simple, provides a sense of control that is alluring, and aligns with traditional management thinking. It also can work in ordered environments, as defined in Chapter 5, "Risk." However, top-down control depends so heavily upon both a reliably predictable dynamic between the cause and effect of actions and the ability of the person managing the work to maintain a clear and accurate level of situational awareness across the ecosystem that any slip of either can cause a cascading failure. If this were not bad enough, this approach also counts on the manager-type to find and correct any faults and drive improvements through the team. Either of these is difficult when your awareness degrades. It also does not help that such failures also tend to degrade trust between management and the team.

Alignment Through Iterative Approaches

Moving across the spectrum are the more Agile-style iterative approaches, whether in the form of more cyclical approaches like Scrum or more flow-based approaches like Kanban. Rather than trying to control everything centrally, iterative approaches accept that not everything in the ecosystem is going to be clear and instead rely upon the fact that those performing the work likely will have the most up-to-date contextual information in the immediate area they are in. These approaches employ methods that try to optimize the flow of this contextual information across the delivery team to allow the team to self-organize, make informed decisions, and make improvements themselves to deliver more effectively.

The Scrum Sprint Model

The standard Scrum model leverages frequent cyclical mechanisms to align team work to customer objectives, while also allowing for work coordination to take place more tactically at daily standups. These cyclical mechanisms are then supported by both the show-and-tell at the end of the sprint, in order to get feedback from the customer on how well the work aligns to their expectations, along with the retrospective, which allows the team to reflect on their own challenges, make adjustments, and learn.

All of this does a much better job of helping keep everyone informed and aligned with each other and the priorities of the stakeholders. It also does a reasonably good job of encouraging the team to reflect and improve.

Unfortunately, this model's weakness is that it does not deal particularly well with the unplanned reactive operational work that is core to DevOps. In order to both build a reliable iterative rhythm and get regular useful feedback from the customer, this model counts on work being planned and prioritized up front and then remaining static for the duration of the sprint.

When there is too much unplanned work hitting the team, there is a risk of all of this breaking down. Where this seems to be felt most deeply is in the cyclical alignment mechanisms. Most alignment activity tends to occur at Sprint planning, where the product owner can work with the team to figure out dependencies and areas where team members need to coordinate with one another. While an excellent Scrum Master or product owner might be able to help somewhat to untangle messes caused by unplanned work during a sprint, they often are hindered by the lack of a sufficiently deep level of visibility and situational awareness across the ecosystem to really help.

Kanban

Unlike Scrum, kanban thrives when tasks are unpredictable. This is also why many elements of it form important parts of the workflow described in Chapter 12, "Workflow." By focusing on the flow of tasks and the amount of work in progress, it allows tasks to be reordered and new ones to be inserted at any time. There is even a means to expedite urgent work.

However, one of the biggest problems with teams that use kanban is that so many tend to overlook the need for cross-team synchronization, alignment, and improvement. This is not because this need was ignored in the creation of kanban. Kanban, as described by David Anderson, has daily standups much like Scrum, where everyone "walks the board" with someone acting as a facilitator. These daily standups, along with after meetings, allow the team to find and remove blockers as well as stay in synch. There are also queue replenishment meetings, which are similar to Scrum's sprint planning in that they provide an agreed understanding of priorities and objectives, along with release planning, and even review and improvement sessions.

Where the problems begin is that most teams miss the intent behind these mechanisms. Rather than thinking about the target outcomes, how to maintain alignment across the team, and continual learning and improvement, most instead concentrate on the board and how many tasks they are moving through it. Outcomes and priorities are often neglected or forgotten about unless an escalation occurs. Review and improvement tend to be ignored altogether.

Even when the cyclic mechanisms are performed, most fail to achieve their underlying intent. Daily standups tend to devolve into who is blocking whom rather than everyone looking at the whole board to understand what is going on.

Losing the value of these sync points or dropping them completely is so common that it does not take much effort for a skilled eye to scan a board to see that it is happening. It leaves a clear shadow of fragmentation that degrades the alignment and delivery effectiveness of the team using it.

Service Operations Synchronization and Improvement

Now that we know where common alignment methods tend to fall short, what can be done to overcome these problems?

Rather than starting from scratch, we instead build upon the good work that has come from the iterative approaches. This starts with the kanban-like workflow as described in Chapter 12. We then add elements based on the cycles and synchronization points of both Scrum and kanban, but with a couple of important twists.

The first is the introduction of the Queue Master and Service Engineering Lead. As you will see in this chapter, both of these play a major role in overcoming many of the challenges of keeping the entire team situationally aware and aligned.

The second is more interesting. Having to react to unplanned work all the time, teams start to become increasingly tactically focused. This tendency can bleed into the alignment and improvement mechanisms, causing teams to think in a much more short-term way that suboptimizes what improvements and learning they can achieve.

For that reason, I have found that it is more sensible to divide these cycles into two. The first is the shorter *tactical cycle*, much of which has elements familiar to the iterative Agile cycles. The second is a much longer *strategic cycle* that is focused on deeper problem solving and improvement to help the team deliver to meet the target outcomes more effectively.

Let's walk through each to understand them better.

The Tactical Cycle

The tactical cycle is primarily focused on keeping the team informed and aligned on a day-to day-basis. Many aspects of it are similar to a Scrum sprint. It is centered on the workflow and is led by the Queue Master. As the name suggests, the cycle contains mechanisms designed to help with tactical prioritization, resource allocation, event scheduling, and conflict resolution. Reflection and improvement are also important elements, but tend to be tightly targeted to either immediate need or the target outcomes laid out as part of the strategic cycle.

Figure 14.1
Tactical cycle.

The length of the cycle is typically one week in order to improve the opportunities to adjust to findings coming from reactive work.

If development occurs in a separate team, it is helpful whenever possible to align the start of a tactical cycle to the start of the development sprint. This allows SE Leads to quickly assess and align resources and scheduling of activities across teams. If for some reason alignment is not possible, SE Leads will need to work closely with their delivery team before the cycle kickoff to try to determine what might be needed. Even a somewhat inaccurate view can help the Queue Master and team limit potentially damaging surprises.

The Queue Master usually rotates with each cycle. This is useful for two reasons. The first is that it introduces a regular fresh set of eyes into what is going on across the ecosystem. The second is that the work the new Queue Master needs to do in order to get up to speed gives both the new and the previous Queue Masters an opportunity to compare notes and get a fresh perspective about everything from the current state of the workflow to any outstanding activities from the previous cycle and any known blockers or known work coming in. This *Queue Master brief* in the hours before the new tactical cycle begins can help prevent both the Queue Master and the wider team from being lulled into dangerous complacency. Nothing encourages people to sharpen their situational awareness as quickly as the possibility of unknowingly being handed a raging dumpster fire.

Once the new Queue Master for the cycle has been briefed, this cycle begins with a cycle *kickoff*. There are also *daily standups*, and the cycle ends with a *retrospective*. While the resemblance with Agile counterparts is helpful, as noted earlier there are a number of important differences.

Queue Master Brief

Figure 14.2

The brief between current and subsequent QM is an important first step.

While the tactical cycle is a continuous loop, the person holding the Queue Master role is not always the same. For this reason the Queue Master needs to go through a series of steps to prepare for a smooth handoff.

The process begins in the hours before the cycle kickoff meeting and is generally only as long as it needs to be. It starts with the current Queue Master reviewing the workflow board with the new Queue Master. This is usually short, and most of the focus is to provide extra context behind activities across the board that may simply be too lengthy to cover or otherwise not suitable to cover with the rest of the team during the retrospective or kickoff meetings.

The new Queue Master usually follows this by getting a quick rundown from any Service Engineering Leads of any major upcoming events or scheduled work. The intent is two-fold. One is to make sure SE Leads uncover any upcoming work that may not have made its way to the board. The other is to catch any potential resource requirements and dependencies that cannot be resolved by the team alone and require management help to sort out. This helps minimize resource conflicts from suddenly derailing the Kickoff meeting.

From there, the new Queue Master should touch base with management and/or key business contacts. This is to find out about any changing priorities or impending development or business activities that might provide useful context or uncover potential operational risk or constraints during the upcoming cycle. Resource and scheduling conflicts should be escalated here, if required. Sometimes it might make sense to arrange to have someone from management at the kickoff to answer questions and give guidance.

By the time the Queue Master is done, they should have a decent outline to keep the kickoff meeting focused.

Cycle Kickoff

Figure 14.3
The Cycle Kickoff.

The cycle always begins with the *kickoff*. The purpose of the kickoff is to bring the team together to agree upon the priorities and theme of the cycle. This is done in order to help align the team as well as provide a forum to surface potential resource and skillset needs for the coming cycle. As the Queue Master has to ensure the flow of work during the cycle, they are best suited to run the kickoff meeting.

When the kickoff meeting happens, it should first provide a theme for the cycle, if there is one, along with ranked priorities for the team. This is followed by a quick rundown of impeding development, business, and operational activities for everyone to be aware of. Then, each SE Lead goes through upcoming events in their projects, along with any details, context, and resources needed for upcoming work that needs to be scheduled and performed. From there, the Queue Master walks through the workflow, asking any questions and making sure that the team members know of any issues that might prevent scheduled or important work from occurring, or anything that might get in the way or slow down the pace of flowing work. Improvement items that have been agreed to are picked up and put in the *Ready* queue alongside any other ready known work. Once everyone is in order, the meeting ends.

Important Differences Between Kickoffs and Sprint Planning

To some people, the kickoff might just look like a somewhat stripped-down sprint planning or kanban queue replenishment meeting. There are enough similarities that you could overlay the two for teams that have both development and operational duties. However, before doing so there are some very important differences that you need to be aware of.

The first is that the unpredictable nature of operational work means that it is folly to load up a cycle to capacity with preplanned work and expect that it will all be done. There is simply no way of knowing whether capacity will be severely constrained by an operational disaster, high-priority emergency work, or some other event. This makes planning and coordination difficult.

The best way to counter this unpredictability is to limit how much of the team has to be exposed to its interruptions. Establishing the Queue Master role can go a long way to help. Another helpful way to counter unpredictability is to limit the size and uneven distribution of work items. This includes minimizing the number of tasks that require poorly distributed specialized skills. Doing so increases team flexibility by making the damage caused by any unexpected interruptions that do slip through far less severe.

The workflow itself also is useful for giving you a reasonable idea of not just the likely slack in capacity the team might have for interrupts but also what impact certain types of interruptions might have. This is useful for expectations setting and risk mitigation.

Another important difference is that, unlike in Scrum, there is rarely a stable set of prioritized work items coming from one stakeholder. The unpredictable nature of customer, infrastructure, security, and even organization demands means that newly incoming work can easily displace other high-priority tasks mid-cycle. The Queue Master and SE Leads should help reduce this unpredictability quite a lot, though it is unlikely to go away entirely.

The accompanying sidebar provides an example of a Cycle Kickoff meeting to help you understand its typical dynamics.

The Kickoff

It was Ed's turn to be Queue Master. Queue Master weeks were always a bit disruptive, but Ed had really grown to appreciate the bigger-picture view they provided. They also helped him feel like he was really contributing to the team.

He knew that he had to get prepared for the kickoff meeting later that day, so he grabbed a pen and a pad of paper and walked over to the workflow board to take a look. He was already very familiar with its current state, but knew that there was always the possibility of something he hadn't noticed while handling his own work. Taking some quick notes, he could then ask about anything he felt he might need details on.

The board was as busy as ever. The team had managed to get through a lot of tasks over the last week, though there were some things that could have been in better shape. For instance, Kathy's oncall shift had been far busier than normal, meaning that she had a significant backlog of work still left to do to investigate the latest cloud caching technologies. There were also some tasks from the group that Beth was the SE Lead for that she had handed off to Simon while she was Queue Master that hadn't gone quite as planned. Ed was sure that this would be brought up in the retrospective. Everyone needed to know if there were communication or handoff problems, or even if that annoying "this isn't our Lead" trust problem popped up again in the delivery teams when work got picked up by others.

Ed could see that Emily was already loading up the *Ready* column with a bunch of work that needed to happen in preparation for the Feeds team's upcoming release. She was always the most proactive SE Lead on the team. Ed was always amazed at how thoroughly she was on top of everything. Having said that, he noticed that there were a couple of items that she had put up that looked like they might touch some services that were being worked on by the team Beth was Lead on. He made a note to ask whether they were aligned on it.

After reviewing the board, it was time to visit the current week's Queue Master. Beth was busy collecting her notes from the week and wrapping up some of the remaining Dark Matter items.

"Hey, Beth, how's the week shaping up?"

"Mostly okay," replied Beth. "I had to defuse another 'oh-my-God you have to do this thing I have forgotten to tell you about for two weeks right now' issue from Product. They had completely forgotten that they needed a beta of the new reporting engine and enough data to populate it for the trade show next week. If we hadn't already integrated Danela's environment management tools into the build process, they would have been completely out of luck."

"At least that was taken care of" mused Ed.

"Yeah, definitely. Anyway, the workflow is in decent shape. I have some archiving Dark Matter tasks to finish up, and I probably ought to go talk to Simon before the retro."

"Oh, I noticed that some of Emily's work is touching on your project."

"I noticed. Thanks for reminding me!" replied Beth. "I will bring it up in the kickoff if Simon doesn't know about it."

Ed swung by Billie's office to see if there was anything important going on next week. He also went over to Janet to make sure that everything was more or less in place for the trade show. He then met up quickly with each of the Leads just before the retrospective kicked off.

The team had agreed that it made the most sense to have the new week's kickoff on workflow Friday afternoons immediately after the retrospective. Some team members found this a little awkward. Most were pretty tired by the end of the week, and even though the board and Queue Master usually caught everything by Monday, they might forget some of the context of what was discussed. There was also the problem that some of the bigger customer-effecting releases tended to happen on the weekend to minimize customer impact. This sometimes left fallout that needed to be cleaned up on the following Monday. Mondays were always busy, making it hard to set aside the time for a kickoff. Holding the kickoff next to the retrospective was also very useful as it allowed the learning of the previous week to be immediately incorporated into the following iteration. There were also times that starting right before a weekend was useful, if nothing more than to let people get ready for the next week.

To deal with the "forgetting problem," they agreed that Monday immediately before the standup the Queue Master would do a 5-minute recap.

When the kickoff started it was clear that the two main themes for the upcoming week were the buildup for the release Emily was on, and for people to help Kathy with her project. With Beth's help, Ed quickly covered the scope of the trade show. Even though Janet was involved and the code was still beta, most of what was going to be demonstrated at the trade show was fairly static and therefore not likely to cause much in the way of problems.

Emily then started to go through the items she had coming up. "OK, guys, I have six tasks that I am teeing up for next week. The top two are things that I definitely want to handle. This third item gives a pretty good overview of what the release is about, so it should be done by someone other than me. This fourth one needs to be done before the last two, so I marked it as a dependency."

Beth pointed at the last one and said "that one looks like it touches the transfer service, which folks on my team are working on."

"Yep, it does," replied Emily. "You might want to tackle that one. Let's meet after this and talk. I would love to make sure we aren't causing problems."

"Sure," responded Beth.

After that, Kathy went through her caching project items. Sam offered to try to pick some of them up to help.

Beth then went through the three items that she had, and said that there were likely to be a few more coming in, but as the team hadn't worked through the details for their next sprint yet, it didn't make sense to put any more up.

Once everyone finished, it was Danela's turn. Danela was the Tools & Automation Engineer for the team. She took on building anything that the others didn't have the time or skills to do. Much of her work would arise from problems discussed in the retrospective that the team agreed needed automation help to resolve. These would then be prioritized by the team in the kickoff. It wasn't very often that she had to react to anything during the iteration, so she was usually able to commit to a stable set of work items.

For this iteration, Danela was going to continue to work on some of the logging and auditing functionality for the automated deployment tooling. Much of this came out of the need to authoritatively report on the configurations of instances and services on particular dates, as well as to list who installed which changes present on them on which dates. As there were no other pressing matters, the team asked a few questions about her approach and plans for delivering it, but mostly left her to it.

Ed was feeling pretty good about the iteration once they wrapped up the meeting. Everything seemed to be in far more control and visible than before they started running the iterations. Even the predictable unplanned demand from Product was now far easier to deal with.

Daily Standup

The second of the iteration mechanisms is the daily standup. The daily standup is conducted to reinforce awareness across the team. Like its development counterpart, it happens daily and is intentionally short. It is intended to bolster the team's ability to uncover and sort through any rising problems, conflicts, or coordination opportunities that might otherwise be missed or happen later than is optimal.

Figure 14.4
The daily standup.

Just like its development counterpart, the daily standup is *not* a status meeting and must not ever become heavyweight. The key is to only mention things that others ought to be aware of.

There are a few minor differences in the structure of the service operations standup that are worth mentioning. The first is that the Scrum Master facilitation role is taken up by the Queue Master. The objectives of the Queue Master bear many similarities in keeping the standup short (preferably no more than 15 minutes) and focused on synchronizing team members as well as helping people with blockers and conflict. Where the differences come in is that the Queue Master uses the workflow as a tool to inform and to help spot conflict.

Standups start with a brief report from whoever was oncall during any production incidents that are noteworthy to mention. These are really short heads-up mentions of problem areas, whether or not a problem is still ongoing, who if anyone is still engaged on it, and if there is any incident report that people can look at. The key is to stay brief. Deeper discussion can happen afterward if necessary.

The Queue Master then takes the lead. They mention highlights on the workflow, including any interesting, important, or high-priority work that people need to be aware of in the queue, whether they have spotted a potential problem in one or more tasks that need to be brought to people's attention, and if there are any dependencies or blockers that people need to be aware of.

Following the Queue Master, the chance to speak goes around the team. For double-duty development and operational teams, this can be just like any normal standup. For dedicated operational teams, this often can be a lot quicker than a normal standup. With all the work on the board, each team member only needs to mention specific items that they think people should know about regarding either what has been done or what is coming up. They can also bring up questions or problems about a particular matter, which then should be addressed after the standup.

The Standup

It was now Tuesday, and Ed's week as Queue Master was going fairly well so far. Sure, there were still the usual vague requests like "Can you do that thing with the server?" tasks that every QM had to throw back for clarification. But for the most part the flow of tasks through the workflow was going fairly smoothly.

Simon was oncall this week, so Ed had Simon start.

"There were a couple of failures with the scheduler last night," grumbled a rather groggy Simon. "Nothing serious. I know that the release Beth is on touches it, so I will let her know if I find anything interesting."

Next was Ed's turn. Usually the Queue Master starts by bringing attention to any escalated or expedited work, then asks about any blocked or problematic work in the workflow. Today the only items to note were some important pieces of work that had been put in the queue for the deployments that Beth and Emily were leading. He mentioned them, but then let those two fill in any details.

Sam was next. "I might pull in the prerequisite task from Emily's team today, if it is okay and nothing else major comes up. I'll sync with Emily after this."

"Ok, sure," replied Emily.

Emily was next. She had cleared the first item she had to do, but a couple of other items came up that she still needed to load into the queue.

"We are looking to deploy next week," stated Emily. "Unlike Beth's, there aren't all that many important changes. I have already updated the Arsenal wiki, and will point out some of the interesting bits at the retrospective."

Thomas then spoke. He noted that he had two tasks in progress because he had inadvertently grabbed one that had a prerequisite of the second. He noted that he wanted to discuss how to prevent that in the retrospective at the end of the week.

Beth was next. "Well, the timing of the scheduler failure was pretty convenient. Mike has been deep in that code." She then reached out and moved two tasks out of the *Ready* column. "We need to hold off on these two tasks until Simon, Mike, and I have a chance to dig into what happened. The others are still a go. I might also add a couple more later today. As always, let me know if you have any questions on any of these tasks."

Danela was last. "I am getting ready to update Depot and Mister Forensics later today. The changes so far are minor. As always it would be good to get any feedback. I am planning on updating the staging side first. If everything is fine I will roll it out in production. I will be sure to swing by and talk to Emily and Beth before I do anything. Let me know if any of you are interested in knowing more."

Ed then wrapped it up and everyone started their day.

Retrospective

The retrospective is run at the very end of the iteration. It is an opportunity for the team to reflect upon the previous week, talk about what has happened, and look for improvements to be put in place:

- Were the priorities incorrect, or was important information missing that was unexpectedly uncovered during the course of the week?

- Were the goals and the amount of work that the team thought they would accomplish overambitious, or were tasks unexpectedly quick to complete, allowing the team to tackle additional work?
- Were there tasks accidentally handled in the wrong order, or were there instances where tasks required significant avoidable rework?
- Were there times when there was too much work in progress, and if so, why?
- Are there upcoming developments that the team needs to know more about or needs to adjust to?
- Are there discoveries or developments that might help the team?

Figure 14.5
The retrospective.

Together, the retrospective creates a formal mechanism for team members to learn from both events and from each other and improve for the next iteration. It can also act as a natural inspection point and potential firebreak to allow for problems and dysfunction to rise to the surface closer to when they are happening. This provides better context for the problems, as well as allows them to be dealt with in a way that reduces the potential damage that they might otherwise cause. It can also help the team better articulate situations where management help and support might be required. This could be to receive additional guidance, to help in removing an impediment, or to obtain resources in an improvement that requires investment.

For investments, the retrospective can help collect evidence to build a case for management to review.

The retrospective also marks the end of the term for the current week's Queue Master. The advantage of this is that it is an expected break point for the team. This allows the current Queue Master to make sure that any important Queue Master items are handled properly and not lost.

General Meeting Structure

The length of the retrospective is heavily determined by the number of items that the team feels they need to discuss and agree to next steps on. Generally, you should aim for it to take an hour, but padded so there is the ability to spill into a second hour when necessary. Keeping it brief helps everyone stay focused and engaged. Anything longer tends to become less impactful, and most team members generally like having any free excess time in their schedules.

Everyone should be invited to attend the retrospective, though active participation is required by the following roles, which each have a commitment to fulfill:

- The current week's Queue Master
- Next week's Queue Master
- Service Engineering Leads (if the role exists)
- Any incident details (or important on-call findings)
- Key individuals who fielded significant items during the iteration that may require discussion. These people can be brought in as necessary and do not need to stay for the whole meeting.

It is important that notes are taken during the retrospective to ensure that what is discussed is captured and can be subsequently tracked. In order to help make sure that the next week's Queue Master is up to speed, it is usually good practice to make that person responsible for taking notes for the meeting for publishing afterward. These notes should at the very least include the list of potential discussion items, details of the ones discussed, along with any decisions and next steps with assigned owners. These notes should be published via a wiki with links to any work items that are referenced. These notes provide a useful insight into problem patterns, history, and progression that can be used to support further discussion in the strategic review.

The current week's Queue Master starts the meeting by providing a summary of key workflow details from the last week, as well as a review of whether the theme for the week held. This summary should be brief, with the primary focus on any anomalies that are worthy of further discussion or further investigation and follow-up, *not* a rehash of everything that happened over the entire week. The Queue Master should lay out each item on a board or a Post-it Note with a 30-second summary of why it is noteworthy (which could be anything from making people more aware of a situation, an area that should be targeted for improvement, a failure or conflict that needs to be further investigated, a Dark Matter item that appears to be part of a bigger problem, etc.). The team can add to the list. After that is complete, the team votes on the top three to five items to discuss.

The next step is for the Service Engineering Leads to summarize details from their engagement with either a delivery or operational project. The focus is primarily on new developments, learning, or questions that may be of interest to the rest of the team. They might point to any new documentation, any demos or reviews, and any impending installation, configuration, or operational work that might be coming up to be entered into the workflow.

It is good to keep the SE Lead updates as brief as possible. Any need for a deeper dive into details can and should be done separately.

The SE Lead, along with the Queue Master and rest of the team, should look for and point out any opportunities for others to get exposure that can help the team come up to speed on the engagement. If the team feels that a single point of failure is developing in the team, it should be pointed out here so that remedies can be discussed.

Once the SE Leads are done, anyone who handled any production incidents or were part of an on-call rotation is given an opportunity to mention any items that are noteworthy for the team to think about. Again, like the Queue Master, this shouldn't be a rehash of the week. It should instead target such things as problem areas with the production services that might warrant additional awareness, discussion or investigation, as well as potential areas to improve oncall itself. The target is to look to improve service "ilities," while improving the effectiveness of incident management and the difficulty of on-call rotations for everyone.

Tools & Automation Engineering follows the production incident and management section with any updates or feedback that they feel is worthwhile to give the rest of the team. Sometimes this will be a mention of new tools or capabilities available to the team, along with establishing a time to go through them with team members. Other times it might be to ask questions or provide feedback to the team on particular problem areas that might require further discussion.

The final bit that gets covered before going into the top three to five discussion items is a quick run through of the tallies for Dark Matter items by the Queue Master. The main goal here is to see if the numbers are increasing or decreasing, and if anything new has popped up. As Dark Matter is often a target-rich environment for self-service automation, the team can use this time to discuss whether workflow backlog items should be created for Tools & Automation Engineering to consider tackling, and whether they should take a higher or lower priority to other work.

Once that is done, the team goes back to the top discussion items. If something that was brought up in the other parts of the meeting becomes more pertinent to discuss further, the team can vote to include it.

The Learning and Improvement Discussion

When the team gets to the top discussion items, there is often a tendency for the team to spend it complaining. While that can be therapeutic, it is not a great use of the team's retrospective time. The team should instead dedicate this part of the retrospective to articulating the problem and assigning next steps to tackle it.

The structure of the discussion of each item should be as follows:

- Initial statement of the problem.
- How the problem measurably detracts from the team's ability to progress toward outcomes.
- Ways that the problem can be further investigated (in cases where the root cause is not clear); or, as in the case of the scheduler problem described in the upcoming sidebar, deeper explanation might come as part of the retrospective.
- If the problem is a tactical change, determine what countermeasures can be or have been put in place to minimize or eliminate the problem. This determination should include by whom, at what cost (time, money, resources), and in what timeframe. It should also include how the effect of the countermeasure will be measured, by whom, and when the measures would be reviewed.
- If the problem requires a more strategic change, determine whether it is an item that should be brought to the next strategic review meeting. If so, what evidence needs to be collected, and by whom, to help?

The discussion should be time boxed, generally to an agreed-upon time in the team, and moderated to keep everyone on topic. The moderator can be the next week's Queue Master (assuming they are not the one actively pushing the topic), the manager of the team, or, in cases where it is a lively topic, a neutral third party.

Once the team has gone through the structure, a vote should be held to see whether everyone is satisfied with the result. If they are not, the topic can either be taken to a separate agreed-to meeting with the respective parties or escalated up the management chain for resolution.

Ed and the Retrospective

Finally it was nearing the end of the iteration for Ed. The week had been long and a bit bumpy. He was looking forward to handing over Queue Master to Sam, who was already starting to pull together the information he needed for the Kickoff meeting.

The team got together around the workflow board. Simon and Beth invited Mary to the retrospective to cover some of the issues that had been happening around the scheduler, as well as to answer any questions from the team around it and their upcoming release. Normally, Mary would be brought in when the scheduler topic came up, but Mary decided it would be interesting to sit in on the whole meeting to see what was going on in Operations in general.

Billie also decided to pop in for the meeting. The team was used to her showing up. She usually didn't participate, though it was helpful having her there when big items came up that needed to be escalated up to her.

Once everyone was there from the team, Ed got started.

"This week was a bit less of a wild circus than last week. From a workflow perspective we appeared to make a lot of good progress on the two themes. Emily managed to get all of her work items done, and Kathy's project made up most of the slippage from last week.

"I heard that there might be a new project kicking off soon that will need a Lead. I think Sam is next to get one. We haven't received a request yet, but just be aware it is coming.

"I noticed a few odd things this week. Thomas had a big buildup of WIP this week. I know one of them was caused by a missed dependency, but there are still several items in the *Doing* column. It would be good to know if there is a bigger issue there we need to look into.

"There was also a problem where developers from the team Beth is Lead for kept trying to cram work into the workflow without going through Beth. I know those guys have been a little problematic. It would be good to discuss to understand if the problem is particular to them or needs to be more widely addressed.

"The scheduler problem we had this week is probably also another useful topic to put out there, especially as Mary is here.

"We had one expedited item off of the back of the scheduler outage. There are also a couple of items in the *Ready* column that have languished for the entire iteration. It would be good to know if we need to do anything specific to get those pushed through, as well as if we need to make any changes to how we handle work to prevent that from happening.

"Finally, there was a flood of tickets that came in about unlocking accounts. It would be good to know if it is a potential bug that development needs to take care of or the start of something we should create a self-service tool around."

Ed put up Post-it Notes, one about WIP, one for Lead work problems, one for languishing tasks, and one for unlocks. "Does anyone have any others to put up before we vote?"

Beth raised her hand. "I have one, especially as Billie is here. What do we do when two teams are releasing changes on the same component immediately after each other? I am not sure if we can solve it ourselves, but it is an issue Emily and I have suddenly found ourselves facing."

"OK, great! Let's add that," responded Ed. "Now everyone vote. Each gets to vote for three of them."

After everyone voted, it was clear that the three winners were Lead work problems, the scheduler, and Beth's overlap issue. Simon had put all of his votes on the scheduler item, as he was still concerned it might fail again, and wanted the team to know more about it.

Emily spoke up. "Let me go first. I might need to step out early to take care of some of the launch things that are coming together right now."

"Sure," replied Ed.

"Thanks. As you guys know we are launching this weekend. I think most of you made the run-through I did on Wednesday on the key changes. Fortunately, there aren't many. I will be around all weekend in case anything goes wrong. Thomas and I agreed to sync up after the Kickoff meeting, and then at 9 p.m. on Saturday and Sunday. If any of you are dying for an excuse to go to a work meeting over the weekend, let me know."

Beth muttered, "Actually, I might pop in on Saturday just to check on the status of the overlap items between our releases. Otherwise I will probably be thinking about it all weekend."

"OK, I'll send you the meeting details," replied Emily.

Beth then spoke up: "I probably ought to go next. As you all know, my team is also getting ready to release. Originally we were hoping for next week. However, between the overlaps in Emily and my releases, and the problem with the scheduler we had this week, it looks like it might get pushed out. I will let all of you know when we have a better idea."

Beth continued, "I'll leave the scheduler topic for the discussion later. I know that we are also going to talk about the problems I have been facing with my team later, but I thought I'd say a couple of things now. My team is still clearly struggling with the SE Lead idea. I know that Kathy, who is probably the best Lead we have, was their Lead last time."

"Yeah, they are a pain," replied Kathy. "Are they still forgetting stuff and having planning problems?"

"Yes, that is part of it," stated Beth. "Their work also touches a lot of services, which I don't think everyone quite appreciates. Anyway, it would be really great if we can find some ways for us to help them help all of us."

Kathy then thanked everyone for helping her gain back some time in her caching project. "We will be running some trials soon. Let me know if you have any questions or interest in knowing more about what we are up to. We are still about a month or so from any real action."

It was now Simon's turn as the on-call person. "We're covering the scheduler later, which was this week's albatross."

When Simon was done, Danela updated the team about the Tools & Automation area. "OK, the Depot and Mister Forensics updates went well, as all of you know. We now have a much better track record of changes moving forward. I created a little widget that some of you might find useful for showing configuration churn over a block of time. I also updated the chatbot to better annotate anything we post up to Arsenal. It is also a little more user-friendly to use. Let me know if you guys have any feedback.

"On the account unlocking, it would be good to know a bit more about what is causing the problem. We shouldn't create a tool that just deals with symptoms. I will talk with Ed afterward this, and maybe propose some investigative work for me for next week."

"Great, thanks!" replied Ed. "OK, here are the Dark Matter tallies. As you can see, account blocks shot way up. Restarts are still going down, which is good. Now that Danela's tools are out there to allow development to rebuild and restore most things on-the-fly, most of the requests we get are for more obscure things that need additional permissions. It is an area we might want to investigate more to see whether or not we can also automate that chain. Everything else was mostly fine."

Ed continued: "OK, it is time to go through our discussion topics. As Lead issues got the most votes, let's start there.

"The problem is about teams not working effectively with SE Leads. There is the issue of unknown or unqualified work hitting the Queue Master without the Lead's knowledge. This, of course, usually creates a lot more work for the Queue Master. But the bigger problem is why the Lead is being left out of the loop. Not all work needs to go through the Lead. But in the case of the Zephyr team, they seem to habitually not engage with their Lead. As a result, we cannot help catch problems like the release overlap problem, or effectively help guide "ility" targeting or even ensure that the release goes smoothly."

Kathy then spoke. "Part of the challenge I noticed was that the Zephyr folks are a little militant. They seem to think they know everything, and won't listen to any comments we might have. They seem to think that we are just nontechnical janitor types or something. It is very weird."

"I know that I definitely have been trying," responded Beth. "Another issue that I think is more pertinent to the problem of unqualified tasks going around the Lead is that some teams, and Zephyr in particular, like to approach sprint planning as an all-or-nothing commitment. I continue to get pressure to commit myself 100% to the sprint, and I'm told that only I can do the tasks and no one else. The other problem is that, contrary to my understanding of Scrum, they feel that they can decide what I do and how I do it. That is a big problem, especially when what they demand cannot be done."

Beth continued, "Here are two examples from this week. One ticket was for production data to be put into the development environment, even though it included PII (personally identifiable information) that we simply cannot expose like that. The other was a demand for administrator access to the servers hosting the scheduler. The Zephyr team refused to believe that even we try to minimize our own shell access to production!"

Ed replied, "I saw those tickets come through. What countermeasures can we put in place to help?"

As Zephyr was the team that she was on, Mary decided to speak up. "I know there are some strong personalities on our team that can make us a bit of a handful at times. It might be helpful to 're-onboard' us. That way everyone can be exposed to what is supposed to happen."

"Another thing we could consider doing is putting in place some sort of 'SE maturity' rating for teams," replied Emily. "We did have something sort of like that when we first started, where we gave specific benefits for teams hitting specific targets. Maybe we can use something like that to nudge Zephyr in the right direction. We just need backing from management."

"I can probably help with that," said Billie. "Come up with a proposal and we can go through it. I think having some sorts of maturity measures can be helpful in general if they are crafted well."

Emily responded, "I can start crafting something. I might need help from Kathy, Beth, and anyone else who might want to participate. Then we can go through it with Billie for her approval and then roll it out."

"Count me in as well," said Simon.

Ed smiled. "That sounds like a good plan to me. Is everyone okay with that proposal?"

Everyone agreed.

Ed then moved on to the scheduler problem. With Simon's help, Mary gave some background to the problem, how to detect when an incident was happening, and what to do to fix it. She then went through what they were doing to put in a more permanent solution. It meant that their upcoming release would be pushed out, but with some of the other challenges going on, that was probably going to happen anyway. Mary agreed that she would provide an update in the next Retrospective.

Finally, the team went through the overlap issue. The general agreement was that the problem came down to a general lack of visibility of the code being worked on, as well as a lack of information sharing across development teams. They agreed to put repository transparency into the maturity work that Emily was doing. Billie also agreed to speak with the senior engineers of each team.

With that the team adjourned the meeting.

The Strategic Cycle

Operationally oriented work by nature tends to be both constant and heavily tactically focused. In such a reactive atmosphere people can unknowingly become inured to being in perpetual firefighting mode. This can cause people to not only fail to take a step back to understand and eliminate the underlying problems, but also lose sight of the target outcomes that key stakeholders are trying to achieve.

Many of us have seen various manifestations of this shortsightedness in our professional and personal lives. It could have been an overworked clerk turning away a customer in order to complete some paperwork, services that randomly interrupt and close important customer sessions, causing them to lose work, or a team intentionally leaving an important server in production that has become an irreproducible snowflake because no one has time to figure out how to rebuild it.

While retrospectives do help teams reflect and improve, it is far too easy for a team to become so focused on fixing the immediate tactical problems (like making the filling out of paperwork faster) that they miss the larger patterns of what is happening around them (e.g., having to fill the paperwork out at all, or having its completion being so urgent that it affects customer engagement and sales).

The strategic cycle tries to break this pattern. It does this in two ways. One is by explicitly dedicating some portion of team bandwidth to allow the team to take a step back from their day-to-day tactical activities to look more critically at whether there are more effective ways to achieve the outcomes desired. This time allows for deeper exploration of systemic problems and experimentation with larger or more radical improvement efforts that can break the cycle of limited half measures that so often hobble needed change.

The other way the strategic cycle tries to break the pattern is by giving the team ownership of improving themselves and their own efficacy. This subtle yet important shift in perspective moves the onus of improving away from management and to those who are more likely to make effective and lasting change. It also helps individuals and teams feel more empowered to initiate change, as well as feel pride for any improvements they enact.

Giving teams the bandwidth and responsibility to improve doesn't mean that improvement is a disorganized free-for-all. The strategic cycle relies upon three mechanisms to help bring and maintain focus throughout.

The first of these mechanisms is the improvement and problem-solving kata, as explained in Chapter 7, "Learning." The improvement kata is used by the members of the team to organize and explore improvements toward an agreed target condition. Work that gets generated as part of the kata gets integrated into the workflow much like any team project so that it can be tracked and team members avoid becoming unnecessarily overloaded.

Team members working on strategic cycle items can sometimes need help and guidance to stay on track and progress. This is where the second mechanism, the coaching practice, comes in. The coaching practice, also covered in Chapter 7, is a way for coaches, managers, and team leads to help team members shape and progress their improvement kata efforts. Sometimes help is in the form of problem analysis. Other times it might be helping the team shape investment cases, providing resources to help their efforts, or redirecting tactical work to give them the bandwidth to progress.

What pulls the whole strategic cycle together and provides the target conditions that are fed into these improvement katas come out of the *strategic review*. The strategic review, described in detail in the next section, is the main formal event of the strategic cycle and the one that it begins and ends with. It is the mechanism that involves the whole team where they review and reset target outcomes, reflect on larger or more stubborn retrospective discussion topics, wargame or run a hack-a-thon to rough out potential new solutions to a common problem, as well as improve cross-team alignment.

Together, these activities create the atmosphere necessary to promote the sort of learning and professional growth that help individuals and the team succeed.

The strategic cycle is intentionally longer than the tactical cycles it overlays, with the optimal length being monthly. This not only helps create a break from the day-to-day pressures that get in the way of looking objectively across the ecosystem, but also gives the team a chance to gain support to tackle bigger problems that hold it back.

For busy teams, using a double strategic cycle loop can be a workable option. In these situations there is a major cycle to tackle large problems and significant transformational efforts that runs quarterly, and minor cycles that tackle either smaller strategic items or, for distributed teams, local aspects of the larger cycle item. This model is far from ideal, and is only recommended if the regular approach simply isn't working.

Let's take a look at the mechanics of the strategic review and the different forms it can take to understand how it anchors the entire strategic cycle.

Strategic Review

Figure 14.6

The Strategic Review.

The intent of the strategic review is to establish the focus for the strategic cycle by defining one or more target conditions to achieve. The topic or theme behind these conditions is typically chosen by the team about one or two weeks before holding the session, either by having a dot vote (where each person on the team is allotted three to five votes they can put on one or more items, with the topic having the most votes being chosen) or by taking the most urgent or important topic on the list. Choosing the topic beforehand maximizes the amount of time in the review that can be dedicated to working through the problem. It also allows the team to prepare by gathering evidence, materials, and/or people who might prove valuable for the session.

There are three typical sources of topics. The most common source is the tactical cycle retrospectives. Often there are larger or more involved items that need more focused time to solve than can be provided in a tactical cycle. Another possible source is a major shift in service offerings or organizational structures. Such a shift often has very real impacts on the team that need to be explored and understood so that appropriate adjustments can be made.

The third source is past strategic cycle topics that need review to determine whether they need to be explored further or if new target conditions need to be set. Typically, a topic should be sized with conditions that can be reached in one to two strategic cycles. A topic that needs more than one cycle should be reviewed at the next strategic review to see if it is on track or requires adjustments. If it cannot be completed by the end of the second cycle, either the target condition was mis-scoped or those working on it were not given enough assistance to complete it. In the case of the latter, the strategic review should be dedicated to coming up with new ways to ensure sufficient assistance can be secured in the future.

One very important point is that the review is not a mechanism for management to kick off some business-driven initiative that has little to do with the team learning and improving itself. The review is for the team. This is an important point to make, especially as the person leading or moderating the meeting is often the leader or manager of the team. For this reason, especially in the early forming/storming days where there are lots of issues and little understanding or alignment on how best to use the meeting to solve them in a way where the team can learn and improve, using an outside facilitator or balanced party well versed in such reviews to help moderate is a good idea.

The review is arguably one of the most important events for the team. It not only helps improve team cohesion and cross-team alignment, but also is an opportunity to bring everyone together out of their everyday roles to learn and break free of potentially flawed mental models though exposure to the insights that others have of the operating ecosystem. For this reason, it is important to invite everyone on the team.

Many teams find such regular strategic reviews extremely difficult to do, especially when teams first start on their DevOps journey. Meetings that can be long and take you out of your day-to-day activities always seem like a painful distraction no matter how helpful they end up being in the end. There is also the challenge of having everyone involved. It is not uncommon for teams to be big, busy, and geographically separated with poor telecommunications setups.

Those teams that are truly geographically split (such as US-India, US-Europe, US/EU-Asia) with sizeable numbers on both sides face a far bigger problem. Some can get by with cross-coordinated local strategic reviews where each location focuses on specific areas and then shares with the other. Even with those, having at least quarterly joint reviews has a lot of value. This can be accomplished by rotating the hosting between locations and supplementing with some travel of key staff from the remote location to help with cross-pollination. It is still not ideal, and can still fall foul of cultural disconnects, but it is far more effective than not doing it at all.

General Review Structure

The typical strategic review is broken into three parts. The first is a very quick review of progress on the measures that came out of the last review. Typically, any updates are posted regularly for the whole team to see so that any significant problems can be flagged for discussion later in the Review. The purpose of the first part is to have a short and focused update to add any needed additional color on the topic from those acting on them. This is usually timeboxed to no more than 5 minutes each.

The second part of the review is the main subject matter itself. This begins with an initial statement of the topic or theme, along with some explanation as to why it is important to cover for the session. This does not need to be particularly long, just enough to set the scene for the rest of the meeting.

One thing to keep in mind is that a review does not necessarily have to be purely problem-based. Sometimes it might be devoted to exploring a new technology, doing a deep dive in an environment or subsystem, or meeting with a customer. In each of these cases there needs to be a clear and measurable objective agreed to at the beginning that must be met by the conclusion of the cycle. These are typically one of the following:

- Insights to improve team situational awareness with next steps that alter the team's approach and ways of working
- New technology, tool, or process approaches to be adopted or extended to help the team improve situational awareness, or decision and delivery efficacy to meet target outcomes

When a problem is the topic, the discussion should follow a somewhat similar structure to that of the retrospective, including an initial statement of the problem and how it measurably detracts from the team's ability to progress toward target outcomes. This discussion should be capped to no more than 15 minutes.

Once the team agrees to a statement, the team moves to the third part of the review, which is to dig into the problem to come up with a path for resolving it. This should employ blame-free problem-solving tools to determine the problem's root causes and explore potential workable solutions to reach the target condition. Sometimes a root cause will not be totally apparent, in which case experiments should be framed up to discover more. Like any improvement initiatives, these should be set up with clear target conditions that can be fed into a learning kata.

Depending on the problem you are trying to solve, there are a number of problem-solving tools that can work well to help. For instance, value stream mapping works well for analyzing flow and handoff problems.

Perhaps one of the most versatile tools for structuring a general problem-solving discussion is the *A3*.

A3 Problem Solving for the Strategic Review

Often root cause analysis takes more than simply talking about a topic to get through its various elements objectively. Sometimes to get to the root cause and help with putting together countermeasures to improve, you need a tool or a guide to help. This is where a number of Lean tools can help.

A3 problem solving is one such tool to help structure a review topic. The A3 is a simple template that traditionally lives on an A3-size sheet of paper, or roughly the equivalent of a sheet of American legal-size paper. The size is helpful in that it is both portable and keeps the team focused and brief, noting only what is important and relevant. Some teams resort to including diagrams and pictures on their A3s to convey richer information more compactly. The A3 can also be used with great effect in weekly retrospectives, normal day-to-day problem solving, and even in incident postmortems. The A3 can be employed during the Strategic Review for bigger structural and strategic items, though it can also be valuable to help organize your thinking around any sized problem-solving activity.

Figure 14.7 shows an example of an A3. I have included a more readable version of the A3 in the appendix.

Figure 14.7

Example A3.

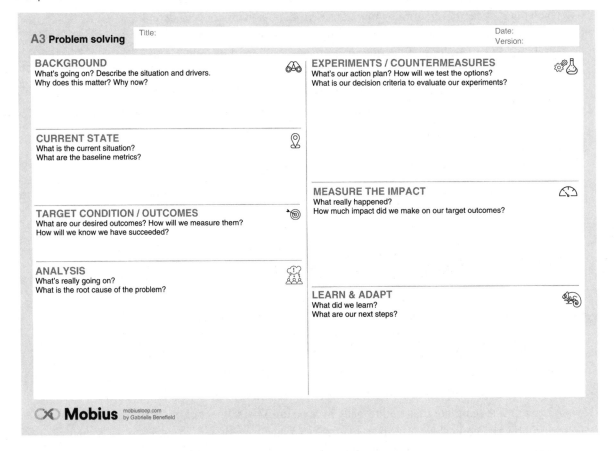

The title of the A3 is typically the theme being targeted. The theme must not be a solution, like "We need more automation" or "We need XYZ tool," but should be more the problem you are trying to solve (like "Installing software is too time/people intensive" or "Troubleshooting XYZ problem is error prone").

From there, the A3 is broken into the following sections:

1. **Background:** Why is this topic important, and what is the business case? It needs to be relevant to the organization's objectives, as well as concise in order to communicate the value in trying to address this

problem. If there are other side benefits to working on this topic, such as learning, those can also be listed. This section basically needs to be clear enough not only for the team to care, but also to start to frame up the case for investing time and/or money in the problem.

2. **Current Conditions:** What is currently going on, and what is the actual problem with the current situation? This should be fact based and clear, and quantified with baseline metrics if at all possible. Graphs and other visual indicators can help.

3. **Goal or Target Condition:** What is the measurable or identifiable target outcomes(s) you are aiming to achieve? Be specific, and make sure it ties back to the business case and indicators captured in your current conditions. It is also useful to indicate how the outcome will be measured or evaluated.

4. **Root Cause Analysis:** This is where the team spends time to get to the bottom of the problem. Some people go crazy and employ various problem-solving tools to help. The important thing is not the technique, but that you uncover why the problem is happening, and what the root cause is. Oftentimes, especially in Operations, the problem is a symptom of an even deeper issue.

5. **Proposal or Countermeasure:** If the team has done an effective job of getting down to the root cause, you can now work together to put together one or more proposed countermeasures for solving the problem or improving the current situation. The countermeasures should address one or more aspects of the root cause. They should be accompanied by measurable or observable criteria to verify their impact and determine whether the action will prevent the recurrence of the problem.

6. **Plan:** Who is responsible for doing what, by when? The answers to these questions need to be clear and agreed upon. Also, the implementation order is both unambiguous and reasonable.

7. **Results Confirmation:** This details the results of the countermeasures to determine whether their effectiveness met expected targets and measures improved in line with the goal statement. If measures have not improved, the reasons why are detailed. This section is filled in at an agreed-upon future date, usually during a subsequent review.

8. **Follow Up:** What did we learn about this situation, and in light of this new knowledge, what should we do? What is necessary to prevent a recurrence of the problem? What remains to be accomplished? Is any communication required, and if so, to whom and in what form(s)?

The theme, as well as some background and available supporting information regarding the current condition, is often agreed upon and gathered before the review. This allows the team to quickly review the information and agree upon a reasonable goal, then focus most of the time on performing root cause analysis, developing proposed countermeasures, and creating an agreed plan for moving forward.

During the root cause analysis, the team should take the opportunity to examine the relevant parts of the environment to help better understand the situation and give better context to any data. This may include gemba walks, engaging directly with a customer or other areas of the business that may help provide an external perspective of the situation.

Note

Gemba walks consist of walking through the relevant parts of the ecosystem. This can be anything from looking at the specific details of a process through a worked example, looking at the development process and underlying conditions within it, analyzing build or deployment environment construction/creation/hygiene to understand the situation and any potential issues it may have, examining logging or monitoring noise, investigating deployment issues in order to find and eliminate their causes, understanding how customers engage with services in order to improve their ability to achieve their target outcomes, and the like.

If at all possible, these discussions should be structured and time boxed to ensure that the team can agree upon the root cause(s), and then have sufficient time to develop and agree upon countermeasures and a plan forward before the end of the review.

The results from any countermeasures can be reviewed either at a subsequent strategic review or at some other agreed-upon point in time. I tend to prefer reviewing at the next strategic review whenever possible, because it both helps maintain momentum and allows for a convenient time to discuss and schedule any follow-up activities.

Here is an example of an A3:

Title: Environment setup is too time and people intensive

Background:

- Setup requests require significant advanced notice, or else cause change delays.
- Team capacity is heavily impacted with each request, causing other work to build up and be delayed.
- Development, customers, and the business are complaining at the long lead times required to turn around an environment.

Current Condition:

- [Value stream map of current process]

Goal:

- Environment setup time reduced to one day or less
- 80% reduction in rework caused by setup mistakes
- Operational team intensity reduced by 75%

Root Cause Analysis:

- [This could be a mind map of some variety, a fishbone diagram, or something else that you find helpful.]

Countermeasures:

- Operating system installation automation
  - Turnaround time reduction target to less than 2 hours
  - Reduction of operating system installation rework by 90%
- Cloud virtualization with an Image library
  - Turnaround time reduction target for frequently used preset configurations to less than 2 hours
- Standardized packaging of all software
  - Reduction of installation rework by 90%
- Software deployment automation
  - Reduction of people intensity

Plan

- [High-level action plan with next steps]

As the typical problem levels begin to shrink, the team should start to find that they have a bit more capacity to tackle ever bigger or more complex items within the strategic review.

Summary

Creating a natural rhythm of synchronization and improvement events is a great way of turning alignment, reflection, and learning into a continuous habit, one that is shared by the entire team. The events along the shorter tactical cycle aid the team with planning, workload balancing, maintaining shared awareness, and making tactical improvements, while the longer strategic cycle help build in time for steady learning and improvement. Together they bring all the elements together to help the team succeed.

Chapter 15

Governance

If you want people to think, don't give instructions, give intent.

David Marquet

IT governance is an important but often contentious topic within IT service delivery. Few would argue with the statement that managers and investors alike need to make sure that IT investments are being implemented and operated both efficiently and in line with the needs of the organization and its customers. Regulated industries such as banking, healthcare, food, energy, telecommunications, and transport also need a means to ensure that stringent legal and regulatory requirements are being met to minimize health, financial, legal, and personal risks.

Governance procedures themselves are typically seen as slow and cumbersome. It does not help that they often appear to conflict directly with more iterative delivery approaches like Agile and continuous delivery. Some governance procedures even go so far as to discredit these Agile approaches, saying they make governance impossible and therefore cannot be used for anything but the most trivial or least important of environments.

This chapter seeks to show how you can ensure any governance mechanisms you have within your organization are both effective and minimally disruptive to your DevOps journey. We begin by covering the key factors for successful governance, how they fit with many of the themes throughout this book, and how so many organizations fail to meet them. We then move to the common reasons governance implementations fail. Finally, we finish the chapter with important tips for how to improve the efficacy of your own governance.

Factors for Successful Governance

Few things tend to focus the mind like being the subject of a full audit. For some, an audit represents failure. Others compare them to a long slog through mountains of files, complete with intrusive questioning by nosy auditors to justify the most minor of transgressions. Adopting a different perspective, audits offer an opportunity to step back and know whether your governance mechanisms are both effective and meet the requirements of your organization.

Audits have long been a steady feature throughout my career. I actually feel fortunate to have spent considerable time on both sides of an audit. Those audits have spanned everything from legal disputes and regulatory investigations to certification, conditions tied to venture capital investments and M&A activities, as well as in-depth reviews driven by executive boards. While most of the them have been relatively uneventful, I have always found them to be good learning and improvement opportunities for myself and the organization being audited.

One of the most valuable lessons to come from audits is that governance quality doesn't seem to be related to whether an organization uses a particular practice or governance framework, how many governance boards are in place, who is on them, or how often they meet. Governance quality also doesn't seem to be determined by how detailed processes are, how much documentation there is, or whether the organization or the people in it hold any process or methodology certifications. What does matter is that the following key factors are in place:

- The *intent* behind any legal, regulatory, and business requirement is widely understood and adhered to by everyone across the delivery ecosystem.
- Governance and reporting processes and controls must aid and not interfere with organizational efforts to achieve target outcomes.
- Governance processes and controls must always support and never damage organizational situational awareness and learning.

Let's walk through each to show how the absence of any one of these factors can erode the overall efficacy of any governance mechanisms you have in place.

Meeting Intent

Making sure that governance processes meet the underlying intent of a requirement seems like an obvious objective. Most audits begin by laying out the requirements under review, often with a short statement or discussion regarding the intent of each requirement. This makes it easy to then compare how well any mechanisms meet the intent.

Consider, for example, the intent of checking on the return on an IT investment. The best way to measure this would be to check if, and how well, the target outcomes were achieved, although some find measuring outcomes hard to do or imprecise. A common shortcut is to instead use a proxy measure like function points or story points delivered. Unfortunately, such measures do little to tell you whether the actual intent was achieved. To demonstrate this, I once showed two implementations of the same service, one with more function points than the other. The one with fewer function points was faster, more stable, and did a far superior job in delivering what was required; however, by just measuring function points, the poorer implementation with more function points would be considered a better investment.

Intent misinterpretations, disconnects, and measurement errors can occur even more frequently when trying to handle regulatory and legal requirements. Assume that your organization must fulfill a separation of duties requirement. These requirements are designed as a check to make sure someone cannot put in a change without the full knowledge and approval of the organization and participation of separate organizational parties. This limits the potential for fraud, theft, sabotage, and error.

To implement the separation of duties principle, most organizations separate the development team that builds the software from the operations team that deploys and runs it. An approval process with a governance board whose members are suitably accountable sits in the middle to review any changes.

This might look great from the outside, but how effectively do the processes meet the intent behind the requirement of minimizing the risk for potential fraud, theft, sabotage, or error?

Understanding the contents of any changes and the reasons behind them helps determine whether there is a risk. Facilitating this understanding is usually done by presenting the board with a summary of the changes, along with any detailed requirements documentation, test results showing any known service behavior changes, release notes, deployment procedures, and an overview.

While this approach appears sound, there are a number of troublesome flaws. The first is that it assumes the details presented are complete and adequately capture any risks. Anyone knowingly trying to violate the intent is unlikely to document it. This means that you need some other mechanism to find and present any potential risks. While there is a possibility the testing processes might stumble across a hidden risk, the only means to confidently do so would be by going through the actual code and configuration implementations directly. Unfortunately, it is extremely rare that anyone outside of the development team ever does this.

This leads to the second challenge. While governance board members might be suitably accountable, they often lack the skills, time, and even situational awareness necessary to parse all the documentation and relevant technical details provided to make a sufficiently informed decision. This means that actual governance is left to a mix of the following:

- Trust that anything potentially prohibited was eliminated by those doing the work
- Dumb luck that any risk is so visible and obvious that it immediately comes out of the data presented

The final flaw of this approach is that it assumes that all the deployment activities performed by the operations team align perfectly with the deployment procedures presented. This can happen, but more often than not there are some differences. Sometimes these differences might be caused by a minor mistake such as a miskeying or misordering of steps. Other times there are errors or gaps in the instructions themselves that require unplanned (and frequently uncaptured) work. These errors/gaps might manifest in a tweak to a configuration file, a file permission change, or some other activity needed to get everything working properly.

While it is unlikely that an operations person would knowingly commit sabotage, fraud, or error, few bother to capture what actions they performed, let alone check whether those actions align with the deployment procedures presented. This creates potential unknowns that can introduce hidden risks into the ecosystem.

If you are lucky, you can still avoid undermining your own efforts with such flaws. However, you must also be aware that many of the traditional fixes put in place to fill such gaps, such as increasing the amount of documentation or bringing in even more senior people to the governance board, do little to help.

No Target Outcome Interference

Not meeting intent effectively is far from the only problem with any governance and reporting mechanisms you might put in place. They can also interfere with the second factor, your efforts to achieve your larger service delivery target outcomes.

Being able to achieve target outcomes is obviously important. As you might expect, governance mechanisms usually introduce a level of delivery friction through the combination of extra work, handoffs, and approval gates required to meet it. Such friction will inevitably have some impact on your delivery capabilities that can and should be actively managed to minimize its effect. There are many ways this can be done through some combination of regular monitoring and streamlining of processes, intelligent tooling, and other improvements.

Unfortunately, few organizations bother to do much more than nibble around the edges of the problem. In one organization, I was brought in to try to optimize an 18-month-long delivery cycle. What I discovered was that all the technical aspects, including architectural designs, coding, testing, and deployment, made up at most 6 weeks of the 18-month period. The remaining time was spent in all the governance approval processes surrounding it.

While few organizations are quite that dysfunctional, many still find themselves pressed between an urgent need to deliver changes to meet customer demands and the slow grind to work their way through governance processes. This is not helped by the fact that governance processes usually require valuable time from important people who are often short of it, resulting in further delays and frustration. Not only are such delays wasteful, anyone who has been caught between a governance process and an impatient customer knows that they often look ridiculously incompetent to those on the outside.

All of this can be incredibly frustrating to many of those being pushed hard to deliver. This can build to the point where delivery people look for ways to work around the governance procedures. The least subversive method is to simply batch up all changes into one large delivery, meaning that governance processes only have to be done once. Such large batching also means that only bigger changes will get noticed, allowing other ones to slip through. Other organizations simply try to avoid or actively thwart governance altogether through emergency patches or backchannel activities to achieve objectives on the sly.

None of these actions do much to both achieve governance intent and progress toward target outcomes.

Maintain Situational Awareness and Learning

It might seem odd to have to consider the effect of governance on situational awareness and learning. Governance processes should, if anything, be mechanisms that capture and bring to light the ecosystem dynamics you need to know about and learn from. Yet it is surprisingly common for governance to be implemented in ways that both directly and indirectly hinder the sorts of information flow and understanding critical to maintain them.

Direct Interference

Most cases of direct interference tend to occur when organizations interpret legal and regulatory requirements in overly stringent ways. Take the example of data handling requirements such as those around personally identifiable information (PII). Some believe that such requirements preclude any sharing or exposure to the data or data factors, even those that convey important data characteristics but are not in themselves directly identifying. This is especially true for sensitive data like patient medical records, something that even more data-liberal countries like the United States have stringent regulations for.

But cutting off all types of data sharing not only is the wrong approach but can even be potentially dangerous. In the case of hospital patient records, it would be ridiculous to assume that such protections prevent hospitals from reporting critical public health data. While the patient's name cannot be revealed, other factors that many might consider identifiable, such as the type of disease, where and how the patient might have contracted it, the community the patient resides in, the patient's sex/ethnicity/occupation/sexual orientation, how the disease affects the patient, and treatments used and their effectiveness, not only can but must be exposed. These help health officials determine the disease's source, its prevalence in the community, the likely direction and rate of spread, the potential mortality rate, as well as what might be required to treat and contain it.

The same is true for separation of duties. While duties might need to be separated, such requirements do not typically preclude build and run teams from working together or sharing information and expertise.

Indirect Interference

While far more subtle, indirect interference can be just as destructive. All the various workarounds that inevitably get put in place to overcome governance friction, from the large release batches and emergency patches mentioned earlier to other workarounds such as breaking large changes into smaller ones to avoid extra governance scrutiny or avoiding going through governance oversight outright, all have a tendency to hide or obfuscate details. This makes it difficult to be aware of the current situation, understand its dynamics, and use that knowledge to learn and improve.

The other form of indirect interference is even more problematic. It is extremely easy to be lulled into assuming all the documentation and reporting created for governance is in itself effective for maintaining situational awareness and learning on its own. It would be great if this were true. But even the most comprehensive governance processes are designed to be snapshot checks on specific requirements or conditions. As such, any documentation collected tends to only provide a static fragmented view with at best an incomplete view of ecosystem dynamics that few people both read and understand fully. This makes it a low-quality mechanism for maintaining active situational awareness and learning.

These dysfunction examples are both common and have a tendency to quietly sneak in and cause significant damage before they are noticed. For this reason, it is important to check for them through regular reviews and retrospectives where they are likely to surface.

Common Governance Mistakes

All of the shortcomings of traditional governance approaches do not come out of nowhere. The vast majority are caused by common governance mistakes that are very easy to fall into.

Recognizing their existence is half the battle. While you might not be able to immediately correct them, understanding how they cause problems can help you flag the issue and possibly help minimize the resulting damage. The sections that follow highlight some of these common governance mistakes and offer some guidance on how to mitigate them.

Poor Requirement Drafting and Understanding

The vast majority of the requirements that determine the shape of many governance processes are ultimately defined by the lawyers who write the regulations and contracts that contain them. Unfortunately, not everyone is well versed in all the technical nuances of the spaces for which they are writing regulations and contracts. Legal language also has a tendency to be written in ways that are incomprehensible for the technical teams to interpret and follow.

Legal contracts that companies enter into are the biggest source of these sorts of headaches. Not all organizations have their own in-house legal counsel, and even when they do, they interface primarily with management and teams such as Sales and Vendor Management. This limited exposure to the technical delivery side makes it that much less likely that contracts and other legal agreements will be drafted and agreed to in a way that avoids causing big technical implementation problems.

The best way to avoid these sorts of quandaries is for technical teams to get to know Legal staff early and build strong relationships with them. By introducing what your team does and articulating your desire to avoid unnecessary grief befalling you and the rest of the organization, you can create a bridge that can help everyone. Legal is usually staffed by smart people who themselves want to be seen as working in the best interest of the company. They know the contracts that have been signed and can help you understand their conditions as well as the legal terms and intent behind them. They can also help do the same with any regulations you need to follow, possibly even pointing out potential pitfalls and loopholes that are useful to be aware of. This can help you both highlight their impacts and find effective ways to abide by them.

By being a known friendly contact, Legal staff are also far more likely to seek you out whenever there is a contract being negotiated. They might ask for help to interpret technical details and proactively avoid creating problems. They can also provide insights into negotiations, giving you some advanced warning of their dynamics and sticking points, which is very useful in improving situational awareness.

Being even a supporting part of negotiations can help you locate awareness gaps within your organization. For instance, Sales and Marketing team members may misunderstand a key capability, or the risk associated with certain commitments. Negotiations also provide useful insights into likely target outcomes of potential customers, as well as point out possible problem areas to watch out for from your suppliers.

Helping Legal Help You

Many technical people grumble at the idea of voluntarily reaching out to Legal, either not seeing the point of it or worried that they might unexpectedly add to their own already heavy workload. I have found that it is always worthwhile to reach out and put in a little bit of effort to turn Legal into powerful forces of good for you, and ultimately for your customer.

One instance where this came in handy was when I was working at a service provider that was negotiating a contract renewal with their largest customer. Both companies needed each other. While not the only customer, the contract made up nearly 50% of the revenue for the supplier. For the customer, the services provided were key to helping deliver their most important products to market.

Such a heavy co-dependency often creates an unhealthy dynamic. For the supplier, having so much hinging on one customer leads to a tendency to bend over backwards to accommodate them. This can be made worse if Sales, which often is incentivized to close a deal no matter how big the discrepancy between top-line and bottom-line numbers, has a strong influence in company decision making. Such conditions greatly increase the risk of a contract being signed with onerous delivery requirements.

The customer also knew how important they were to the supplier. While they had a clear interest in making sure the supplier didn't go out of business, it was still important to negotiate a contract that gave the customer plenty of leverage to help them achieve their two key outcomes.

Being that the delivered services were so important to the customer, they first wanted to ensure that the services were sufficiently available and performant to meet their needs. Downtime and service problems were not just frustrating but could actually risk their own product delivery schedules. This was especially important at certain critical points in their product lifecycle. They needed to make sure that we minimized that risk.

The customer also wanted to make sure that any additional features they might need would receive a suitably high priority. Being so intricately tied in their product delivery meant there were times that they were dependent upon our ability to deliver certain capabilities. Any lack of responsiveness on our part could cause problems on their side.

As they came to the negotiating table, they sought to structure the contract to optimize for their needs. The problem came with the way that they sought to achieve them.

To ensure service availability, they asked for a 99.99% service uptime guarantee measured from their side, with harsh financial penalties on us as the supplier whenever they were broken. To secure the features they needed, they demanded the ability to view, prioritize, and even add features going into any new service release.

From the customer's perspective, such demands seemed reasonable. Our Sales team, which was eager to push the contract through, provided little resistance, so the customer quickly became confident their demands were reasonable. However, our lawyer knew this was no ordinary contract. She wanted to make sure we were not signing up for anything that would later prove problematic, so she sought me out to go through the legal language.

It was clear from the beginning that there was no way we could sensibly make such commitments. However, the team couldn't just say "no." The team needed to really understand the intent behind the customer's requests and then shape the contract terms in a way that worked for both sides.

The team started with the service uptime guarantee. While it was clear that service uptime and reliability were important, a blanket uptime number was not terribly useful. For one, it wasn't clear what it measured. The way the guarantee was worded did not specify whether the service was usable. A less ethical company trying to work around the onerous terms could meet the measure by putting in place a service that responds but does nothing whenever there is a problem.

Another challenge common with such crude uptime guarantees is that they do not reflect usage patterns. Like most businesses, usage patterns vary by time of day as well as the time of year. There were periods when uptime was critical to the customer. Being down for even one minute then, let alone for our whole annual downtime allocation, would cause serious damage to their business. However, there were also lots of times when the customer's offices were closed or business was quiet and usage was so low that our services could be down for hours or even days with few noticing.

There was also a problem that important upgrades and maintenance activities, especially those that require significant data manipulation, often needed some downtime to reduce risk. A strict reading of the uptime guarantee would inevitably result in fewer and potentially riskier upgrade and maintenance activities of the sort that would run counter to the customer's own objectives.

With this knowledge, the team went back to the customer to work out something that would more closely meet the service availability and reliability intent they were seeking. An easy first step was to expand the mechanisms used to coordinate our maintenance activities. This gave each side much more awareness of the situation on each side, providing a means to proactively determine the critical times when high uptime and usability was necessary. Such awareness went a long way to reduce potential conflict. The visibility they had of our own activities also increased their flexibility to allow upgrades and maintenance activities outside of critical windows.

For the service level agreement itself, the team worked with the customer to define usability metrics for key services that were meaningful to both sides. The team created probes that would collect and present metrics from important locations in their environment. When a problem was found, supporting data was also collected to help troubleshooting. This allowed both sides to identify problem areas and develop ways to improve them.

The demand to control our work and prioritize our feature delivery was far more problematic. It was dangerous to both us and all of our other customers to have one customer in control of our work prioritization. Our services were extremely complex. It would be difficult for someone outside the company to understand the importance of some of our core work and why such items were higher in importance than items the customer was advocating.

If such control was so important, the only sensible solution would be to fork over their version of our services. But, as with the uptime guarantee, the result would also run counter to their objectives. Each additional live version effectively doubles delivery and support efforts, resulting in a far less stable set of services with a far slower delivery cadence.

Instead, the team did three things to address the customer's concerns. The first was to create a regular summit with key people from their organization to talk through their needs as well as discuss elements of our roadmap that were particular to them. This helped improve mutual understanding and trust.

To maintain roadmap balance the team also created a more generalized summit where we invited other key members of our customer community to review our roadmap and provide feedback. Interestingly, over time as everyone became far more comfortable sharing ideas and discussion, even with others that they viewed as major competitors, the need for individualized summits fell away.

The third item was to open up our services more widely and provide a software development kit (SDK) that enabled customers to extend many of our services themselves. This accomplished a number of things. It gave customers the ability to deliver many of the features they wanted faster. It also improved the engagement and camaraderie between our engineers and theirs. Several customers decided to share their own extensions with others, and in many cases even started to work collaboratively with each other to extend our services.

Using Off-the-Shelf Governance Frameworks

Figure 15.1
Governance needs are rarely so generic that they can be developed by outsiders with little understanding of your situation or target outcomes.

Not having a say in shaping a regulation or contract is far from the only problem technical teams face. A lot of the time we aren't even made aware that one is coming until we are confronted by a demand to find a way to comply with it as soon as possible. When we ask for details, we often get hit with documents full of impenetrable legal language. With such an immediate need, what options are available?

One solution is to find a consultancy or out-of-the-box solution that can take the problem out of our hands. There is no shortage of providers claiming to deliver everything you might need. Many themselves take a shortcut by adapting a preexisting practices framework to do so. Those looking for a more IT-centric bent may be presented something like ITIL or COBIT that include modules for incident handling, service design, security, and change management. Those wanting more project and program management might see Prince2 or PMI that stress planning, risk assessment, business case, and portfolio management.

Such an offering can be quite compelling. Taking the ready-made approach opens up a whole range of value-added processes with prebuilt examples that can be used to structure, record, and govern any delivery and operational activities you might have. Not only does this seem cost effective for everything you get, it has the added bonus of following widely recognized standards. These come complete with their own training curriculums, certification levels, and skilled practitioner communities that can be drawn upon. Many contracts and regulations will even reference them directly or point to them as examples to follow. Who wants to reinvent the wheel when there is no need to?

As you might expect, such an approach comes with some serious challenges that few fail to consider.

The first is that these sorts of external solutions emphasize process adherence over outcome delivery. In fact, you might argue that process adherence is the target outcome of these solutions. That isn't to say they ignore what is delivered, just that the emphasis is toward checking the process boxes.

Part of the reason for this is that most are grounded in method-driven management approaches. They assume delivering outcomes can be assured through controlling how work is performed and by whom. In such a world, policing process adherence is a good way to maintain this control. It also happens to align with how many view the role of governance, especially in cases where the organization must ensure it meets any legal or regulatory requirements.

The problem is that most modern service delivery ecosystems are complex domains where it is difficult for management to tightly detail and choreograph every task in advance, especially when this information is requested weeks or months in advance of actual implementation.

All of this makes the processes themselves too brittle and slow to deal effectively with the unknown and unforeseen. With new requirements emerging all the time, a process-driven framework forces managers with two bad choices. Either become a bottleneck by trying to micromanage everything, knowing you will become overwhelmed and miss important details, or hire knowledgeable and situationally aware people who know what is necessary to meet target outcomes and force them to navigate the processes.

Process-heavy governance frameworks also impose a lot of extra friction in the form of extra up-front planning, documentation, and approvals, all of which result in the added pressure of time and effort. Reviewers get put under intense pressure to push through anything that is proposed without enough time to build a sufficiently deep understanding of the details to do so effectively.

This results in a terrible result for everyone. Those outside see an organization that is dangerously slow to deliver and yet still blind to how reliably it can adhere to its legal and regulatory requirements. Those on the inside face a sea of dysfunction, with those trying to deliver finding most of their time and effort being wasted on seemingly useless work, while those responsible for governing sensing they are one decision away from disaster.

Mistaking Process for Governance

It is important to note how commonly held the misperception is that tight sequential process adherence equates to effective governance. Time and again I have been told this is the one and only reason an organization cannot use any form of iterative or continuous delivery mechanisms, only for me to have to prove otherwise.

This concern was so strong at one company where we were rolling out Agile delivery techniques that government regulators were invited in to perform an audit to make sure we were not in violation of the regulations we had to follow.

Dutifully, the government sent a number of auditors to our office.

Their first request was for us to show detailed documentation laying out our delivery requirements. We pointed them to the various team backlogs, showing them each of the work items and explaining how the product owner prioritized them. Being a large organization, we also had a Chief Product Owner for a larger business area who held the area's prioritized backlog. That person coordinated with the team product owners who pulled work into their area's backlog from the larger backlog.

Their next request was to demonstrate that all work aligned with delivery requirements. We showed how teams planned and pulled work into their sprint, then tied the artifact or record of the work performed to the work item. For code, this could then be followed through the build process, where the results and artifacts created were also captured and associated with the work item. Testing was mostly automated, with work only passing if it met the requirements necessary to meet the stated definition of done. These were also recorded and associated with the work item.

Their next request was for us to demonstrate how change management and deployment was handled. We had traced all linkages and dependencies across our service ecosystem and had labeled areas by both risk and whether or not explicit approval was required to meet any known legal or regulatory requirement. Changes with low risk and not associated with anything needing approval could technically be deployed at any time. Most of these were either data and minor configuration elements or part of some minor support subsystem unaffiliated with a regulated service. Despite no approval being necessary, the details of every change, its purpose, and who executed the change and when it was executed were recorded and tracked for later review.

For changes that were either considered higher risk or contained some legal or regulatory element that required official review and signoff, the process was a bit different. Unlike many typical change management reviews, those required to review and sign off on a particular change would receive a Notice for Approval. This notice included a high-level summary of why review and approval of the change by that person was necessary, along with a collection of reports detailing everything that would be impacted by the change, references to the work item IDs explaining why the change was deemed necessary, along with build and test results and an analysis of the relative risks associated with the change, the services affected, how those services might be impacted, as well as any details explaining when and how the change, if approved, would be released. Most of these details would be generated from the various automated systems that could be queried further as necessary.

The approval request also included a date and time for a review meeting if it was deemed necessary. This date and time was also the deadline for approval or denial of the change. If there were no concerns, those reviewing could simply log in and click their approval, allowing for the items to be released. If there were any additional questions, those could be posed to the teams requesting the change to answer and document through the tool or at the review meeting.

If the approver missed the deadline, a notification of the missed deadline would be documented and quickly escalated through the management chain. We found that it took very few escalations for such deadlines to cease being missed.

The final question from the government auditors was about post-program/release review. We showed that reviews were in fact rolling and were part of the delivery team's retrospectives. These were also captured and stored for review. Work items, releases performed, and incidents were also referenced in order to provide additional transparency. If any activities came out of the retrospective, these would also be referenced within the resulting work items.

When we finished answering their questions and demonstrating how each mechanism worked and how all regulatory requirements were followed, the auditors said that they were more than satisfied. In fact, they claimed that they had never seen such an effective governance and reporting mechanism in their careers. Later we heard that there were efforts within parts of the government to follow a similar approach.

Out-of-the-Box Process Tooling and Workflows

Figure 15.2

Out-of-the-box process tooling can seem alluring from the outside.

I am always reticent to recommend specific tooling solutions without a detailed understanding of the ecosystem in which they will be deployed. Tooling choices can have a big impact on whether you achieve the intent behind a set of legal or regulatory requirements. In many cases a tooling choice can provide the very documentation, controls, and tracking that are needed.

Some organizations go a step further and use tooling as a means of enforcing a set of processes in order to effectively govern artifacts and activities that can exist within a delivery ecosystem. This can be extremely helpful. I have myself used tooling to prevent everything from manual environment configuration changes, to check-ins, to software repositories that are not associated with a specific task.

However, governance through tooling can be tricky. Once tooling becomes firmly embedded in your delivery ecosystem, it can be difficult to extract. For that reason, and in order to avoid creating chaos and dysfunction, you have to make sure whatever is being enforced fits your ecosystem neatly, clearly meets the intent you are trying to achieve in a way that is obvious to most, and is flexible enough to adjust as conditions change.

Unfortunately, just as with processes, it is extremely tempting for organizations to put in place a ready-made governance-through-tooling solution. Some see built-in "best practice" process workflows as a compelling feature of an out-of-the-box tool, or are lured into it as a value-add as part of an off-the-shelf governance process framework adoption. Others simply stumble across them in whatever ticketing tool they have. This "insta-process" approach is appealing. They are easy to implement and are officially recognized.

You might be lucky and find a set of workflows that work for you; however, their one-size-fits-all approach tends to force process flows, gates, dependencies, and completion criteria that might not fit the realities of your ecosystem.

With process workflows, what might suit the masses might not suit your individual needs. In service delivery, such mismatches can cause massive amounts of friction and frustration that constrain the service delivery process, making it far more difficult for those in it to know what is going on to do their job effectively.

I have been in many organizations that have adopted such tools and workflows, only to deeply regret doing so only after it was too hard and time consuming to extract them from the delivery ecosystem. Inevitably people work around them, either by performing and tracking work using other means outside the tool, double-keying when necessary, or simply not tracking anything formally at all. This creates the worst of all scenarios, which is having a set of governance processes and tools that does not capture and govern all the activities in the ecosystem effectively.

It is also worthwhile to point out that you should not be fooled into thinking that using a tool or set of workflows that is a poor fit is okay as long as the process methodology followed is a more iterative Agile one. I have seen many tooling and workflow monstrosities with "Agile" monikers that enforce such heavyweight dependencies and completion criteria that they create terrible organizational dysfunction. In more than one case I have seen some of the most mild-mannered Agilists in the industry curse in frustration and refuse to use them.

The Tool

As part of a company reorganization, the senior leadership decided to have me integrate the group responsible for IT service management tooling into my organization. As most of my focus up to that point was with my teams on the development and release engineering sides, I knew relatively little about the tooling team. I decided to pay them a visit to get to know a bit more about them, their tools, and the initiatives they were working on.

One of the first initiatives I was introduced to was a new service management ticketing system. It used a tool from a well-known company in the space, and the team had worked closely with the supplier to build out all the workflows along with a rollout strategy.

I was intrigued. The workflows were modeled on ITIL version 3, which attempts to manage the entire IT service lifecycle from inception, including deep into product management and development. The project itself claimed to be only a few short weeks from rollout across the whole company, yet this was the first time I had ever heard about it.

I asked whether they had worked with any of the product management or engineering teams that would be affected by the workflows. They replied that because the tool used a well-known and respected process methodology that made all the governance processes clearer and easier to track, they didn't need to. Clearly everyone would want to adopt it.

So I decided to walk the process flows with them.

There were a number of oddities with the first step. There was an assumption that all work would start with an investment case. Yet most of the work that teams performed involved ongoing improvements, additions, and fixes to existing products and services. So we agreed to move on. The next steps were even more strange. Process gates were set up with various advisory boards who were supposed to review documents and work items that either didn't exist or would not exist in the form needed until further in the lifecycle. There were also members on their boards to whom they gave ultimate approval authority that organizationally not only had no such power but had it in a process flow that would not give them enough information to be able to make such a decision.

At this point it was clear that the project was on a very bad trajectory. Even if the project could overcome all the organizational and rollout hurdles it would certainly encounter, the amount of dysfunction it would ultimately cause was breathtaking. But it was clear from all the effort and enthusiasm the team had that I would have to show them why.

We ran simulations through their process flows from very real projects taken from my teams. The scenarios compared how work was handled today with the way that it was expected to progress from the workflows in the tool. In many cases the progression of work in the tool would be misdirected for nonsensical change approvals or needless handling by teams not typically involved at the defined point in the delivery process. This naturally caused work to unexpectedly stop, with important information failing to flow to the correct people at the right times. The simulations showed how the processes could not deal with the continuous flow between developers, testers, and operational people.

Even as it became increasingly obvious to the tooling team that this project was not going to work, the supplier kept trying to say that the fact it used ITILv3 meant it was superior to our own processes and therefore would succeed. The supplier decided to try to go over my head to plead to the CIO. The CIO took one look at the processes, asked why the processes had him sitting on over 800 review board meetings a week, and threw them out.

Tips for Effective DevOps Governance

Having effective governance is actually far less complicated than most people make it out to be. It really comes down to targeting the following three key factors without equating process adherence with governance or falling for any quick fixes:

- Meeting your requirements intent
- Not interfering with organizational efforts to achieve target outcomes
- Supporting organizational situational awareness and learning

But we are busy people. So here are some quick tips and tricks that I heavily rely upon that allow me to maintain high levels of governance while still allowing delivery teams the flexibility and freedom to do what they need to do in order to deliver the services customers need to achieve their target outcomes.

Understand Governance Intent

Understanding the intent of any governance or legal/regulatory requirement is critical. Most delivery teams get hit with demands for good governance, or worse, get told they have to implement some horrible process, with no explanation as to why. Few teams bother to ask for any details behind the outcomes or underlying intent desired. Occasionally, it is possible to figure out the intent even if the mechanisms proposed are clunky or outright bad, such as with a return on investment or quality review. Other times the reasons are unclear or wrapped in impenetrable legalese. Sometimes, the entire requirement gets enveloped in a fog of mostly false rumors, as so often happens with Sarbanes-Oxley compliance reporting.

When things are unclear, ask nicely for clarification of the underlying intent. If the intent is to implement internal policies, try to find out where they came from and the history behind them by seeking out a friendly manager for guidance.

For legal and regulatory matters, you might want to try reaching out to the Legal or Compliance team for some help. Ask for any details on what the legal or regulatory requirements are and who they are for, as well as clarification on what they might mean.

I have done this a number of times, with HIPAA, Sarbanes Oxley, and GDPR being the most common legal/regulatory hobgoblins. Consulting the Legal or Compliance team will help you find that there are important nuances relevant to your ecosystem that you might not have considered. You might need to ask a number of questions to tease these nuances out, so be sure to remain friendly. Your goal is to understand the intent behind the legal and regulatory requirements so that you can achieve them in the best way possible.

Make It Visible

There are times when no one can really explain the intent behind governance processes coherently. Sometimes, the person or group demanding that the processes be followed will insist upon equating performing the processes themselves as the intent. This lack of a clear understanding of what is being governed not only results in shoddy governance, but can also have a larger impact on overall service delivery.

Figure 15.3
Sometimes it takes looking deeper to really understand.

A great way of solving this issue is to make what the process accomplishes, and its impact on service delivery, visible. It is a must for any new process, but it can also be done to review existing ones.

I usually start by building a value stream map that shows the various steps, who performs them, and the amount of time it takes and/or is available to perform them. On this map I also lay out what is done and try to detail the assumed intent behind the work.

Along the way I note any known or potential areas for failure. For existing processes, these might include missed or misunderstood details, the use of a low-quality proxy measurement, or some process element or detail that might violate the intent behind a requirement.

It is also worthwhile to look at the efficacy of the processes themselves and the various artifacts within them. For instance, what material evidence is collected, what is it used for, and does it create sufficient situational awareness to make an informed decision or to learn from? Are the people who are part of the process sufficiently equipped to perform their duties and make effective decisions? Can they do this on their own, or do they need support from someone/somewhere? If external support is required, does the process help with securing it?

Finally, I look for any review mechanisms for the process that allow for problems to be spotted and improvements to be put in place. If these review mechanisms exist, who runs them, how often, and how is the efficacy of the process and any improvements determined?

Making the process visible is always an eye-opening experience, especially for management and those leading governance. Just as in the earlier story of the 18-month approval process, most simply do not realize the level of dysfunction, instead directing their attention to more tangible activities like code creation and deployment.

Propose Reasonable Solutions

Identifying a problem and collecting evidence is great. But anyone who has run a team or project knows that rather than just point out or complain about a problem, the most valuable thing someone can do is propose a reasonable solution to the problem. This is especially important in a situation where governance is causing delivery problems or is ineffective at fulfilling its intended purpose. Better still is when a proposal is a group effort, or at least has strong buy-in from others.

The best proposals start with outlining the intent of the governance process. You can do this either to put forward a new governance proposal when it is needed or to fix an existing one. You do not need to lay out all of the detail, but be sure to do your homework in case you are asked any questions about it.

If you are pointing out an existing governance problem, highlight the elements that are problematic or are being missed. Give an overview of the current problem, whether it is with governance, the friction caused, meeting outcomes, or situational awareness and learning. Give some examples but try to be brief.

Then lay out some ideas of ways to solve the issue. How does your proposal address it, and how does it maintain or improve overall governance efficacy? Be sure that you have covered your bases on the governance intent side.

Whenever I do this, I never do it alone or in a bubble. I always try to find others who either feel the problem themselves or have a strong interest in the efficacy of the process to work with. This helps build buy-in and will likely strengthen the proposal and ultimately the efficacy of whatever is proposed.

One example of this is the vicious change management–automated deployment struggle. I frequently see companies that automate deployments before establishing environment or configuration hygiene, resulting in unexpected failures and unknown states as changes are deployed into production. A common reaction to this is to put in place an even stricter change management approval process with more steps, documents, and approvers. These do little to solve the underlying problem (deploying what I often call "random bits onto shifting sand"). Instead, I uncover the problem of the unknowns and their effects, as well as show how the added process does little to solve it. I then build a step-by-step approach for resolving the underlying problems (make the underlying infrastructure and configurations both known and automatedly re-creatable from scratch, make packaging and configuration atomic, etc.), as well as reforming the change approval process to be more useful.

Sometimes your proposal might not be accepted at first. That is okay. Try to find out where any problems exist in what you put forward and see if there are ways you can address them.

Automation and Compliance

While tooling can certainly cause problems, it can also really help with governance and requirements compliance. Processes will inevitably need to evolve over time, so it doesn't make sense for tooling to be only an enforcement mechanism with little value to the person doing the work. Instead, I try to shape automation to be flexible and helpful, collecting details and driving transparency that can also be used to aid the person doing the work at the same time. By using automation as a flexible aid that makes people's lives easier while helping them complete tasks the correct way, the tooling is far more likely to remain used rather than worked around.

For instance, forcing people to tack on a task ID to a code check-in might sound annoying at first; however, it can save a great deal of time and effort when you try to figure out what code you changed for a given piece of work, or why you changed it the way you did. If you have heavyweight compliance requirements, intense security reviews, or are being audited for some reason, task IDs can also prove to be an extremely handy way to automatically generate all the documentation and reports about what was done, what tests were run against it and their results, and what packages were created and when they were released.

Another instance of useful automation tooling comes from the deployment side. When done well, fully automated deployments allow you to know exactly what was released and what changes were made where, all without worrying about potential variations, missed steps, or untracked extra work being performed by human hands. Delivery pipelines can also be configured to allow for change thresholds to be set so that higher-risk and requirement-dependent work gets reviewed by the right parties with the right information to make a sensible decision, while lower-risk and unregulated changes can be rolled out with fewer controls.

Be Flexible and Always Ready to Improve

Whether you are an individual contributor, a manager, or an executive responsible for maintaining good governance, it is important to remember that achieving the three critical factors for good governance is more important than the means you use to do so. There are many ways to achieve them. It is your job to work with the rest of your organization to find the means that are best for you. As the people, services, customers, and their target outcomes change, the means will likely also likely need to change and adjust over time to compensate.

Figure 15.4
Flexibility and improvement take practice.

To do this, you will need to be flexible. Regularly review your governance commitments, how well you meet them, and how much the mechanisms you use to manage them affect the organization's responsiveness and awareness in achieving and improving the means you use to meet the target outcomes. To improve your ability to meet them, you might need to experiment from time to time or rip out a trusted tool or process and replace it with a new one.

Finally, there will be times that you might want to put in a new tool or way of doing things that seems to actively conflict with a governance requirement. For instance, the one team DevOps approach often falls afoul of separation of duties requirements. Look at the intent of the requirement alongside your own objective. Most who want to use the one team DevOps model hope to reduce delivery friction while maintaining awareness, responsiveness, and ownership of the running service by those developing it. While you might not be able to have everyone doing everything at the same time, there are a number of creative ways that you can use tooling and create organizational structures that can still achieve both the desire and requirement intent.

Summary

Governance is both an important and necessary element that many IT delivery and operational teams need to deal with in order to help the larger organization comply with various legal and regulatory requirements. Unfortunately, it is common for the underlying intent behind any legal, regulatory, and business requirement to not be communicated, let alone understood, by those within the delivery ecosystem who are meant to abide by it. This often leads to unnecessarily cumbersome governance and reporting processes and controls to be put in place that deter organizational situational awareness and learning, as well as interfere with organizational efforts to achieve target outcomes. These problems not only cause considerable frustration among delivery teams, but also are erroneously viewed as impenetrable obstacles toward adopting DevOps and continuous delivery tools and techniques.

By ensuring that there is a clear and current understanding of the intent behind the legal and regulatory requirements, it is possible to have sufficient governance controls as well as allow delivery teams to build a delivery ecosystem that enables them to pursue and deliver the target outcomes that matter effectively.

Appendix

Example A3

A3 Problem solving

Title:

Date:
Version:

BACKGROUND
What's going on? Describe the situation and drivers.
Why does this matter? Why now?

CURRENT STATE
What is the current situation?
What are the baseline metrics?

TARGET CONDITION / OUTCOMES
What are our desired outcomes? How will we measure them?
How will we know we have succeeded?

ANALYSIS
What's really going on?
What is the root cause of the problem?

EXPERIMENTS / COUNTERMEASURES
What's our action plan? How will we test the options?
What is our decision criteria to evaluate our experiments?

MEASURE THE IMPACT
What really happened?
How much impact did we make on our target outcomes?

LEARN & ADAPT
What did we learn?
What are our next steps?

∞ **Mobius**
mobiusloop.com
by Gabrielle Benefield

Index

Numerics

5S, 261–262
    for large Internet service companies,
        281–283
    seiketsu, 273–277
    seiso, 270–273
    seiton, 266–270
    shitsuke, 277–278
    sort (*'seiri'*), 262–266
    for start-ups, 278–281

A

A3 problem solving, 427–432
accountability, governance and, 435–436
accuracy, 43, 169–172
action, 26
after action reviews, 79–80
Agile, 4, 10, 41, 77, 102, 447, 451
agility, 10
Alexander the Great, 57
alignment
    service operations synchronization
        and improvement, 400
    strategic cycle, 421–423, 424–432
    tactical cycle, 400–402
        daily standup, 408–411
        kickoff, 403–408
        Queue Master brief, 402–403
        retrospective, 411–421
    through iterative approaches, 397
        kanban, 399
        Scrum Sprint model, 398
    top-down approach, 397
all-in-one tools, 275–277
ALM (Application Lifecycle
    Management), 277
analysis paralysis, 134
analytics, data collection and, 292
anchoring bias, 46, 162

Anderson, D., 351
Andon, 350–351
anti-goals, 68–69
APIs, 121
assessment. *See also* maturity model
    review processes, 187–188
    standardized testing, 185–187
automation, 257–258, 261, 318. *See also*
    Tools & Automation Engineering
    bias, 47, 162
    build and CI system, 311
    ecosystem conditions, 258–260
    governance and, 458
    implementing 5S principles
        for large Internet service
            companies, 281–283
        for start-ups, 278–281
    tools, 268
availability, 223–224
    bias, 46
awareness, 95–96, 99, 115, 214. *See also*
    situational awareness
    development, 312–314
    fog, 205–207, 222
        eliminating, 209–214, 219–220
        identifying what you can or
            cannot know, 214
    operational, 206–207
    SE Lead and, 246–248
AWS, 124

B

Babel, 11–12
backbriefing, 63, 69–71, 194
Battle of Kasserine Pass, 176
best practices, 273–274, 451
bias, 161–162
    anchoring, 46
    automation, 47

availability, 46
cognitive, 46–47
confirmation, 290
execution, 35–36
hindsight, 47, 51–52
representativeness, 46
solution, 34, 35
Big Data, 43, 289, 326
Blockbuster Entertainment, 7
Boyd, J., 4, 18, 23, 24–25, 28, 33, 36,
    40–41, 74, 77, 83. *See also* OODA
    loop
    Aerial Attack Study, 24
    "Destruction and Creation," 77
bugs, 271, 305, 314
bullwhip effect, 116–118
business continuity planning, 204, 236
Business Intelligence, 43, 69, 214, 289

C

CABs (Change Advisory Boards), 14–15
CEO, 68
change management, 317–319,
    447–449
Chaos Engineering, 47, 79, 216–217
chaotic contexts, 137–139
    dictators, 139–141
    firefighter arsonists, 141–142
clear contexts, 131–133
cloud environments, 96–97, 124, 202
Clousewitz, C., 62
coaching practice, 193–195
code(ing), 10, 13, 41, 48–51, 92, 95–96,
    112–113, 136, 233, 241, 251, 252, 268,
    271, 319. *See also* software
    defects, 89
    metrics, 311
    Power Peg, 266
    quality, measuring, 224–225
    queryable, 321
cognitive bias, 46–47, 161–162. *See also*
    bias
collaboration, incentivizing, 251–252
color coding, 90
Commander's Intent, 63–66, 211
communication, 95. *See also* information
    disconnects and, 348–349

implicit, 73
Queue Master role and, 385
competitive objectives, 96
complexity, 135–137, 351
    environment, 128–129
    kanban board and, 360–362
    unpredictability and, 61
complicated contexts, 133–134
configuration management, 274, 277,
    317–319
confirmation bias, 162, 290
confusion, 143
constraints, 68–69, 345
context, 43, 141–142, 261, 306
    chaotic, 137–139
        dictators, 139–141
        firefighter arsonists, 141–142
    clear, 131–133
    complex, 135–137
    complicated, 133–134
    of confusion, 143
    disconnects and, 347–349
    target outcomes and, 144
continual improvement, 75–77, 84
    coaching practice, 193–195
    kata, 191
        day-to-day, 191–192
        improvement and problem
            solving, 192–193
    outcome-directed learning, 188–190
continuous delivery, 4, 10, 41, 218–219
continuous integration, 233, 259, 280,
    283, 312
contracts, 442–445
coupling management, measuring,
    239–241
CRM, 39
C-suite, 116
culture, information flow and, 177–178
customer engagement, 242
cycles. *See* strategic cycle; tactical cycle
Cynefin, 129–130, 210. *See also* context

D

daily standup, 408–411
Dark Matter, 340–342. *See also* friction
    preventing, 359–362

Queue Master role and, 379–380
dark pools, 266
dashboards, 312, 314
data
    collection, 291–292
    determining the purpose and value of,
        293–294
        buying furniture online,
            294–295
        getting successfully treated at the
            hospital, 295–297
    knowing the consumer, 297–299
        capture and presentation
            distortions, 301
        language mismatches, 299–301
    monitoring, 324–325
    presenting, 321–322
    service, 326–327
    sources, 302–303
        timeliness, 305–306
        trustworthiness and consistency,
            303–305
day-to-day *kata*, 191–192
DBAs (datase ddministrators),
    specialization, 100–101
DBE (Database Engineering), 101
decision-making, 21, 22–23, 144,
    221–222, 396. *See also* Mission
    Command; situational awareness
    on the battlefield, 25
    cognitive bias and, 46–47
    contexts
        chaotic, 137–142
        clear, 131–133
        complex, 135–137
        complicated, 133–134
        of confusion, 143
    execution bias and, 35–36
    friction elimination, 39–42
    improving, 53–54
    information
        accuracy, 43
        context, 43
        dis-, 45–46
        timeliness of, 43
    knowledge and, 44

learning and, 48–51
making the best choice the easiest
    choice, 145–147
OODA loop, 25
    action, 26
    decide, 26
    nonlinear looping, 28
    observe, 26
    orient, 26
    PDCA cycle and, 28
    risk, 129
    situational awareness, 42–44
    solution bias and, 34, 35
    target outcome, 30–33
    target outcome and, 16
    trust and, 44
    unpredictability and, 58
defects, 47, 88–91. *See also* failure(s)
    causes of, 89
    in code, 89
    spotting, 90–91
"Defend against the Madman" approach,
    121–122
delivery, 221–222
    "as code," 284
    continuous, 4, 10, 41, 218–219
    ecosystem, 197
    fog, 205–207
        eliminating, 209–214, 219–220
        identifying what you can or
            cannot know, 214
    friction, 37, 57
        dependencies and, 41
        eliminating, 39–42
        feedback and, 42
        multitasking and, 42
        reducing, 9–11
        targeting, 11–12
    hygiene, measuring, 232–234
    ilities, 207–209
    metrics, 36–39
    "mistake proof," 90
    outcome-directed approach, 190
    pipeline, 238
    speed, 201
    teams, 15

demand
    bullwhip effect, 116–118
    unexpected variability in, 114–116
Demming, E., 28
dependency(ies), 41, 357
    failures and, 237
    instrumenting, 314–316
    management, 269–270
    serial loopback, 102
    team, 313
deployment, automation and, 260
development environment,
    instrumenting, 310–314
DevOps, 4, 9, 10, 15, 18, 33, 40, 53, 76,
    151, 168, 197, 199, 251
    Einheit, 74–75
    governance, 453
        flexibility and, 458–460
        intent, 454
        proposals, 456–457
        requirements compliance, 458
        transparency, 454–456
    production services and,
        253
    retrospectives, 192–193
    Strategic Reviews, 192–193
    uptime, 65
    waste. *See also* waste
        defects, 88–91
        excessive processes, 106–109
        handoffs, 101–103
        overproduction, 91–93
        overspecialization, 97–101
        systemic impediments, 94–97
        task switching, 105–106
    WIP ("work in progress"), 103–104
dictators, 139–141
direct interference, 438–439
directive briefing, 66
    anti-goals and constraints, 68–69
    execution priorities, 67–68
    situational overview, 67
    statement of desired outcome, 67
disaster recovery, 236
disconnects, 343–346
    communication, 348–349
    resolving, 347–349

disinformation, 45–46
Docker, 97
Donaldson, L., 296
downtime, 123

E

ecosystem, 183, 204, 221, 222
    5S, 261–262
        seiketsu, 273–277
        seiso, 270–273
        seiton, 266–270
        shitsuke, 277–278
        sort (*'seiri'*), 262–266
    automation and, 258–260
    complexity, 61
    delivery, 197
    development environment,
        instrumenting, 310–314
    dynamics, 169–172
    hygiene, 232–234
    IT, instrumenting, 331–333
    logging, 323–324
    monitoring, 324–325
    observability, 147–151, 307–309
    rebuilding, 323
    situational awareness and, 154–156
    transparency, 243–244
    unknowns, 310
education, formal, shortcomings of,
    51–52
effectiveness, 57–58, 198
Einheit, 71–75
EM (Energy-Maneuverability) theory,
    24, 83
engagement, measuring, 241–243
entry management, Queue Master,
    378–379
Equifax, 9
execution bias, 35–36
execution priorities, 67–68
experimentation, 135–137
exploits, 8

F

failing to learn, 48–51
failure(s), 181, 211

dependencies and, 237
 single point of, 239–241, 314
feedback, 46, 135–136
 friction, 42
 timeliness of, 306
Fingerspitzengefühl, 74
firefighter arsonists, 141–142
flexibility, governance and, 458–460
"fog of war," 58. *See also* awareness
"follow the sun" model, 384–385
 other work when on duty, 386–389
 sync point management, 385
formal education, shortcomings of,
 51–52
Fortran, 48–51
Fowler, M., 119
frameworks. *See also* Mission Command
 Cynefin, 129–130
 governance, 445–449
 maturity model, 222, 223–224
  areas of interest, 228–229
  configuration management and
   delivery hygiene, measuring,
   232–234
  engagement, measuring,
   241–243
  incentivizing collaboration and
   improvement, 251–252
  information flow and
   instrumentation, measuring,
   229–231
  levels, 225–228
  measuring code quality, 224–225
  single point of failure mitigation
   and coupling management,
   measuring, 239–241
  supportability, measuring,
   235–239
 OKR (Objectives and Key Results), 37
 service management, 13–14
framing, 164, 204
 finding and fixing problems in
  organizations
   customer engagement, 165–167
   locally focused metrics, 168–169

output metrics, 167–168
Fredendall, L., 176
friction, 9, 14, 37, 57, 83, 84, 459–460.
 See also waste
 configuration, 204
 dependencies and, 41
 elimination, 39–42
 feedback and, 42
 governance and, 437–438
 multitasking and, 42
 reducing, 9–11, 359–362
 speed and, 40
 targeting, 11–12
 waste and, 85–86

G

"gemba walk," 307–309, 430–431
Gilb, T., 208
Gitlab.com, 12
goals
 anti-, 68–69
 competitive objectives, 96
governance, 13, 112
 accountability and, 435–436
 common mistakes, 440
  out-of-the-box process tooling
   and workflows, 450–453
  poor requirement drafting and
   understanding, 440–445
  using off-the-shelf frameworks,
   445–447
 DevOps, 453
 factors for successful, 434–435
  maintaining situational awareness
   and learning, 438–440
  meeting intent, 435–437
  no target outcome interference,
   437–438
 flexibility and, 458–460
 intent, 454
 process and, 447–449
 proposals, 456–457
 requirements compliance, 458
 transparency and, 454–456

H

handoffs, 101–103
hindsight bias, 47, 51–52, 162
Hölzle, U., 123
hooks, queryable, 321
human brain, 154–156. *See also* mental
 models, situational awareness and

I

IDE (integrated development
 environment), 90
IKEA effect, 47
ilities, 207–209, 217–218, 221–222, 223,
 224
 known manageables, 214–215
 known unmanageables, 216–217
 unknowns, 217–219
implicit communication, 73
improvement and problem solving *kata*,
 192–193
incident management, 179, 238, 338
indirect interference, 439–440
industry best practices, 13–14
information, 396. *See also* data
 accuracy, 43
 capturing, 290
 context, 43
 flow, 169, 198–199
  cultural disconnects, 177–178
  disconnects, 347–349
  ecosystem dynamics and, 169–172
  measuring, 229–231
  SE Lead and, 246–248
  tracers, 172–173
  transmission mismatches, 173–176
  trust and, 178–180
  visualizing, 349–351
 timeliness of, 43
innovation, 7, 8, 48–51
instrumentation, 291, 293–294, 295, 305,
 306
 configuration management,
  317–319
 dependency, 314–316

development, 310–314
interpreting, 300
IT ecosystem, 331–333
measuring, 229–231
observability and, 310
packaging, 314–316
production, 320
security, 325–326
testing, 319–320
tool, 316
wastewater management, 328–331
intent, governance and, 434, 435–437,
 454
interference
 direct, 438–439
 indirect, 439–440
 target outcome, 437–438
internal cloud, 97
intuition, 73, 74
Invisible Gorilla, The, 155
irregularity, 83
IT, 197
 cloud environments, friction and,
  96–97
 ecosystem, instrumenting, 331–333
 failures, 8, 13
 friction, 86
 governance, 433
 information flow, 175
 mura ("irregularity"), 113–114
 overproduction, 92
 risk, 127
 service management, 337
 service providers, data resilience and
  recovery, 204
 snowflakes, 119–120, 121
 specialization and, 100–101
 task switching, 105–106
ITIL, 13, 452–453

J-K

JM (Job Methods), 84
JMX (Java Management Extensions), 321
kaizen, 272, 356
kanban, 10, 349–352, 399
 flow and, 368

kaizen, 356
    limits of a workflow board, 367
    managing the board, 367–368
    simplicity and, 360–362
    state columns, 352–355
    swim lanes, 355–358
    tally boards, 359–360
    task cards, 358–359
    timestamping tasks, 364
    using the board, 362–363
    WIP (work in progress), 365–367
    work blockages, 364–365
kata, 191, 272
    day-to-day, 191–192
    improvement and problem solving,
        192–193
kickoff, 403–408
Klein, G., 158
Knight Capital Group, 9, 263–266, 301
knowledge. *See also* learning
    decision-making and, 44
    -execution mismatches, 108
    operational, 206–207
    "single points of failure," 120
    skills and, 185
    unpredictability and, 59–60
known
    knowns, 131
    manageables, 214–215
    unknowns, 133
    unmanageables, 216–217
Koçulu, A., 11–12
Korean War, 23, 24, 40–41
Kubernetes, 10, 97

L

large Internet service companies,
    implementing 5S principles, 281–283
leadership, 55
    Commander's Intent, 63–66
    effective, 57–58
    service delivery, 3
    top-down approach, 58
Lean, 77, 80, 83, 125–126, 145,
    147–148, 350
    5S, 261–262

seiketsu, 273–277
seiso, 270–273
seiton, 266–270
shitsuke, 277–278
sort (*'seiri'*), 262–266
kanban, 349–351
    flow and, 368
    kaizen, 356
    limits of a workflow board, 367
    managing the board, 367–368
    simplicity and, 360–362
    state columns, 352–355
    swim lanes, 355–358
    tally boards, 359–360
    task cards, 358–359
    timestamping tasks, 364
    using the board, 362–363
    WIP (work in progress), 365–367
    work blockages, 364–365
kata, 272
    day-to-day, 191–192
    improvement and problem
        solving, 192–193
mura ("irregularity"), 113–114.
    See also unpredictability
    bullwhip effect, 116–118
    minimizing, 120–122
    snowflakes, 119–120
    unexpected demand variability,
        114–116
    unmanaged variability, 118
Muri ("overburden"), 109–110
    overloading releases, 111–113
    people and, 110–111
outcome-directed learning, 188–190
"stop the line," 90
"walking the gemba," 307–309
waste and, 84, 90
learning, 48–51, 183
    continual improvement and, 75–77
    effective leadership, 57–58
    formal education, 51–52
    hindsight bias and, 51–52
    kata, 191
        day-to-day, 191–192
        improvement and problem
            solving, 192–193

outcome-directed, 188–190
skills and, 184–185
standardized tests and, 185–187
Legal and Compliance teams, 300–301,
442–445, 454
locally focused metrics, 168–169
logging, 323–324

M

MacArthur, D., 85
managers, 210–214, 277–278, 371–372.
See also Queue Master; Service
Engineering Lead; teams
managing
micro-, 278
risk, service delivery, 12–15
waste, overproduction, 91–93
manufacturing
waste. *See also* waste
defects, 88–91
excessive processes, 106–109
handoffs, 101–103
overspecialization, 97–101
task switching, 105–106
waiting, 94–97
WIP ("work in progress"), 103–104
maturity model, 222, 223–224
areas of interest, 228–229
incentivizing collaboration and
improvement, 251–252
levels, 225–228
measuring code quality, 224–225
metrics
configuration management and
delivery hygiene, 232–234
engagement, 241–243
information flow and
instrumentation, 229–231
single point of failure mitigation
and coupling management,
239–241
supportability, 235–239
Maven, 270
Meltdown, 8
mental models, 45, 157–158
cognitive bias and, 161–162
data interpretation issues, 160

disinformation and, 45–46
problems with, 158–160
resilience, 160–161
mentoring, 194–195, 211
method-driven management, 340,
446–447
metrics
availability, 223–224
code, 224–225, 311
configuration management and
delivery hygiene, 232–234
delivery, 36–39
engagement, 241–243
information flow and instrumentation,
229–231
interpreting, 300
locally focused, 168–169
output, 167–168
single point of failure mitigation and
coupling management, 239–241
for success, 294–295
supportability, 235–239
Microsoft Azure, 13
misalignment, 60–61, 396. *See also*
alignment
Mission Command, 3, 33, 55–56
after action reviews, 79–80
anatomy of, 62–63
backbriefing, 69–71
Commander's Intent, 63–66, 211
continual improvement and, 75–77
directive briefing, 66
anti-goals and constraints, 68–69
execution priorities, 67–68
situational overview, 67
statement of desired outcome, 67
Einheit, 71–74
organizational impacts of, 80–81
origins of, 56–57
staff rides, 78–79
target outcome, 62–63
unpredictability, 58–59
ecosystem complexity and, 61
misalignments and, 60–61
through knowledge and awareness
weaknesses, 59–60
unpredictability and, 56–57

Mobius outcome delivery approach, 3
Moltke, H., 62, 66, 72, 77, 78, 80, 83
monitoring, 324–325
MTBF (Mean Time Between Failure), 123
Muda, 86–88, 115. *See also* waste
multitasking, 42
mura ("irregularity"), 113–114. *See also* unpredictability
    bullwhip effect, 116–118
    minimizing, 120–122
    snowflakes, 119–120
    unexpected demand variability, 114–116
    unmanaged variability, 118
Muri ("overburden"), 109–110, 115
    overloading releases, 111–113
    people and, 110–111

N

Napoleon, 57–58, 72
negative events, 75
Netflix, Simian Army, 122–124, 216–217
Node, 11–12
nonlinear looping, 28

O

observability, 295
    ecosystem, 147–151, 307–309
    instrumenting for, 310
observation, 26
office hours, Queue Master, 382–383
off-the-shelf tools, 303–304, 305
Ohno, T., 83, 85
OKR (Objectives and Key Results) framework, 37
on-demand service delivery, 205
OODA loop, 25, 135
    act, 26
    decide, 26
    nonlinear looping, 28
    observe, 26
    orient, 26, 43–44
    PDCA cycle and, 28
open source software, 10

Operation Millennium Challenge, 25, 40
optimism bias, 162
ordered systems
    clear contexts, 131–133
    complicated contexts, 133–134
organizational impacts of Mission Command, 80–81
organizations
    finding and fixing framing problems
        customer engagement, 165–167
        locally focused metrics, 168–169
        output metrics, 167–168
    overburden and, 110–111
    specialization and, 98–99, 100–101
orientation, 26
origins of Mission Command, 56–57
outages, 122, 272
outcome-directed learning, 188–190
output metrics, 167–168
overburden, 83, 109–110
    overloading releases, 111–113
    people and, 110–111
overproduction, 91–93
overspecialization, 97–101
ownership, building a sense of, 199

P

PaaS (platform-as-a-service), 10
partially done work, 103–104
Parvin, A., 35
PDCA cycle, 28
performance, 207, 208. *See also ilities*
PII (personally identifiable information), 438–439
"playing it safe," 76
POMs (project object models), 270
Pony Test, 64–65
Power Peg, 266
pride, building a sense of, 199
process(es), 201. *See also* governance
    excessive, 106–109
    failure, 48–51
        CRM, 39
        OODA loop and, 28
    governance and, 447–449
    review, 187–188

standardization, 275
workflow and, 337–339
production, instrumenting, 320
productivity, 84
Puppet, 10, 97
pure waste, 86–88

Q

QA (quality assurance), 319
queryable hooks, 321
Queue Master, 75, 91, 104, 106, 147–148, 175, 181, 220, 372–373, 404–405
daily standup and, 408–411
"follow the sun" model, 384–385
other work when on duty, 386–389
sync point management, 385
retrospective and, 414, 415
role mechanics, 374
Dark Matter handling, 379–380
entry management, 376–377
maintaining flow, 380–381
office hours, 382–383
pattern recognition, 381–382
rotation, 374–376, 386
sorting and dependency discovery, 378–379
rollout challenges, 389
junior team members as Queue Masters, 391–393
pushy Queue Masters, 391
sync points, 394
team members not seeing the value, 389–390
traditional managers thwarting rollout, 390–391
tactical cycle and, 400–403
typical day of, 386–389

R

rebuilding the ecosystem, 323
reflection, 396
releases, overloading, 111–113
reliability, 207
representativeness bias, 46

resilience, 160–161, 204
retrospective, 192–193, 411–413
general meeting structure, 413–415
learning and improvement discussion, 415–421
review, 187–188
kaizen, 356
strategic, 424–432
risk management, 127, 143–144
decision-making, 129
chaotic contexts, 137–142
clear contexts, 131–133
complex contexts, 135–137
complicated contexts, 133–134
confusion and, 143
making the best choice the easiest choice, 145–147
ecosystem observability, improving, 147–151
ilities, 208
service delivery, 9
downsides of targeting, 14–15
managing, 12–14
rotation of duties, 142, 240
Queue Master, 374–376, 386
Service Engineering Lead, 244–246

S

SaaS (Software-as-a-Service), 200
satisficing, 47
Scharnhorst, D., 72
On War, 58
Scrum, 10, 77, 214, 314, 398, 404–408
SDK (software development kit), 445
security
breaches
Equifax, 9
SolarWinds, 128
tracking and analysis, 325–326
seiketsu, 273–277
seiso, 270–273
seiton, 266–270
"Selective Attention Test," 155
separation of duties, 435–436, 439
serial loopback, 102
serverless architecture, 136

service delivery, 3, 4, 15, 17, 204–205,
    221
  agility, 10
  availability, 223–224
  data, 326–327
  on-demand, 205
  disconnects, 343–346, 347–349
  fog, 205–207
    eliminating, 209–214, 219–220
    identifying what you can or
      cannot know, 214
  friction, 57, 83
    dependencies and, 41
    eliminating, 39–42
    feedback and, 42
    reducing, 9–11
    waste and, 85–86
  ilities, 207–209
  known manageables, 214–215
  known unmanageables, 216–217
  leadership, 3
  maturity model, 223–224
    areas of interest, 228–229
    configuration management and
      delivery hygiene, measuring,
      232–234
    engagement, measuring,
      241–243
    incentivizing collaboration and
      improvement, 251–252
    information flow and
      instrumentation, measuring,
      229–231
    levels, 225–228
    measuring code quality, 224–225
    single point of failure mitigation
      and coupling management,
      measuring, 239–241
    supportability, measuring,
      235–239
  measuring, 17
  metrics, 36–39
  Mission Command, 33
  outcome-directed approach, 190
  risk
    downsides of targeting, 14–15
    managing, 12–14

situational awareness, 205–207
  speed, 9–10, 201
  systems thinking, 80
  target outcomes, 16, 18, 293–294
  unknowns, 217–219
  uptime and, 65
Service Engineering Lead, 243–244, 380
  challenges, 250–251
  on the delivery team,
    250, 253
  duty rotation and, 244–246
  operational, 249–250
  organizational configurations and,
    248–250
  overcoming the operational
    experience gap, 254–255
  retrospective and, 414–415
  tactical cycle and, 400–402
  team awareness and, 246–248
Shingo, S., 87
shitsuke, 277–278
silos, 136–137
Simian Army, 124, 216–217
single point of failure, 120, 239–241
situational awareness, 2–3, 4, 16, 42–44,
    111, 114, 115–116, 120, 206. *See also*
    kanban
  backbriefing and, 69–71
  cognitive bias and, 161–162
  Dark Matter, 340–342
  disconnects, 343–346, 347–349
  Fingerspitzengefühl, 74
  framing, 164, 165–169, 204
  governance and, 438–440
  human brain and, 154–156
  information flow, 169, 206
    cultural disconnects, 177–178
    ecosystem dynamics and, 169–172
    measuring, 229–231
    tracers, 172–173
    transmission mismatches,
      173–176
    trust and, 178–180
  mental models, 157–158
    data interpretation issues, 160
    problems with, 158–160
    resilience, 160–161

method-driven management and, 340
operational knowledge, 206–207
strategies for improving, 163, 181–182
unpredictability and, 59–60
workflow and, 336–337
Skillman, P., 183
skills, 184–185
SLAs (service-level agreements), 202,
203, 445
Snowden, D., 129, 131
snowflakes, 119–120, 121, 136
software
buggy, 271
customization, 279
development, overloading releases,
111–113
open source, 10
packaging, 234
SMARS, 266, 301
SolarWinds, Sunburst exploit, 128
solution bias, 34, 35
sort ('seiri'), 262–266
specialists, 98
specialization, 98–99, 100–101, 102–104
Spectre, 8
speed
friction and, 40
service delivery, 9–10, 201
Spotify, 99
sprints, 214, 404–408
staff rides, 77, 78–79
standardization, 273–275, 281
all-in-one tools, 275–277
test, 185–187
start-ups
development awareness, 312–314
implementing 5S principles, 278–281
state columns, 352–355
strategic cycle, 421–423
review, 192–193, 424–425
A3 problem solving, 427–432
structure, 426–427
success, 24, 294–295
Sun Tzu, 25
sunk cost fallacy, 162

supply chain friction, bullwhip effect,
116–118
supportability, measuring, 235–239
swim lanes, 355–358
sync points, 400
synthetic transaction monitoring, 304
systemic impediments, 94–97
systems thinking, 80–81

T

tactical cycle, 400–402
daily standup, 408–411
kickoff, 403–408
Queue Master brief, 402–403
retrospective, 411–413
general meeting structure,
413–415
learning and improvement
discussion, 415–421
tally boards, 359–360
target outcomes, 16, 17, 18, 30–33,
62–63, 67, 214, 293–294
Commander's Intent and, 63–66
context and, 144
current state and, 188–189
governance and, 437–438
metrics, 36–39
Pony Test, 64–65
task(s), 371. See also kanban; workflow(s)
black holes, 346
cards, 358–359
Dark Matter, 340–342
identifiers, 311
structured approach, 183
switching, 105–106
team-based approach, 189
Taylor, F. W., The Principles of Scientific
Management, 37
TCO (total cost of ownership),
146–147
TDD (test-driven development), 122
teaching to the test, 186–187
teams, 198, 199. See also Queue Master;
Service Engineering Lead
dependencies, 313

eliminating fog, 219–220
gauging maturity of, 238–239
Legal and Compliance, 300–301
operational experience gap,
    254–255
rotation of duties, 142, 240
seiketsu and, 274
separation of duties, 435–436, 439
Service Engineering Lead,
    243–244, 253
    awareness and, 246–248
    duty rotation and, 244–246
    organizational configurations and,
        248–250
telecommunications, legacy voice
    products, 92–93
Terraform, 97
testing, instrumenting, 319–320
Three Mile Island, 159–160
tiger teams, 194
tight coupling, 96, 97, 102
tools, 24, 43, 44, 90, 95–96, 203, 207,
    217, 221–222, 250, 251, 274.
    See also Cynefin
    A3 problem solving, 427–432
    all-in-one, 275–277
    automation, 258–260, 268
    Dark Matter and, 342
    instrumenting, 316
    off-the-shelf, 303–304, 305
    out-of-the-box, 450–453
    problem-solving, 193
    seiketsu and, 274
    Simian Army, 124
    target outcome and, 16
Tools & Automation Engineering,
    283–284
    organizational details, 285
    retrospective and, 435
    workflow and sync points, 285–287
top-down
    alignment, 397
    leadership, 58
Toyota, 74, 83, 85, 87, 125–126
tracers, 172–173, 309
trading systems, 272–273

transparency, 121, 136, 207, 214,
    243–244
    governance and, 454–456
    standardization and, 273–277
trust, 52, 73
    decision-making and, 44
    information flow and, 178–180
TWI ("Traning Within Industry")
    program, 4, 84

U

unknown unknowns, 135
unordered systems, 134–135
    chaotic contexts, 137–139
        dictators, 139–141
            firefighter arsonists, 141–142
    complex contexts, 135–137
    confusion, 143
    observability and, 148
unpredictability, 56–57
    continual improvement and, 75–77
    ecosystem complexity and, 61
    "fog of war," 58
    managing through, 58–59
    misalignments and, 60–61
    through knowledge and awareness
        weaknesses, 59–60
    workload, 335
uptime, 65, 202, 207, 445

V

variability, 123
    demand, 114–116
    minimizing, 120–122
    standardization and, 273–277
    unmanaged, 116–118
visualizing, workflow, 349–351.
    See also kanban

W

"walking the gemba," 307–309, 430–431
war-gaming, 78–79, 182
waste, 83, 84–85, 106–109
    defects, 88–91
        causes of, 89

in code, 89
    spotting, 90–91
friction and, 85–86
handoffs, 101–103
mura ("irregularity"), 113–114
    bullwhip effect, 116–118
    minimizing, 120–122
    snowflakes, 119–120
    unexpected demand variability,
        114–116
    unmanaged variability, 118
Muri ("overburden"), 109–110
overproduction, 91–93
overspecialization, 97–101
partially done work, 103–104
process, 106–109
pure, 86–88
systemic impediments, 94–97
task switching, 105–106
waiting, 94–97
wastewater management ecosystem,
    instrumenting, 328–331
WIP (work in progress), 103–104,
    365–367
Woolworths Australia, 17

work environment, 95
workflow(s). *See also kanban*
    board, 362–363
        flow and improvement, managing,
            368
        limits of, 367
        managing, 367–368
        simplifying, 360–362
        state columns, 352–355
        swim lanes, 355–358
        task cards, 358–359
        timestamping tasks, 364
        WIP (work in progress), 365–367
        work blockages, 364–365
    Dark Matter and, 340–342
    disconnects, 343–346, 347–349
    managing organically, 339–340
    out-of-the-box, 450–453
    patterns, 381–382
    processes and, 337–339
    Queue Master role and, 380–381
    situational awareness and, 336–337
    visualizing, 349–351
World War II, 24, 79, 85, 176